Highland Warrior

Alasdair MacColla and the Civil Wars

I had many stories to write on the events of
the times if I undertook to do it, but what
induced me to write even this much was
when I saw that those who treated of the
affairs of the time have made no mention of
the Gael, the men who did all the service.

Neil MacMhuirich

Other books by David Stevenson:

The Scottish Revolution 1637-44 (Newton Abbot 1973)
Revolution and Counter-Revolution in Scotland, 1644-51 (London 1977)
Scottish Covenanters and Irish Confederates (Belfast 1981)
The Covenanters: the National Covenant and Scotland (Edinburgh 1988)
The First Freemasons: Scotland's early lodges and their members (Aberdeen 1988)

Highland Warrior

Alasdair MacColla and the Civil Wars

by
David Stevenson
Professor in History, University of St. Andrews

SALTIRE
SOCIETY

First published 1980 by John Donald Publishers.
This paperback edition published 1994 by
The Saltire Society, 9 Fountain Close,
High Street, Edinburgh EH1 1TF

The publisher acknowledges subsidy from
the Scottish Arts Council towards the
publication of this volume.

A catalogue record for this book is available from
the British Library

ISBN 0 85411 059 3

Front cover illustration: detail showing a romantic
nineteenth-century impression of the Retreat of Montrose
at Philiphaugh reproduced by permission of the Mansell Collection

Designed by Gourlay Graphics, Glasgow

Printed and bound in Great Britain by Bell and Bain Limited

Preface

THIS book tries to do three things. Firstly, it provides the first biography of Alasdair MacColla who, though one of the greatest warriors of Highland tradition, has remained a shadowy figure where written history is concerned, only emerging from obscurity in 1644-5 when he acted as the Marquis of Montrose's second in command. Secondly, explaining Alasdair's part in the Montrose campaigns and assessing his achievements as a soldier provides an opportunity for a general reassessment (long overdue) of these campaigns. They are usually only examined from Montrose's point of view; to take instead the contribution of the Irish and the Highlanders to the campaigns as a starting point helps provide (it is hoped) new insights into events, and raises doubts about Montrose's own accounts of his actions, as well as about accounts by those whose starting point has been uncritical hero-worship of him. Thirdly, in placing the lives of Alasdair and his father in the broader context of seventeenth century Highland history, an attempt has been made to interpret the remarkable (and remarkably neglected) political changes which transform many clans from leaders of resistance to the growing power of James VI into ardent supporters of James VII. It is argued that the events of the 1640s, in which Alasdair took a central part, saw the dramatic beginnings of this emergence of Highland Jacobitism. It seems to me that such a fresh look at the seventeenth century Highlands is rendered necessary not only because of past neglect, but also because the one work which does attempt a sustained study and over-all interpretation of the topic is based on fundamental misunderstandings. Audrey Cunningham's *The loyal clans* (1932) advanced theories based almost entirely on a single work, John Drummond's *Memoirs of Sir Ewen Cameron of Locheill* (Abbotsford Club, 1842). From Drummond himself Miss Cunningham took the projection back into the early and mid-seventeenth century of eighteenth century Jacobite attitudes to the Stewart dynasty (Drummond wrote c.1733); and from the editor's introduction (by James Macknight) she took an argument about the total incompatibility of 'patriarchy' and 'feudalism', and belief that this incompatibility was the cause of most of the troubles of the Highlands. Explicitly in my first and last chapters, and implicitly in much that lies in between, I have argued against these interpretations.

In writing on Highland history I lack at least one basic technical qualification; I am totally ignorant of the Gaelic tongue. All I can do is offer two excuses for my presumption. Firstly, those who are skilled in Gaelic have not written much on the themes that this book is concerned with, and sometimes it can be useful for a fool to rush in if no angels show interest in treading in the direction in which he wishes to go. Secondly, I have been fortunate to receive generous assistance from those Gaelic scholars whom I have approached for help. Dr Colm O Boyle and Mr

Donald Macaulay of the Department of Celtic, University of Aberdeen, have borne patiently with endless questions from me. Dr O Boyle has provided me with translations of several Gaelic poems, and with corrections to existing translations of other Irish and Gaelic sources. In addition he has read my whole typescript, and saved me from many errors, both major and minor. He cannot, however, be blamed for any misuse of Gaelic of which I may be guilty; and in particular he is not responsible for the forms of names of Gaelic Irish, Highlanders and clans that I have adopted (and explain below). My compromise decisions here must, I fear, pain any Gaelic scholar. Finally, the following have kindly given me permission to quote their translations of Gaelic poems: Dr John Lorne Campbell, Dr Annie Mackenzie (Mrs Murray), Dr J. A. MacLean, and Professor Derick Thomson. To all these Gaels my gratitude for their help to an ignorant *Gall*. My limping Latin has also required help on occasion. Here I am grateful to Mr Thomas Pearce, Department of Classics, University of Aberdeen, and to my wife, Dr Wendy B. Stevenson. The latter has also, by a careful reading of the typescript, saved the reader from much in the way of awkwardness of expression, obscurity of meaning, and error or inconsistency of argument.

The spelling of both Irish and Highland place and personal names presents many problems of convention and consistency; no single solution is possible which will satisfy all. My main consideration has been that this is a book written in English which will be read mainly by readers whose first language is English. In place names I have accepted anglicised versions where these are generally accepted (thus Knocknanuss, not Cnoc na nDos). With personal names I have generally used anglicised spellings of Gaelic names (thus Angus, not Aonghas; Randal or Ranald, not Raonull or Ragnald; MacDonald not MacDhomhnuill). Often where completely different English and Gaelic (or anglicised-Gaelic) names are regarded as equivalents (for example, Alasdair = Alexander; Gilleasbuig or Gillespie = Archibald), complete consistency would lead to confusion. Few would recognise the Marquis of Argyll as Gillespie Campbell, for outside the Highlands he was Archibald Campbell; on the other hand to call Coll Ciotach's father Archibald would be absurd since Coll was commonly known as Coll MacGillespie. I have therefore sought to use the names, or variants of names, by which individuals are most commonly referred to in surviving sources; but some decisions on this are unavoidably arbitrary. The form 'Mac' has always been preferred to 'Mc' or 'M'', and the prefix has always been followed by a capital letter (thus MacLean, not Maclean). In using the variants of the same name, 'MacDonnell' and 'MacDonald', I have sought to confine the former to the MacDonnells of Antrim, the latter to Highlanders, though again such decisions are sometimes arbitrary.

David Stevenson.

List of Maps

Contents

Prologue: What's in a Name?

IT is disconcerting for a biographer to find that the first question that he has to settle is what to call the individual he is writing about. But in this case the difficulty is a very real one. The subject of this book was known by several names (or versions of names) during his life.

On the one hand, for those whose first language was English, he was at the time of his death (or should have been, for as we shall see many found it difficult to decide what to call him) Lieutenant General Sir Alexander MacDonald — or perhaps MacDonnell,[1] the former prevailing in Scotland, the latter in Ireland. Thus our subject is clearly identified by military rank, by title, by an acceptable Lowland Scots christian name, and by a fixed (apart from the troublesome fluidity of the last few letters) surname. But to most of those among whom he lived the same man was usually identified simply as Alasdair MacColla (or MacCholla). Rank and title are rejected as irrelevant and alien; the christian name is Gaelic; and there is no fixed hereditary surname, MacColla being used in the literal sense of 'son of Coll'. Alasdair's father's nickname might be added for additional clarity — 'Alasdair MacColla Chiotaich'[2] — or his grandfather's name might be added to his father's, giving 'Alasdair MacColla mhic Gilleasbuig'[3] (often anglicised as 'MacGillespie' or 'MacGillespic'). Names of other ancestors in the male line could be listed, turning his name into a recital of his genealogy without its being clear when the one changed into the other. Thus precisely what a Gael called Alasdair depended on the context, on precisely how much information in addition to the personal name Alasdair he needed to distinguish (to those he was talking to) this particular Alasdair from others of the same name. This Gaelic system of nomenclature confused most of those to whom Gaelic culture was alien; and this includes most of those who wrote about Alasdair's exploits in his lifetime.

To understand one aspect of the confusion over 'Alasdair's' name one has to go back to his father. Coll's name appears on a paper supposedly signed by him (though in reality he could not write) as 'Coll Macgilespik',[4] and he was generally known by some variant of this or as Coll MacDonald. At some time he acquired in addition the sobriquet 'Ciotach', a word which has several different meanings — the main ones being left-handed; ambidextrous; and cunning or crafty. Most writers have taken it to mean in this context 'left-handed', a few have favoured 'ambidextrous'; but only two have suggested 'crafty' as a possible interpretation.[5] Yet there is a strong argument to be made for this last interpretation being correct. The nickname only appears late in Coll's life; its first appearance is in 1629, in a Latin translation of a Gaelic letter (now lost) by Coll in which he refers to himself as 'Ego Collatius Kiotach Macdonell'.[6] Had the name referred to a physical characteristic like left-handedness one would have expected it to have been used

1

much earlier; it never appears in the years of Coll's greatest fame, 1614-15. But these years closed with an incident which might well have earned him the half-hostile, half-admiring epithet of 'the crafty'; Coll saved himself from the penalties of treason by betraying his allies.

Both Coll's christian name and his nickname proved difficult to non-Gaels. Almost inevitably, some English speakers jumped to the conclusion that 'Coll', a name unknown to them, was an abbreviation of his military rank, and that 'Ciotach' was a surname. Thus was foisted on the world a motley band of officers, 'Colonell Kittoghie', 'col. Kittack' and 'Collonell McGillespick'.[7] From these variants, a late seventeenth century source created 'Colonel Coill M'Donnell alias M'Gillespick', an eighteenth century historian 'Col. Killa', and a nineteenth century editor 'Colonel Macdonald'.[8] Other historians carried confusion further by deciding that Coll or Coll Ciotach were places, thus introducing 'MacDonald of Kolkitto', and 'MacDonald of Coll'.[9] Many other writers, though at least knowing that they were dealing with names and not ranks or places, distorted poor Coll almost out of recognition, presenting such weird variants as 'Coawkittoche', 'Cailkitoch', and 'Coall Kittoch'.[10]

John Milton felt 'Colkitto, or Macdonnel, or Galasp' to be outlandish enough to be mentioned in a sonnet as 'rugged names'.[11] But, though Milton here used the names of Alasdair's father and grandfather, it was the exploits of Alasdair himself which had brought them to his attention. This is appropriate, for the confusion over what to call the father was nothing to that which arose over the name of the son; and this arose through a tendency to assign some of the father's names to the son as well as through the normal uncertainty over how to use or translate Gaelic names. Even in so formal a context as the 1645 act of the Scottish parliament condemning Alasdair to death for treason there is some confusion. The act generally calls him Alexander MacDonald (though his christian name also appears as Alasdair), sometimes with the addition of 'alias Colkittoches sone'. But once he appears as 'alias Colkittoche'.[12] This is doubtless an example of the usual reason for Alasdair becoming 'Colkitto'; the careless omission of the word 'son' after that name (or of 'Mac' before it). It has sometimes been argued that Alasdair was left-handed or ambidextrous like his father[13] and was thus entitled to the same nickname. But, even if Alasdair was 'ciotach' (in any of its meanings) he would never have been called 'Coll Ciotach'. It is true that the marquis of Argyll inherited the epithet of Gillespie 'Gruamach' from his father, the seventh earl,[14] but this is quite a different matter, since both men had the christian name Archibald (Gilleasbuig in Gaelic) as well as somewhat morose dispositions which earned them the epithet 'the sullen' or 'the gloomy'.

The erroneous attribution of the name Colkitto to Alasdair seems to have arisen during his first period of fame, in Ulster in 1641-2. Most sources refer to him, correctly enough, as Alasdair MacColl or Alexander MacColl MacDonald, frequently adding that he was Colkitto's son. But in June 1642 he is referred to simply as 'Colkittagh', which is simplified by the following October to 'Col Kitto'.[15] So Alasdair was launched on his career as Colkitto, though some writers were not entirely happy with the name and resorted to such phrases as 'commonly called Kilkittoth', 'known vulgarly by the name Colkitto', 'whom they call Colla Killagh' and 'called by an Irish appellation Calkito'.[16] Once the name is applied to Alasdair it undergoes precisely the same wild distortions that it experiences when applied to his father. Alasdair becomes 'Col. Kittoch'.[17] His men become 'Colcatochies forces'.[18] He is 'Kolkitagh', 'Colkiltoth' and 'Colekintoe'.[19]

In Latin Alasdair appears as 'Alexander Mac-Donaldus, Colli cognomento sinistri filius',[20] which is accurate enough (though, interestingly this takes Ciotach to mean left-handed). But in one French source he is disguised as Major General 'Colquete',[21] while in Italian he wins promotion, becoming earl of 'Ciletto' or 'Kilketto'.[22] Harder to explain is why in one source he becomes 'Alexander M'Donald, *alias* Alaster M'Leod, *alias* Colcattochie's son',[23] for Alasdair was no Macleod. Equally puzzling is why two usually reliable sources call Alasdair 'Mr. MacDonald' and 'Maister McDonald',[24] since in Scotland the prefix 'Mr.' was reserved for those holding a master's degree from a university.

Out of this great mass of names what are we to call 'Alasdair'? Clearly many forms are erroneous or distorted and can be rejected. 'Colkitto' and the many variations on that theme must be rejected as belonging properly to his father — even though this was the name by which Alasdair was probably most widely known to non-Gaels in his lifetime. Even while both men were still alive the erroneous use of this name caused confusion, leading to the father being distinguished as 'old Colkittoche' (or 'old Collgillespick'),[25] a practice which some modern historians have copied by designating Alasdair 'Young Colkitto'.

'Alexander MacDonald' (or 'MacDonnell') and 'Alasdair MacColla' are the forms we are now left with. The man himself would have found either form acceptable. The three surviving examples of his signature all read 'Allexander Mcdonnell'.[26] This at first appears decisive; he is consistent in signing his name. Surely he would sign with what he regarded as the correct form of his name, and historians should accept this. But, on the other hand, all of these three signatures are appended to documents written in English, and therefore in them he probably used what he regarded as the English version of his name. How would he have signed a Gaelic letter, addressed to a fellow-Gael? No evidence survives that allows a definite answer to this question, but he would probably have signed with some spelling of 'Alasdair MacColla', perhaps adding 'Ciotach' and/or 'MacDonnell'. It is as Alasdair MacColla that he appears in Gaelic poetry and Gaelic folklore, and this is doubtless the name by which he thought of himself when among his own people — as well as the name by which most of those who knew him personally thought of him. As he lived in the Gaelic world, fought for it, and spoke mainly its language (and English only occasionally), it seems by far the most appropriate name to give him — even in a biography written in English.

Hence this is a biography of Alasdair MacColla.

But, what's in a name? Does it matter that this man was known by a wide variety of names, or which of them one chooses to use? It does matter. The very fact that there was such confusion over what to call Alasdair — and, indeed, over what he called himself — tells us a good deal about him and his environment. The confusion of names is a vivid demonstration of the fact that he was a man whose exploits brought him fame in two worlds, two cultures and languages; the Gaelic culture of the native Irish and Highland Scots on the one hand, the English-speaking world of the English, the Lowland Scots and the Anglo- and Scoto- Irish on the other. The differences between the name-systems of the two cultures, christian name and fixed surname on the one hand, christian name and sobriquet or patronymic on the other, illustrate the difference between two cultures based on separate languages. And the difficulty English speakers found in understanding the Gaelic names and name-system which Alasdair's exploits brought to their attention illustrates the depth of their ignorance of the Gaelic world, and thus quite how different the two worlds were. Arguably this is what the wars Alasdair MacColla and his father fought in were mainly about; the differences and tensions between the two basic cultures, centred on two languages, which existed in the British Isles.

NOTES

1. J.T. Gilbert (ed), *A contemporary history of affairs in Ireland from 1641 to 1652* (3 vols in 6, Dublin 1879-80), i.159, 176.

2. Eg, 'Alastrann mac Colla Ciotaigh', T. O'Donnchadha (ed), 'Cin lae O Meallain', *Analecta Hibernica*, 3 (1931), 12.

3. Eg, 'Alasdair mac colla mic Giolla asbuig', A. MacBain and J. Kennedy (eds), *Reliquiae Celticae* (2 vols, Inverness 1892-4), ii.176.

4. Macdonald, A.J. and A.M., *The Clan Donald* (3 vols, Inverness 1896-1904), iii, second plate after p.641. This is presented as a facsimile of Coll's signature, but it is not original — see Chapter 2 note 91.

5. J.R.N. Macphail (ed), 'Extracts from the . . . Denmylne MSS', *Highland Papers*, iii (SHS 1920), 295n: W.R. Kermack, *The Scottish Highlands. A short history* (Edinburgh and London 1957), 129n.

6. C. Giblin (ed), *Irish Franciscan Mission to Scotland, 1619-1646. Documents from Roman archives* (Dublin 1964), 125-6.

7. *A true and exact relation of divers principall actions* . . . (London 1642), 4; W. Cobbet, *State trials*, v (1810), 1396; *Acts of the parliaments of Scotland*, vii (1820), 232.

8. J. de V. Loder, *Colonsay and Oronsay in the Isles of Argyll* (Edinburgh 1935), 234-5 quoting J. Anderson (ed), *Calendar of the Laing Charters* (Edinburgh 1899), 663; J. Lodge (ed M. Archdall), *The peerage of Ireland* (7 vols, Dublin 1789), vii. 116; J.G. Fotheringham (ed), *Montereul correspondence* (2 vols, SHS 1898-9), i.46n.

9. J.H. Burton, *History of Scotland* (8 vols, Edinburgh and London 1876), vi.369; D.P. Menzies, *The red and white book of Menzies* (Glasgow 1894), 273.

10. Cobbet, *State trials*, v.1411, 1439; M. Napier (ed), *Memorials of Montrose and his times* (3 vols, Maitland Club, 1848-50), ii. 165, 167.

11. R. Black, 'Colla Ciotach', *TGSI*, xlviii (1972-4) 201; R. Baillie, *Letters and journals* (3 vols, Bannatyne Club, 1841-2), iii. 499.

·12. *APS*, VI.i (1870), 317-23, checked with original in SRO, PA. 2/23.

13. Eg, M. Napier, *Memoirs of Montrose* (2 vols, Edinburgh 1856), ii.416, 417.

14. J. Wilcock, *The great marquess. Life and times of Archibald 8th earl and 1st (and only) marquess of Argyll* (Edinburgh and London 1903), 6.

15. Bodleian Library, Oxford, Carte MSS, 3, ff.239-40; T.W. Moody and J.G. Simms (eds), *The bishopric of Derry and the Irish Society of London*, i (IMC 1968), 245.

16. *A mighty victory in Ireland* . . . (London 1647), 3; *A perfect narrative* . . . (London 1647), 7; H. Cary (ed), *Memorials of the great civil war* (2 vols, London. 1842), i.362; E. Hyde, earl of Clarendon, *History of the rebellion and civil wars in England*, ed. W.D. Macray (6 vols, Oxford 1888), iii.523.

17. *An extract of severall letters from Scotland* . . . (London 1645), 6; E.S. Shuckburgh (ed), *Two biographies of William Bedell* (Cambridge 1902), 174.

18. T.H. Marshall, *History of Perth* (Perth 1849), 194; [J. Cant], *Memorabilia of the City of Perth* (Perth 1806), 167.

19. HMC 63: *Egmont*, I.ii.414; *A declaration published in the Scots army . . .* (London 1646), 13-14; *A declaration of the proceedings of the new moddel'd army in the kingdome of Scotland . . .* (London 1646/7); *Three great victories . . .* (London 1645).

20. D. O'Connell and B. O'Ferrall, *Commentarius Rinuccinianus* (6 vols, IMC 1932-49), i.460.

21. J.T. Gilbert (ed), *History of the Irish confederation and the war in Ireland* (7 vols, Dublin 1882-91), vii.331.

22. *State papers and manuscripts relating to English affairs, existing in the archives and collections of Venice . . . 1643-7* (1926), 313, 316, 317.

23. D. Peacock, *Perth; its annals and archives* (Perth 1849), 269.

24. J. Spalding, *Memorials of the troubles* (2 vols, Spalding Club 1850-1), ii.386, 402, 478; R. Baillie, *Letters and journals* (3 vols, Bannatyne Club 1841-2), ii.217n, 321.

25. J.D. Marwick (ed), *Extracts from the records of the burgh of Glasgow, 1630-62* (Scottish Burgh Record Society, 1881), 509; SRO, PA.11/5, f.51.

26. Bodleian Library, Oxford, Carte MSS, 12, f.82 (letter to Ormond, 13 August 1644); Hamilton Muniments, Lennoxlove, C.1/1956 (letter to Charles I, 15 August 1646); SRO, GD.220/3/184, Montrose Muniments (Kilcumin band, 1645). These three documents are printed in Gilbert, *Ir confed*, i.795-6, HMC 21: *Hamilton*, i.113, and Napier, *Memorials* ii.173 respectively, but in each case Alasdair's signature has been transcribed inaccurately. The same is probably true of the surviving copy of his 1647 commission to his father, which gives his signature as 'Alexander McDonald', SRO, PA.7/23/2/49.

1

The Highlands in the Early Seventeenth Century

THE Gaelic world into which Alasdair MacColla was born at the beginning of the seventeenth century was a world of violence, instability and change. For both Gaelic Ireland and the Gaelic Highlands of Scotland (especially the Western Highlands and Isles) the later sixteenth century had been marked by bitter internal wars and by attempts at domination or conquest from outside. The Tudor conquest of Ireland had been completed in 1603; for the first time English claims (maintained since the twelfth century) to rule all Ireland corresponded with reality. The Highlands had not been conquered by the Scottish crown but were gradually being forced to accept rule from Edinburgh in fact as well as in theory.

The collapse of the political autonomy of the Gaelic areas of Ireland and Scotland in the face of attack by the monarchies of England and Scotland was hastened by internal warfare and feuding among the Gaels themselves; they lacked any central political or military authority to unite them in their struggle. By contrast their opponents achieved greater unity than ever before. By the union of the crowns of 1603 James VI of Scotland became also James I of England and Ireland; a united monarchy could now co-ordinate action against the linked Gaelic societies of the Highlands and Ireland.

Looking back, it tends to be assumed that the Gaelic world, fast losing its political autonomy, had begun the decline of the separateness of its way of life from the rest of Britain which was to lead to the complete disappearance of its language and culture from many areas. Military conquest and political domination would lead to outside economic, social, cultural and religious influences becoming, in many cases, irresistible. The Gaelic world was doomed. But though with the benefit of hindsight we may judge that in some respects this process had already begun, this was far from clear at the time. Gaelic political autonomy might be collapsing, but many Gaels believed — or at least hoped — that it could be revived; the setbacks experienced need not be final. Moreover, though political separateness might be in decline, other features of Gaelic separateness showed no sign of decay. In religion Roman Catholicism, often associated with the Gaelic cause (though by no means all Gaels were Catholic), was showing a marked revival in Gaeldom in the early seventeenth century. In culture the Highland world was remarkably healthy; it is true that the great medieval tradition of stone carving in the West Highlands disappears after the Reformation crisis of the mid-sixteenth century, but in poetry and music the picture is very different. Changes were certainly taking place, new forms of poetry

emerging, but this was a sign of life, not of decline. The seventeenth century was to produce a great variety and richness of Gaelic poetry, some of it among the best ever composed in the language. The classical music of the bagpipe was to reach new heights in the hands of pipers like the MacCrimmons in Skye.[1]

Gaelic culture in the Highlands thus not only survived but was thriving in the seventeenth century. It was able to do this, in spite of political change, of violence and instability, largely because the social structure on which the culture rested proved flexible enough to adapt itself to new conditions. The clan changed, but it survived as the basic local political and social unit. This brings us to the vexed question, what were 'clans'? Surprisingly, the problem has received little detailed attention from historians so far as the sixteenth and seventeenth centuries are concerned. It tends to be assumed that clans then were the same as the clans that were to be destroyed in the eighteenth century. But, though much further research is needed, it seems clear that the clan was no more fossilised than Gaelic culture was, and that many of the later myths about the nature of the clan do not apply to the reality of earlier clan structure, and were probably not even applied to it in theory.

The clans of late medieval and early modern Scotland had their origins in the fourteenth century or later. They were not, as is sometimes still assumed, survivals of primitive tribes with an existence stretching back to distant antiquity. Nearly all chiefs claimed such distant roots, and sometimes there was truth in the claims in a strictly genealogical sense; the chiefs could trace as their ancestors great leaders of earlier ages. But these ancestors had not been 'chiefs' of 'clans' such as existed from the fourteenth to the eighteenth centuries.

The clans arose to fill a power vacuum. At the end of the thirteenth century the Lowlands and parts of the Highlands had a political and social system in common. The Western Isles (only ceded to Scotland by Norway in 1266) and most of the Western Highlands still had not been feudalised; but it seemed that these areas would gradually be integrated more closely with the rest of the country (though without abandoning their cultures, their language, or many features of their social system). Local landholders would in time add (under royal pressure) to their existing acceptance of dependence on the monarchy a feudal definition of their rights to their lands and their obligations to the crown. The basic idea underlying feudalism was that all land belonged ultimately to the king. He made grants of land to his leading subjects, but they did not own such land outright; they held it from the king in return for payments and services (especially military service), and they were his vassals, owing loyalty and obedience to him. Those who held land directly from the king, the tenants 'in chief', would in turn grant or let it (or most of it) out to lesser men, who became their vassals, and so on down the scale until the small tenants who actually farmed the land were reached. Social status and political power alike were based on relationship to land. The king's authority was largely dependent on his claim to the ultimate ownership of all land, and the most powerful men in the kingdom were almost invariably (except for clerics) tenants in chief. Such men built up their power through the obedience and service due to them from their own vassals, and through the wealth accumulated from the rents and dues paid to them by such lesser men, and by tenant farmers to whom the tenants in chief would rent some land directly. Thus was created the 'feudal pyramid', a (theoretically) neat, orderly hierarchy of landholders spreading downwards and outwards from the king at the top to the actual cultivators of the soil at the bottom.

Needless to say, the reality was not so simple as the theory. Feudalism was constantly evolving and changing. Pre-feudal survivals and local practices often complicated the picture. And, above all, kinship ties based on blood relationship were strong. In one sense indeed kinship quickly came to be an essential element in feudalism, in that feudally held land came to descend from father to son; but in addition to this, men naturally tended to favour their own relations in granting land and making political alliances. One of the best ways of extending one's power and influence was to arrange beneficial marriages for oneself and one's kin. Such a feudal 'system' modified by kinship prevailed in most of Scotland, and seemed destined to be extended to the remoter Highland areas.

In the fourteenth century, however, the power of the monarchy declined. Weak kings were followed by a disastrous succession of child rulers. Between 1390 and 1625 no monarch of Scotland had reached adulthood on ascending the throne. During extended royal minorities the power of central government tended to decay as factions competed viciously to rule in name of the infant monarch, often granting out power previously exercised by the king to great men in order to win their support. The work done by even the most competent rulers in restoring royal power seldom survived the subsequent royal minority. Moreover, the resources of the crown often had to be concentrated on fighting the long wars with England rather than on asserting royal authority throughout the country.

As the power of the monarchy decayed, so men had to fend for themselves — especially in areas like the Highlands and Isles relatively remote from the centre of government. Landholders had to protect themselves without reference to their ultimate feudal superior, the king, for he could no longer offer them effective protection or justice. In such circumstances the landholders who survived and prospered were those who acted aggressively, extending their power at the expense of neighbours, striving to increase the number of followers who, willingly or unwillingly, would obey and serve them. Such activities could be indulged in with little fear of retribution from central government. There were many ways in which ruthless men could thus aggrandise themselves, but only three basic ways in which they sought to legitimise their actions. Feudal authority could be extended by forcing lesser neighbours who held land directly from the king to agree to hold it in future as their vassals, and charters obtained from the crown sanctioning this. Or they could claim authority as head of kin groups or families, insisting that seniority gave them power over all their relatives. Finally, extension of power could be given the legitimacy of written agreement through banding or bonding. Such bonds could be between equals, binding themselves together in friendship or to act as allies; or between a great man and a lesser one, the latter by a bond of 'manrent' obliging himself and his followers to obey the former in return for protection.

Feudalism; kinship; bonding. These became the basic social ties throughout

Scotland, Highland as well as Lowland. Where do 'clans' fit into this picture? As royal authority declines one begins to hear of 'clans' in the Highlands, and commentators begin to divide the inhabitants of Scotland into two types; Lowlanders, speaking the Scots variant of the English tongue and relatively 'civilised' and law-abiding; and Highlanders, speaking Gaelic, warlike and unruly, barbaric compared to Lowlanders, organised in 'clans'.

'Clan' means literally children or offspring, and the clans were the social and political groups which emerged in the Highlands in the fourteenth and fifteenth centuries in response to the lack of effective royal authority. As the name suggests, the idea of kinship, of authority based on the headship of a kin, was the dominant feature of the clan in theory. But in practice the origins and structures of clans varied greatly. In the west the chiefs of clans generally traced their ancestry back to great men, Celtic or Norse, of earlier ages; their families had accepted the authority of the 'feudal' monarchy but now, as royal power decayed, they revived and emphasised older claims to pre-eminence. In the east many clans were almost entirely feudal in origin; the Gaelic speaking chiefs who emerged were the descendants of French speaking Anglo-Normans whose first claim to authority in the area they dominated was the grant of land to them by feudal charter, but who as generations passed had 'gone native', become gaelicised. As this happened they tended to buttress the authority they claimed by feudal grant from a declining monarchy by claiming also a kinship right to the obedience of their men, thus appealing to an older form of legitimacy and partly adopting the culture of the local population. The parallel with the way in which many of the early Anglo-Norman settlers in Ireland 'went native' is striking.

The origins of clans were thus diverse and complicated. Quite what the clans were in practice is both complicated and controversial. The modern popular image of the clan is of a body of people related by blood, descended from a common ancestor, inhabiting a clan territory, ruled by a chief who is head of the kin, wearing a clan tartan and all having the same surname.

The last two of these characteristics can easily be disposed of; tartans were worn, but there were no fixed clan tartans, and clansmen did not share a common surname, for the very good reason that until the seventeenth century most Highlanders had no fixed surnames. As to descent from a common ancestor, it does seem that by the eighteenth century it was usual for those who followed a chief to claim such kinship with him. This was a myth, but a useful one, since men believed in the truth of it and it provided a very strong social bond. Nonetheless, it was a myth, and the further one looks back in the history of clans the more obviously mythical it becomes. Originally the 'clan', in the strict sense of the children or descendants of the man held to be the founder of the clan, was the dominant or ruling group in the 'clan' in the wider sense of all who gave obedience to a chief.

Thus a 'clan' usually consisted of several distinct groups: the 'clan' proper, those with close blood ties with the chief; lesser subordinate 'clans', 'septs' or kin groups often with their own chiefs, which accepted the authority of a greater chief; dependants or 'native men' who obeyed a chief, often inhabitants of land a chief had taken over by conquest or other means; 'broken men', refugees from feuds in other clans or from small clans which were collapsing under outside pressure; and, finally, a group of officials whose functions had become hereditary in their families, ranging from pipers and harpers to boydguards and to senachies (genealogists and historians). The growth of the power and size of a clan was certainly reliant on kinship, but conquest and the offering of protection in return for loyalty were at least equally important. An Irish historian has pointed out that the clan in the 'Scottish sense' of all the subjects of a chief or ruler having kinship with him never existed in Ireland, and suggested that the idea of 'the homogeneous clan in Scotland appears to be seated upon foundations no more secure than those which support its offspring in Ireland'.[2] 'Scottish' clanship thus did not exist even in Scotland! The clan 'in its larger sense was . . . heterogeneous in composition. It was based as much on a binding lord-vassal relationship such as occurs in all feudal societies as on kinship'.[3]

Of course in time, as the various elements in a clan grew used to working together and intermarried, such separate origins tended to be forgotten, or the importance of them to be minimised; but nonetheless one can make the generalisation that the central feature of the 'clan' in the wider sense of all the men who followed a chief was not kinship but obedience. A chief's clansmen were those who, willingly or unwillingly, obeyed him. But the word 'clan' in different contexts had different meanings. In the early seventeenth century, for example, men still often referred to the Clan Donald as if it were a single unit, but in practice the MacDonalds were by this time split into several separate groups each of which was an autonomous clan with its own chief — the MacDonalds of Glengarry, Keppoch and Sleat, the Clanranald, the Clan Donald South or Clan Ian Mor. Smaller groups within these subdivisions could also be referred to as MacDonald 'clans'; the MacDonalds of Colonsay (a branch of the Clan Ian Mor), or even the 'clan' of Coll Ciotach. And at each level these references sometimes include only the dominant kin, but on other occasions all the followers of that kin as well. All this seems very confusing, but really is no more so than the range of meanings of the word 'family' in the Lowlands, which could mean anything from all with any blood relationship down to parents and their children, and which could be extended to include servants living in a household with the 'kin' family.[4]

If all members of a clan, in the sense of the following of a chief, were not related by blood, how — and why — did the belief that they were arise? In part it was a natural development; the authority of a father was regarded as the most basic of all forms of authority, so it was natural for any leader to try to lay claim to it, just as kings claimed to be fathers of their people. By claiming to be a father or head of kin to all his followers, a chief was both flattering his dependants by recognising them as his kin, not mere subjects, and was putting them under an additional obligation to him. To claims to obedience based on conquest, tradition or feudal grant he was adding claims to the natural authority of the head of the kin. Chiefs' 'subjects' were proud to be allowed to claim such 'kinship' to them, and many went further and adopted their chiefs' surnames, adding outward plausibility to the claim of relationship. At first this relationship might clearly be seen as fictitious or honorary, but in time the metaphor of kinship tended to be converted into belief that real blood kinship existed.

Moreover, over the generations genuine kinship of blood would tend to spread ever wider in the clan. The ruling kin group might at first be a very small body, but it tended to grow with each generation as brothers and sons of chiefs were granted lands and founded cadet branches of the main family. Chiefs took it for granted that the most powerful positions within the clan should be reserved for their 'real' kinsmen, who thus came to be leaders and organisers of the clan at a local level. These were the *daoine uaisle*, the gentry of the clan, holding land from the chief in return not only for rent but for their services as military leaders and as advisers to the chief. Many of the *daoine uaisle* came to hold their land hereditarily though they had no formal leases; custom gave them security, and many disliked the increasing tendency in the seventeenth century of chiefs to insist on written leases or 'tacks'. Even the longest of leases were seen as limiting their rights in the land. Nonetheless, the tack eventually triumphed everywhere, and by the eighteenth century the *daoine uaisle* were generally called simply tacksmen.[5]

As chiefs advanced the claims of their kinsmen to land, so the dominance of their kin group grew. Thus in the Highlands as in Ireland 'One of the most important phenomena in a clan-based society is that of expansion from the top downwards'. As a seventeenth century Irish scholar noted, 'as the sons and families of the rulers multiplied, so their subjects and followers were squeezed out and withered away'. The ruling kin extended and took over land from dependants, depressing their social status.[6] Real kin were favoured rather than fictional kin. Thus the size of the clan proper, the kin group, tended to grow even greater, until the point was reached at which all important men in a chief's following, the wider clan, were kin of the chief. So were some lesser men, members of cadet branches which had not thrived and distant relatives. But still many, probably the majority, of lesser men who followed a chief were not really his kin.

Nonetheless it is obvious that kinship, real or fictitious, lay at the centre of clanship and the power of the chief. But kinship was never the whole story. From the first — and indeed in many cases especially at first — other elements were inherent in the structure of the clan and the power of the chief. Clanship emerged as the power of 'feudal' monarchy declined, but feudalism did not disappear from the Highlands. Kinship claims to authority were often added to existing feudal claims, not substituted for them, when the latter alone became inadequate as the king could no longer enforce the law and feudal rights. A chief would advance kinship claims to power, but he would not lightly neglect or abandon feudal claims. If a chief conquered new territory for his clan he would usually try to get official legitimisation of this through a subsequent feudal grant from the king.

Kinship and feudalism thus could go hand in hand in the growth of a clan. But the two could come into conflict, and this has led some to blame most of the troubles in the Highlands in the sixteenth and seventeenth centuries on feudalism. It was, we are told, a 'peculiarly artificial system of land tenure',[7] differing in principle from the older Celtic institutions which gave birth to the clan. Claims to authority in Celtic society were 'patriarchal', based on kinship, while feudal authority was based on rights to the land on which people lived. 'Natural' clanship began with people, 'artificial' feudalism with property. The insistence of central government on trying to force feudalism on the Highlands (especially the Western Highlands and Isles) led to the people of the Highlands being in constant revolt, rejecting the 'feudalism' which contradicted their 'patriarchal' principles.

Now it is certainly true that the authority of a Gaelic chief and that of a feudal lord can be said to rest on different principles, the former on a hierarchy of blood, the latter on a hierarchy of land-holding, but this does not mean that the two were completely incompatible in practice. In fact the structures of society produced by the two systems could be similar. Maybe in the kinship traditions of the Gaels 'rights to land depended on personal status, and not as under feudalism status upon holding of land', but in practice the distinction was usually unimportant. In both systems status and power were linked to the holding of land. Whether status gave you land or land gave you status is an interesting theoretical point, but little more.[8]

Furthermore, the use of the word 'patriarchal' to describe Gaelic ideas of political authority is potentially misleading, because it leads to the conflation of two different theories under a single name. In a sense the authority of a chief was 'patriarchal'; he was the head of his kin, and was regarded as the father of his clansmen. But traditionally his authority was limited in some respects. He was expected to rule in consultation with his leading clansmen, and they had in theory the right to depose him if this was regarded as necessary for the good of the clan. Moreover chiefs were (again, at least in theory) chosen by the leading clansmen from among the previous chief's immediate male kin. But the essential point of patriarchal political theory as it developed in the seventeenth century was that it claimed absolute power for a ruler as the power of a father over his family is unlimited.[9] And such patriarchal ideas enjoin strict adherence to primogeniture in the succession of rulers. Yet sometimes these differences have been ignored, and a conflation of traditional Gaelic kin-based authority with absolutist patriarchalism has been made. This has then been used to explain why many clans came to support the Stewart monarchy. The exalted theories of absolute royal power put forward by James VI were very similar to Celtic ideas of the powers of rulers, it is argued, and they therefore won an immediate sympathetic response in the Highlands, chiefs swinging round to support the dynasty against its enemies.[10] The monarchy is thus held to have rejected a 'feudal' theory of political obligation which the clans were bound to resist, in favour of a 'patriarchal' one which they were bound to support. But the argument rests entirely on the false assumption that the word 'patriarchal' is always used with the same meaning.

The main problem raised by the monarchy's determination to impose feudal landholding throughout the Highlands arose from weak, inconsistent and inefficient government. In a number of cases feudal charters to disputed territory were granted successively to both parties concerned through official ignorance or incompetence. The trouble thus lay not in any inherent weakness in (or alienness of) feudal landholding but in the much wider problem of bad government. James VI's government 'bestowed an infinite benefit upon the chiefs and their clans' by sorting out much of this confusion over feudal rights to Highland lands.[11] But this benefit came not from James suppressing the 'feudalism' often held to have caused such troubles but, on the contrary, from a firm and consistent (though not always just) imposition of feudal landholding.

In some instances, through official bungling, feudal rights to Highland lands could be claimed by more than one party. But even this was seldom the cause of disputes; it was rather a symptom of existing ones, for the two parties concerned would usually both claim traditional rights as well, and often sought eagerly for feudal charters to back up such existing claims. Similarly, when one party only in a land dispute can claim feudal rights, this does not necessarily mean the other party is championing traditional clan rights against alien grants; the 'right' of such rival claimants is often right of conquest which it is hoped eventually to legitimise by gaining a feudal charter from the distant king. What really mattered in the Highlands in the sixteenth century in the absence of any effective central government was power. Whether the exercise of this power was justified by feudal or kinship arguments was secondary.

Yet, as already stated, there could be conflict arising from the differing principles and practices of the two 'systems'. The most common, and intractable, was that the feudal superiority of land could pass to one man, who thus had the feudal right to the service and loyalty of the men living on it, while these men in practice remained loyal to another man, whom they regarded as their chief. Thus the Camerons and the MacDonalds of Keppoch lost the feudal right to virtually all their lands but retained the loyalty of their clansmen. Such situations could cause disputes lasting for generations; but though in some cases these were disputes between Highland clan chief and Lowland feudal superior, it was much more common for the rival demands for loyalty both to come from clan chiefs, for even the most Gaelic of chiefs showed no hesitation in pressing feudal claims when it suited them; feudalism could be a useful alternative to naked conquest in extending a chief's power. The Campbell earls of Argyll (followed closely by the MacKenzie earls of Seaforth) proved masters at the art of aggressive feudalism. Financial difficulties of neighbouring chiefs could be exploited by lending them money on security of the feudal superiority of their clan's lands; when the loan was not repaid the chief might find himself holding his land not directly from the king but from the earl of Argyll, or he might be squeezed out altogether. Disorder or revolt by other clans could be encouraged, and then crushed in name of the king in return for a grant of the feudal superiority of the lands concerned. Once feudal superiority was obtained, the process of absorbing the inhabitants into their new 'clans' could begin; the breaking down of traditional loyalties, the expulsion of the recalcitrant.

Differing customs in determining succession could also lead to feudal superiority and chieftaincy becoming separated. By feudal custom land descended to the eldest son, or if a man had no sons, jointly to his daughters. In Gaelic custom the chief should be the most suitable of the immediate male kin of the previous chief. This might well be his eldest son, but it could be a younger son or a brother; the chief men of the clan should decide the matter. In practice, however, disputes were fairly rare. In the great majority of instances the eldest son, the feudal heir, was accepted as chief without question, for though this might not conform to older tradition, such a system of primogeniture did have advantages. Choosing the best qualified candidate might sound more sensible than automatically accepting the eldest son; but in practice it tended to lead to bloody succession wars between rival claimants, such as were common in Gaelic Ireland. Cases did occur in which the claims of a chief's eldest son were set aside, and the feudal rights of daughters in instances where a chief had no sons were generally ignored; and occasionally existing chiefs who proved inadequate were deposed and replaced. But very often the monarchy was willing to turn a blind eye to these aberrations, and granted feudal recognition to the new chief. Thus feudalism could be flexible, for monarchs often preferred to uphold the realities of power in the Highlands rather than support the legitimate claims of those deprived of their 'feudal' rights.

To sum up, feudalism was often as central to a chief's power as kinship. Chiefs used feudalism willingly when it worked to their own advantage, and only made the discovery that it was something alien and unnatural if it happened to work against their interests. When feudal ties did not exist, chiefs often found it convenient to invent quasi-feudal ones to bolster their authority. Dependants of chiefs were obliged to pay 'calps' to the chief on the death of each head of the family as a token of their dependence. This consisted usually of the best horse of the dead man, and thus paralleled the heriot often exacted in the Lowlands.[12] Or such dependants could be bound to their chief by bonds of manrent, promising service (sometimes including the payment of calps) and acknowledging superiority 'as native men ought' in return for protection.[13] As well as such quasi-feudal ties, quasi-kinship ones were created; not just through the general myth of kinship wider than that which acutally existed, but also through the artificial kinship of fosterage. Sons were frequently sent to foster parents for at least part of their childhood, and elaborate arrangements made to share the cost of their upbringing. Fosterage could be used to strengthen real kinship ties, as when Lord Lorne (the son of the earl of Argyll) sent his heir to be fostered by Sir Colin Campbell of Glenorchy in the 1630s.[14] Or it could be used to create an entirely artificial kinship, as when a son of Campbell of Glenorchy in 1580 fostered his son with a 'native servant' or dependant.[15]

All these different social ties failed to bring peace and order to the Highlands. The growth of clanship was largely a response to increased lawlessness, but it came to seem (to Lowlanders at least) that it was clanship which was causing and perpetuating disorder and violence. Clan became 'a bad word in Lowland mouths; clans did wicked things'.[16] There was a good deal of prejudice in such opinions, but also (especially in the sixteenth century) an element of truth. Most clans would extend their territory at the expense of their neighbours if possible, and would act ruthlessly in pursuit of traditional feuds or in vengeance for insults. Even when no major conflicts were in progress, plundering cattle raids were endemic and could lead to serious bloodshed. Violence, aggression and plundering came to have a central part in the ethos of the clan; in the most violent periods and areas a clan could become virtually a society of warriors, for whom warfare or raiding were necessary to prove their manhood and bind the clan together in the elation of aggression, the pride of success, the determination of defeat. Periodic violence was an essential and honourable part of life. The Highlands were experiencing a heroic age in which the warrior was the dominant element in society, in which the warrior bands of neighbouring communities fought each other and individuals gained renown in warfare 'of an aggressive and predatory character', in which literature (written and oral) was much concerned with the deeds of warriors, with the feats of strength and courage of individual 'heroes'.[17]

How did this society of the Highlands differ from that of the Lowlands? In basic social structure the two parts of Scotland were in many ways surprisingly alike. The contrast between feudalism and clan kinship was not as great as has sometimes been claimed, and just as when the Highland clan 'system' emerged it often included strong feudal elements, so the Lowland 'feudal system' was simultaneously becoming permeated by increasingly important kinship bonds. 'The development of the Highland clan was accompanied by that of the Lowland families or "kins"',[18] for 'in neither region was feudalism by itself capable of providing the secure social grouping necessary for survival in the time of lawlessness over which the early Stewarts presided'.[19] The Lowland family or 'name' came to be almost as important as the Highland clan. In the Lowlands as in the Highlands groups bound together by kinship (real or mythical) and feudalism feuded and fought for power in hierarchic societies similar in basic structure. Yet there were some significant differences in structure, and by the late sixteenth and the seventeenth centuries social changes in the Lowlands were leading the two societies to diverge. Kinship was in decline as a social and political bond, a process which was eventually to make Highland emphasis on it seem another symptom of the area's backwardness. Large-scale transfers of church lands both before and after the Reformation encouraged in the Lowlands the development of an increasingly active land market, and of an increasingly commercial attitude to land. Such dealings in land enriched many existing lairds and created many new ones; the wealth and independence of such lesser landowners was growing, a process that inevitably weakened the traditional pre-eminence of the greater nobility. The slow rise of other groups in wealth and status — lawyers, administrators, merchants and ministers of the reformed church — confirmed the gradual movement away from a society dominated by a few great families. The Highlands had no equivalent to the burghs of the Lowlands, the larger of which had substantial communities of merchants leading settled, urban lives; and such burghs were growing in size and wealth.

The growing importance of the middle ranks in Lowland society — the lairds, merchants, and members of the professions — was widening the gap between Highland and Lowland social structures. Moreover, though the basic structures of society retained many similarities, they were nonetheless very different societies in other respects — in religion, in language, in culture, in economy, in lawlessness and in relationship to the monarchy.

Religious differences were the last to appear. In many Highland (especially West Highland) areas organised religion collapsed after the Reformation of 1560.

Except in parts of the east and Argyllshire the new reformed church failed to establish an effective ministry for several generations. Many western clans remained loyal in name to Catholicism, but through lack of priests the remnants of the old religion became increasingly corrupt and in places pagan practices revived. Meanwhile most of the Lowlands accepted Calvinism, and the parish minister became a dominant figure in the local community. Thus, though some southern and eastern clans accepted protestantism, religion came in the late sixteenth century to be a new and bitter source of hatred between Lowlander and Highlander.

Of all the differences between Highland and Lowland, that of language was the most obvious. Almost inevitably men who cannot understand what each other is saying come to look on each other as alien. The Scottish state and monarchy might be largely Celtic in origin, Gaelic might once have been the most widely spoken language in the kingdom, but by the sixteenth century most Lowlanders thought of Gaelic speakers as not really Scots; the language they spoke was usually called 'Irish', and the same word was often applied to the people of the Highlands as well, stressing their alien nature.

The alienation caused by the linguistic division was heightened by the cultural divide which coincided with it. To the Lowlanders who formed the majority (perhaps two thirds) of Scotland's population the Gaelic culture of the Highlands, with its close links with native Irish culture, hardly seemed worthy of the name 'culture' at all. How could Highland literature, written or oral, have any merit when it was expressed in 'barbarous' Irish? How could Highland music be worthy of serious consideration when it used different scales from those which had become standard in western music? How could one believe in the learning of the scholars of a society which had no schools or universities recognisable to a Lowlander, and whose learning was often oral and not dependent on the printed word, the emerging symbol of civilisation? Even the very dress of Highlanders, with their long plaids and bare legs, made them seem foreign in Lowland eyes. And, like most people in most ages, the Lowlander assumed that a culture different from his own must be inferior.

The Highlander in turn was no less prejudiced; proud of his own culture and heritage, he had no doubt that it was superior to that of the decadent, soft-living Lowlander. Moreover, many Highlanders felt a deep resentment at the way in which their language and culture had become limited geographically to the Highlands. Many Lowlanders who now spoke Scots were indistinguishable in blood from Highlanders who spoke Gaelic, but for centuries Gaelic had been slowly retreating, and Highlanders came to look on Lowlanders as men of a different race who had stolen the lands of the Gaels, driving them into the remoter, poorer parts of the kingdom. Scotland was rightly their kingdom, but the Lowlander had cheated them of much of their birthright.

Cultural and linguistic differences coincided fairly closely, by the fifteenth and sixteenth centuries, with the division between the two main types of economy in Scotland, which were largely determined by geography and climate. Gaelic speech and culture were largely confined to the areas of the north and west in which agriculture was predominantly pastoral. Grain (oats and barley) was grown wherever possible, but the economy was dominated by cattle. Sheep and goats rivalled them in numbers, but not in the central place they had in the life, the culture and the warfare of the population. Sale of cattle in the Lowlands was the main source of the money with which clansmen bought necessities they could not produce for themselves, and with which chiefs purchased luxury goods, fine clothes, guns, French wines. In the Lowlands by contrast arable farming, the growing of crops, tended to be supreme, though always combined with pastoral farming. Probably even without other differences, this difference in emphasis in the main economic activity, agriculture, between Highlands and Lowlands would have led to tension and misunderstanding. Pastoral and arable farming tended to foster different attitudes and ways of life. Pastoral agriculture took less of a man's time in the course of the year than arable. Cattle herding was a life of movement from pasture to pasture, with whole communities often moving to sheilings, summer pasture, for several months of the year. By contrast the life of the arable farmer was more fixed and static. Disorder — local feud or warfare — tended to be more disruptive to arable than to pastoral farming. Cattle were conveniently mobile, and could often be driven to safety in case of attack, while crops, whether still in the field or already harvested, could not so easily be saved from destruction. Equally, from the opposite point of view, that of the aggressor, cattle were a most convenient form of booty; wealth in less mobile form, like crops or grain, once captured often had to be destroyed for lack of transport. Thus cattle raiding could become an institution in Gaelic life, hallowed by tradition and given a central place in mythology, because it was not so economically destructive as similar raiding by warrior bands would have been in areas of settled arable agriculture.

The effect of the contrast inherent in differing economies can be over-exaggerated, but it is more than a coincidence that the Lowland region which produced a society most like that of the Highlands was also an area of hill and moor, of pastoral economy: the Borders. There as in the Highlands the predatory raid and violence flourished to an extent unknown in the rest of the kingdom; there too kin loyalties thrived to such an extent that men referred to Border as well as to Highland clans. But, before this leads one to carry economic determinism too far, it must be added that the Borders shared more than a pastoral economy with the Highlands. The geography of the Borders, like that of the Highlands, made communications difficult and the assertion of the power of central government laborious. The Borders might be much less remote from Edinburgh than most of the Highlands, but they were almost as difficult to govern since (until 1603) this lack of remoteness was compensated for by the political sensitivity of the international boundary with England, which made central government reluctant to act decisively in the area.

Relationship to central government and the monarchy is the final major factor in differentiating Highlands from Lowlands to require consideration. On the whole the Gaelic-speaking Highland areas were less obedient to central government, more disorderly and violent, than the Lowlands. The fact that the Borders often formed a partial exception to this generalisation shows that it cannot be carried too far, but it is nonetheless basically true. Many Lowland areas suffered from feuds which caused intermittent bloodshed and could last for generations; and the monarchy often proved ineffectual in suppressing such disturbances. But such violence was usually very limited in scope, casualties confined to a few individuals at a time. This was very different from the full scale inter-clan wars which became endemic in the Highlands, with territory being conquered and held by right of conquest, with pitched battles and (in the late sixteenth century at least) occasional massacres of whole communities, men, women and children. The Lowlands did of course experience organised warfare from time to time: civil wars between factions fighting to control central government. But this was, from a national point of view, essentially different from clan warfare in that the fighting concerned national political issues. Admittedly such civil wars often had in them large elements of traditional feud, but nonetheless they always had a direct connection with national politics; only this could justify warfare. Sixteenth century Highland warfare needed no such justification, and usually had nothing to do with national politics. The same point can be made in another way by stating that the great landlords of the Lowlands strove to control central government, and were at times ready and able to defy it with impunity when they could not get their own way; but many Highland chiefs showed little interest in the central government at all. Lowland magnates might bully the king on occasion; the chiefs of the West Highlands and Isles tended simply to ignore him. In the first half of the sixteenth century such chiefs made occasional appearances in national affairs and politics. In 1513 many Highlanders fought at Flodden; in the 1540s those favouring the revival of the lordship of the Isles were plotting with the English. But in the second half of the century the westerners and Islesmen (apart from the Campbells) played no significant part in national affairs, concentrating instead on their own internal feuds and those of the native Irish. To the monarchy, and from the point of view of the unity of Scotland as a nation, those who thus ignored national politics were an even greater threat than those who sought to control them for selfish ends.

What was the attitude of Highlanders to the monarchy? They acknowledged that they were Scots, subjects of the Stewart kings of the Scots. But this kingship was seen as a distant overlordship which was virtually without practical implications, which did not necessarily include any obligation to give obedience or to pay dues or taxes. It is thus bewildering to be told that most Highland gentlemen had 'an innate reverence for kingship'[20] unless one immediately qualifies this by stating that such mystical reverence was strictly confined to theory and was not allowed to interfere with the autonomy of the clan in practice. It would be just about as meaningful to claim that the covenanters had an innate reverence for kingship since though they revolted against Charles I they never denied that he was king. This is not to say that chiefs never obeyed the king; if it was convenient or useful, or (increasingly, as royal power grew in the early seventeenth century) if they were forced to, they would do so, and lard their obedience with fulsome protestations of loyalty.

It has been well said that the problem which emerged in the fourteenth century (and which was not even partially solved until the seventeenth) was 'not merely the superficial problem of upholding law and order in the Highlands but the more fundamental problem of holding together in one nation the two parts of Scotland that were divergent in language and culture'.[21] There seemed at times a real danger that Scotland might not survive as a single state; the fact that, with the benefit of hindsight, we know that it did survive should not blind us to the fact that it might not have.

However, in trying to define the ways in which Highlander differed from Lowlander there is always the danger of making the divide appear too simple, too clear cut. Generalisations which are, on the whole, accurate and enlightening can conceal great diversity and complexity. The difference between, say, settled inhabitants of the peaceful area round Edinburgh in the late sixteenth century on the one hand and the warring clansmen of the Western Isles in the same period on the other, is obvious. But the difference between the generally more settled clans of the Eastern Highlands and their still fairly turbulent Lowland neighbours is not nearly so great. One may draw the 'Highland line', the border between Highlands and Lowlands, on a small-scale map with some confidence; on any large-scale map it would be foolhardy to commit oneself to paper. Rather than a border line there is a border zone, varying in width, in which features of both societies and cultures can be found, in which there may at times be violent conflicts between the two, but in which cooperation and even mutual respect are possible. Some men could be equally at home on either side of the border. An essentially Lowland landlord like the earl of Huntly could take on the character of a chief on his more remote estates. The Gaelic speaking chiefs of the Campbells could, as earls of Argyll, be Lowland nobles taking a major part in national politics. Even a king, James IV, might be able to speak Gaelic and appreciate some aspects of Gaelic culture.[22] But James VI's very different attitude to all things Highland a century later indicates the increasing depth of the Highland/Lowland split. For him Highlanders living on the mainland were 'barbarous for the most part' though 'mixed with some shewe of ciuilitie', while the men of the Isles were utterly barbarous 'without any sort or shew of ciuilitie'.[23]

Thus though the generalisations must be qualified, they retain their force; when Alasdair MacColla was born, most Lowlanders regarded Highlanders as savages, more Irish than Scots, lacking all but the slightest tincture of civilisation.[24]

Among the clans which emerged in the late fourteenth century, supremacy undoubtedly lay with the MacDonalds. Part Norse and part Celtic in origin, the ruling kin of the clan had held political power in the Western Isles for centuries. Now it expanded its power greatly at the expense of a weak monarchy and created what was almost an independent state, the lordship of the Isles. At its greatest extent the lordship extended over all the Hebrides from Islay in the south to Lewis in the north. On the mainland it included Kintyre and Knapdale in the south, Morvern, Ardnamurchan and Lochaber around the southern end of the Great Glen, and, through absorbing the great earldom of Ross, a huge block of land extending north to Sutherland and east to the east coast. The weakness of the central Scottish government enabled this state within a state to emerge, but it obviously posed such a threat to the unity of the kingdom that its abolition had high priority for Scottish kings. At last the forfeiture of the lordship was achieved by James IV in 1493, and he led naval expeditions to the Isles several times later in the decade.[25]

In some senses the forfeiture was a success; in others it was a disaster. With the destruction of the united political authority of the lordship the direct threat posed by the Western Highlands and Isles to the monarchy disappeared. But the collapse of the lordship's authority was not followed up by the extension of royal power to replace it. James IV found such an extension beyond his resources, and of the ninety years between his death in 1513 and the union of the crowns in 1603 only about forty saw Scotland ruled by an adult monarch. Struggling to assert their authority even in the Lowlands, monarchs and regents could only give the Highlands intermittent attention (as in James V's expedition to the Isles of 1540). One central authority, the lordship, had been abolished, but nothing effective had been put in its place. The result, predictably, was chaos. The great Clan Donald, deprived of its head, split into sections which became separate clans and fought with each other for supremacy. This disunity among the MacDonalds allowed many other clans, which had been emerging as political and social units but which had previously been subordinate to the Lordship, to throw off their dependence on the MacDonalds and wrest land from them. Neither feudalism nor kinship was strong enough to restore order, and neither was capable of determining where justice lay in the morass of conflicting claims to the possession of land and the loyalty of men. The century and a half between the late fifteenth and the early seventeenth centuries was thus the most turbulent and violent period of Highland history, a heroic age of instability, war and raid, with the relative positions of the various clans fluctuating constantly. Population growth creating pressure on land and therefore aggression against neighbours has often been suggested to account for this violence, but (though certainty is impossible) there is no evidence to support this theory. The Highland wars of these generations gave rise to intense loyalties, to epic deeds of courage and martial skill; but also to treachery, ruthless oppression, and atrocity.

The attempts of the monarchy to deal with this situation were not only intermittent but also frequently counter-productive. Recognising that they had not power to control the Highlands directly, kings took to granting authority to great men in or near the Highlands whom they thought they could trust to represent the monarchy and to try to impose at least some semblance of order. James IV began this practice, creating the Campbell earls of Argyll king's lieutenants in the south, the Gordon earls of Huntly king's lieutenants in the north. Such grants of semi-regal power were renewed at irregular intervals to the same families throughout the following century.[26] Increasingly the government had little choice but to renew the commissions, for the Campbells and the Gordons had used their powers as agents of the king to consolidate and extend their own power, making themselves ever more indispensable to the monarchy. The government well knew that they were using their positions to aggrandise themselves but tolerated it because royal power was insufficient to suppress such abuses, because the more powerful these families became the more effectively they could help the government in remote areas, and because gaining such personal power was regarded as a natural and legitimate reward for service to the crown.

The rise of the Campbells, who had long been well established in mainland Argyllshire, was 'particularly spectacular', achieved by marriages to heiresses, by manipulation of feudal law, by action on behalf of the crown, and by naked aggression (sometimes disguised by provoking neighbours into rebellion and then suppressing them in name of the crown). At first the Campbells may have themselves aspired to become lords of the Isles but, fear of such ambition having brought them temporary royal disfavour, in the later sixteenth century they contented themselves with the title of earl and the piecemeal acquisition of territory.[27] By this time the Campbells were the most powerful clan in all the Highlands. They had absorbed or dispersed many smaller neighbouring clans, until only one clan remained which might still prove a rival to their power in the Southern Highlands, the Clan Ian Mor.

The Clan Ian Mor (or Clan Donald South as it is sometimes called) took its name from Ian (or John) Mor (killed 1427), a younger brother of Donald, lord of the Isles. Ian Mor's Scottish possessions were centred on the castle of Dunyveg in Islay, and he acquired by marriage to an heiress the area of north and east Antrim known as the Glens, the part of Ireland closest to Scotland. Thus the chiefs of the Clan Ian Mor are known as either the MacDonalds of Dunyveg and the Glens, or as the MacDonalds of Islay and Antrim. On the fall of the lordship in the 1490s both Ian Mor's grandson and his great-grandson were executed, but the clan survived, and indeed thrived, becoming in the early and mid-sixteenth century the most powerful of the branches into which the Clan Donald was now split. However, in the last decades of the century the power of the clan crumbled through internal division and external attack. A younger brother of James MacDonald of Dunyveg and the Glens (died 1565), variously known as Somhairle Buidhe, Somerled or Sorley Boy, seized possession of the clan's lands in Antrim and passed them on to his son Randal (Ranald) on his death in 1589. Thus was founded as a separate 'clan' the MacDonnells (as the name was usually spelt in Ireland) of Antrim, or of Dunluce, who by skill and judicious trimming emerged from the vicious internal wars and subsequent English conquest of Ulster in secure possession of both the Glens and the Route (or north west) of Antrim. Later Randal MacDonnell obtained sufficient royal favour to be created earl of Antrim in 1620.

Thus the Clan Ian Mor split, and Sorley Boy's nephew, Angus, who had succeeded his father as MacDonald 'of Dunyveg and the Glens' was reduced to being 'of Dunyveg' alone. But in spite of this political split between the Irish and Scots branches of the clan, social and personal ties remained strong. Nor were these the only links between Ireland and the Highlands. There had always been links between the two parts of the Gaelic world, but these became particularly close from the fourteenth to the sixteenth centuries. The fourteenth century 'Gaelic revival' which nearly drove the English out of Ireland has obvious parallels with the development of clans and the emerging gulf between Highlander and Lowlander in Scotland in the same period.[28] MacDonnells settled in Antrim in large numbers, and in the late sixteenth century MacDonalds, MacLeans, Campbells and other Highland clans intervened directly in the wars in Ulster, serving English or Irish masters, frequently changing sides with 'frivolous ease'. Throughout the century Highland mercenaries served in Ireland by the thousand, uprooted by disorder in the Highlands and drawn to Ireland by the opportunities for employment there provided both by wars among the Irish lords and by the resistance to English conquest.[29] To the English these Highland mercenaries became known as the 'redshanks' as their dress left their legs bare; by the seventeenth century the name was sometimes applied to all Highlanders.

Cultural ties between Ireland and the Highlands were also close, with free movement of poets, musicians and scholars; many Highland families of learned or professional men had Irish origins. Irish and Highland Gaelic might differ significantly, but in practical terms they formed a single language, holding men together rather than separating them. To many Gaels, almost equally at home in native Ireland and in the Highlands, the fact that England claimed to rule the former, Scotland the latter was an artificial division which made little sense. An illustration of how far the Western Isles and Gaelic Ulster formed one world was provided by Rathlin Island, off the Antrim coast. Final decision on whether the island was part of Scotland or Ireland was not reached until 1617, when the 'Irish' claim of the MacDonnells was accepted, the 'Scottish' claim of the Campbells being rejected.[30]

The final downfall of the Clan Ian Mor began with a feud with the MacLeans. The quarrel, between Angus MacDonald of Dunyveg and his brother-in-law Sir Lachlan Mor MacLean of Duart, centred on the possession of the area of Islay known as the Rhinns. The war spread quickly, and soon involved most of the clans of the Western Isles. The Clan Ian Mor won the support of the MacDonalds of Clanranald and Sleat, the MacDonalds (or MacIans) of Ardnamurchan, the MacLeods of Lewis and the MacPhees of Colonsay, while the MacLean claim was supported by the MacLeods of Harris, the MacNeills of Barra and the MacKinnons. Nor were Highlanders alone involved in the fighting; Angus MacDonald at one point hired English mercenaries, while MacLean enlisted part of the crew of a stray ship from the 1588 Spanish Armada.

In some ways the government of James VI was not sorry to see 'barbarous' Highlanders engaging in a bloody civil war and thus weakening themselves, but the speed with which the quarrel spread throughout the Isles and the involvement of foreign mercenaries soon made the feud a threat to central authority which no government could afford to ignore. After various attempts to promote an agreed settlement had failed, the government tried to force an end to the war by acting as unscrupulously as the warring clans themselves. MacDonald and MacLean were summoned to Edinburgh under the protection of safe conducts, but were then seized and imprisoned. After paying fines and promising good behaviour for the future they were released (1591); but Angus had to leave two sons in Edinburgh as hostages.

In spite of this, Angus was soon in trouble again. In 1594 he and other western chiefs were declared to have forfeited their lands for refusing obedience to the king's orders. The chiefs simply ignored this, and Angus' son James was released from captivity in Edinburgh so he could try to persuade his father to submit. When Angus and the others continued recalcitrant, a military expedition was prepared to enforce obedience. News of this led the chiefs at last to submit, but Angus held out for so long that royal forces had already landed in Kintyre before they received news that he had sent his son James back to Edinburgh with his submission. Moreover, James VI had by this time been exasperated by Angus' conduct into deciding to settle the dispute over the Rhinns of Islay by granting a lease of the lands to MacLean of Duart; and two plans were being considered for further decreases in Angus' territory — either that he be deprived of all Islay, being left with Kintyre, or that on the contrary he be confirmed in possession of Islay (except the Rhinns) but give up Kintyre.

The latter plan was eventually accepted. Angus came to Edinburgh to offer his submission, and was only allowed to return home on binding himself to find security for payment of arrears of rent due to the crown, to remove his clansmen and dependants from Kintyre and the Rhinns of Islay, and to hand Dunyveg Castle over to the king. His son James remained in Edinburgh as a hostage, but was knighted, doubtless as a reward for having helped to persuade his father to submit.

A further complication now arose to threaten Angus' position. In 1596 both Angus and James VI had appealed for military aid (against each other) to the former's kinsman, James MacDonnell of Dunluce. Dunluce had avoided involving the MacDonnells of Antrim in the quarrel, but was encouraged by Angus' declining fortunes to intervene in another way. He put forward a claim that Angus was illegitimate and that his own claim to Islay and Kintyre should be accepted. Dunluce's claims were eventually rejected, but they provided a useful threat for the king to use in negotiating with Angus; Dunluce was knighted and granted some lands in Kintyre. This puzzling favour shown to Dunluce, though his right to Angus' lands was denied, may suggest that there is some truth in the allegation that he had offered to do more than take over Islay and Kintyre; it was said he also offered to become King James' vassal for his Irish lands, and to persuade other Irish lords to do the same.[31] Dunluce had been cooperating with the rebellious Ulster Irish against the English, and now contemplated some of the Irish lords transferring their allegiance from England to Scotland. James cannot have seriously contemplated accepting the offer; that would have led to war with England. Nonetheless the offer may have led him to show favour to Dunluce in order to retain his support. James was not above meddling in Irish politics secretly in order to try to win support for his claim to succeed to the English throne, as his later contacts with the earl of Tyrone demonstrated.

In spite of the difficulties Angus had brought on himself by holding out longer than the other western chiefs in 1596, and the new threat posed to him by Dunluce, he seems to have made no attempt to carry out his agreement with the king. Evidently he hoped that prolonged passive resistance would force the king to reach a compromise settlement with him. His experience of earlier attempts by the government to assert itself in the Highlands had convinced him that if he held on long enough the regime would accept his position, as it would be too much trouble, and too expensive, to take decisive action against him. Unfortunately for Angus this policy, though sometimes effective in the past, was no longer adequate. Angus was assuming that James VI's efforts to restore order in the Highlands would be as sporadic and ineffectual as those of previous regimes. In fact in the previous decade royal power in Scotland had grown greatly, as James came of age and won support for his policies in both church and state. His power still fell far short of the absolute power he dreamed of, but he was showing his determination to assert his authority over all persons and all areas of the country. Already his power was greater than that of any ruler since James V more than half a century before. For James the problem of disobedience and disorder in the Highlands was a major threat to his authority which he had to deal with effectively if he was to retain his credibility as king.

Symptomatic of James' determination to sort out the political chaos of the Highlands was an act of parliament of 1597 ordering all who claimed any right to land in the Highlands to produce their title deeds and find security both for the payment of rents and other dues to the crown and for the orderly behaviour of themselves and their men. Trying to settle disputes over land ownership, exact payment of crown rents, and make chiefs responsible for the behaviour of their clansmen had all been attempted in the past; now all three were combined into a concerted programme, and those who failed to obey the act were to forfeit all right to their lands. Probably it was accepted that some chiefs would be unable to produce adequate feudal titles to their lands or to find sureties, and was intended that large areas of land would thus be made available by forfeiture which could then be used to 'civilise' the Highlands by the introduction of Lowland colonists. Another act of the same year pointed in this direction by ordering the founding of royal burghs in Lewis, Lochaber and Kintyre — the last of these indicating the strategic importance held by Kintyre and the determination of the government to transform it into a centre of Lowland influence.

To all these signs of the changing attitudes — and capabilities — of Edinburgh, Angus MacDonald was evidently blind. But his son Sir James was not; his years as a hostage in Edinburgh had doubtless given him the opportunity to gauge official attitudes to Highland problems, and to the Clan Ian Mor in particular. To Sir James it must have seemed that his father's policy of trying to ignore the government (and his own promises to it) was sheer folly, almost certain to bring the king's wrath on his clan. The clan was already regarded as a major troublemaker, the territories and powers of which must be reduced; further defiance might well lead to its complete destruction. Such beliefs, as well as personal ambition, probably lay behind Sir James' conduct in 1598. He was again sent west by the government to try to persuade Angus to submit to the crown. Angus was living in his house of Askomel at Ceann Loch (Campbeltown); Sir James knew his parents were there but nonetheless set fire to the house at night. Angus managed to escape, badly burnt, whereupon he was seized by Sir James' men and kept prisoner for some months. Sir James took over leadership of the Clan Ian Mor, and managed to get royal approval for having arrested his own father. But Sir Lachlan Mor MacLean now decided to take advantage of this internal feud among his enemies by making good his royal lease of the Rhinns of Islay by driving out the MacDonalds. This Sir James was not prepared to allow. Negotiations with the MacLeans having failed, a battle was fought at Loch Gruinart in August 1598: Sir Lachlan Mor was killed and the MacLeans routed, over three hundred men being killed. But in revenge the MacLeans organised a new devastating invasion of Islay, helped by Camerons, MacLeods, MacKinnons and MacNeills.

Meanwhile Sir James was seeking to legitimise his position. In 1599 he went to Edinburgh and offered to take over his father's lands and carry out the latter's former promises — to remove his followers from Kintyre, hand Dunyveg Castle over to the king, and pay crown rents. In addition, he would pay his father Angus a pension. The government at first favoured a settlement on these terms but in the end nothing was done. The king's attention, so far as the Highlands were concerned, was concentrated on his plans for Lowland colonisation of Lewis, forfeited by the MacLeods on their failure to produce title deeds. Perhaps too there was a reluctance to confirm Islay, the most fertile of the Western Isles, in MacDonald hands even in return for the surrender of Kintyre; if colonisation succeeded in Lewis, would not Islay be an excellent site for a new colony?

Another contribution to the failure to confirm the settlement with Sir James probably lay in the attitude of the Campbells, for the growing weakness of the Clan Ian Mor had roused their ambitions. Until this point there is no evidence that the Campbells had played any direct part in the recent troubles of the clan, though they can hardly have failed to feel satisfaction at seeing their former rivals for supremacy in the South West Highlands in difficulties, and to have hoped ultimately to benefit from this. But previously the Campbells had been beset with their own internal troubles which had left them in no condition to pursue their ambitions. Since 1584 the child 7th earl of Argyll had been chief of the clan, and until the early 1590s rival cadet branches of the clan feuded for control of the young chief, the feuds culminating in the murder of Campbell of Calder in 1592. By the late 1590s, however, the earl of Argyll had reached adulthood. Undoubtedly he hoped the king would add Kintyre to his estates, as the Campbells had long been regarded as the leading agents of the government in the South West Highlands, and he may well have felt that he could never be safe in possession of Kintyre while the Clan Ian Mor continued to hold Islay. This would explain the earl's opposition to Sir James' 1599 proposals, even though they involved a MacDonald withdrawal from Kintyre; the Campbells might gain more in the long run by opposing Sir James' plans and thus leaving the future of all his clans' lands unsettled for the moment. A kinsman of Argyll's, John Campbell of Calder, was also taking a close interest in MacDonald affairs. His sister married Sir James at about this time, and he may already have had his eye on Islay.

Sir James MacDonald was later to blame most of his misfortunes on the Campbells, and so far as events after 1600 are concerned there was much truth in his allegations. But it was internal feuding among the MacDonalds (the separation of the MacDonnells of Antrim from the MacDonalds of Dunyveg, and the feud between Sir James and his father Angus) and quarrels with other clans (especially the MacLeans) which had reduced the Clan Ian Mor to such a weak state that it could fall prey to Campbell ambitions. The Campbells were certainly masters of the disreputable art of encouraging or provoking disorder among neighbouring clans and then intervening in the name of law and order to their own advantage. But though they did employ such tactics on occasion, it may be doubted if they used them quite so frequently as is often alleged. By their very nature such secret intrigues could not be expected to leave hard evidence to prove their existence, and it sometimes appears that any chief in the South West Highlands accused of misdeeds almost automatically put the blame for his acts on secret Campbell provocation or persuasion. The Campbells were often enough guilty of such practices for the charge to seem plausible and thus spread doubt and confusion even if no evidence could be produced to substantiate the charge.

The first major intervention by the earl of Argyll in the dispute over the leadership of the Clan Ian Mor came in 1603. In the years since 1599 it seems that Angus and Sir James had both maintained their claims to leadership, though neither had been able to obtain royal approval. By 1600 Angus was no longer a prisoner and was evidently leading his clan,[32] and in 1603 he managed to seize his son and handed him over to Argyll, who sent him to be imprisoned in Edinburgh; since Sir James' proposals had never received royal approval, it was now evidently assumed that he was in the wrong in the feud with his father.

Once Sir James had been removed from the scene, action was taken to force Angus into submission. In 1605 a military expedition landed in Kintyre, and the southern chiefs renewed former promises of loyalty to the king. Among them was Angus MacDonald, who paid off all arrears of crown rent for both Islay and Kintyre. Suspicion of him remained, however, and was doubtless stirred up by Argyll, for while (in 1606) Angus complained he could get no answers from the privy council in Edinburgh to his petitions and offers of obedience, arrangements were being completed for Argyll (in reward for his services to the crown) to take over Kintyre and Jura from the MacDonalds. Hearing rumours of this, Sir James MacDonald tried to escape from Edinburgh Castle to aid his clan (though he himself had proposed to surrender Kintyre in 1599), but he was unsuccessful, and merely brought on himself closer imprisonment than before.

A royal charter was duly issued in 1607 assigning Kintyre and Jura to Argyll, one of the conditions of the grant being that he should not lease land to MacDonalds. Rumour said that the MacDonalds were preparing to resist Argyll, so he was appointed king's lieutenant of the Southern Isles to subdue them. But no violence occurred, probably because Angus MacDonald had come to accept that the loss of Kintyre was inevitable. His son made a second unsuccessful attempt to escape from Edinburgh Castle, presumably hoping to supplant his father and raise the clan in arms. As a result he was brought to trial for both his attempted escapes and his attack on his father in 1597. He was found guilty and condemned to death in 1609, but the sentence was not carried out, it probably being calculated that Sir James alive but under a sentence of death which would allow his execution at any time would be more valuable as a restraint on MacDonald conduct than his death would be. The death sentence was doubtless intended as a lesson not just to the MacDonalds but to other clans as well, for the regime was making yet another major attempt to settle the problem of the Western Highlands.

The previous year, 1608, Lord Ochiltree had led an expedition to the Isles, acting as king's lieutenant. Angus MacDonald surrendered Dunyveg Castle and his fort on Loch Gorm to him; the former was garrisoned, the latter destroyed. Ochiltree then sailed on to Mull, where he summoned a meeting of all the chiefs of the Isles. When they had assembled he invited them on board a royal ship to be edified by a sermon from the bishop of the Isles. Once on board, however, they were taught a rather different lesson from that which they had expected, being carried off to captivity in Lowland prisons. Angus escaped this fate, either being sent home before the seizure of the other chiefs or being released before Ochiltree returned to the Lowlands. Whichever was the case, the fact that Angus was allowed to remain at liberty presumably indicates that he had shown his willingness to submit completely to the king.

This kidnapping of the Island chiefs provided — and presumably had been planned in order to provide — an excellent opportunity for trying to make a new start in bringing order to the Isles. In 1609, after a winter in prison to teach them the limits of their power, the chiefs were freed on finding sureties to guarantee that they would return to Edinburgh by a certain date and that in the meantime they would actively help the bishop of the Isles (who was acting as the king's agent). Though Angus MacDonald was not among the kidnapped chiefs, he had been summoned to Edinburgh; after appearing before the privy council he was incarcerated for a time in Edinburgh Castle before being sent to join the other chiefs in meeting the bishop on Iona. There they swore to observe nine 'statutes' or proposals for reform.

These 'statutes of Iona' are frequently held to have brought about the transformation of the Western Highlands; they are held to be responsible for this time being a turning point at which the power of central government and the influence of Lowland culture finally begin to prevail over the autonomy of the chiefs and Gaelic culture. It would, however, be more accurate to say that, at most, the statutes mark or symbolise a turning point, rather than that they are actually responsible for the changes which were to come in the years ahead. What was increasingly to incline chiefs to obey the king was not the existence of the statutes but the sustained pressure on the chiefs, year after year, of an increasingly efficient central administration based on the privy council. No longer does one expedition to the Isles have to satisfy the ambitions of central government for a generation or more; instead such expeditions become for some years almost annual events. Not all are successful, some achieve nothing, but over the years the sustained interest of central government in Highland affairs has an effect. The statutes of Iona mark the maturing of this intervention in the Highlands, the point at which vague general aims — excluding the natives in favour of Lowland colonists, or demanding obedience from chiefs — give way to a detailed programme for reform bringing together and extending the policies of previous years. Simply demanding general promises of obedience from the chiefs was not enough. Trying to replace the natives with Lowlanders by force was (as the Lewis venture proved) too difficult and too expensive. Therefore the chiefs were now to be forced or persuaded to act as agents for the introduction of policies which would reform Highland society and, in time, remodel it on Lowland lines. Highland chiefs would be transformed gradually into Lowland lairds.

As well as signing a general band swearing obedience to the king, the laws of the land and the established church, the chiefs at Iona swore to carry out nine specific reforms. They would aid the spread of the organisation of the reformed church, repairing churches, paying ministers' stipends and suppressing immorality. They would establish inns for travellers to prevent the country people being obliged, in addition to paying rent, to provide hospitality for travellers and idle men with no regular source of income. As an extension of this, 'sorning' (the exaction of food and lodging by threat of force) was to be suppressed. Connected with these statutes were limitations placed on the size of the households of chiefs; Angus MacDonald, for example, was to maintain no more than six gentlemen in his household. The motive given for doing this was, again, to reduce the burden on country people in supporting such idlers; but doubtless more important in reality was the belief that such retainers supported by a chief provided a nucleus for his armed forces and that, being men with no settled estates or professions, they were restless men who tended to stir up feud and violence. At other levels of society, too, idle men with no settled, respectable livings were to be suppressed — 'sturdy beggars' or vagrants, and especially bards; of all elements in Gaelic society the bards were regarded with most suspicion, it being suspected that their poems of flattery of chiefs and clans encouraged arrogance and aggression, while their poems of satire and ridicule stirred up hatreds and feuds. Other statutes directly concerned with the suppression of violence sought to limit strictly the trade in wines and spirits and to ban the carrying of arms (the government was already engaged in trying to reduce the number of galleys in the Isles, to make the transport of armed forces more difficult). More positively, education was to be added to religion in spreading Lowland culture and civilisation. All Highland gentlemen were to have at least their eldest sons (or eldest daughters if they had no sons) educated in Lowland schools until they could speak, read and write English. Finally, each chief undertook to be responsible for the obedience to the statutes of his kin, friends and dependants, his clansmen.[33]

The negative aspects of the statutes of Iona, the attack on Gaelic life and culture, are often those which are most stressed; but there is more to them than this. Central government was undoubtedly trying to extend its own power and Lowland 'civilisation', but it was also genuinely trying to improve the lives of the people of the Highlands. The concern for poor tenants open to arbitrary exactions by their superiors or by sorners was sincere, even though some misunderstanding was involved; such 'sorning' doubtless often seemed to the Highlander the fulfilment of traditional obligations of hospitality to strangers or to a chief's guests. When a band of loyalty signed along with the statutes by the chiefs spoke of 'the grite miserie, barbaritie and povertie unto the quhilk for the present our barrane cuntrie is subject' which 'hes proceidit of the unaturall deidlie feidis quhilkis hes bene foisterit amangis us this lait aig', it was referring to a real problem, one which no authority within the Highlands was strong enough to solve. Destroying the autonomy of the chiefs, if it brought peace, could benefit Highlanders as well as central government. If the work of bards contributed to disorder, then attacking them was more than just a sign of cultural prejudice — just as trying to ensure that the upper ranks of society could understand the language in which the government of the country was conducted was more than just linguistic prejudice.

Moreover, policies similar to those contained in many of the statutes had been, and continued to be, pursued in Lowlands as well as Highlands — suppression of travelling entertainers and sturdy beggars, curbing of over-powerful subjects, suppression of feuding, limitations on the carrying of weapons, and attempts to get men of status to provide their children with formal education. Certainly many features of Highland life and culture were under attack; but much the same could be said of many features of traditional Lowland life and culture.

The statutes of Iona were never enforced fully throughout the Western Isles. Disorder, disobedience to the king, blood feud and occasional clan war continued for many years to come. To talk of a 'Transformation' being 'wrought in the temper of the wild chiefs' by the 'amazingly successful' statutes is absurd.[34] Nonetheless after about 1610 or 1615 the scale of violence, the extent to which chiefs ignored or defied the king, did (with a few notable exceptions) decline through the sustained attention (of which the statues are one aspect) to Highland affairs. Chiefs still had wide autonomy in local matters, but they were answerable to the council and often appeared before it to answer complaints against them. The holding of hostages in Edinburgh, the threat of financial penalties and the fear of further military expeditions to the Isles and of forfeitures of property all contributed to persuading the chiefs to moderate their conduct. The Clan Ian Mor's loss of Kintyre had shown what might happen to a clan which tried government patience too far. Even more frightening as a warning was the ease with which six counties in Ulster had recently been forfeited from their native Irish holders to the crown and were now being planted with Lowland Scots and English settlers. The final downfall of the Clan Ian Mor which was soon to follow emphasised the same message. It was these demonstrations of royal power rather than the statutes of Iona which were primarily responsible for the main changes in the conduct of chiefs in the West Highlands in the years ahead. The statutes are fascinating for the insight they give into official thinking on Highland problems, but most of them had little practical significance.

By this time Angus MacDonald seems to have been resigned to the disappearance of his clan as a major social and political unit. He had already agreed to the surrender or Kintyre (though he evidently made no attempt to remove his followers), and in 1612 he agreed to transfer Islay to Sir John Campbell of Calder, evidently partly in exchange for land elsewhere, partly for cash to pay off his debts. Freed from both his creditors and government suspicion of his continued presence in Islay, Angus could then spend his remaining days in peace. But the agreement with Calder evidently stipulated that Angus could withdraw from it, and thus retain Islay, if he could repay the money advanced by Calder. This he managed to do in September 1612, through the intervention of Sir Randal MacDonnell of Dunluce, who had won Angus' agreement that he and not Calder should take over Islay. Thus the island continued in MacDonald hands for the moment, Calder's first attempt to gain possession having been thwarted. Sometime in the following year Angus died; a report of September 1613 on the state of the Isles reveals this, and that Sir Randal had subsequently taken possession of Islay.[35] At first he only occupied the island on a short lease from the crown (issued in the name of Sir George Hamilton, as Sir Randal was not a Scot), but he began negotiations for a more permanent tenure. All this must have been done with royal approval. As Sir Randal was known to be a loyal subject in Ireland, there was no objection to his taking over Islay, and it may have been hoped that, as Angus' cousin, he would be acceptable to the MacDonalds and would be able to control them. However, difficulties soon arose. The inhabitants of Islay soon complained that Sir Randal was oppressing them with 'Irish' exactions.[36] Behind this may have lain opposition to his claim to Islay, based on resentment at the rise of the Antrim branch of the ruling family. It had been Sir Randal's father, Sorley Boy, who had deprived Angus MacDonald of the Clan Ian Mor's Antrim lands. In the 1590s Sir Randal's brother, Sir James, had attempted to take over Kintyre from Angus. Now Sir Randal was attempting to take over Islay, disinheriting Angus' sons.

Angus MacDonald left two legitimate sons, Sir James (still a prisoner in Edinburgh Castle) and Angus Og, and one illegitimate son, Ranald Og; or at least it was claimed that Angus was the latter's father, but Angus had refused to recognise him and he is frequently referred to as Ranald MacAllester. The death of their father and the attempt of Sir Randal to take over Islay[37] stirred the three sons of Angus into rival bids to seize the island and then negotiate with the government from a position of strength. It is worth stressing that it was thus an attempt by Sir Randal MacDonnell of Dunluce to take over Islay with royal approval which precipitated local resistance and then the rebellions of Angus MacDonald's sons, and thus brought about the final destruction of the Clan Ian Mor, not the plots of the Campbells. As in the past, the Campbells had only to wait until the internal feuds and rivalries of the MacDonalds discredited them, then take advantage of this for their own ends.[38]

NOTES

1. K.A. Steer and J.W.M. Bannerman, *Late medieval monumental sculpture in the West Highlands* (Edinburgh 1977); D. Thomson, *An introduction to Gaelic poetry* (London 1974); F. Collinson, *The bagpipe — the history of a musical instrument* (London 1975), 141-57; I.F. Grant, *The MacLeods. The history of a clan* (London 1956), 243-7.

2. G.A. Hayes-McCoy, 'Gaelic society in Ireland in the late sixteenth century', *Historical Studies*, iv. (1963), 49; G.A. Hayes-McCoy, *Scots mercenary forces in Ireland* (Dublin 1937), xii-xiii.

3. E.R. Cregeen, 'The changing role of the house of Argyll in the Scottish Highlands', in I.M. Lewis (ed), *History and social anthropology* (London 1968), 164; W.F. Skene, *Celtic Scotland* (2nd ed, 3 vols, Edinburgh 1886-90), iii. 318-25. What is perhaps the best account of the clans in the sixteenth century appears in I.F. Grant, *The social and economic development of Scotland before 1603* (Edinburgh 1930), 472-550. For a detailed narrative history see D. Gregory, *History of the Western Highlands and Isles to 1625* (Edinburgh 1836; the 2nd ed of 1881 is that cited below). The most stimulating short history of

the Highlands is W.R. Kermack, *The Scottish Highlands* (Edinburgh 1957). For the Highlands in the fifteenth and early sixteenth centuries see J.W.M. Bannerman, 'The lordship of the Isles' in J.M. Brown (ed), *Scottish society in the fifteenth century* (London 1977), 209-40; Bannerman, 'The lordship of the Isles: historical background' in Steer and Bannerman, *Late medieval monumental sculpture*, 201-13; R.G. Nicholson, 'Domesticated Scots and wild Scots: the relationship between Lowlanders and Highlanders in Medieval Scotland', *Scottish Colloquium Proceedings*, i (University of Guelph 1968).

4. For similar variations in the meaning of 'clan' in Ireland see K.W. Nicholls, *Gaelic and Gaelicised Ireland in the middle ages* (Dublin and London 1972), 9.

5. Cregeen, 'Changing role', in Lewis, *History and social anthropology*, 161; A. McKerral, 'The tacksman and his holding in the south west Highlands', SHR, xxvi (1947), 10-25.

6. Nicholls, *Gaelic and Gaelicised Ireland*, 10-11; Hayes-McCoy, 'Gaelic society', *Historical Studies*, iv. 49.

7. A. Cunningham, *The loyal clans* (Cambridge 1932), 15.

8. Ibid, 25; Grant, *Social and economic development*, 514.

9. See G.J. Schochet, *Patriarchalism in political thought* (Oxford 1975).

10. Cunningham, *Loyal clans*, 196. Gregory, *History*, 333 similarly ascribes the support of the clans for the Stewarts to the exposure of the sons of chiefs to Lowland education (after the statutes of Iona and later regulations) which taught 'high' church and state ideas. But there is little sign of obedience to the regulation demanding Lowland education for sons of chiefs, and anyway (as pointed out in Grant, *MacLeods*, 234) how such education 'converted' Highlanders to royalism is far from clear: why did it not prevent so many Lowlanders turning against the crown by becoming covenanters?

11. Ibid, 233.

12. Skene, *Celtic Scotland*, iii. 318-20; A.J. and A.M. Macdonald, *The Clan Donald* (3 vols, Inverness 1896-1904), iii. 118.

13. Skene, *Celtic Scotland*, iii. 320.

14. J. Willcock, *The great marquess. Life and times of Archibald . . . marquess of Argyll* (Edinburgh 1903), 25-6.

15. Skene, *Celtic Scotland*, iii. 321-3.

16. R.G. Nicholson, *Scotland. The later middle ages* (Edinburgh 1974), 207.

17. See C.M. Bowra, *The meaning of a heroic age* (Newcastle 1967) and H.M. and N.K. Chadwick, *The growth of literature* (3 vols, Cambridge 1932-40), iii. 729-49.

18. Nicholson, *Later middle ages*, 207.

19. Ibid, 206.

20. W.C. Mackenzie, *The Highlands and Isles of Scotland* (Edinburgh 1949), 225.

21. Nicholson, *Later middle ages*, 205.

22. Ibid, 541.

23. C.H. McIlwain (ed), *The political works of James I* (New York 1965), 22.

24. For some recent assessments of the differences between Highlands and Lowlands see Nicholson, *Later middle ages*, 205-9; G. Donaldson, *Scotland. James V to James VII* (Edinburgh 1965), 13-14; W. Ferguson, *Scotland's relations with England. A survey to 1707* (Edinburgh 1977), 46-7; and T.C. Smout, *A history of the Scottish people, 1560-1830* (London 1969), 42-7.

25. Nicholson, *Later middle ages*, 542-4.

26. Ibid, 544-9.

27. Bannerman, 'The lordship of the Isles' in Steer and Bannerman, *Late medieval monumental sculpture*, 211-13; Cregeen, 'Changing role' in Lewis, *History and social anthropology*, 155-9.

28. Nicholson, *Later middle ages*, 236-7.

29. Hayes-McCoy, *Scots mercenary forces*; A. McKerral, 'West Highland mercenaries in Ireland', SHR, xxx (1951), 1-14; Mackenzie, *Highlands and Isles*, 185.

30. W. Clark, *Rathlin. Disputed island* (Portlaw, County Waterford 1971), 108-15.

31. A.I. Cameron (ed), *Warrender papers* (2 vols, SHS 1931-2), ii. 429-30.

32. Hayes-McCoy, *Scots mercenary forces*, 314.

33. For the statutes of Iona see *RPCS, 1610-13*, 25-30.

34. Mackenzie, *Highlands and Isles*, 207. An interesting discussion of the importance of the privy council, rather than the king, in forming Highland policy in this period can be found in M. Lee, 'James

VI's government of Scotland after 1603', *SHR*, lv (1976), 49-53, but the success of the government in bringing peace and order to the Highlands is exaggerated — there is no mention of the 1614-15 MacDonald rebellion, of the destruction of the MacGregors, or of the Campbell take-over of Ardnamurchan, for example.

35. C. Innes (ed), *The book of the thanes of Cawdor* (Spalding Club 1859), 223-7; *RPCS, 1613-16*, 818. MacDonald, *The Clan Donald*, ii. 586 and R. Black, 'Colla Ciotach', *TGSI*, xlviii (1972-4), 206 both state (the latter citing a Gaelic manuscript) that Angus died in Rothesay on 21 October 1614. But the report to the council cited above indicates he had died much earlier, and that this was so is confirmed by many references to 'umquhil' ('the late') Angus long before October 1614. If the report is correct in stating that Sir Randal only possessed Islay after Angus' death, then the latter must have been dead some time before 17 March 1613, as on that date the privy council acted on complaints that had reached them about Sir Randal's oppressions in Islay, *RPCS, 1613-16*, 13-14.

36. Ibid, 13-14.

37. That Sir Randal had not abandoned his claim to Islay before the 1614-15 rebellions is proved by references in J.R.N. Macphail (ed), 'Extracts from the . . . Denmylne MSS', *Highland papers*, iii (SHS 1920), 150, 158, 168.

38. For the misfortunes of the Clan Ian Mor up to 1614 see the relevant sections of Gregory, *History*, A. McKerral, *Kintyre in the seventeenth century* (Edinburgh 1948), Macdonald, *The Clan Donald*, and G. Hill, *A historical account of the Macdonnells of Antrim* (Belfast 1873).

2

Coll Ciotach: A Most Zealous Catholic and Most Warlike Man

ALASDAIR MacColla's ancestors were closely involved in the misfortunes of the Clan Ian Mor and the rise of the MacDonnells of Antrim. His great grandfather, Colla nan Capull (Coll of the horses), was a younger brother of James MacDonald of Dunyveg and the Glens (died 1565), and an elder brother of Sorley Boy, who seized the Antrim lands of the Clan Ian Mor. Colla nan Capull settled in Ireland, and his eldest son Gillespie (Archibald) Fiacal (a nickname indicating that he had been born with teeth) married into the Ulster family of O'Quin. According to tradition, shortly after the marriage Gillespie's coming of age was celebrated (1570) at Ballycastle. The festivities included bull baiting, and one of the bulls broke loose. In the course of the efforts to subdue the bull Gillespie was wounded in the thigh by a sword; he was taken to Rathlin Island for medical treatment, but there he died. Rumour darkly hinted that Sorley Boy had had Gillespie poisoned, fearing that he would prove a rival in the struggle for the control of the Route.

Sometime after Gillespie's death his wife gave birth on Glasineerin Island on Lough Lynch in north-west Antrim to a son, Coll MacGillespie, later to be known as Coll Ciotach. Responsibility for Coll's upbringing seems to have passed to his father's younger brother, Ranald (Randal). Ranald spent some time as a mercenary in Ireland — he is recorded fighting in Munster in 1586 — but later settled in Colonsay. There Coll spent most of his childhood.[1]

The island of Colonsay occupies an important strategic position; it lies between the two largest and richest islands of the Southern Hebrides, Islay to the south and Mull to the north, and directly opposite the Firth of Lorne which leads north-eastwards to Loch Linnhe and the Great Glen. The nearest land lies eight miles away in Islay, and in good weather many of the Hebrides and both mainland Scotland and the hills of Donegal in Ireland can be seen. The island is about eight miles long and one to three miles broad; except at high tide it is joined to Oronsay, adding another three miles of length. Most of the island is low-lying, no hill exceeding 470 feet in height, and though much of the land is covered with broken rocky hills, the soil of some areas is very fertile.

Colonsay had been held under the lords of the Isles by the family of MacPhee (Mac a Phi, MacDuffy or MacFie), who acted as hereditary keepers of the lordship's records. After the fall of the lordship the Clan Ian Mor obtained title to the island, and it was presumably with the consent of Angus MacDonald of Dunyveg that Ranald settled there. Quite what the relative positions of Ranald and the MacPhees were is obscure; it may be that this is an example of the process whereby the chief of an expanding clan or kin (in this case Angus MacDonald) grants land to his own kin which has previously been held from him directly by a dependant family (the MacPhees), thus depressing the social status of the latter. By the early seventeenth century, however, the declining power of the MacDonalds posed a threat to the position of Coll Ciotach (who had succeeded his childless uncle) on Colonsay. In March 1610 the earl of Argyll obtained a royal grant of the barony of Ardnamurchan, and this was held to include Colonsay. Argyll appears to have made no attempt to gain immediate possession of the island, but obviously both Coll and the MacPhees must have felt increasingly insecure.[2]

Nothing whatever is known of Coll's early life beyond the bare facts of his birth and removal to Colonsay. The earliest dated reference to him does not occur until 6 February 1609, when Coll was already thirty-eight or thirty-nine years old. On that day Lord Ochiltree, who had returned to Edinburgh some months previously with the chiefs he had kidnapped from Mull, promised to produce before the privy council on 16 March Angus MacDonald of Dunyveg, two of Angus' sons, and 'Coill McGillespik'.[3] This indicates that Coll was already regarded as an important figure in the Clan Ian Mor. How he had risen to this position is unknown, but it seems likely that he had emerged as a courageous fighter and able politician in the struggle with the MacLeans and in the efforts of the clan to gain a secure title to its lands — though it is notable that according to tradition it was the MacPhees, not Coll or his uncle, who led resistance on Colonsay to MacLean raids.[4] In the event it seems that neither Angus nor Coll appeared before the privy council on 16 March. Angus eventually appeared in May, but Coll evidently was not with him. It seems quite likely that Coll was present with Angus when the latter accepted the statutes of Iona in August — many of the special friends, dependants and tenants of the chiefs were present though their names are not recorded. After the tantalising reference of February 1609 five more years were to pass before Coll again appears in surviving records.

In March 1614, following the death of Angus MacDonald of Dunyveg and the bid by Sir Randal MacDonnell of Dunluce to gain possession of Islay, Ranald Og (alleged to be Angus' bastard son) seized Dunyveg Castle from the small garrison established there in the king's name by the bishop of the Isles.[5] Presumably Ranald Og's action was intended to win him some advantage in gaining recognition as Angus' heir. If so, he behaved remarkably stupidly. The seizure of Dunyveg inevitably brought the wrath of the government down on him, and the fewness of his supporters suggests both lack of planning by him and lack of enthusiasm for his cause. He may of course have entertained some wild hope that the Clan Ian Mor would rally to him once he had possession of the ancient seat of its chiefs, but if this was so he was soon disappointed. His legitimate half-brother, Angus Og, was living within a few miles of Dunyveg, and immediately he heard of Ranald Og's action he raised his followers under Coll Ciotach and laid siege to the castle. After six days Ranald Og and his men escaped by sea and Angus Og placed Coll in command of a new garrison, to hold the castle in the king's name.

Two different explanations were subsequently given of Ranald Og's conduct.

When he and four of his men (who were put to death) were later captured by Angus Og, he is said to have told Angus and Coll that he had been urged to seize Dunyveg by Donald Gorm, a bastard son of the imprisoned Sir James MacDonald, his half-brother (and Angus Og's full brother).[6] Ranald Og soon escaped, and whether he really told this story or not remains uncertain; but it is obvious that it was very much in Angus Og's interests to get this version of events accepted, since it demonstrated that Ranald Og and, by implication, Sir James, were plotting against the king's government, while he, Angus Og, had intervened to foil their plots. That this story was so convenient for Angus was doubtless one reason for the rise of an alternative interpretation of events later put forward by Andrew Knox, the bishop of the Isles; he suggested that it had been Angus Og himself who had persuaded Ranald Og to capture Dunyveg,[7] thus providing the former with an incident which he could exploit to prove his own loyalty to the crown and discredit Sir James. The truth will never be known, so 'saturated with falsehood and intrigue' were events in Islay in 1614-15.[8]

After garrisoning Dunyveg, Angus Og offered to surrender the castle to the bishop of the Isles, provided he first received a pardon for any offences he might have committed in suppressing Ranald Og. In many ways this condition was a reasonable one to ask for; but his insistence on it inevitably meant that he appeared to be bargaining with the government about the restoration to it of a castle which he said he had only captured so he could restore it. This led to immediate suspicion of Angus' motives; as far as the privy council in distant Edinburgh was concerned, the essentials of the situation appeared to be that Dunyveg Castle was back in the hands of MacDonalds for the first time since 1608, that the MacDonalds were refusing to surrender immediately, and that (according to a report from the bishop of the Isles) the castle was being prepared to withstand a siege.[9] The privy council quickly concluded that Angus Og's claim to be acting in the king's interests was made simply to confuse the issue and gain time while he strengthened his own position. It had, after all, been Angus Og who had last commanded the castle when it was held by the MacDonalds, and in 1608 he had been very reluctant to hand it over to government forces on his father's orders.[10]

It was natural that it should be suspected that Sir James MacDonald lay behind any plots of his kinsmen, so the privy council had his belongings in Edinburgh Castle searched and all papers seized; but examination of them proved that far from encouraging rebellion Sir James had been urging Angus Og to submit. At this the council decided to test Angus' sincerity and discover his 'drifts and projectis', whether he would 'render obedience or profess him selff a rebell and disloyall subject'. Orders were therefore issued on 9 June that he surrender Dunyveg to the bishop or be denounced as a rebel.[11] However, nothing was done to implement this order immediately, and early in August after further consideration it was agreed that Angus Og should be offered the pardon he had demanded.[12] This was no doubt partly a recognition of the reasonableness of his request, partly also a realisation that offering a pardon would remove all doubts about his intentions if he still remained in arms.

In September Bishop Knox landed in Islay with fifty soldiers paid by himself, twenty men provided by Sir Aulay MacAulay of Ardincaple, and some MacDonalds who said they were willing to support him. The bishop had sent Sir Aulay and Donald Gorm MacDonald of Sleat (who had agreed to use his influence in favour of a peaceful settlement) ahead to persuade Angus Og to withdraw from Dunyveg. But he refused to surrender and many of the bishop's men began to desert him while increasing numbers of hostile MacDonalds appeared in the area. Soon forces under Coll Ciotach and Ranald MacJames (or Ranald of Smerby, a brother of old Angus MacDonald of Dunyveg) 'did ly about the bischop's house', and proceeded to burn the boats which had brought him to Islay. Cut off and surrounded, he was forced to negotiate. Humiliating concessions were forced from him. He had to promise to do his best to secure for Angus Og a seven-year lease of Islay (in place of Sir Randal MacDonnell of Dunluce) and ownership of Dunyveg Castle, while Coll Ciotach was to be confirmed in possession of some church lands he held in Islay. All involved in the rising were to be pardoned, and to keep the bishop to his promise Angus Og seized his son, Thomas Knox, and his nephew, John Knox of Ranfurlie, as hostages.[13]

Angus Og's action in September 1614 makes it probable that, in spite of his protestations, his intention all along had been to force the king to accept him as tenant of Islay. His demand for a pardon had been met, only to be rejected and new demands made. He later tried to excuse his conduct by saying that Coll Ciotach and Ranald MacJames had acted against the bishop without his knowledge, and that he only took hostages because he was angry at hearing that the bishop had imprisoned Sir James' son Donald Gorm, but these explanations are hardly convincing.[14] He also claimed, both in September 1614 and later, that the earl of Argyll had urged him not to surrender Dunyveg, and had promised to help him to secure possession of Islay.[15] It is possible that there was some truth in this, for it is easy to see several reasons why Argyll should have acted in this way. In general he wished to complete the ruin of the MacDonalds, long his rivals. Of all the MacDonald claimants to Islay, Argyll must have been most opposed to the powerful Sir Randal MacDonnell of Dunluce, and continued trouble on the island would discredit Sir Randal as it seemed the rebellions were directed partly at least against him. Finally, the earls of Argyll had long been used to acting as the chief agents of the crown in the southern Isles, but in recent years they had been increasingly ignored by the government, with first Lord Ochiltree and then Bishop Knox supplanting them. In making such changes the government had indicated both its determination to be represented by men it could control fully, and its suspicion that use of the Campbells as agents often caused more trouble than it prevented and might lead to the Campbells becoming as powerful and as serious a threat to royal authority as the MacDonalds had once been. Bishop Knox was undoubtedly hostile to Campbell expansion, so Argyll had a strong vested interest in discrediting him by encouraging the MacDonalds to humiliate him and thus show that he was powerless without large-scale and expensive military help from the king. Thus it is possible that Argyll intervened as Angus Og alleged. But it is interesting that there were no allegations that Argyll had encouraged Ranald Og's original seizure of Dunyveg, which indicates that if he did intervene it was after the crisis began; he may have exploited it for his own ends, but he did not instigate it. In any case, it is hard to believe that Angus Og can really have been much influenced in his conduct by any secret contacts with Argyll; any MacDonald would have been a fool to put much faith in Campbell promises.

Argyll personally gained little from Angus Og's defiance of the bishop; the main benefactor was his kinsman Sir John Campbell of Calder. Calder requested Islay in feu from the king, offering a large feu duty and undertaking to bear much of the cost of subduing the MacDonald rebels on the island himself. This the privy council accepted. Calder was to lead an expedition against the rebels composed of his own men, levies from Argyllshire, and artillery and two hundred soldiers sent by the king from Ireland. On 22 October Calder received a commission to act as king's lieutenant against the rebels, replacing the bishop of the Isles.[16] The bishop denounced as folly the making of the name of Campbell greater in the Isles than it already was; this was simply 'to root out one pestiferous clan, and plant another little better'. Instead Islay should be planted with 'honest men' like Ulster.[17] But, as so often in the past, as far as the council was concerned delegating action to the Campbells had the overriding advantages that it was cheap and (at least in the short run) saved trouble.

The decision to award Islay to Calder presents one puzzle; why was the earlier acceptance of Sir Randal MacDonald of Dunluce as old Angus MacDonald's successor in Islay now being ignored? It might have appeared that he was the obvious person to turn to for help against the rebels. Yet the council made no approach to him, and indeed strongly opposed his even visiting Islay.[18] The explanation for this is presumably that accepting Sir Randal as tenant of Islay had been intended to provide the island with a 'civilised' and loyal landlord who was also a MacDonald and therefore acceptable to the islanders. Instead, it now seemed the lease to Sir Randal had helped provoke MacDonald rebellion. This must have much strengthened the hand of those who claimed that Islay would never be quiet until the MacDonalds were excluded. Moreover, the council may well have had second thoughts about the wisdom of encouraging the reunification of the Clan Ian Mor's Irish lands with some of its Scottish ones. That the union of the crowns had provided new opportunities for coordinating action against Gaels in both kingdoms had long been recognised as of great value. Lowland Scots were participating in the plantation of Ulster; Scots forces had helped crush Sir Cahir O'Doherty's Ulster rebellion in 1609, and forces from Ireland were now to be employed on Islay. Bishop Andrew Knox combined the Scots bishopric of the Isles with the Irish bishopric of Raphoe in recognition of the fact that the problems of the two areas were linked. But such government coordination was aimed at cutting the ties between Gaelic Ireland and the Highlands, not at fostering them, as the lease of Islay to Sir Randal would be bound to do.

That such fears of links between the disaffected of both areas were justified is illustrated by the Irish dimension of the 1614 Islay rebellion. The extent of the links did not become known until 1615, but they may well have been suspected the previous year. The precise nature of the contacts is far from clear. Ranald Og had been at Dunluce in Antrim immediately before his seizure of Dunyveg in March

1614;[19] there is no evidence that his stay in Ireland had anything to do with his conduct at Dunyveg, but subsequent developments suggest that there may well have been a connection, for the later stages of the 1614-15 MacDonald risings undoubtedly 'had some connection with the movements of the discontented in Ulster, but these intrigues are very obscure, and perhaps scarcely worth unravelling'.[20] Various plots had been brewing for some years among the Ulster Irish, bitter about the plantation imposed on six counties by King James, and these plots became linked to events in Scotland through the discontents of some Antrim MacDonnells unhappy at Sir Randal MacDonnell's leadership. These men were led by Alexander MacDonnell, the son of Sir Randal's elder brother, Sir James, who had died in 1601. Alexander had quarrelled with his uncle over land, and was ready to put himself at the head of a rebellion aimed (like that in Islay) against both the government and Sir Randal.

The Ulster plot of 1614 involved members of such leading families as the O'Neills and the O'Cahans, and aimed at gaining possession of Con O'Neill (the son of the exiled Hugh O'Neill, titular earl of Tyrone), the taking of hostages to be exchanged for imprisoned Irish leaders, and the capture of Derry, Coleraine, Lifford, Culmore and Limavady; by some accounts there was also to be a general massacre of the colonists in these places. Of thirty-eight conspirators eventually identified, several were MacDonnells and one was 'Coll MacGillaspic MacDonnell' — Coll Ciotach. Confessions later exacted from some of the plotters told of a meeting held in May or June 1614. By one account the rising was to have taken place the following August, and it was decided that 'when they went to burn and surprize Coleraine, they would send for Coll MacGillenaspie into Scotland, who was sure to assist Alexander and his kinsmen in that action'. Another account stated that Alexander MacDonnell was to raise men in the Scots Isles as well as in Antrim and that Lother MacDonnell was to be sent to get the assistance of Coll Ciotach. Finally, it is said that it was agreed that 'those of Scotland should begin the war first'.[21] These plots for a joint Irish and Isles rebellion may have predated Ranald Og's capture of Dunyveg, but it is perhaps more likely that the Ulster plot was sparked off by news of the trouble on Islay. And it sounds very much as if the plotters knew in advance (in May or June 1614) that Angus Og was going to fail to carry out his promise to hand over Dunyveg on being promised a pardon, such open rebellion being the beginning of the war referred to.

In the event no Ulster rising took place in 1614. Angus Og was thus left isolated as Calder gathered his forces and preparations were made to send him help from Ireland. But before military force was employed against him one further intrigue complicated the already labyrinthine plottings which surround the fall of the Clan Ian Mor. The chancellor of Scotland, the earl of Dunfermline, dispatched one George Grahame of Eryne (a Gaelic speaker acquainted with Angus Og) to persuade the rebels to release their hostages, the son and nephew of Bishop Knox. Grahame reached Dunyveg in November, and is said to have promised that if Angus Og submitted and freed the hostages, Dunfermline would do what he could to get him a grant of Islay, and would ensure that he received a pardon. Angus Og then (by his own account) released the hostages and handed over the castle to

Grahame, whereupon Grahame authorised him to act as constable of Dunyveg in name of Dunfermline. Further, according to Angus, Grahame authorised him to resist the king's lieutenant (Calder) and to defy a herald who was approaching to demand the surrender of the castle.[22]

What is one to make of this bewildering intrigue? It is possible that Dunfermline had hopes of securing Islay for himself and had therefore opposed the grant to Calder — he had evidently refused to help Calder secure the island by agreement with old Angus MacDonald in 1612.[23] It may have been that Dunfermline wished to ensure that Angus Og continued to resist and thus had no hope of reaching any compromise with the king; but it is haid to see how this would have advanced Dunfermline's own claims to Islay — it would still be Calder who conquered the island. It is perhaps more probable that he hoped to gain official support for the unauthorised promises he had got Grahame to make to Angus Og. Calder would thus find his orders to subdue Islay cancelled as Dunfermline had persuaded Angus Og to submit without bloodshed. Through his services in thus ending a rebellion (and through his high office) Dunfermline could then put in a strong bid for Islay, supported by those who opposed the extension of Campbell power to Islay. Once granted Islay, Dunfermline could either abandon Angus Og, or perhaps accept him as a tenant on the island. However (if this interpretation be accepted), Dunfermline failed to win official backing for his planned negotiated settlement with Angus Og; he therefore proceeded to deny that he had sent Grahame to do more than get the hostages in Dunyveg freed so that Calder could attack the castle without putting them in jeopardy.[24] Grahame had succeeded in doing this, and Dunfermline's influence was sufficient to ensure that the rebels' version (revealed after their capture) of Grahame's actions was not too closely investigated — Grahame himself naturally denied that he had encouraged Angus Og to resist Calder.[25] Several Campbells supported some of the rebel allegations against Grahame,[26] which indicates that they were not entirely inventions of rebels trying to justify their conduct. But on the other hand it is significant that Angus Og and Coll Ciotach never produced the original of Grahame's written instructions from Dunfermline, which they claimed to possess, but only a copy.[27] On balance, the safest verdict is that Grahame was involved (with or without Dunfermline's knowledge) in making false promises to Angus Og in order to get the hostages released; and that Angus and Coll then proceeded to exaggerate the extent of these promises in order to try to exculpate themselves.

Shortly after Grahame had persuaded Angus Og to release his hostages, Robert Winrahame, Islay Herald, appeared and demanded the surrender of Dunyveg. On Grahame's suggestion Angus sent Coll forward with him and three or four men to talk to the herald. A quarrel then took place, 'some cvill language' passing between Coll and Winrahame, during which Coll 'abusit the herauld' who then withdrew frustrated.[28]

On 21 November 1614 a charter was issued granting Calder Islay in feu. Late in the same month his forces reached Islay and closed in on Dunyveg.[29] But the reinforcements expected from Ireland had not arrived, and after waiting for a fortnight for them Calder withdrew his men to the mainland. Two days after he left, the Irish forces arrived under Sir Oliver Lambert — who found the Highlanders fine men 'yet more barbarous than the rudest that ever I saw in Ireland'.[30] Early in January 1615 Calder brought his forces back to Islay and began joint operations with Lambert against the MacDonald strongholds. Ranald MacJames surrendered the fort on Loch Gorm when summoned on 21 January, and the bombardment of Dunyveg began on 1 February. It produced immediate results; the following day Angus Og, though still protesting that his resistance had been authorised by Dunfermline, talked with Calder and agreed to surrender. On returning to the castle, however, he changed his mind — influenced, it was said, by Coll Ciotach. Further bombardment having convinced him a second time that resistance was useless, Angus Og and some of his followers emerged that evening and surrendered unconditionally. But Coll and others held out, demanding guarantees that their lives would be spared before laying down arms. They then made a daring escape by boat under heavy fire, pursued by government galleys. Coll's boat was eventually forced ashore on the Oa of Islay (the south-west extremity of the island) and sunk. Calder ordered the breaking of all boats on the island to prevent the fugitives escaping. On 6 February he captured and executed six of Coll's men, and he estimated that this left uncaptured only a group of four MacDonald rebels (presumably led by Coll) and nine or ten men of other clans who had scattered individually. Of those who had surrendered earlier, six of the garrison of Loch Gorm and fourteen from Dunyveg were executed immediately. Angus Og and others were sent to Edinburgh for interrogation, and there in July he and five of his followers were hanged.[31]

It is hard to arrive at any judgement on Angus Og, so little emerges of his personality and motives. But it does seem that he was a remarkably bad politician, with a taste for intrigue not backed up by skill, and an uninspiring leader of rebellion, simply shutting himself up in Dunyveg and awaiting attack. Though it can be no more than speculation, it does seem likely that much of the inspiration and driving force behind the rebellion came from Coll Ciotach rather than Angus Og. It had been Coll the Irish plotters looked to for help, not Angus, Coll who had besieged and taken Dunyveg from Ranald Og, Coll who had abused the herald, and Coll who had persuaded Angus to go back on his promise to surrender and then, when Angus had changed his mind again and surrendered, had continued defiant and then escaped.

Coll was more able, more daring and more lucky than Angus Og. His escape from Dunyveg was quickly followed by his escape from Calder's manhunt on Islay. By 16 February it was known that he, Malcolm MacRorie MacLeod and a few others had fled to other isles, and a proclamation was issued against him.[32] Coll may have landed first on Jura; there are various traditions of Coll and his men routing a party of Campbells there.[33] In late February he may have spent a few days in Antrim (though the reference may be to his visit some weeks later).[34] Early in March he captured a cargo ship belonging to Henry Robinson of Londonderry; this was a stroke of good fortune not just for Coll but for historians, for on board the ship was one Robert Williamson (a servant of Robinson's) who was kept prisoner by Coll for the next ten weeks to help to sail the ship, and after his escape Williamson gave an account of his adventures which gives us a more detailed picture of Coll in this period when he wandered the seas seeking safety than survives for any other period of his life.[35] Daringly, Coll first returned to Islay, landing on the little island of Texa within a mile of Dunyveg and sending some of his men to confer with friends on the main island. The news they brought back must have indicated that it was not safe to try to hide there, and the executions carried out by Calder indicated that there was little hope of submitting and obtaining a pardon, so Coll sailed on. First he went to Colonsay, where he went ashore, then on to Mull, where he anchored for four days. On Canna Coll and his men feasted and drank with friends for about eight days before moving on to North Uist, which was owned by Donald Gorm MacDonald of Sleat. There Sleat's wife and nephew sent them four horseloads of food, perhaps as much out of fear of being plundered as from hospitality.

To get rid of their unwelcome guests they suggested that these outlaws might be safe from the long arm of the government if they sailed to the remote island of Hirta or St Kilda, lying thirty miles out to the west of the Outer Hebrides. After about eight days Coll took the hint and, having been provided with guides, set sail westwards. Not surprisingly this aroused the fury of Sir Rorie MacLeod of Dunvegan, who owned St Kilda; according to his account Coll's men killed all the cows, sheep and horses on St Kilda and carried off all the spoil they could, leaving some in North Uist with the guides to reward the islanders for their help.[36] By Robert Williamson's account St Kilda had only about twenty inhabitants at this time, and Coll took from them a great store of barley and about thirty sheep. He stayed about a month on the main island of the group, Hirta, and then sailed three and a half miles north-east to the great stack of Boreray; 'there Coll had a purpose to keep himself, for it is of such strength as not to be gained but by famine'. Boreray covers about 189 acres and is surrounded by black cliffs rising to peaks of between 300 and 1000 feet, the west side consisting of sheer cliffs, the east mainly of steep grassy slopes.[37] On this great rock Coll the outlaw dreamed of establishing an impregnable pirates' lair, where he could live safe from the enemies who had driven him from Islay and Colonsay, preying on Hirta and other islands and on shipping. Though Boreray had probably been inhabited from time to time (rebels from the authority of MacLeod's steward on Hirta are said to have withdrawn there on one occasion),[38] it was not really suitable for Coll's purpose, lacking both a harbour and a beach for drawing up boats. That Coll considered such a plan even for a moment indicates his desperation, and perhaps also his awed reaction to Boreray's towering peaks and pinnacles; the stack looks as if it ought to be a grim fortress.

Traditions of Coll's visit to St Kilda survived into the nineteenth century, but it is doubtful if they contain much accurate information. An early eighteenth century tradition claimed that when Coll landed, the inhabitants hid in caves; that is plausible enough, but it goes on to state erroneously that Coll had lost his right hand in battle (an attempt to explain his nickname), that he arrived in 1641, and that he stayed nine months. The same tradition gives Coll a place in the religious history of the island. There was a Catholic priest on St Kilda, the story runs, but he was so ignorant that he could not teach the people the Lord's Prayer, the Creed or the Ten Commandments. Coll, shocked at this, taught the people correctly on these points and rebuked the priest; but when the people wished to depose the latter, Coll stated that he had never known a priest deposed merely for ignorance.[39] Unfortunately this anecdote seems to be a confused version of a later incident concerning Roderick, a local religious teacher on St Kilda. In 1697 the islanders agreed to abandon Roderick,[40] and were soon converted to protestantism. Sometime later this story was combined with traditions of Coll's visit to provide anti-Catholic propaganda; the ignorant impostor Roderick becomes a Catholic priest, Coll is made to admit that priests are usually ignorant.

After his sojourn on St Kilda, Coll returned south through the Isles, calling at North Uist, Canna, Iona (where he went ashore and bought some powder and shot) and Colonsay. On 9 May he seized Rathlin, capturing the principal men of the island and breaking all the boats on it so that no word of his presence could reach the mainland of Ireland. Next day Coll secretly landed on the Antrim coast at Bonamargy, sending his boat back to Rathlin. Coll stayed two days in Antrim, moving south as far as Lough Neagh. On 12 May he lit a beacon fire to summon a boat to take him back to Rathlin; with him now were Alexander MacDonnell (leader of the proposed Ulster rising the previous year), the latter's half-brother Sorley and others. His talks with these men seem to have restored Coll's flagging spirits, for before he had landed in Antrim he had said he was resolved to disband his men and live in Islay and Kintyre 'in secrett manner amongst his friends' with a small boat always ready to carry him to safety if necessary. Now, revived by the support of his Ulster kinsmen and friends, Coll was vowing 'to pilladge and rifle all those that he could overcome without spareinge of any'; he would recapture Dunyveg and kill all the Lowlanders in Calder's garrison there. Coll's force had been strengthened by the capture of a fishing boat of five or six tons (carrying oats to Scotland) while he had been in Antrim, and by the cargo of a Glasgow ship of about twenty tons which his own boat captured while returning to Rathlin after picking him up in Antrim; the rewards of piracy in this case were wine, beer, whisky, fishing gear and money. However, Coll soon lost the newly acquired fishing boat; on the night of 12 May Robert Williamson escaped in it, and next day was revealing to the authorities in Ireland that rebels and pirates were occupying Rathlin. He put Coll's strength at thirty men and boys[41] armed with fourteen guns (with powder and shot for about twenty rounds each), twenty-four swords and seventeen targets (shields), in addition to which all had knives.

The plan of the men on Rathlin was evidently to hold the island and raid passing shipping[42] while (presumably) trying to whip up support in Ulster and the Isles. But Alexander MacDonnell was soon arrested at Dunluce (he was later freed, though several of those involved in the Ulster plot were executed) and Coll Ciotach and Alexander's half-brother Sorley sailed north, abandoning Rathlin. Coll may have left for fear that Williamson's revelations would lead to his being trapped on Rathlin; to date efforts to track him down had been thwarted by his keeping on the move. Or he may have been seeking support in the Isles. Finally, news may have reached him which suggested that all was not lost for the Clan Ian Mor; a new MacDonald rising in the Isles was being organised, led by Angus Og's elder brother, Sir James. In the event, the new rebellion was to be a disaster for the MacDonalds, but it was to provide salvation for Coll Ciotach, by putting him in a strong enough position to purchase a pardon from the government.

From his prison in Edinburgh, Sir James MacDonald must have followed the antics of Ranald Og and Angus Og with mounting frustration. In about October 1614 he had made a series of offers to gain himself freedom and settle the Islay problem. He would lease Islay from the king (for seven years in the first instance, so his loyalty could be tested). If this was not acceptable he would go to Islay, get Angus Og to give up Dunyveg, make Islay worth 10,000 merks a year (how was not explained — the rent he himself offered was 8000 merks), and then transport himself and his kin to Ireland (or wherever else the king ordered) on being given the equivalent of a year's rent of Islay to buy new land with. If this too was rejected, all Sir James asked was a pardon and permission to transport himself and his kin abroad. Surprisingly one of the cautioners Sir James named who would guarantee his performance of his promises was Sir John Campbell of Calder — who presumably hoped that the offer to rent Islay would be rejected but that one of the offers of Sir James to withdraw his kin from Islay would be implemented, thus making Calder's task in taking over the island easier.[43]

Sir James' offers were ignored, and Calder proceeded to crush Angus Og's rebellion and occupy Islay. But late in May 1615 Sir James at last succeeded in escaping from Edinburgh Castle and making his way back to the Highlands. The privy council took his escape as proof of a guilty conscience; he had fled out of fear that Angus Og and his followers, then under interrogation in Edinburgh, would reveal his complicity in their treason. Sir James' own explanation was very different: he had heard that Calder had procured from the king a warrant for his immediate execution. While Calder certainly had good reason to wish Sir James dead — to prevent future trouble in Islay — there is no evidence that such a warrant actually existed. Moreover, the help Sir James received in escaping indicates that there was more to his action than the wish to preserve his own life. He was helped by Alasdair MacDonald of Keppoch and by the eldest son of the captain of Clanranald.[44] This suggests that Sir James had received promises of at least some assistance from the other MacDonald chiefs for an attempt to drive Calder's men from Islay before the Campbell hold on the island could be consolidated. Such help would not be given simply to support the wronged Sir James but out of fear for their own future. In less than a decade the Campbells had gained Kintyre, Islay, Jura, Colonsay, Ardnamurchan and Sunart, all at the expense of the MacDonalds; how long would it be before, having destroyed the Clan Ian Mor and the MacDonalds of Ardnamurchan, the Campbells turned on other MacDonald chiefs?

At Sleat in Skye Sir James conferred with MacDonald of Sleat, who did not join him personally but allowed some of his men to do so. Sir James then sailed south to Rhum and on to the island of Eigg. There he met Coll Ciotach and his men, and an elaborate ceremony of greeting took place. Coll's men, said now to number about

140, marched round Sir James and his followers for half an hour, firing shots in the air, after which each man came forward and shook hands with him. Among those present were Donald Gorm (Sir James' bastard son) and Sorley MacDonnell from Antrim. The rebels, who may now have numbered 300 men altogether, sailed on to Colonsay, where they stayed four nights and built a fort on an island in Loch Sgoltaire. While they were there, one Duncan MacDougall and three of his brothers landed on Oronsay; they formed part of the garrison of Dunyveg under Alasdair MacDougall, who had been appointed constable by Calder. Duncan wished to marry the daughter of the prior of Oronsay (a MacPhee) but her father had refused his permission, so Duncan had now arrived 'resolved to haif revisched and tane hir away'. To his horror he found the island in rebel hands, and he and his brothers were seized by Coll Ciotach and carried before Sir James MacDonald, who proceeded to order their execution, doubtless as much because they were helping the Campbells as through their intended abduction of the prior's daughter. Later Sir James agreed to spare their lives, but this involved him in a serious quarrel with Coll, who urged immediate execution.[45]

It was late June when the rebels left Colonsay and landed secretly on Islay. They managed to lure the constable of Dunyveg, Alasdair MacDougall, and some of his men out of the castle and then ambushed them. As they fled, the constable and some of his men were killed, and the rebels managed to capture some of the castle's defences and its water supply before effective resistance could be organised. Next day the castle surrendered, the rebels having lost only three men in gaining possession — among them Ranald Og, who had initiated the series of MacDonald rebellions the year before. Calder's men were driven from all Islay, while MacDonalds flooded in to help Sir James. At last, he hoped, he could negotiate with the king for possession of Islay from a position of strength, not as a helpless prisoner, and the island would be preserved from the Campbells — 'I will die befoir I sie a Campbell posses it'. Rather than, like Angus Og, awaiting counter-attack passively in Dunyveg, Sir James resolved to retain the initiative by occupying Jura and Kintyre.[46]

Meanwhile action against the rebels was being organised. The privy council put a price of £5000 on Sir James, with 5000 merks on Coll Ciotach. Once news arrived that Sir James had taken Dunyveg and that he seemed to be winning much more support than Angus Og had ever done, it was decided that it was necessary that the earl of Argyll should lead forces against the rebels in person, replacing Calder as king's lieutenant. But Argyll had little interest in such work. Some years before he had married (as his second wife) an English Catholic, and increasingly he seems to have found the quiet life of an English gentleman preferable to that of a Highland war leader. Moreover, he was much in debt, and was reluctant to cross the border for fear of his Scottish creditors. Many of the leading Campbell gentry were also in financial difficulties through acting as sureties for his debts. Eventually, on the direct orders of the king, Argyll did agree to return to Scotland, and until he arrived Sir Dougal Campbell of Auchinbreck was commissioned to act against the rebels — having first been released from prison, where he had languished in connection with his chief's debts.[47]

By the time Auchinbreck was ready to take action the rebellion had spread to the mainland. On 26 July Donald Gorm, Sir James' son, and twenty-four men had seized the house of Ceann Loch in Kintyre, and Sir James and Coll soon occupied the rest of the peninsula with 400 men, receiving an enthusiastic welcome from many of the inhabitants. Jura was also in rebel hands, and Malcolm MacPhee of Colonsay and all his men had agreed to support the rising. From further afield men seeking adventure came from the northern Hebrides. Sir James was now master of all the Scottish lands of the Clan Ian Mor which had once belonged to his father. The rebels, elated by their successes and by the failure of Argyll yet to appear in the field against them, talked of advancing into Campbell territory to strengthen their bargaining position, but nothing came of this; having occupied the lands they claimed a right to, the rebels ran out of steam, and allowed the initiative to pass to the Campbells and the government. Auchinbreck's men found no difficulty in preventing the rebels advancing from Kintyre while they awaited the arrival of Argyll.[48]

By early September Argyll had assembled his forces at Duntroon, and was ready to advance against Sir James' main camp on the west side of Kintyre, opposite the little island of Cara, where he had about 1000 men and his ships at anchor near by. Argyll dispatched Calder with seven or eight hundred men by sea to capture the rebels' ships while he himself advanced to Tarbert and merged his forces with Auchinbreck's. Meanwhile Sir James MacDonald had sent Coll Ciotach with about sixty men in three boats to seek news in West Loch Tarbert of the enemy's movements. There Coll encountered Colin Campbell of Kilberry, who was probably similarly engaged in reconnaissance, and captured him and three or four of his men. Coll then withdrew towards Sir James' camp, but on his way was warned that Calder had occupied the island of Gigha, north of Cara. On venturing near Gigha to test the accuracy of the report Coll's boats were attacked by Calder's. Closely pursued, Coll was forced to beach his boats on mainland Kintyre and flee, losing fifteen or sixteen of his own men but retaining his Campbell prisoners. In Sir James' camp panic had spread on news arriving that Argyll and Calder were advancing, and his forces completely dispersed. He himself made good his escape to Rathlin before returning to Islay to try to organise resistance. But Argyll quickly shipped his men first to Jura and then on to Islay, and two English warships (along with a boat carrying an artillery train) arrived to assist in the destruction of the rebels. Despairing, Sir James asked Argyll for a four-day truce, promising to surrender unconditionally before it expired. Argyll rightly regarded this as a delaying tactic designed to give the rebel leaders time to escape; Sir James seems to have intended to flee to the northern Hebrides, but was being held up by contrary winds. Argyll therefore only agreed to a truce on condition that Dunyveg and the fort on Loch Gorm were surrendered within twenty-four hours. Reluctantly Sir James accepted this, but by this time Coll Ciotach had escaped from Kintyre and had taken over command of both the castle and the fort, and he refused Sir James' orders to surrender them. In thus acting Coll was, it seems, largely moved by considerations of expediency. He could see as well as Sir James that the rebellion had failed, and was determined that he and not Sir James should gain the credit for voluntarily surrendering Dunyveg — and he had his Campbell prisoners as hostages to strengthen his bargaining position. He therefore made his own approaches to Argyll, while Sir James had to admit that it was no longer in his power to bring the rebellion to an end. Argyll therefore planned a night attack on Sir James' camp, but the latter received warnings of this and fled to Ireland with his son Donald Gorm, Alasdair MacDonald of Keppoch, Sorley MacDonnell, and about forty men. His other followers scattered in all directions.

The next day Coll agreed surrender terms for himself and a few of his friends. He would surrender Dunyveg and Loch Gorm, free his prisoners, and would then help in rounding up his fellow-rebels, in return for his life being spared. Under this agreement he handed over in all nineteen of his former companions-in-arms, including Malcolm MacPhee of Colonsay. Some of these men he betrayed were among the nineteen or so rebels Argyll executed in Islay before moving back to Kintyre to terrify the MacDonalds there by further executions.[49]

Thus ended the confused series of Clan Ian Mor risings of 1614-15 which had begun largely as attempts to keep Islay out of the hands of Sir Randal MacDonald of Dunluce and had developed into attempts to preserve the island from the Campbells and regain other lands. The government was quick to follow up its victory, not just by trying to punish the rebels but also by binding other chiefs to closer obedience than ever before while they were still demoralised by the example of the complete destruction of the Clan Ian Mor. In 1616 the privy council renewed many of the provisions of the statutes of Iona and added new regulations to them. The island chiefs were to appear annually (and more often if summoned) before the council with their leading kinsmen, to answer any complaints against them. They had to agree to limit strictly the size of their households, to reside in named houses and themselves supervise the cultivation of home farms 'to the effect they might be thereby exercised and eschew idleness'. No chief was to have more than one large galley, and on their voyages they were not to oppress the country people; indeed they were to lease all their lands (except the home farms) to tenants at fixed rents, instead of vague traditional exactions, and were to free their lands of all sorners and idlers who lacked lawful occupation. Carrying of arms was closely regulated, and the annual wine consumption of chiefs' households was limited. Schools were to be established in every parish so that 'the Irishe language, which is one of the chief and principall causis of the continewance of barbaritie and incivilitie amongis the inhabitantis of the Iles and Heylandis, may be abolisheit and removit'. Chiefs were to send all their children aged over nine years to be educated in the Lowlands; sons who had not received such schooling would not be allowed to succeed their fathers. In 1617 parliament joined in the attack on Highland 'barbarity'; the exaction of calps was forbidden.[50]

These reforms of 1616-17, and the destruction of the Clan Ian Mor which immediately preceded them, probably mark a more important turning point than the 1609 statutes of Iona and the rather farcical kidnapping of the chiefs. It was now that most chiefs came to accept some government interference in their private lives, their dealings with their own clansmen, and their relations with other clans. They now begin to give at least some outward show of obedience to such regulations; none, perhaps, were ever obeyed to the letter (and the government can hardly have expected them to have been), but chiefs felt it necessary to regulate both their own behaviour and that of their clansmen much more strictly than before. Feuding (let alone full-scale inter-clan wars) and defiance of the king had to be avoided or government action against a chief was likely when he next appeared in Edinburgh — which most of them now did with some regularity. Dues payable to the crown were now paid much more regularly than before. But though this was, from the government's point of view, a notable advance, there is much truth in the view that King James' policies 'had no more than superficial success';[51] the underlying problem of integrating the Highlands (socially, linguistically, politically and in religion) with the Lowlands had not been solved, though superficial obedience had been exacted from the chiefs.

Moreover in one respect the limited success that had been achieved may have contributed to future instability. Paying crown dues cost money. So did journeys to Edinburgh. Legal costs could make settling disputes by recourse to law more expensive (in terms of money) to a chief than a resort to clan war would have been. The first sign of a chief becoming more 'civilised' in his way of life was often his acquiring a taste for expensive Lowland and foreign luxuries and remodelling his castle on larger and more luxurious lines. Such assimilation of chiefs to the money economy of the Lowlands was no doubt welcome to the government, but many chiefs, used to exacting more from their men in services and produce than in cash, soon found their conspicuous consumption leading them into permanent heavy indebtedness. The evidence for this process is fragmentary; and doubtless many chiefs of earlier generations had had financial problems. But it does seem that the debts of many chiefs were increasing rapidly in the early seventeenth century, in spite of the fact that in many cases their cash incomes probably grew substantially with more settled conditions and the fast expansion of the cattle trade with the Lowlands and England. To stave off bankrupcy, chiefs began to resort to selling off some of their lands, or to raising loans on the security of land through wadsetting, or to surrendering feudal superiority over their lands to others; or land could be seized from them by the legal process of apprising to pay their creditors.[52] In a society in which such transfers of rights to land did not necessarily entail a transfer of the loyalty of those who lived on the land, this was bound to give rise to tension and dispute. Having lost land through extravagance or financial incompetence, chiefs were apt to try to maintain their former power by appealing to the traditional loyalty of their clansmen.

On the Clan Ian Mor's former lands a few MacDonalds survived the 1614-15 risings as men of some standing, though now as tenants of the Campbells: the MacDonalds of Largie in Kintyre, the MacDonalds of Sanda (an island off the south coast of Kintyre), and the MacDonalds of Colonsay, for Coll Ciotach soon established himself there. For a time it even seemed that the MacDonalds might recoup some of their losses by benefiting from the troubles of the Campbells. In 1618 the earl of Argyll made his way to the Spanish Netherlands without royal permission and announced his conversion to Catholicism; for this he was declared guilty of treason, and control of his estates passed to Campbell lairds acting for Argyll's child heir, Lord Lorne. While in the Spanish Netherlands Argyll met with two of the rebels he had driven from Scotland a few years before, Sir James MacDonald and Alasdair MacDonald of Keppoch. There were fears that the three men were plotting some new rebellion, but nothing came of such rumours, and on the whole the disgrace of Argyll worked in favour of the MacDonalds for it underlined the fact that the Campbells had come to have unrivalled power in the south-west Highlands, power which might be used against the king's interests. To King James, an adept at the art of balancing and playing off against each other rival forces and interests, the obvious solution seemed to be to show renewed favour to the MacDonalds. Sir James and Keppoch were therefore summoned to London in 1620 and given royal pensions. The Scots privy council was instructed to pardon them for all past offences; but though the pardons were granted, many of the king's advisers were reluctant to see the leader of a major rebellion a few years before return to Scotland where he might again stir up trouble. Agreement was therefore reached, it seems, that Sir James should not return to Scotland, and he lived in London until his death in 1626. Keppoch was more fortunate, being allowed eventually to return quietly to his clansmen.[53]

That the refusal to let Sir James back to Scotland had been wise was indicated by a new MacDonald rebellion in 1625. For some years the MacDonalds of Ardnamurchan had been trying to escape from the tightening grip of the Campbells, and their resistance culminated in open rebellion. This was promptly suppressed and Donald Campbell of Barbreck-Lochow established as landlord, feuing Ardnamurchan and Sunart from Argyll.[54] Had Sir James been back in the Highlands, the rising might well have been a much more serious matter; the temptation for him to spread it by trying to raise the remnants of the Clan Ian Mor in arms would have been very great.

Sir James made no further attempt to regain his father's lands. The MacDonnells of Antrim did not give up so easily, though their greed for Islay had contributed to its passing into Campbell hands. In 1627 Sir Randal MacDonnell (who had been created Lord Dunluce in 1618 and earl of Antrim in 1620) tried to buy Islay from Sir John Campbell of Calder,[55] who was not finding Islay and its largely hostile population so profitable an investment as he had hoped and who, having recently been converted to Catholicism, may have had more sympathy for the MacDonalds than in the past. Nothing came of this attempt, perhaps because the government was unwilling to accept Antrim as tenant of Islay. Certainly this was the reason for the failure of the earl's attempt to secure Kintyre in the 1630s.

In 1617 Argyll had ruled that Kintyre and Jura should pass on his death to his son by his second marriage, James Campbell (created Lord Kintyre in 1622), while the rest of his estates went to Lord Lorne. While in the Spanish Netherlands, Argyll had transferred Kintyre and Jura to Lord Kintyre, and this gift was ratified by royal charter in 1626 — Argyll had by then made his peace with the king and come to London, though (like Sir James MacDonald) he never returned to Scotland.[56] In 1631 Lord Kintyre agreed to sell his lands to Lord Lorne for £10,000 sterling, but though Argyll seems to have agreed to this,[57] the sale was not carried out. Antrim later claimed that Lorne had refused in the end to buy the lands and had agreed that Kintyre could sell them to whoever he wished,[58] but the truth probably is that Lorne, himself in financial difficulties, was unable to fulfil his side of the bargain.

In 1635 Lord Kintyre found another buyer, Antrim, who worked through his agent Archibald Stewart of Ballintoy (a Scots protestant whose family had long been settled in Antrim). Kintyre was bought in name of Antrim's son, Lord Dunluce; but though the sale had been completed and possession formally transferred, the privy council cancelled the sale at the request of Lord Lorne on the grounds that the original grant of Kintyre to Argyll had included a stipulation that it should never be transferred back to a MacDonald. The following year the matter was finally settled — though not to the satisfaction of the MacDonalds — by Lord Kintyre selling his lands to Lord Lorne.[59]

The 1614-15 risings have been described as 'the last great struggle' of the Clan Ian Mor to retain 'the ancient possessions of their tribe'.[60] This is not so; the last such struggle lay thirty years in the future, and it is ironic that the attempt then made was to be organised and led by, respectively, the second earl of Antrim (son of the man whose bid for Islay had provoked the earlier MacDonald risings) and Alasdair MacColla (son of the man whose treachery had ignominiously brought the last of these risings to an end).

Surprisingly, Coll Ciotach's conduct in 1615 in betraying his fellow-rebels did not permanently damage his reputation in the eyes of his clansmen; he had betrayed others as the only way of saving his own skin, and while that was not entirely honourable, nonetheless to have found an effective way of saving himself by intrigue when all seemed lost was perhaps seen as just as essential to a leader as skill in fighting and valour in battle. As suggested in the Prologue above,[61] it may well be that it was such craft and cunning, a capacity for intrigue, that earned Coll the nickname 'Ciotach' rather than the left handedness or ambidexterity which are the other meanings of that word and are usually attributed to him. After the collapse of the 1615 rising Coll Ciotach evidently tried to establish himself as master of Colonsay. This led to a conflict with the MacPhees, exacerbated by the fact that their chief, Malcolm MacPhee, was being held in prison after his betrayal by Coll. In 1618, however, Malcolm received a pardon and returned to Colonsay to recover his lands. It was perhaps in order to bolster his own authority by gaining official favour against MacPhee that Coll opened negotiations with agents of the government, especially as the temporary disgrace of Argyll might lead the king to compromise rather than risk further trouble in the Isles.

By March 1619 Coll had received a remission or pardon from Thomas Knox, who had been dean of the Isles since 1617 and had just succeeded his father as bishop of the Isles. The privy council, however, evidently refused to ratify this, as Coll had not bound himself to the standard terms being demanded from chiefs; he had not found sureties to guarantee that he would keep the peace and appear before the council whenever summoned. Indeed some thought was given to trying to bring Colonsay and other lands into the direct possession of the crown as Argyll had been condemned for treason; but the advice that 'small beginnings of discontent in that barbarous cuntrie, may breed more tumult nor the proffit of so much land' evidently prevailed with the king. Trying to gain actual possession of such lands from their present holders would stir up more trouble than they were worth.[62] When, therefore, Coll declared himself willing to appear before the council to answer any complaints against him as he had resolved to become 'ane obedient and dewtifull subject', the council accepted his offer. On 8 June 1619 the council granted him a safe conduct provided he appeared by 12 July.[63] The date was later extended to 20 July, but in the event he did not appear until 14 March 1620. He then undertook to live peaceably and to appear before the council whenever summoned to answer complaints; as sureties for this he produced Alexander MacDonald of Largie and Hector MacAllister of Loup.[64]

In spite of such promises Coll was soon in trouble again, through the feud between him and Malcolm MacPhee. Traditions of a prolonged feud suggest that Coll carried out a series of piratical raids on the island, but only the culmination of the feud is known from contemporary written sources (which show that here, where they can be checked, the traditions are remarkably accurate).

In February 1623 the prior of Oronsay, Donald MacPhee, lay dying, and his kinsman Malcolm MacPhee came to visit him. But Coll heard of the intended visit, and secretly landed on Oronsay with his eldest son, Gillespie, and about twenty men armed to the teeth with bows and arrows, two-handed swords, dirks, muskets and pistols. On Oronsay they hid ready to ambush Malcolm, who came from Colonsay by boat. But on landing Malcolm sent two servants ahead of him to announce his appraoch, and Coll's men opened fire on them, killing them both, thus warning Malcolm that something was wrong. Instead of fleeing, however, he moved forward to investigate, and came under heavy musket fire. One of his companions, Donald Og MacPhee, fell dead, but Malcolm managed to escape. His line of retreat to his boat must have been cut off, however, for he fled to the southern tip of Oronsay. Cornered there, he scrambled over the rocks and swam out to low rocky Eilean nan ron, the Isle of the Seals. There the last chief of the MacPhees of Colonsay spent his last night, alone and without food or shelter in wet clothes in mid-winter. The following morning Coll and his men came out by boat and, according to tradition, after a long search found Malcolm hiding under seaweed on the shore. He fled but his enemies caught up with him after he had been twice hit by musket bullets, and finished him off with swords and dirks. The thrifty murderers then carefully dug the musket balls out of the corpse: lead was scarce. Another leading MacPhee, Dougal, had surrendered on Oronsay on promise of his life; but after twenty days of captivity on Colonsay he too was murdered.

In due course Coll, Gillespie and their men were summoned to appear and stand trial for these five murders. When they did not appear they were 'put to the horn', sentenced to confiscation of their moveable goods. This was the only punishment imposed (and even it could not be enforced) for their crimes. The much vaunted 'law and order' imposed by James VI through the statutes of Iona proved incapable of bringing to justice the murderers of a chieftain even in the relatively accessible southern Hebrides. Nor were either king or Campbells capable of preventing Coll enjoying the fruits of his crime. With Malcolm MacPhee murdered and the prior of Oronsay dead, Coll took control of both islands. In the register of hornings he was described as 'ane broken heilandman quho thir many yeiris bygane hes beenne ane outlaw and fugitive fra our lawis for dyveris slauchteris' and other crimes, living obscurely in 'desert plaices'. Now he had conquered lands on which to settle and, as so often happened in the Highlands, those concerned soon accepted the situation.[65] William Stirling of Auchyle, an agent of the earl of Argyll, bought Oronsay from the bishop of the Isles in 1623, but in 1624 found it expedient to grant a feu of the island to Coll Ciotach, and in 1629 he transferred his feudal superiority of the island to Lord Lorne.[66] Lorne was already legally the superior of Colonsay, and he too accepted Coll's *fait accompli* and was willing to recognise him as his tenant there. Here Coll doubtless benefited from temporary weakness in the direction of the Clan Campbell. Argyll had retired to London, and his son and effective successor as chief, Lorne, was only about sixteen years old.[67]

It comes as no surprise to find that Coll proved an unsatisfactory tenant, and eventually, in 1635, Lorne raised an action against him in the court of session. Coll, it seems, was denying Campbell claims to the islands and trying to avoid paying rents and other dues, while Lorne was trying to establish that he was a vassal of the Campbells. Lorne may have been stung into action at this time by Coll's involvement in a cattle raid directed against Campbell property. In February 1635 Coll (now aged about sixty-five) was one of those accused of taking part in a cattle raid on the lands of Crossaig, on the east coast of Kintyre, which were held by one Alexander Campbell. However, he was probably only a minor partner in this exploit, as action was only taken against one of the other accused, an Arran man who was ordered to return the cattle and horses stolen.[68] In the following month the case raised by Lorne was decided in the court of session. On the court's orders the Campbells had produced title deeds supporting their claims, while Coll had produced none. On 25 March 1635, therefore, the court issued a decreet of improbation declaring any titles Coll might have to the islands null as he had failed to produce them.[69]

Coll now faced forcible expulsion by the Campbells from Colonsay. To prevent this he and his eldest son, Gillespie, were forced to accept a humiliating agreement with Lord Lorne. On 25 March 1636 at Roseneath Castle they agreed to make to Lorne a down payment or grassum of 10,000 merks (£6,666:13:4 Scots) in return for a lease of Colonsay for Coll's lifetime, and to pay 880 merks (£586:13:4) a year rent for the island — as opposed to the £453:6:8 that the Campbells had previously been demanding. But it was not these financial clauses in the agreement that hurt most; in addition Coll and his son had to swear to serve Lord Lorne faithfully in all his lawful employments and affairs in the Highlands and Isles, by both land and sea. They were to behave and carry themselves with all dutifulness towards him, and were to be ready at all times to contribute their best help and assistance to him in all things tending to the honour, profit and advancement of the house of Argyll.

To encourage Coll to be a dutiful servant, a rebate of 80 merks a year would be granted of the 880 merks rent due for Colonsay. No mention was made in the agreement of Oronsay, Coll's title to a feu of the island being accepted as valid.[70] The bitterness with which Coll accepted these terms, making him a servile dependant of his hereditary enemies, may be imagined. But his position was too weak to enable him to retain his lands in any other way.

No information survives as to Coll's political activities in the 1620s and 1630s; he probably approved of the attempts of the MacDonnells of Antrim to buy former Clan Ian Mor lands, but there is no evidence that he took any part in them. One development in which Coll did play a major part was, however, to be of great political significance: the revival of Catholicism in the Western Highlands and Isles. In September 1623 Pope Urban VIII appointed four Irish Franciscan priests to be missionaries in the area — Edmund MacCann, Paul O'Neill, Patrick Hegarty and Cornelius Ward. For some years attempts had been made to establish such a mission, but only in and after 1624 was the success of the missionaries significant, and in 1631 a permanent headquarters was set up at Bonamargy Friary in north Antrim.[71] Probably the mission was, from the first, under the patronage of the earl of Antrim, and he may well have seen its work partly as a way of reviving the unity and morale of the MacDonalds in the hope of an eventual revival of their power.[72]

Most of the MacDonalds, and many of the other inhabitants of the Isles, were Catholics, but their religion often consisted of a vague adherence to traditional ways rather than an active and organised faith, for in many areas no priest had been seen for generations — since the Reformation of 1560 or even before that. Within a few years the Irish Franciscans changed the situation dramatically and could claim to have made thousands of 'converts'; not, usually, converts from protestantism but men eager to revive their nominal Catholicism and receive the sacraments now that at last they had priests to administer them. Coll Ciotach's reputation as an enthusiastic supporter of the faith had evidently spread even before the missionaries appointed in 1623 arrived, for instructions issued to them by the papal nuncio in Brussels (which probably date from 1623-4) told them that Coll, the lord of Colonsay, was a Catholic who could provide them with information, and with directions on how to reach other islands. The instructions also mention the 'governor' (*gubernator*) of Colonsay as someone who would help the missionaries; this may be a reference to Malcolm MacPhee, who in fact had just been murdered by his zealous fellow-Catholic, Coll Ciotach.[73]

Once the missionaries reached Scotland they soon needed to call on Coll Ciotach's help. Ward, O'Neill and Hegarty landed on Sanda in July 1624 and proceeded to Kintyre. They were received enthusiastically, but a local protestant minister tried to organise the arrest of two of them. 'Colla MacDonnell, catholicus', was in Kintyre at the time and arranged their escape to Cara and thence to Oronsay. They stayed several days on Oronsay and Colonsay and made some converts, but there seems to have been considerable hostility to them and they were forced to move on to Mull after spending their last night in the open, gathering shellfish for food. It seems Coll had not accompanied them to his islands, and it may be that in his absence the islanders feared to give hospitality to priests; or they may have been in no mood to help priests sent by Coll as the latter was engaged in murdering and driving out the MacPhees, their former leaders. Later in this same journey Ward stayed for three days with the 'heretic' Campbell of Calder disguised as a travelling Irish poet and harper. In the end he revealed his identity to Calder, who promised to become a Catholic; his conversion was completed the following year by Patrick Hegarty.[74]

In October 1624 and spring 1625 Patrick Hegarty visited Colonsay and had more success than he and his colleagues had had a few months earlier; large numbers of the inhabitants were converted, as well as many men on other Clan Ian Mor lands. In the summer of 1625 Ward also was back in the Isles, making hundreds of converts in Kintyre (with an excursion to Arran), Islay, Texa, Jura and Colonsay. The last of these islands he left almost entirely Catholic, though he could spend only three days there as the bishop of the Isles was pursuing him. It was Ward who described Coll as *catholicus zelosissimus . . . vir bellicosissimus*, 'a most zealous Catholic . . . a most warlike man'. From Colonsay Ward moved on to Mull; MacLean of Duart was hostile, but MacLean of Lochbuie and, further to the north, Ian Muideartach, captain of Clanranald, had been 'converted' to Catholicism the year before and welcomed him.[75]

The conversion of Clanranald well illustrates the political implications of the work of the Franciscan missionaries. In February 1626 the captain wrote to Pope Urban VIII offering to subdue the greater part of Scotland for the true faith provided he received help from the pope or the Catholic powers in defending the area conquered from the king. Once such help arrived the remainder of Scotland could be conquered. 'All the Gaelic speaking Scots and the greater part of the Irish chieftains joined to us by ties of friendship . . . will begin war in each his own district to the glory of God.'[76] Revived Catholicism gave many Highland chiefs who were trying to retain their supremacy and resist Lowland cultural influence a wider cause than that of clan to fight for. An element of this already existed; many chiefs had resisted new-fangled protestantism, as they saw it as a Lowland religion being pressed on them by the central government. But such negative suspicion and rejection of protestantism was very different from the positive counter-reformation religious zeal now expressed by the captain of Clanranald. Moreover, this revived Catholicism was spread by native Irish priests teaching in Gaelic, which naturally tended to strengthen West Highland links with Gaelic Ireland, which had been weakened by the plantation of Ulster and the destruction of the Clan Ian Mor. And, as Clanranald's letter shows, such links were more than just religious and cultural; he looked on the Irish as his natural political and military allies. Nothing came of his great plan, but it is of interest as an indication of the extent to which some chiefs, though tamed for the present, actively resented domination by Lowland, protestant central government and hoped to throw it off as soon as an opportunity arose.

Cornelius Ward was back on Colonsay in 1629, and Patrick Hegarty in 1630 and 1631,[77] but after this the missionaries spent most of their time at Bonamargy; protestant efforts to capture the missionaries had made life in the Isles too hazardous for them. In 1629 Coll was among those who wrote testimonial letters for the priests detailing their activities; Ward had, he affirmed, visited Colonsay three times, and he, Hegarty and O'Neill had converted nearly all the islanders. But Ward had nearly been captured by the heretics during his 1629 visit, only being saved by the intervention of Coll himself, who had been seriously wounded in the incident. The original Gaelic letter is lost, and it survives only in a Latin translation in which Coll appears as *Collatius Kiotach Macdonell* — the earliest known use of his nickname.[78] However, though the missionaries after 1631 made fewer and briefer visits to the Isles than before, the results of their labours were not destroyed; each year up to 1640 hundreds of Highlanders made their way to Bonamargy to receive the sacraments.

Ward records that in 1625 he administered communion to Coll Ciotach and all his family.[79] What family did Coll have? Unfortunately it is impossible to give any more connected an account of Coll's private life than of his involvement in more public affairs. His marital career is confused; various traditions credit him with wives from the O'Cahans of Dunseverick in Ulster, the MacNeills of Barra and the MacDonalds of Sanda, and with marrying daughters of Campbell of Auchinbreck (which sounds distinctly improbable) and of Ranald MacJames of Smerby. Most or all of the traditions may well be true, for marriage was still far from being a 'till death do us part' institution in the Gaelic world; 'associations of varying degrees of permanence persisted, from pure concubinage to the "marriageis contractit for certane yeiris" proscribed by the Iona Statutes . . . to marriages fully consecrated by the Church'.[80] Marriages were made and dissolved according to custom, without reference to either the religious or the civil laws of the kingdom.

However, the wife by whom Coll had all — or nearly all — his children can be identified. Ranald MacJames of Smerby's daughter, evidently named Mary, married Ranald MacDonald of Benbecula, and bore him a son, Angus Mor. But about 1603 he repudiated her — altogether he was to repudiate three of his five successive wives. After this she married Coll Ciotach and bore him three sons, Gillespie, Ranald and Alasdair, and 'a good family of daughters, who were married to good gentlemen'.[81] Of the daughters, all that is known is that one, Jean, married MacKay of Ardnacroish, and that another is said to have married a brother of MacDonald of Largie. In addition Coll had a fourth son, Angus; he was illegitimate, and therefore is not mentioned among the children of Mary.[82]

The dates of birth of Coll's children are unknown, but if we accept 1603 as the earliest date that Coll could have married Mary, and combine this with the fact that Alasdair was his third son by her, then 1605 is the earliest possible date that Alasdair MacColla could have been born. As he was old enough and experienced enough to be entrusted with leadership of a raid on the Isles in 1640, he can hardly have been born much after 1620. In all probability he was born some years before 1615, and was one of the sons of Coll who were held prisoner in the Lowlands in that year. All we know for certain is that two sons of Coll were being held in May 1615;[83] government forces seeking Coll after his escape from Dunyveg in February of that year would naturally have searched Colonsay, and it seems probable that, failing to find Coll himself, they took hostage those of his children that they found. The sons captured are not named; but a Gaelic poem addressed to Coll by Cathal MacMhuirich refers to the former's offspring being 'away from you without attendants' and begs that God preserve from evil and enemies 'three youngsters who have taken part in no great evil'. Gillespie 'of the spirited nature is held captive from you', Angus and Alasdair 'are parted from you'.[84] The poem is not dated, but as 1615 is the only known date on which some of Coll's sons were held captive as children, it seems highly likely that it is concerned with the immediate aftermath of the 1614-15 risings, and that a third son had been captured later than the two referred to in May 1615. Internal evidence supports this dating. The poem refers to Coll as a fugitive at sea, who does not dare to land at any harbour because the MacDonalds have been suppressed and enemies are watching for him. It is said that 'were it not for the warriors of the Gael — for all their fine boasting — failing to turn up', Coll's sons 'would not be in the Lowlanders' noisy towns' — surely a reference to the failure of other clans to support the MacDonalds in 1615.[85] Thus it seems that Alasdair MacColla was captured and taken as a prisoner to the Lowlands in 1615; how long he remained there is unknown.[86]

Vague as this is, it is the most concrete evidence we have of any incident of Alasdair's childhood; the rest is supposition and tradition. Coll's home on Colonsay was a house known as *An Sabhall Ban*, the White Barn, near the present Colonsay House in the north of the island. There Alasdair and his brothers and sisters were evidently born and spent most of their childhood — though the unlikely tradition which credits Coll with marrying a daughter of Campbell of Auchinbreck places his birth in Glendaruel in mainland Argyll. Another traditional connection between Alasdair and the Campbells of Auchinbreck is provided by the story that he lived with them for some time as a child. There is possibly some truth in this; it would have been natural for the Campbells, in attempting to reconcile the family of Coll Ciotach to their rule, to have forced him to let his sons be brought up partly by Campbells, even if no formal agreement for fosterage was made. This supposition would also make sense of an otherwise inexplicable reference to Alasdair in a poem by Ian Lom MacDonald: 'You were fattened in a manner appropriate to swine by the race of Diarmaid of the Boar' (the Campbells). Perhaps, indeed, such an attempt to bring up Coll's children as Campbells, partly educating them in the Lowlands, is their 'captivity' referred to by Cathal MacMhuirich. If, however, such conditioning of the young Alasdair was attempted, it failed — as events were to prove; and tradition asserts that while staying with the Campbells of Auchinbreck Alasdair accompanied each stroke of his reaping hook as he cut bracken with the words 'if you were a Campbell, I would treat you in this manner', though this is perhaps a little too appropriate a touch to be plausible: Alasdair was to behead the laird of Auchinbreck in 1645.[87]

All the other traditions of Alasdair's childhood which survive are of the sort that probably — in some instances certainly — were invented once he became a heroic figure in order to provide appropriate signs and portents in childhood which had indicated future greatness. On the night he was born all the swords in the house rattled in their scabbards, and the locks on the guns snapped. Coll took these supernatural happenings as a warning that the new-born child would grow to be exceptionally evil, and therefore — always the man of action, with a quick and preferably drastic solution to any problem — proposed that the baby be drowned. He was only dissuaded by a nurse who put forward a more convincing interpretation of the omens: they meant the child would grow to be a great warrior. Other such predictions followed in later years. Another nurse, one Hallowe'en, performed a divination by placing a blue thread in a kiln, a traditional procedure, after which she predicted that he would be successful and perform deeds of great valour until he raised his standard at the mill of Gocam-go. As the standard was driven into the ground a coin would jump from the soil; after that Alasdair would never be successful again. One tradition places this last prediction in Ireland; others talk of Alasdair spending part of his childhood on Rathlin. There may be some truth in them — it would be surprising if Alasdair had not visited his MacDonnell kinsmen in Antrim.

Alasdair's actions as a child, tradition affirms, soon added weight to predictions of his heroic future. He ate a toad, a repulsive traditional feat for a budding hero which was also to be ascribed to Alasdair's commander in later years, the marquis of Montrose. Other actions, if correctly attributed to him, might be thought more truly to foreshadow the man he was to become, as they illustrate his strength and fiery temper. When cutting peats on Colonsay he was chided for not cutting fast enough, whereon he so bombarded the unfortunate complainant with peats that he was knocked down; Alasdair then beat him up for good measure. He so goaded a horse in a plough team for working too slowly that it died. He caught a cow that had gone berserk, and held it with one hand while he killed it with an axe — in reward for this he is said to have been given his first shoes, stockings and bonnet, Highland children even of high social status being brought up barefooted. On Rathlin on the orders of an evil stepmother — who also fed him the flesh of his own dog — he twisted the feet or legs off the carcase of a bull, another traditional feat through which Gaels displayed their heroic potential.[88]

Tradition asserts that Alasdair grew up to be a man of almost superhuman stature and strength, and it seems that this reflects more than just the natural tendency to exaggerate such attributes in heroic figures. Patrick Gordon of Ruthven, who had probably met Alasdair, relates that he was 'of such extraordinarie strenth and agilitie as there was non that equalled or came neire him'. Alexander Clogie, who in Ireland in 1642 heard many accounts of Alasdair's exploits, describes him as a son of Anak; and the only thing the bible tells us of these otherwise obscure figures is that they were gigantic — 'the giants, the sons of Anak' (Numbers, 13.33); 'A people great and tall, the children of Anakins . . . who can stand before the children of Anak' (Deuteronomy, 9.2).[89]

From his youth Alasdair would have been trained in the use of spear and knife, of bow and arrow, of pistol and musket, and perhaps above all, of sword (the single-handed basket-hilted sword which was replacing the two-handed sword) and the targe or target (a small round wooden shield covered in leather and studded with nails). His earliest memories probably included the turbulent events of the second decade of the century — the fall of the Clan Ian Mor, and his own capture and detention in the Lowlands. Whether at home on Colonsay or visiting kinsmen elsewhere, he must have been brought up in an atmosphere of nostalgia for the great days of MacDonald power and of bitterness at how his own Clan Ian Mor, still in the mid-sixteenth century the most powerful in the Highlands, had lost its land through treachery and deceit on the part of both the government and the Campbells; in such tales the major contribution the MacDonalds had made to their own downfall by internal feuding was doubtless conveniently forgotten. Stories, poems and music relating his father's exploits in trying to uphold the Clan Ian Mor, and describing the cunning which had enabled him to survive disaster, must have surrounded Alasdair throughout his youth.[90] Of his formal education all that can be said is that he learned how to write — an ability not shared by either his father or his eldest brother, Gillespie.[91]

By the time Alasdair reached adulthood in the 1630s his father was already an old man. He may still have dreamed of a revival of the Clan Ian Mor, but the West Highlands and Isles seemed in reality to be firmly under the control of central government, giving no real hope of a change in the clan's fortunes. The power of the government might still seem fairly remote, but that of the Campbells was inescapable. Their Highland empire now stretched from Kintyre in the south to Ardnamurchan in the north, from Islay in the west to Breadalbane in the east; and the earls of Argyll combined feudal authority as great landlords and clan chieftaincy under the traditional title of MacCailein Mor, with the offices of sheriff of Argyll and justice general of Argyll and the Isles, and could expect in any crisis the additional office of king's lieutenant. Coll, settled in Colonsay as a puppet of the Campbells, seemed destined for a peaceful old age after his adventurous and bloodstained life, a relic surviving from an age of violence and clan war which now seemed to be over.

Coll was deprived of his peaceful old age by the revolt of the covenanters against Charles I, a revolt which was to bring about revolutionary changes in the political position of the clans which were to be of immense significance for generations to come. More important to Coll, no doubt, the revolt seemed briefly to give the Clan Ian Mor a chance to reclaim its rightful pre-eminence in the West Highlands.

NOTES

1. For Coll's ancestry and birth see R. Black, 'Colla Ciotach', *TGSI*, xlviii (1972-4), 202-5 (a most interesting article that I have used extensively in this chapter); Hill, *Macdonnels of Antrim*, 54-5; Macdonald, *Clan Donald*, iii.399; S. Grieve, *The book of Colonsay and Oronsay* (2 vols, Edinburgh 1923), i.268.

2. J. de V. Loder, *Colonsay and Oronsay in the Isles of Argyll* (Edinburgh 1939), 108, 219-20. One 'Donald MacFie in Collonsaye' was present in 1609 when the statutes of Iona were signed (though he did not sign them himself), but it seems probable that he was not himself the chief of the MacPhees but his representative, Loder, *Colonsay*, 95.

3. *RPCS, 1607-10*, 747.

4. Loder, *Colonsay*, 97-107.

5. The most extended accounts of the 1614-15 risings are in Gregory, *History*, 349-90 and Loder,

Colonsay, 108-29. Most of the sources are printed in *RPCS, 1613-16* and Macphail, *Highland papers*, iii.

6. Ibid, iii.194-5.

7. Ibid, iii.143-4.

8. Macdonald, *Clan Donald*, ii.587.

9. Macphail, *Highland papers*, iii.144-5.

10. Macdonald, *Clan Donald*, ii.582-3.

11. *RPCS, 1613-15*, 695-7; Macphail, *Highland Papers*, iii.145.

12. *RPCS, 1613-16*, 706,710.

13. Macphail, *Highland papers*, iii.149-52.

14. Ibid, iii.197.

15. Gregory, *History*, 353-5.

16. *RPCS, 1613-16*, 716-24.

17. Gregory, *History*, 356.

18. Macphail, *Highland papers*, iii.168,203.

19. Ibid, iii.195.

20. R. Bagwell, *Ireland under the Stuarts* (3 vols, London 1909), ii.144.

21. M.A. Hickson (ed), *Ireland in the seventeenth century* (2 vols, London 1884), i.15-17,20, ii.260; *CSPI, 1615-25*, 42-3; Black, *TGSI*, xlviii.207,237 n.9, Bagwell, *Stuarts*, i.144-6.

22. Gregory, *History*, 359-61.

23. Innes, *Cawdor*, 225.

24. Macphail, *Highland papers*, iii.170-2.

25. Ibid, iii.236-8.

26. Eg, ibid, iii.239-41.

27. Ibid, iii.187-8.

28. Ibid, iii.208-9,213,237-8; Gregory, *History*, 360-1.

29. *Register of the great seal of Scotland, 1609-20* (1892), no.1137.

30. Bagwell, *Stuarts*, ii.144.

31. Macphail, *Highland papers*, iii.176-86; Gregory, *History*, 361-6; R. Pitcairn (ed), *Ancient criminal trials in Scotland* (3 vols, Bannatyne Club 1833), iii.364,365.

32. *RPCS, 1613-16*, 303,728-9.

33. A. Campbell, 'The manuscript history of Craignish', ed. H. Campbell *Miscellany* iv (SHS 1926), 244-5; A. Matheson, 'Traditions of Alasdair MacColla', *TGSG*, v (1958), 17-19; J.D.S. Campbell, marquis of Lorne (ed), *Adventures in legend* (n.d.), 213-14. The last two of these sources date the incident to the 1640s, presumably through confusing Coll with his son Alasdair.

34. *CSPI, 1615-25*, 60-1; Black, *TGSI*, xlviii.207-8.

35. Williamson's account is calendared in *CSPI, 1615-25*, 58-9. Black, *TGSI*, xlviii.208-10 summarises the account and corrects some personal and place names.

36. Macphail, *Highland papers*, iii.242.

37. F.G. Thompson, *St Kilda and other Hebridean outliers* (Newton Abbot 1970), 19,23.

38. Ibid, 102-3.

39. Black, *TGSI*, xlviii.209-10. See also A.J. and A.M. Macdonald (eds), *The Macdonald collection of Gaelic poetry* (Inverness 1911), xliii and Thompson, *St Kilda*, 44 for later versions of this story.

40. M. Martin, *A voyage to St Kilda* (4th ed, London 1753), 68-77.

41. Information from Glasgow put Coll's strength at eighty 'broken hieland men', Macphail, *Highland papers*, iii.226.

42. Black, *TGSI*, xlviii.212.

43. Macphail, *Highland papers*, iii.165-6.

44. Gregory, *History*, 367.

45. Loder, *Colonsay*, 97,122; *RPCS, 1613-16*, 441-2.

46. Macphail, *Highland papers*, iii.243,254-6,260,262-70; Gregory, *History*, 367-9,372-3; Black, *TGSI*, xlviii.212-13.

47. Gregory, *History*, 369-78.

48. Ibid, 378-80; Macphail, *Highland papers*, iii.276-8.

49. Ibid, iii.287-8,290,291,293,294,300,301; *RPCS, 1613-16*, 758-9,763-4; Gregory, *History*, 373-

90; Black, *TGSI*, xlviii.213-14.

50. Ibid, 214-15; Gregory, *History*, 392-7; *RPCS, 1613-16*, 671-2.

51. J.M. Brown, 'Scottish politics 1567-1625', in A.G.R. Smith (ed), *The reign of James VI and I* (London 1973), 32. The best account of James' Highland policies and their effects is Grant, *The MacLeods*, 173-254.

52. F.J. Shaw, 'Landownership in the Western Isles in the seventeenth century', *SHR*, lvi (1977), 34-48; Kermack, *Scottish Highlands*, 142-3.

53. Gregory, *History*, 399-402.

54. Ibid, 405-12.

55. Innes, *Cawdor*, 270-1.

56. McKerral, *Kintyre*, 29-31.

57. SRO, GD.112/39/459, Breadalbane Muniments.

58. Hill, *Macdonnells of Antrim*, 241.

59. Ibid, 237-45; McKerral, *Kintyre*, 34-6. McKerral wrongly identifies Antrim's agent as Stewart of Blackhall.

60. Gregory, *History*, 390.

61. See also Macphail, *Highland papers*, iii.295n.

62. J. Maidment (ed), *State papers and miscellaneous correspondence of Thomas, earl of Melros* (2 vols, Abbotsford Club 1837), i.204. This letter is only dated 18 March, and the editor has suggested 1615 as the year. This is clearly wrong; it was written during the period between Argyll's condemnation (February 1619) and his pardon (November 1621). It cannot have been written on 18 March in 1620 or 1621, as Coll's submission had been accepted four days before the first of these dates; it must therefore have been written on 18 March 1619. The only objection to this is that the letter does not refer to Thomas Knox as bishop; but as he had only been elected and provided a few weeks before, this is probably just a slip of the pen, a failure to remember his new title.

63. *RPCS, 1616-19*, 590; Loder, *Colonsay*, 128,130; Black, *TGSI*, xlviii. 219; R. Black, 'A manuscript of Cathal MacMuireadhaigh', *Celtica*, x (1973), 203.

64. *RPCS, 1619-22*, 21-2,231.

65. SRO, DI.1/38, General Register of Hornings, June — July 1623, under date 27 June 1623; Grieve, *Colonsay*, i.320-3; Pitcairn, *Criminal Trials*, iii.553; Loder, *Colonsay*, 224; Black, *TGSI*, xlviii.220.

66. Loder, *Colonsay*, 225-7; HMC 3: *4th Report*, appendix i.479; Black, *TGSI*, xlviii.220-1 citing SRO, R.S.1/18, General Register of Sasines, July — December 1625,f.237v. Loder misdates the bishop's transfer of Oronsay — 1633 instead of 1623.

67. There is a tradition that Coll's son Angus murdered an unpopular Campbell factor on Colonsay. Black, *TGSI*, xlviii.217 dates this event to the 1620s, Grieve, *Colonsay*, 269-72, perhaps more plausibly to the 1640s.

68. Loder, *Colonsay*, 228.

69. SRO, CS.7/476, Register of Acts and Decreets (Scott: Decreets), January — June 1635, ff.287v-289r; Loder, *Colonsay*, 228.

70. SRO, RD.1/492, Register of Deeds (Scott), February — June 1636, under date 13 April 1636; Loder, *Colonsay*, 228-30.

71. C. Giblin (ed), *Irish Franciscan mission to Scotland, 1619-1646* (Dublin 1964), ix-xi.

72. D. Mathew, *Scotland under Charles I* (London 1955), 193-6; D. Stevenson, *Scottish Covenanters and Irish Confederates* (forthcoming).

73. Giblin, *Irish Franciscan mission*, 24-5.

74. Ibid, 50-4.

75. Ibid, 37-45,60-3; Black, *TGSI*, xlviii.223.

76. J.L. Campbell (ed), 'The letter sent by Iain Muideartach, twelfth chief of Clanranald, to Pope Urban VIII, in 1626', *Innes Review*, iv (1953), 110-16.

77. Black, *TGSI*, xlviii.223.

78. Giblin, *Irish Franciscan mission*, 125-6.

79. Ibid, 60,62.

80. Black, *TGSI*, xlviii.215. For the flexibility of marriage in Gaelic Ireland see Nicholls, *Gaelic and*

Gaelicised Ireland, 73-7. A.E. Anton, 'Handfasting in Scotland', *SHR*, xxxvii (1958), 89-102 proves that it is incorrect to use the term 'handfasting' of temporary marriages, but his conclusion that the forms of limited marriage customary in the Highlands were no more than concubinage, as no such 'peculiar customs of marriage' were recognised in Scotland, is misleading. Such marriages might not be accepted as valid by lawyers and clerics in Edinburgh, but they were a long-established and recognised part of Highland life, and children of such unions were considered legitimate.

81. *Rel.Celt.*, ii.173.

82. Macdonald, *Clan Donald*, iii.277,401-2; Black, *TGSI*, xlviii.216-19. Black argues that Angus was Coll's stepson, he being the Angus Mor of his wife's previous marriage to MacDonald of Benbecula. Persuasive as the argument is at some points, I have rejected it; all sources which refer to Angus' ancestry call Coll his father, none calls Mary his mother. In a society which placed such emphasis on kinship this seems impossible to explain away, and makes it much more likely that he was Mary's stepson, not Coll's. See Chapter 9, notes 86-7 for references to a bastard son of Coll, evidently Angus, in 1647.

83. Macphail, *Highland papers*, iii.202-3.

84. Black, *Celtica*, x.197.

85. Ibid, x.194-200.

86. Black argues that the poem, with its three captive sons, cannot refer to 1615 as only two are then mentioned. He therefore suggests the alternative date of 1623-4, suggesting that Coll's three sons were captured in the efforts to bring Coll to justice for the murder of Malcolm MacPhee. This argument seems very dubious; instead of involving the creation of one extra imprisoned son in 1615, when it is at least certain that two were prisoners, it involves creating three captive sons at a time when there is absolutely no evidence that any were prisoners, captured presumably in an entirely unknown raid on Colonsay. The only evidence Black cites to support his theory (*TGSI*, xlviii.216,239, citing SRO, RS.1/18, f.237v; *Celtica*, x.221) is that the sasine granting Coll possession of Oronsay in 1624 names Ranald, specifically described as Coll's second legitimate son, as his heir. It is argued that this must have been because his other two sons (the ones named in the poem) were captive. This is unconvincing; why should Coll disinherit his eldest son because he was for the moment a prisoner? The naming of Ranald as heir can be explained far more simply and plausibly: Coll wished to leave his second son Oronsay because he assumed that his eldest son would inherit his much richer property, Colonsay. Finally, the internal evidence of the poem, cited above, fits 1615 but makes little sense in 1623-4.

87. Grieve, *Colonsay*, ii.236,237,277; Campbell, *Records of Argyll*, 196; A.M. Mackenzie (ed), *Orain Iain Luim. Songs of John Macdonald, bard of Keppoch* (Scottish Gaelic Texts Society 1964), 36-7.

88. Matheson, 'Traditions', *TGSG*, v.13,15,89; Campbell, *Adventures in legend*, 209,211; Loder, *Colonsay*, 136; S. Laoide (J. Lloyd), *Alasdair MacColla* (Dublin 1914), 53-4. A poem describing the young Alasdair competing in various sporting events in North Uist is to be found in D.A. Fergusson (ed), *From the farthest Hebrides* (London 1978), 100-3; but it is far from certain that the poem dates from the seventeenth century, so it does not provide reliable evidence about Alasdair's activities.

89. P. Gordon, *A short abridgement of Britane's distemper* (Spalding Club 1844), 64; E.S. Shuckburgh (ed), *Two biographies of William Bedell* (Cambridge 1902), 173.

90. In addition to the poem referred to above, addressed to Coll c.1615 — though evidently not delivered until 1636! — (Black, *Celtica*, x.202), there survive a waulking song (to be sung as a work song while fulling cloth), part of which has Coll as its hero (Macdonald, *Macdonald collection*, xliii-xliv, 275-7), and a pipe tune evidently associated with Coll's part in the 1614-15 risings (Black, *TGSI*, xlviii. 231-6).

91. For examples of Alasdair's signature and two letters in his handwriting see above, Prologue, note 26. The evidence that Coll and his eldest son could not write occurs in the agreement with Lord Lorne they made in 1636; the agreement was signed by Coll and his son with their hands led by a notary public 'becaus we can not wryte our selffis', SRO, RD.1/492, under date 13 April 1636. Evidence that, on the contrary, Coll could write seems to be provided by the publication of a facsimile of what is said to be his signature in Macdonald, *Clan Donald*, iii, 2nd plate after p.641. Examination shows that this facsimile is taken from a document dating from 1614, NLS, MS. Adv. 31.1.2, no.86 (printed in full in Macphail, *Highland Papers*, iii.187-8). But this document is merely a copy of a lost original; the text and the two 'signatures' appended to it (those of Coll and Angus Og MacDonald) are thus all in the same hand.

3

The Apprenticeship of Alasdair MacColla

THE Scottish revolt against the rule of Charles I began in 1637, and reflected a wide variety of discontents: fear that the union of the crowns was leading to Scotland being ruled in England's interests; dislike of anglicisation in both church and state; constitutional grievances against an absentee and increasingly absolutist monarchy; complaints at high taxation; the bitterness of the nobility at an alien, anglicised monarchy which sought to undermine their power and interfered with their property rights; and, most important of all, religious grievances. James VI had successfully tamed the more extreme protestants of the reformed church of Scotland, the presbyterians, and had successfully imposed royal control on the church and restored the power and status of bishops, who acted as his agents. James had also made a start towards reforming the worship of the kirk, to restore to it many traditional features which had been abandoned at the reformation, but strong opposition to this had emerged and James drew back and compromised. His son Charles, who succeeded him in 1625, had less tact; it was his attempts to impose a new prayer book on Scotland which sparked off revolt in 1637, for it was the last straw in a long series of changes which had gradually persuaded many Scots that his ultimate aim was not the creation of a conservative protestantism but a return to Catholicism. The exaltation of bishops in civil as well as religious affairs, the adoption of new theological ideas which undermined Calvinist predestination, the increasing elaboration of ritual and ceremonial, all seemed to suspicious Scots protestants to point in this direction.

By early 1638 the opponents of the king had won widespread support throughout the Lowlands (except in parts of the North-East), and the national covenant was drawn up and signed with enthusiasm as a band of union among those determined to resist the king's policies. An absentee monarchy ruling through a privy council in Edinburgh proved incapable of dealing with the crisis, and the covenanters soon won control of most of the country. King Charles' reaction was to decide to raise an army in England to invade Scotland.

At first the crisis was almost entirely a Lowland one, but as civil war approached and both king and covenanters began to seek support wherever they could find it, the attitude of Highlanders became a matter of great importance; and it soon emerged that many clans had more sympathy for king than for covenanters. The rule of Charles I had given them less reason than that of his father for discontent; not because he showed them greater understanding or favour, but simply because his rule proved increasingly ineffectual in the Highlands. Charles' attitude to Highlanders was (until he found it expedient to appeal to them for

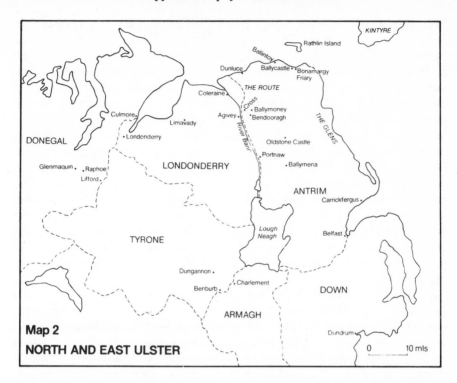

Map 2
NORTH AND EAST ULSTER

support) as contemptuous and hostile as his father's had been, and under him Highland policy remained unchanged. Thus his reign opened with strong government support for the suppression and final dispersal of the MacIans or MacDonalds of Ardnamurchan, whose violent resistance to the Campbell take-over of their lands led briefly to fears of a major rebellion in the Western Isles. The following year, 1626, official approval of Campbell supremacy in the west was reaffirmed when the earl of Argyll was, as part of a programme of administrative reform, deprived of his hereditary office of justice general of Scotland; for Argyll was allowed to remain justice general of Argyll and the Isles. In the same year Charles renewed orders that English language schools be provided in every parish 'for the better civilising and removing of the Irish language and barbaritie out of the heighlands', and he ordered the establishment of a college at Chanonry of Ross to help counter the barbarity and ignorance of Highlanders. Two years later came further orders for planting schools, building churches and imposing ecclesiastical discipline. In 1630 Charles welcomed a novel plan for Highland clearance through emigration. Sir William Alexander had reached agreement with 'some of the headis of the cheiff clannes of the heighlandis . . . for transporting themselves and there follouers to setle themselues into New Scotland'. Charles approved the plan as it would relieve the kingdom of the burden of 'that race of people which in former times hade bred soe many trubles ther'.[1] The scheme came to nothing as the Nova Scotia colony was soon abandoned, and the following year Charles was lamenting 'there is no order amongst thame [the Islanders] for increasing ather of religioun or civill policie'. Yet in spite of this 'great barbaritie' of the islanders nothing effectual was done. The king ordered the privy council to revive the summoning of chiefs to appear annually in Edinburgh, but most chiefs failed to appear, and after 1631 Charles seems to have shown no interest whatever in Highland problems. Thus the comment that Charles 'throughout the years of peace never seems to have given any thought to a country [the Western Highlands and Isles] whose lords had never penetrated to his presence' is only a slight exaggeration. Yet not only was the area failing to show the increasing 'civilisation' hoped for, there were clear signs that the government's hold was weakening. The captain of Clanranald could use violence to protect Catholic priests from persecution and take part personally in the wrecking and plundering of an English merchant ship, and the council seemed powerless to punish him. Other chiefs defied the government, though rather less blatantly, with impunity. Throughout both east and west Highlands cattle raiding and brigandage increased dramatically, and though the council devoted much time to the problem, nothing effective was done.[2]

Thus many chiefs did have very good — though negative — reasons for preferring King Charles to King James. That he had allowed the attack on the autonomy of chiefs and on Gaelic culture and tradition to lose impetus must have inclined many chiefs to support him -- or at least to refuse to join in revolt against him. Moreover, many Highlanders saw a positive reason for favouring the king in his religious policies. If many Lowlanders feared, wrongly, that Charles' policies were leading towards a restoration of Catholicism, many Highlanders, equally wrongly, looked forward to this and therefore tended to support him.

The revolt of the covenanters hastened this process of reconciliation between the king and many chiefs, for the new regime which emerged in the Lowlands established presbyterianism and was bitterly anti-Catholic. Forced to choose between this revolutionary regime and a conservative, seemingly pro-Catholic king, many chiefs naturally chose the latter. The Stewart kings might, in the past, have led the attack on the power of chiefs and their way of life, but Charles had not pursued such policies with any enthusiasm; indeed, it was now the new covenanting regime which seemed to stand for such traditional Lowland attitudes towards the Highlands. Charles was thus at least the lesser of two evils. He and many chiefs had enemies in common, the covenanters, and even — so some believed — an interest in common, the advancement of Catholicism.

For most of the clans in the Western Highlands and Isles, however, the decisive factor in determining their allegiance in the coming civil war was not national political or religious issues but their own, much narrower clan interests, especially in relation to the Campbells; would civil war give them a chance to challenge Campbell supremacy by breaking the alliance of the Campbells with the monarchy?

The question of which side the Campbells would support was not only of importance within the Highlands; it was central to the national scene, for Lord Lorne was regarded as the most powerful man in all Scotland in terms of the number of men he could raise. It was no secret that Lorne's personal religious outlook inclined him to sympathise strongly with the covenanters, but at first he sat firmly on the fence as the revolt of the covenanters spread. His motives for this were various. He was by nature a cautious man, slow to commit himself (though tenacious once he had done so), and he may well have hoped to be able to let the crisis pass without declaring himself, confident that his power was such that neither side would try to force him to support it for fear that this would drive him into the opposite camp. Moreover, Lorne's position was complicated by the fact that his father, the earl of Argyll, lived on in London and, as a convert to Catholicism, staunchly supported the king. If Lorne declared for the covenanters, might not Charles send Argyll back to Scotland to try to supersede him as chief of the Campbells?

In April 1638 Lorne visited London at the king's request and told him bluntly of Scotland's religious and other grievances. It is possible that Charles had been considering employing Lorne in Scotland as his commissioner to negotiate with the covenanters; Lorne's status and power would win him respect, his religious views would gain him the trust of the covenanters. But if this had been Charles' idea, Lorne's outspokenness caused him to abandon it by indicating that Lorne was a covenanter at heart if not in deed. Argyll is said to have warned that his son could not be trusted, and to have urged Charles to arrest him; but Charles refused on the grounds that it would be dishonourable to imprison a man he had summoned to court, and Lorne was allowed to return to Scotland.[3] But the king's honour did not prevent his almost immediately proceeding to sanction the use of force against Lorne. This may not have been dishonourable; but it was folly, as it drove Lorne into the hands of the covenanters in self-defence.

It was probably news of Lorne's quarrel with Charles in April and May 1638 that inspired the former's enemies to begin planning to exploit the troubles in Scotland to their own advantage. The first earl of Antrim had died in 1636, his peaceful efforts to acquire the former lands of the Clan Ian Mor in Scotland having failed. But his son, the second earl, retained ambitions in this direction, and he had the advantage of being a man well known to the king and trusted by him — he had married the widow of the former royal favourite, the duke of Buckingham.

The earliest evidence about Antrim's approach to the king, offering him help in Scotland, comes from Duncan Omey, minister of Kilcholumkill in Kintyre. On 21 July 1638 Omey made a formal statement before Lord Lorne, sheriff of Argyll and justice general of Argyll and the Isles, about matters which he had doubtless previously related to Lorne informally. Omey stated that the previous month he had been sent for by Archibald MacDonald of Sanda to read him some letters which he had recieved — Sanda was thus evidently illiterate. There were three letters. One was from Sir James Stewart, sheriff of Bute, to Sanda, to whom he was closely related by marriage. This letter enclosed two others which were from Archibald Stewart of Ballintoy to Sanda and to Coll Ciotach, the latter being sent to Sanda for forwarding to Coll.

Omey proceeded to read Sanda his letter from Stewart of Ballintoy which was dated from London, so far as Omey could remember, earlier in June. The letter revealed that Antrim had spoken to the king, telling him that none of the Clan Donald in Scotland had signed the national covenant. At this the king had said he was well pleased, for none who had signed would ever get his favour. Charles had then told Antrim to write to his MacDonald friends to thank them for not signing and to assure them that, as to Lord Lorne, 'when he comes next to court he will do no harm to you thereafter' — Lorne was, it seems, to be arrested, as his father had previously advised.

Pleased by this letter, Sanda proceeded to take Omey further into his confidence. The exiled leaders of the great Ulster Irish families, the O'Neills and the O'Donnells, were planning to return to Ireland with an army to regain their lands; they would do this as soon as the civil war in Scotland began. The earl of Antrim would then bring an army of MacDonnells to Scotland, and all the Clan Donald would rise and join him in a war on the Campbells to recover 'their old patrimonies and what mair they might'. Ranald MacAngus Og MacDonald would return to Kintyre;[4] this latter was one of the sons of Angus Og (he had two sons[5] about whom, apart from this reference, nothing is known) and thus would have a good claim to the chieftaincy of the Clan Ian Mor.

In his talk with Omey Sanda may have exaggerated at some points, relating dreams and vague plots as if they were concrete intentions; but Stewart of Ballintoy's letter, written on Antrim's behalf, makes it clear that Antrim was assuming leadership of the cause of the Clan Donald and had begun plotting with the survivors of the Clan Ian Mor to gain revenge on the Campbells by fighting for the king. Moreover, Sanda had already heard rumours that the native Irish, inspired by the covenanters' success and by the weakening of the king's position this had brought about, were planning to take advantage of the situation by raising a revolt in Ireland against the king, though simultaneously many of their fellow-Gaels in Scotland and the MacDonnells of Antrim would be rising in arms to fight for the king.

Antrim was also in touch with the marquis of Hamilton; the two men had co-operated in several projects in Ireland, and Hamilton was now in Scotland negotiating with the covenanters for the king. On 15 June Hamilton suggested to the king that Antrim be made use of in the plans to invade Scotland; he was beloved by some of the MacDonalds and had some claims on — or pretensions to — Kintyre and other lands. If he was encouraged to invade these lands with his MacDonnells, then this would prevent the covenanters of the south-west Highlands from sending men south to help oppose the royal army which was to invade Scotland from England. As to the northern Highlands, Hamilton informed Charles that he had entrusted keeping them loyal — or at least quiet — to the earl of Seaforth, the chief of the MacKenzies. But he cautiously added that the Islesmen in the west would act out of hatred for Lorne, not affection for the king.[6]

There is no doubt that the king gave his backing to Antrim's plans, though the precise terms in which he did so are unknown. Organisation of the proposed royalist alliance in the Western Highlands spread fast. By 24 August Sir Donald Gorm Og Macdonald of Sleat could report to Hamilton that he had met with the captain of Clanranald, Donald MacDonald of Glengarry, and 'our haill name of

Claine Donald'. They had all sworn 'to doe and live with me in the King's service' and Sleat had received letters from Antrim about his plans.[7]

Lord Lorne was well informed about these intrigues against him, both through the revelations of Duncan Omey and from intelligence reports from men at court who sympathised with the covenanters.[8] He wrote indignantly to Hamilton that he knew not why he deserved such treatment, but that if such oppression as a MacDonnell attack on him took place he would resist.[9] To Lord Wentworth, the lord deputy of Ireland, Lorne denounced the MacDonalds 'who has evir takine their Adwantage in trowblesome Tymes to execute thair Rebellionis', and he passed on MacDonald of Sanda's revelation that the O'Neills and O'Donnells were plotting rebellion. In reply Wentworth described the Clan Donald as 'desperate and barbarous enough'; from the first he opposed Antrim's schemes.[10]

Meanwhile Lorne prepared for war. On 2 August, less than two weeks after Omey's statement to him, the barons and gentlemen of Argyllshire met and drew up orders for the defence of the shire. Musters and wapinshaws (weapon-showings) were to be held, to find out how many fighting men were available and what arms they had. All able-bodied men were to be provided with guns, bows, swords and targets. Pikes were to be distributed. Fletchers and smiths were to be set to work making arrows and arrow heads. Veteran soldiers were to be hired in Edinburgh to train the men. Gentlemen were to make ready their galleys, birlins and boats. Men were to watch the land boundaries of the shire and the harbours of Kintyre, and a series cf beacons was to be established to flash out warnings if any invasion took place. A committee of defence was set up, dominated by Campbells but also including leading MacLeans.[11]

Such efforts to put the country on a war footing were soon common throughout Scotland, but the preparations were unusually early and thorough in Argyll, as this was the only area in which a specific threat of invasion had emerged by the summer of 1638. Yet, as we have seen, Lorne was not a covenanter. Perhaps his sympathies would eventually have led him to become one whatever the king had done, but in the event he was forced into becoming one because the king was encouraging his hereditary enemies to attack him. In the autumn of 1638, most inconveniently for the king, the old earl of Argyll died in London, freeing his son from any constraints the fact that he still lived had placed on him; by the end of the year the new earl of Argyll had publicly declared his support for the covenanters, though it was to be several more months before he actually signed the covenant.

Antrim too began preparations for war in summer 1638. He tried to win support by presenting himself, implausibly, as the victim of aggression. Lorne was planning to attack him. 'This man is my Enemy, and what his Intentions are I do not know' — though he added that the Campbells possessed the lands of his predecessors in Scotland, which hinted at his real ambitions.[12] Antrim soon found that he had not the resources to carry out a full-scale invasion of Argyllshire on his own, and that he was not getting the help he had relied on from the government of Ireland. Wentworth was implacably opposed to him, for he was against arming the MacDonnells, because they were Catholics, because he did not trust Antrim, and because he saw little advantage to the king in an invasion of the Highlands. If

Ireland's resources were to be used against the covenanters, then this was a matter for the government in Dublin to organise, not an opportunity for a private subject like Antrim to get his hands on government money and equipment to advance his plans for personal aggrandisement.[13] Thus Antrim's preparations were slow, and the new earl of Argyll was given a breathing space in which to prepare to defend himself and then move on to offensive action, while Antrim looked on helplessly. By the end of 1638 Antrim, in a desperate bid for sympathy, was claiming that the covenanters 'are now putting in Force an Act, that to the End of the World no MacDonell shall be allowed to enjoy a Foot of Land in Scotland'.[14] Early in 1639 Argyll bought a fully armed frigate and other arms in Holland.[15] By February 1639 Wentworth had heard that he was fortifying Kintyre and training men (he eventually constructed a fortified camp at Lochhead with a garrison under Sir Duncan Campbell of Auchinbreck), and remarked sarcastically that Argyll was more likely to invade Antrim's lands than *vice versa*. A month later Antrim got as far as detailing the arms he needed for his proposed army (of 4800 footmen and 200 horse). These arms he asked Dublin to supply, along with wood for building boats, the help of naval vessels, and 500 long bows, each with four bowstrings and twenty-four arrows; these last were to be delivered to Antrim's supporters when he landed in Scotland. But though bows were 'a Weapon much in Use with the Scots', they were regarded as obsolete in Ireland and none were available. The other weapons could have been supplied, but Wentworth made sure that they were not. He helped justify his refusal by casting futher doubts on the wisdom of Antrim's project; some of the Scots lands Antrim claimed because they had belonged 'to his Ancestors (me thought he said) these thirteen hundred Years' might not be in the hands of covenanters but of men loyal to the king. A MacDonnell invasion would force such men into alliance with the covenanters.[16]

In April Argyll began to move against his enemies. Archibald MacDonald of Sanda, his son Archibald Og and two of Antrim's agents in Kintyre were arrested. Antrim renewed his appeals to Wentworth for help in protecting his allies in Scotland from Campbell aggression; he had received several messages from the Isles begging for aid, and he sent the only messenger who could speak English, one 'Donell MacDonell MacRandell Glass' to Wentworth to explain the situation.[17] A month later MacDonald of Sleat arrived in Ireland, evidently at the request of Antrim who had sent Stewart of Ballintoy to him, on his way to see the king in England. With Sleat there landed about 300 MacDonalds (about 100 of them being described as gentlemen) from Kintyre and Islay who had fled from the Campbells. Argyll had not only dispersed his Highland enemies; he felt confident enough to march 'all his Men clad in red Trouse' to the border to oppose invasion from England.[18] Wentworth remained unsympathetic to this tale of woe, contemptuously dismissing the forces Antrim was trying to raise as 'a Company of naked and unexperienced Irishmen' and refusing Antrim help in supporting the refugees from Scotland. To his annoyance Antrim would not tell him precisely why Sleat was going to court, but it was obvious he would appeal to the king for help, so Wentworth intervened by suggesting that Sleat like Antrim might well be incapable of carrying out any promises he might make — an opinion based on no evidence whatever apart from general distrust of Gaels.[19]

The only action in the Isles that Wentworth would support was the sending of naval vessels to cruise there to gather intelligence and encourage the king's friends. From Carrickfergus on 25 June 1639 the captain of one of these ships, Richard Owen, reported dramatic developments. Owen had sailed from Dublin early in June and anchored in the sound of Islay on the 17th. A boat had come out to discover the ship's identity, and Owen had questioned its crew. At first they refused to give him any information, but when threatened with hanging they became more co-operative. They put the military strength of Islay at about 700 men, who were led by Colin Campbell, the tutor (guardian, in effect acting chief) of Calder; old Sir John Campbell of Calder still lived, but some years before had handed over control of his estates to his son John. The latter had recently gone insane, so his younger brother Colin Campbell of Ardesier had taken over.[20] Colin Campbell was not on Islay, and had left the island in the charge of his uncle, William Campbell (a brother of Sir John). On hearing this, Owen sent to William inviting him to come on board. He cautiously declined, but Owen discovered that he was a 'fervent Papist' and used this to win his trust. Owen pretended that he too was a Catholic, and that he had a priest with him; a letter was then forged in name of this fictitious priest urging William to come on board. This time William did so, and his suspicions were so quieted that he returned next day for a second visit, accompanied by his nephew Colin. The latter had just returned, Owen related, from 'Coll's Isle, whither he went, as I well understand, with an hundred men, having brought with him the spoil of the Island, killing all their Cattle, and taking all their Corn, Butter, and Cheese in Boats, which were discerned to come from thence-ward, rowing close along the Shore'. Owen sent a pinnace (which had accompanied his ship from Dublin) to try to intercept the plunder-laden galleys of the victorious Campbells, but they kept so close to the shore that the pinnace was driven off, 'the Islanders pouring off the Hills upon them so thickly their small Shot' — in spite of the fact that, as Owen noted indignantly, the pinnace was clearly flying the king's colours. Owen therefore had to content himself with seizing Colin and William Campbell and sailing for Ireland; he also brought with him a man who was ready to give evidence against his prisoners, he having been present with them 'in Coll's Isle upon this barbarous Usage of the Inhabitants'.[21]

'Coll's Isle' is of course Colonsay; in the old spelling of 'Collinsa' the name was occasionally thus interpreted in the years that Coll Ciotach held the island. The Campbells had thus at last moved against Coll, nearly a year after they had first heard that he was plotting with Antrim. The delay is surprising, but it seems to be a reflection of the fact that Coll (now aged about sixty-nine) and his family were not seen as serious threats; only after Kintyre had been secured and men sent to join the main covenanting army had Colonsay been mopped up, almost as an afterthought.

Further information about the raid on Colonsay and Richard Owen's activities comes from a letter written from Inveraray Castle (Argyll's headquarters) on 25 June. This reports that the king's naval vessels in the sound of Islay had plundered and killed fifty cattle on Jura, and had captured three Islay gentlemen. Sir Donald Campbell of Ardnamurchan, who had just returned from leading the raid on

Colonsay, had been sent to Islay to prevent any attempted landing there. 'Coll Mcgillespick is heere with my Lord [Argyll] but no certaintie quher his sones ar.'[22] On 4 July the same correspondent recorded that Coll was still detained at Inveraray.[23]

Coll Ciotach was now a prisoner; but how had he become one? It is usually assumed that he and two of his sons were captured during the raid on Colonsay. But the letters from Inveraray cited above do not connect Coll's capture with the raid, and also indicate that his sons were still free. A few other scraps of evidence also cast doubt on the accepted story. In 1645 Alasdair MacColla is said to have stated that four years before (this should be six years) Argyll had drawn his father and brother to Inveraray 'upon trust, and then made them prisoners'.[24] Argyll himself was later to claim that he had arrested Coll and his sons as they had failed to find sureties to guarantee their appearance to answer criminal charges against them.[25] A traditional account relates that Coll was summoned with others to Dunstaffnage Castle to pay their rents. Coll came to the meeting but refused to pay rent to Campbells and sailed for home. But a signal summoned him to return, and when he did so he was made a prisoner.[26] These versions of Coll's arrest conflict with one another and are not entirely convincing — Argyll is trying to justify his own conduct, and Coll would surely have been summoned to Inveraray, not Dunstaffnage, to pay rent. But, on the other hand, Coll may well have been failing to pay his rents and feu duties to Argyll, and Dunstaffnage is probably given as the scene of Coll's arrest because that was where Coll was to spend most of his years as a prisoner.[27] Moreover the tradition, Argyll's story and Alasdair MacColla's story do all have one thing in common: in all of them Coll comes peacefully to Campbell territory and is then arrested. It thus seems probable that he was lured away from his own followers and arrested, and that Colonsay, deprived of his leadership, was then overrun with little difficulty; all that one can say with complete certainty is that from mid-1639 onwards Coll and two of his sons, Gillespie and Angus, are prisoners of the Campbells. But the failure to capture Coll's two other sons, Alasdair and Ranald, was to have disastrous consequences for the Campbells in years to come; both evidently saved themselves by fleeing to their kinsmen in Antrim.

The Campbell attack on Colonsay took place a few days before Richard Owen anchored off Islay on 17 June. On 18 June Charles I signed a peace treaty with the covenanters, ending the almost bloodless 'First Bishops' War'. By 4 July Argyll had dismissed his 'host' in Kintyre, keeping only 200 men in arms, and had written to Lord Deputy Wentworth asking for the release of the prisoners Owen had carried off from Islay;[28] his request was granted promptly, for Colin Campbell had returned in time to be in Edinburgh for the meeting of the general assembly on 12 August.[29]

The peace was, however, from the first a precarious one. Neither the king nor the covenanters really expected it to last. Charles had come to the border with his army intending to invade Scotland, but had found himself faced by a larger and much more enthusiastic army of covenanters. Deciding that he was not ready to face the Scots in battle, he negotiated a peace to buy himself time to prepare for a new war. In the days before the negotiations he had continued to encourage plans for a royalist alliance in the Highlands. On 2 May, at Durham on his way north, he had written to William MacKintosh, chief of the Clan Chattan, ordering him not to obey Argyll and promising to free him from all feudal dependence on Argyll in the future. Instead he was to obey the royalist marquis of Huntly 'or such forces as shall be sent from Ireland for our service'.[30] The letter is doubtless typical of many others, now lost, sent to chiefs to encourage their royalist — or anti-Campbell — leanings. On 5 June Charles issued commissions appointing Antrim and MacDonald of Sleat king's lieutenants and commissioners in the Highlands and Isles, to act against the king's enemies there.[31] Inducements to be zealous in the king's service soon followed. A royal letter to Antrim promised him Kintyre,[32] and a similar letter dated 11 June promised Sleat the islands of Canna, Rhum and Muck, Strathswordsdale in Skye, and Ardnamurchan and Sunart on the mainland. These lands were to be made available by the forfeiture of Argyll, Sir Donald Campbell of Ardnamurchan, and John MacKinnon of Strathswordsdale; there is no evidence that the latter was a covenanter, but it may be that Sleat had blackened his name to the king in order to get a right to lands which bordered his own.[33] Charles also promised Sleat a ship and arms for 1000 men.[34]

The king made his offer of Campbell lands to Sleat on the very day that his peace negotiations with the covenanters began, and he made no attempt to cancel his orders and promises to Antrim and Sleat even after the treaty was signed. The peace gave Sleat a chance to continue his plottings unmolested by the covenanters. Since the fall of the Clan Ian Mor, the MacDonalds of Sleat had been regarded as the most powerful surviving Highland chiefs of their name, and Sleat soon brought together a formidable — at least on paper — band of allies. All our information as to his success comes from a confession by one of the plotters, Sir James Lamont, chief of the Lamonts. He revealed that Sleat had been seeking signatures to a bond of loyalty to the king. Among those from the southern Highlands who signed were Lamont himself, Sir James Stewart (sheriff of Bute), and Sir Archibald Stewart of Blackhall. In the north lay the main strength of the 'royalists' — Sleat himself, the captain of Clanranald, Seaforth (chief of the MacKenzies), John (Ian) MacLeod of Dunvegan and Sir Lachlan MacLean of Duart — the latter had been sworn to the conspiracy after Sleat had 'layed the Bible upon his head'. Meetings were held in Edinburgh and elsewhere, and the conspirators agreed to invade Argyll's estates in conjunction with a landing in Kintyre from Ireland — Antrim's contribution. They were spurred on by further promises of reward and favour. Argyll's offices were to be divided up; it was said that Seaforth would replace him as justice general of the Isles, and Sleat produced his commission to show that he was already king's lieutenant. Sleat vowed to ruin Argyll and all who supported him and undertook to raise 2000 men for the king — provided the arms he had been promised arrived.[35]

These grand plans came to nothing. Lamont betrayed them to the covenanters to save his own skin, and Antrim's invasion from Ireland never materialised — his promises had been over-ambitious, and Wentworth's campaign of denigration against him and all his projects continued. Kintyre and the Isles were not worth the cost of conquering them, and Antrim had not got the support there that he pretended, Wentworth argued. The men Antrim was raising were 'in great part the sons of habituated traitors', and though the MacDonnells might pray for the king this meant nothing in practice; they would not obey orders from the government in Dublin.[36] After the June 1639 peace was signed, many of the MacDonald refugees in Antrim — including perhaps Alasdair MacColla and his brother Ranald — tried to return to their homes, but those who landed in Kintyre were beaten off by Argyll's men; and Argyll made no move to free the prisoners he had taken.[37] To his MacDonald captives Argyll soon added Sir Lachlan MacLean of Duart. A MacLean account dates his arrest to 1641, and states that Duart had received letters from Charles I asking him to raise men for the royal cause. Argyll had then invited Duart to Inveraray and, on his refusal to disclose the king's instructions, had arrested him, keeping him prisoner for over a year in the castles of Carrick and Dunstaffnage. While this is probably accurate in other respects, it puts the date of the arrest far too late; there exists a draft order from the king, probably dating from late 1639 or early 1640, forbidding Argyll to hold courts of justice (as he was using them to force men into disloyalty to the king) and ordering him to release Duart and 'archibald macoll'. A blank line after these two names in the draft indicates that it was intended to add other names, perhaps including Gillespie's (Archibald's) father Coll Ciotach and his brother Angus.[38]

If these orders were ever dispatched, they had little effect; Argyll did free Duart (though when is unknown) but he retained his MacDonald prisoners, and in the autumn of 1639 he granted Colonsay and Oronsay in feu to Colin Campbell of Ardesier, tutor of Calder.[39] Coll Ciotach and his family were not to be given another opportunity to use Colonsay as a base for MacDonald plots.

The renewal of war between the king and the covenanters in 1640 gave the MacDonalds and their allies a new opportunity of asserting themselves against the Campbells, but, demoralised by their failures the previous year, they took little advantage of it. Indeed it was the royalists of the eastern, not the western, Highlands who proved most troublesome to the covenanters. Argyll was commissioned to march east to deal with the threats posed by the Stewarts of Atholl, the Ogilvies and the Farquharsons. Between 18 June and 2 August Argyll marched with up to 4000 men through Atholl, the Braes of Mar and Angus, Badenoch, Lochaber and Rannoch. Little opposition was met with, but the march itself was an impressive assertion of power. It also enabled Argyll to combine public duty with private interest. He had recently acquired the feudal superiority of Badenoch and Lochaber from the financially embarrassed marquis of Huntly, and the march gave him an opportunity to assert himself in these areas.[40]

This new extension of Campbell power soon led to trouble, however. On 1 October Argyll had to commission Sir Robert Campbell of Glenorchy and Sir Donald Campbell of Ardnamurchan to act against the MacDonalds in Lochaber and Glengarry and Donald Robertson, tutor of Struan, and their accomplices. They were, it was said, indulging in raiding, theft and other crimes, behaving as traitors to king and kingdom. It seems likely that they were in fact reacting against Argyll's attempts to assert his feudal superiority over Lochaber and Badenoch rather than acting out of any intention of helping the king, but calling them traitors conveniently justified taking proceedings against them at public expense. Remarkably, the commission to the Campbell lairds reveals that Argyll had previously commissioned the captain of Clanranald to act against MacDonald of Glengarry and his sons, friends and tenants.[41] Presumably Argyll had been hoping to spread discord among the branches of the Clan Donald by tempting Clanranald to attack Glengarry with promises of plunder and reward, but it seems that the plot had failed, as Clanranald refused to act.

On 18 November the MacDonalds of Glengarry were still causing trouble, and a new danger to the Campbells had appeared. The previous week Alasdair MacColla and his brother Ranald had come from Ireland with eighty men and raided Islay. They had tried to kidnap George Campbell, the tutor of Calder's brother, but he had escaped and the MacDonalds had been forced to take to their boats and flee.[42] Tantalisingly, this bald account is all we know of Alasdair MacColla's earliest military exploit. Presumably the intention had been to hold George Campbell — or any other Campbells of status whom they could kidnap — hostage to force Argyll to release Alasdair's father and brothers and, perhaps, to return Colonsay to them. Like the troubles caused by the MacDonalds of Glengarry, Alasdair's raid was a private venture, a matter of clan rather than royalist versus covenanter (though he may have received some help from the earl of Antrim), for long before the raid the covenanters had invaded England and forced Charles I to negotiate a truce with them. This was followed up by a permanent peace treaty negotiated in London, and by a royal visit to Scotland in 1641 during which the king accepted the loss of almost all of his traditional powers, heaped honours on leading covenanters to try to win their support, and accepted the existence of a covenanting regime.

Minor disorder among the MacDonalds continued to trouble the Campbells in 1641,[43] but all danger of a major Clan Donald-royalist rising assisted by an invasion from Antrim was over for the moment. The first attempt of the anti-Campbell clans to revive their fortunes through alliance with the monarchy had failed. All the plots of the MacDonalds had served simply to give the Campbells an excuse to weaken the surviving remnants of the Clan Ian Mor. Colonsay was no longer in their hands; Coll Ciotach and two of his sons were prisoners, and his other two sons were exiles in Antrim, seemingly with no chance of reviving their family fortunes.

After the failure of his raid on Islay in November 1640, Alasdair MacColla settled in Antrim, helped by his kinsmen the earl of Antrim and Archibald Stewart of Ballintoy; the latter's precise relationship to Alasdair is unknown, but their kinship is mentioned on several occasions. No sooner had Alasdair settled down in Antrim, however, than he was caught up in the consequences of the great Irish Catholic rebellion which began in October 1641.

The rebellion, which began in Ulster, had its origins in the bitterness of the native Irish at English conquest, persecution of their religion and (in Ulster) confiscation of much of their land. The relationship of their rebellion to that of the Scottish covenanters is both complicated and fascinating. On the one hand the

Scottish rising made the Irish one possible. It inspired the Irish by showing them that the power of Charles I, which had seemed unshakeable, could be challenged successfully from his lesser kingdoms; England had been invaded and the king forced to make virtually all the concessions asked of him. If the Scots could do this, why could not the Irish do the same, especially now the Scots had weakened the king's position? But if the Irish admired and emulated the covenanters, they also feared them. The covenanters were violently anti-Catholic, and had, in 1639-40, been threatened with invasion by Catholic armies from Ireland — first by the MacDonnells and their Irish allies, then by an army raised by the Dublin government. In the same years the Scots protestant settlers in Ulster had been persecuted for their sympathies with the covenanters. Many Irish feared that the covenanters would now intervene in Ireland, in alliance with the equally anti-Catholic English parliamentarians who were now undermining royal power in England, and introduce a much more vicious persecution of Catholicism than anything yet experienced in Ireland. To fears based on the attitudes of the king's enemies were added hopes based on the king's actions. Charles made inept attempts to gain support from Irish Catholics, and there was a plot (in which the earl of Antrim was involved) for an Irish-royalist seizure of Dublin to help the king against his English and Scottish foes. The plot came to nothing, but it encouraged the Irish to believe that, after they had begun their revolt aimed more against the king's enemies than against him, they could persuade him to support their action. Just as in the Western Highlands Gaelic Highlanders and Stewart king, traditional enemies, had suddenly found that they had interests in common, forming the basis of an alliance of convenience, so now in Ireland native Irish and English monarchy found they had at least enemies in common.

Out of this explosive mixture of long-term discontents and short-term political developments, of bitterness about the past and both hopes and fears for the future, came the Irish rebellion which began on the evening of 22 October 1641. Central to the conspirators' plan was the seizure of Dublin, but this part of their plot was betrayed to the authorities and thwarted at the last minute. This converted the rising into a largely Ulster affair at first. Within a few weeks much of the Ulster plantation had been swept away. Only County Antrim, the north of counties Down and Derry, parts of Tyrone and Donegal, and a few scattered outposts elsewhere remained in protestant hands. There was no wholesale massacre of protestants, though rumour quickly created one, but there were undoubtedly murders and atrocities in plenty as the embittered Irish took possession of the lands they had once held.

No rebellion took place in northern Antrim among the MacDonnells and their Irish neighbours and allies, for the earl of Antrim was loyal to Charles I. But his position was a difficult one; after all, he was a Catholic, with ties of religion, kinship and friendship with many native Irish leaders, and had recently been plotting with some of them to seize Dublin for the king. He was therefore automatically suspect in protestant eyes, and he must himself have been confused by the claims made by the Irish that their rising was a royalist one sanctioned by the king. Antrim was in Dublin when the rebellion began, but was soon forced by the anti-Catholic panic that followed the outbreak to withdraw. He then stayed with Catholic friends in what soon became, as the rebellion spread, rebel-held areas. There he remained for some months, avoiding declaring himself either for or against the Irish.

What instructions, if any, he sent to his representatives on his estates in the north we do not know. In any case, they had to react to the first news of rebellion on their own initiative. A later statement by Gilduff O'Cahan of Dunseverick tells us what they did. O'Cahan and his son Manus were drinking in the town of Dunluce when the first rumours of an Irish rising in southern Ulster arrived. The townsmen — mainly Scots protestants — began to arm to defend themselves, but matters were then complicated by a new and, as it turned out, false rumour that 500 of the earl of Argyll's men had landed and were marching to attack Dunluce Castle, headquarters of their MacDonnell enemies. This raised fears that the local Scots protestants were arming so they could help Argyll's men, and that perhaps the story of a rising by the Irish had been put about to give an excuse for such warlike preparations. Antrim had left the castle in charge of Captain Digby, and he now let O'Cahan and some English settlers join him but refused entry to the local Scots protestants who begged for his protection. However, late that evening the true situation became clear, and Digby let Antrim's brother, Alexander MacDonnell, O'Cahan's son Tirlough Og and Archibald Stewart of Ballintoy into the castle to decide what to do.[44] Digby still insisted on retaining control of the castle, refusing to let other forces into it while he awaited orders from the earl of Antrim, so it was agreed to raise a separate force to defend the surrounding country from the Irish rebels. It looks very much as if the composition of the regiment was a compromise thrashed out by the leaders of the three main groups into which the local population was divided — protestant settlers (English and Scots, often referred to as the British), Catholic native Irish, and Catholic MacDonnells. The regiment was mainly protestant — it was the British who were threatened by the rebellion — and the protestant Stewart of Ballintoy commanded it; the natural choice would have been Antrim's brother Alexander, but though he helped form the regiment, his Catholicism was evidently held to bar him from the command, a decision later confirmed by the English parliament. Two companies in the regiment were assigned to Catholics, however: one to an Irishman, Tirlough Og O'Cahan, the other to a representative of the MacDonnells, Alasdair MacColla. The men in these companies were largely or entirely Irish, MacDonnells and 'Highlanders' — MacDonald and other refugees from Scotland. Among the officers under the two Catholic captains were Ranald MacColla, James MacColl MacDonnell (a grandson of Sir James MacDonnell of Dunluce, died 1601), and Donald Gorm MacDonnell (a great grandson of Sir James).[45]

That Tirlough Og O'Cahan should have been one of the Catholic captains comes as no surprise; he was the son of the chief of a leading local Irish family. The appointment of Alasdair MacColla to command a company is harder to explain; surely one of the local MacDonnell leaders would have been the natural choice? Alasdair was closely related to them, but he had only recently settled in Antrim, and one would have thought his appointment would have caused jealousy. Perhaps giving him his post in the regiment was seen as a way of providing for the landless refugee from the Isles, otherwise dependent on the charity of his kinsmen. But the appointment must also indicate that he already had a reputation as a fighter, a leader of men in battle, based on his daring raid on Islay a year before. If the story that he was arrested at the beginning of the rebellion and imprisoned in Carrickfergus, only being freed on the intervention of Stewart of Ballintoy,[46] is true, then news of Alasdair's prowess had spread beyond his kinsmen and friends.

In addition to the two Catholic companies, Stewart's regiment had at least five protestant ones, under captains Glover, Peebles, Kennedy, Robert Stewart and Fergus MacDougall.[47] The strength of the regiment fluctuated. In December 1641 Alexander MacDonnell stated that he and Archibald Stewart had sometimes supported 1500 men, sometimes 1000 and constantly 700; another estimate was that Stewart had 800 men.[48] The regiment clearly represented an attempt to involve local Catholics in defending the country from the rebels. As the weeks passed, however, relations between followers of the two faiths within the regiment grew ever more strained. Many of the Irish and MacDonnells must have had strong sympathies with the Irish from the first, only remaining quiet through loyalty to the earl of Antrim. Certainly the commander of the rebels, Sir Phelim O'Neill, expected support in north Antrim. A week after the rising began he wrote to Father Patrick Hegarty, the Irish Franciscan directing missionary work in the Highlands from Bonamargy Friary. O'Neill joyfully listed his successes, boasted that he would soon advance to join Hegarty in Antrim, and urged him to inspire rebellion in the area. Specifically, he asked Hegarty to contact James MacColl MacDonnell, and to send word to the people of Rathlin Island, to Donald Gorm (which of the many Donald Gorms is meant is not clear) and all Hegarty's friends in the Highlands, inviting them to come and join the rebels. The letter was intercepted, probably by men of Stewart's regiment; its contents must have added fuel to the growing suspicions among protestants in the regiment that all Catholics would ultimately join the rebels.[49]

Nonetheless, for two months Stewart's regiment successfully kept the peace in the Route (north-west Antrim) and central Antrim, and guarded the Bann from Lough Neagh to the sea to prevent rebels from County Derry across the river infiltrating into Antrim. But as the rebellion spread, wildly exaggerated stories of Catholic treachery, atrocities and massacres reached Antrim, often carried by terrified refugees. The protestants of Stewart's regiment reacted by beginning to turn on local Catholics, both in revenge for the atrocities they believed had been committed by Catholics elsewhere, and out of fears that in Antrim as elsewhere in Ulster the Catholics might suddenly rise in arms and kill or drive out protestant settlers. The Catholics of Antrim must therefore be cowed into submission.

The position of the Catholics in the regiment thus became increasingly difficult. By serving in the regiment they seemed to be supporting the harassment of their co-religionists. At the same time their protestant comrades-in-arms became more and more hostile and distrustful towards them as the only Antrim Catholics actually in arms. It seemed only a matter of time before the protestant elements of the regiments turned on them and disarmed them — or even massacred them. By the end of 1641 mutual hatreds and suspicions had brought the tensions within the regiment to breaking point. Protestant fears — and Catholic hopes — were intensified by news of the success of rebel forces advancing northwards in County Derry. The temptation for the Catholic companies to change sides, both to save their own skins and to help the rebels, became irresistible.

In the planning of action to save the Catholics in Stewart's regiment from what they saw as the protestant net closing around them, Alasdair MacColla took a leading part. And when he acted he did so quickly, decisively, and ruthlessly, secretly co-ordinating his action with the Irish beyond the Bann. Nearly all the evidence we have for the events which now took place comes from formal depositions by witnesses, some taken a few months after the events they describe, some more than ten years later. Not all the evidence is reliable, even when it was given in good faith; those on the spot often had only a vague idea of what was happening beyond things they witnessed or experienced themselves. Even when testifying to events they had seen or taken part in, they must often have been too startled, bewildered or terrified by what was going on around them to have retained a clear and accurate picture of them. Much of what the witnesses say is hearsay, things they were told at the time or later. And, of course, they were seldom impartial. Protestants often, without a conscious intention of deceiving, paint the actions of Catholics in the darkest light, while Catholics involved in the rebellion try to exculpate themselves. Not surprisingly, then, the mass of evidence from the depositions often provides confused and contradictory accounts of the same events. In a sense, of course, such an obscure picture is historically valid; to most of those involved, what was happening was bewildering and obscure. But the historian naturally wishes to construct, with the benefit of hindsight, a clearer picture; and, rather surprisingly, it is possible to reconstruct with some confidence a fairly clear picture of events from the chaotic mass of evidence, blurred and doubtful only in detail. But in some ways such a version of events cannot fail to seem cold and lifeless compared with the confusion, the panic and terror, the speed and urgency of developments, conveyed by the individual depositions.

At the end of December 1641 part of Stewart's regiment was called on to deal with what one source calls an insurrection 'which was at that time likely to have been', another 'a rising or uproar' among the Irish in the district known as the Braid (a river valley running north-east from Ballymena). Of the companies left to guard the Bann, most were quartered in and around Portnaw, with one company (Kennedy's) at Cross (or the Cross of the Route) near Ballymoney. Before the companies sent to the Braid returned — or perhaps just as they were returning — Archibald Stewart sent orders that each company of the regiment should send fourteen or fifteen musketeers to Cross. Stewart had just received an urgent plea for help from George Canning, a protestant settler in County Derry, who had refused to surrender Agivey Castle to the rebels but could not hold out for long. It had been decided to send the force of musketeers being assembled at Cross over the Bann to rescue Canning and his garrison and escort them to safety.

The rebels besieging Canning were led by Manus Roe O'Cahan, and it may have been the order to contribute to a force being sent against him that precipitated the Catholic captains in Stewart's regiment into action, for Manus was Tirlough Og O'Cahan's brother, Alasdair MacColla's kinsman. Conflicts of loyalty and fears for their own safety made it impossible for them to serve against the rebels any longer. They therefore refused to send any men to join the force being sent across the Bann. After this they must have known action would be taken against them, so they decided to move first.

Before sunrise on the morning of 2 January 1642 Alasdair, Tirlough Og and their companies, including James MacColl MacDonnell, Donald Gorm MacDonnell and Ranald MacColla, appeared fully armed marching in good order with banners flying towards Portnaw. News of their approach surprised those who were awake in the companies quartered at Portnaw; one explanation suggested (and perhaps spread by the Catholic companies) was that Stewart had suddenly ordered his whole regiment to assemble at Portnaw. Captain Peebles' company, perhaps suspicious, sent one Murdoch out to ask the advancing Catholics what was happening; when he reached them a man stepped forward and killed him with his sword. The Catholics continued their advance, and began to spread out to the right and left of the British protestant companies' quarters. The alarm was now given and the British officers desperately tried to rouse their men from sleep and get them dressed, armed and assembled; the Catholics had achieved almost total surprise. Soon they were 'well nigh encompassing the British' and poured a volley of musket fire on them before charging. Many of the British were killed, though most saved themselves by panic flight. The companies which suffered most were Peebles' and Glover's. Robert Hamill of Peebles' company said that he never heard of any of his company surviving except himself and six others. Shane O'Coll (normally an innkeeper at Ballycastle) of Glover's company put the British death toll at about sixty, only himself and three others from his company escaping to Ballycastle. Fergus Fullarton of MacDougall's company agreed that about sixty had been killed, but said only about twenty were from Glover's company. Virtually all of Captain Robert Stewart's company, about eighty men, escaped to Ballymoney, according to Lieutenant Robert Fathy; he also testified that James MacColl MacDonnell and Donald Gorm MacDonnell had spared the lives of some of the British, and other witnesses confirm that at least some of the Catholics spared protestants whom they knew personally, either letting them go or keeping them prisoner. Fergus Fullarton was wounded by one of Alasdair MacColla's men, but Alasdair himself then intervened and granted him quarter. Donnell MacCart, also of MacDougall's company, stated that he and five or six others in the company were spared because they were Highlanders.[50]

After the British companies around Portnaw had been dispersed, the local Irish population rose in arms and the O'Hagans (on whose land most of the killing had taken place) crossed the Bann; soon they returned with several hundred men sent by the rebels — some of Manus Roe O'Cahan's men and a force under Captain John Mortimer (who was, according to Patrick Gordon, a Scot). Alasdair MacColla and Tirlough Og then advanced with them to spread rebellion in the rest of Antrim, raising the MacDonnells and O'Cahans, driving out or killing protestants and plundering and burning their houses. As news spread of events at Portnaw and of the advance of the rebels, killing 'all they could meet with', 'all the country, so far as it consisted of Scotch, were running to the caves, holes and rocks, for safety of their lives'. The embittered Irish took a terrible revenge on the protestants who had taken much of their land and persecuted them for their religion. The Antrim protestants, already harassing the Catholic population, soon retaliated in kind; the Island Magee massacre, one of the best-documented massacres of Irish by protestants, took place only a few days after the fight at Portnaw.

The advancing rebels burnt Ballymena, Ballymoney and Cross. James MacDonnell, a cooper in Ballymena, claimed to have seen at least one hundred bodies of men, women and children killed by the Irish. A glimpse of the arrival of the rebels in Billy Parish, marching towards Ballintoy, is provided by Janet Neaven. She fled with her child and another woman to the moors 'because that as the Irish rebels marched through the said parish they murdered all the British they could lay their hands on, amongst others this examinants father and mother and brother'. She saw Alasdair MacColla and John Mortimer among the rebels — the latter 'did upon that day ride upon a black horse'. An attempt to storm Archibald Stewart's house at Ballintoy (led by Gilduff O'Cahan) failed, and the rebels moved on to Dunluce. There Captain Digby, commanding for the earl of Antrim, refused to surrender, whereupon Gilduff O'Cahan and John Mortimer burnt the town of Dunluce. Alasdair MacColla, tired of blood and destruction, opposed this and 'went away with his company'. The next day a new quarrel arose between him and his Irish allies. The O'Cahans proclaimed that anyone who spoke English would be hanged; the most Alasdair would do was to order his men and those to whom he had given his protection to obey for twenty-four hours, he 'being ready to fall out with the Irish that made such a proclamation'.

The rebels were not equipped for a siege of Dunluce Castle, so they marched back southwards, reinforced by about 100 bowmen who landed from Rathlin Island. The castle of Clough or Oldstone under Captain Walter Kennedy (probably the Captain Kennedy of Stewart's regiment) was still holding out against the rebels, but now, according to one of the garrison, John Blair, it was surrounded by 'almost all the Irish gentry of the Route' with 3000 men — doubtless an exaggeration. It is said that the rebels first sent one Henry O'Neill to demand the surrender of the castle, but that Kennedy swore that he would never surrender a MacDonnell castle to an O'Neill. The answer delighted Alasdair MacColla, who then allowed Kennedy to surrender to him, promising Kennedy's men their lives, freedom and property. The story fits in well with Alasdair's known annoyance at some of the recent actions of his Irish allies. But either the story is false (which is most likely) or Alasdair failed to keep his word, for John Blair knew nothing of such a bargain, and he and the rest of the garrison were kept prisoner after their surrender. He also claimed that about twenty women and children were killed under the castle walls, and that about sixty women, children and old men were given leave by the Irish to go to Carrickfergus but then murdered within a mile and a half of the castle.[51]

On 10 or 11 January James MacColl MacDonnell wrote a fascinating letter from 'the Catholique Camp at Oldstone' to his 'Cozen Archibald' — Archibald Stewart of Ballintoy; this, the letter of a man closely associated with Alasdair MacColla, brings us as close as we can get to the latter's motives and mood at this point in his career. James MacColl claims there was a plot against the Catholics in Stewart's regiment; he does not believe Stewart himself had any part in it, but 'I gott intelligence from one that heard the plot laying' whereby 'I and all these gentlemen, with my wife and children, had bin utterly destroyed'. Moreover 'those captains of yours whom you may call rather cowboyes were every day vexing our selves and our tennants of purpose to pick quarrels, which no flesh was able to endure'. Without this provocation he and the others would not have rebelled. But James MacColl goes on to show that he was acting from more than just fear; he was positively committed to the rebel cause. Nearly all Ireland, he related, was now in rebel hands so 'it is but a folly' on Stewart's part to continue to resist 'what God pleaseth to happen'. He promised that if Coleraine (whence Stewart had retreated with the remnants of his regiment) surrendered to him he would help the protestants there to flee to Scotland; if they refused, Sir Phelim O'Neill and 10,000 men would storm the town and many would be killed. As to the reports of atrocities committed by the rebels in Antrim, James MacColl denied any part in them but admitted that things had been done which should not have been: 'the Clandeboys soldiers and the two regiments [from] beyond the Bann were a little greedy for pillageing which could not be help't. As for killing of women none of my soldiers dares do it for his life, but the common people that are not under rule doth do it in spight of our teeth.' He also warned Stewart not to attempt to surrender until he himself arrived, for the 700 men he had around the town at present would not grant him quarter. Finally James MacColl stressed that they were not fighting against the king but only 'to have their religion setled and every one his owne ancient inheritance'.[52]

Coleraine did not surrender. On 14 January the town authorities and Archibald Stewart wrote to Dublin reporting James MacColl's letter and begging for help. Stewart had brought three or four hundred men to the town and was raising more, and the town had raised 650 men; but there was a serious shortage of arms, and more than 3000 women and children were crowded into the town, though a start had been made on sending them to safety in Scotland.[53] No help was forthcoming from Dublin, so two weeks later Stewart and the townsmen appealed for aid to Argyll (who had recently been elevated to the rank of marquis), relating the 'tragicall newes' that virtually all Antrim was in rebel hands due to the treachery of James MacColl MacDonnell and the sons of Coll Ciotach, who had been 'trusted for my Lord Antrim his saike'. It was feared they would not have rebelled without Antrim's consent. Those in Coleraine told Argyll that they expected to be closely besieged at any moment, and begged him to hasten over his regiment to aid them, adding a bitter warning that Argyll had little need of; 'your lordship would doe weall to trust none in this Imployment who have relatioune to that name of Mcdonalds for wee ar Informed they proved never trew in Scotland, and we find it by experience'.[54] It is an indication of how disruptive the Irish rebellion was of old alliances and loyalties that in this letter we find Stewart denouncing his own kinsmen, the MacDonnells, and accusing his master the earl of Antrim of treason, and doing this to Argyll after having, just a few years before, taken a leading part in Antrim's plots against the Campbells.

For Coleraine to turn to Scotland — and to Argyll in particular — for help was natural, for the covenanters had reacted to the news of a Catholic rebellion in Ireland by offering to send an army (paid by the English) to Ulster. Their motives were mixed: hatred of Catholicism, the desire to help the Scots protestant settlers in Ulster, and determination not to let Ulster fall into hostile hands — they had been threatened with invasion from there in 1639 and 1640. There were, moreover, fears that a rising among the Gaelic Irish would spread to the Gaelic Highlanders 'who speak the same language the Irishe doe'. And the peace of the Highlands depended on the 'power and actioun' of the marquis of Argyll.[55] From the first it was probably assumed that one of the regiments of the Scottish army being sent to Ireland would be raised and commanded by Argyll; and just as Antrim's projected invasion of Scotland on the king's behalf in 1639 had been aimed primarily at Argyll and the Campbells, so it was obvious that any force under Argyll sent to Ulster would concentrate on destroying his old enemies, the MacDonnells. Indeed, it is possible that one of the motives of the MacDonnells of Antrim in joining the rebels in January 1642 was fear that Argyll intended to attack them whether they rebelled or not.

Argyll must have been delighted to hear that the MacDonnells had joined the Irish rebels; he now would have no need to seek excuses for acting against them, or against their MacDonald kinsmen in Scotland. Ever since 1639 he had kept Coll Ciotach, his sons Gillespie and Angus, and two other MacDonalds, John and Donald Gorm, prisoner on his own responsibility, ignoring the subsequent peace agreed with the king. In January 1642, as soon as he heard that Alasdair and Ranald MacColla and their followers were in rebellion in Ireland, he brought his five MacDonald prisoners to the attention of the Scottish privy council, justifying their detention by referring to the treachery of their kinsmen in Ireland. The council agreed that Argyll should retain his prisoners, and granted him an allowance of forty merks a week to maintain the five prisoners and their five keepers.[56]

The sending of the Scottish army to Ireland was delayed by lengthy negotiations in London, but it had been agreed that 2500 men (out of a total of 10,000) should cross to Ireland as soon as possible, before the negotiations were completed. Here again Argyll exploited the rising of the MacDonnells of Antrim to his own advantage, by using the news to gain similar permission for his own regiment to cross to Ireland as soon as it was ready. Argyll was also given power to appoint a governor of Rathlin Island, a clear indication that it was assumed that his men would land in north Antrim.[57] However, Argyll's commission was not signed by the king until 18 March, and it was several weeks after that before any of the Scots army reached Ireland. The British in Coleraine were therefore at first left to fend for themselves. Desperately short of food for his men and the thousands of refugees, Archibald Stewart led a sortie from the loosely besieged town to scour the countryside for food on 11 February 1642. The day was long to be remembered by local protestants as Black Friday. Estimates of Stewart's strength (almost entirely footmen) vary greatly, from 600 to 1100 men. Stewart's movements became known to an Irish and MacDonnell force of six or seven hundred men led by James MacAlasdair Charraich MacDonnell, James MacColl MacDonnell, and Alasdair and Ranald MacColla. In the area known as the Laney (near Ballymoney) they devised a trap for Stewart — the ambush had been a favourite tactic of the Irish in the wars of the late sixteenth century. Some of the Irish lured the British into pursuing them, and thus drew Stewart's men into boggy ground; there they were suddenly attacked by Alasdair's main force of MacDonnells.

According to the most detailed account of the battle, Alasdair 'having commanded his murderers to lay downe all their fyre-arms . . . fell in amongst them (with swords and durcks or scones [knives]) in such a furious and irresistible manner, that it was reported that not a man of them escaped of all the eight hundred'.[58] All accounts agree that the British, struggling in boggy ground that made it hard for them either to fight or to flee, were cut down by the hundred, their losses being put at between 600 and 948 men. Stewart and the pathetic remnants of his force escaped back to Coleraine, and the Irish, encouraged by their success, soon advanced to a closer siege than before.[59] But the town continued to hold out, and renewed attempts to persuade Stewart's house at Ballintoy to surrender also failed, whereupon the rebels withdrew frustrated to Ballycastle, where further sporadic killings of the remaining British took place.[60]

The battle of the Laney (sometimes known as the battle of Bendooragh) has a much more than local significance, however, for this appears to have been the first occasion on which what was to become known as the 'Highland charge' is recorded, the tactics which were to bring Highlanders repeated success against Lowland and English forces in the century that followed. Of the many descriptions of the Highland charge the best is perhaps that of Lieutenant General Henry Hawley in January 1746, just a few days before he himself was defeated by Highlanders at Falkirk.[61] When the Highlanders come within musket shot of the enemy, he explained, they fire a volley; then they immediately throw down their muskets and charge with their swords and targes. As they charge they try to instil panic by their loud battle cries; and as they approach the enemy they change formation; having originally been drawn up in lines, as they come forward they gather into groups or clusters — 'separate bands, like wedges condensed and firm', as another writer graphically put it [62] — twelve or fourteen men deep. In these clusters or wedges the Highlanders attempt to pierce the enemy lines in many places. Hawley told his officers that such a charge could easily be defeated if they made their men hold their fire until the Highlanders were at point blank range; 'but If the fire is given at a distance you probably will be broke for you never get time to load a second cartridge, and if you give way you may give your foot for dead, for they [the Highlanders] being without a firelock or any load, no man with his arms, accoutrements, etc. can escape them, and they give no Quarter'.

Though this Highland charge was to become so famous, surprisingly little thought seems to have been given to its origins. Often it seems to be assumed that it was a traditional Highland way of fighting or, if it is realised that it first appears in the 1640s, this is noted without explanation; thus Hill Burton simply states (incorrectly, as will be argued below) that Tippermuir in 1644 was 'the first instance of that simple tactic by which many Highland victories were afterwards obtained'.[63]

The 'Highland charge' does not appear before the seventeenth century because in earlier generations Highlanders did not have the weapons essential to it — the musket, the single-handed sword and the targe or target. The older two-handed claymore was a formidable weapon, but its weight and the fact that it took both hands to wield it restricted the mobility and agility of the user. This problem was increased by the need for the warrior armed with the claymore to wear armour of some sort — of sheet metal, mail or padded cloth — to protect himself as he had no hand free to carry a shield, for such armour was heavy and tended to restrict the wearer's movements. Thus the replacement of the claymore by the single-handed sword in the late sixteenth and early seventeenth centuries was accompanied by the abandonment of armour in favour of the targe, the small round shield of wood and leather, and these two changes immediately led to a great increase in the mobility of the Highland fighting man. Lightly armed and dressed (especially if, as often happened, he cast off his plaid and fought in his shirt), he could now charge and fight with a new speed and flexibility.[64]

The word targe or target could be used to describe any small shield, but was particularly associated with small round shields of wood and leather; the word is, indeed, derived from a Spanish corruption of an Arabic word for just such a shield. Use of such targes, combined with swords, was for a time fashionable in early sixteenth century Spain, and by the middle of the century they were well known in England and Lowland Scotland, often under the name of buckler.[65] But neither English nor Lowland Scots adopted these weapons as standard in their armies, and the fashion for them soon passed. To some extent the adoption of the targe in the Highlands may reflect Lowland influence; but it seems that much more important was the fact that many of the native Irish foot soldiers or *kerne* were armed with targe and sword (along with bows and arrows) until use of firearms became common among them in the later sixteenth century. From them the use of such weapons probably spread to the many thousands of West Highland 'redshanks' or mercenaries who fought in Ireland. The use by Highlanders of these weapons, and the increased mobility they gave, for attack by a fast charge was also probably derived from Irish practice — Edmund Spenser, for example, wrote in the 1590s of 'their fierce running on their enemies', and other accounts confirm that the *kerne* sought to get to close quarters as soon as possible.[66]

The adoption of the single-handed sword and targe was one change in weapons essential to the development of the classic 'Highland charge'. The other was the widespread use of the musket in the Highlands, and this may well not have taken place until the early seventeenth century, though here again earlier Irish practice was probably influential; the Highlanders' single volley of musket fire before charging may well be derived from the *kerne's* use of bows and arrows (or sometimes throwing of darts or javelins) before charging. The Highlanders might only use their muskets to fire one volley before abandoning their guns and charging, but this one volley was nonetheless central to their tactics, both because of the casualties and disorganisation it caused among the enemy just before the Highland charge hit them, and because such a volley frequently led the enemy to reply in kind instead of waiting until the Highlanders were at point blank range. Thus the Highlanders could make their charge with relative impunity, while the enemy musketeers were struggling to reload their guns. By throwing down their own muskets after firing only a single volley the Highlanders might be abandoning their most modern weapon in favour of ones which were basically centuries old, but given the limitations of the musket it was a decision that brought them great advantages at a critical moment in the battle. If Lieutenant General Hawley's men with the greatly improved firelocks of the mid-eighteenth century had no time to reload in such circumstances, what hope had the musketeers of the mid-seventeenth century with their matchlocks, which took far longer to reload? Similarly, Hawley thought that his men, if caught by a Highland charge while reloading, would have no hope of defending themselves effectively with their bayonets. The musketeer of a century before had no bayonet at all, and (in the battles in which the Highland charge was used in the 1640s) rarely had enough well-trained pikemen to defend him.

Did Alasdair employ the 'Highland charge' at the battle of the Laney in February 1642? The accounts of the battle lack detail at certain important points, but they do nonetheless say enough for one to conclude that he did. He had commanded his men 'to lay downe all their fyre-arms' before charging. Nothing is said about their first having fired a volley, but this may be implicit in the statement; had Alasdair made his men put down their guns before battle commenced, it seems unlikely that the account of the battle would have mentioned that they abandoned the guns just before it describes their charge. Alasdair's men are said to charge with swords and dirks. Targes are not mentioned, but this is probably not significant; battle accounts often mention weapons but ignore defensive equipment. As targes had earlier been common in Ireland and a swordsman charging musketeers and pikemen would need some shield to protect himself, it seems likely that targes would have been used. A final central feature of the Highland charge noted by Hawley and others, the division of the charging men into clusters or wedges, is not noted in accounts of the Laney battle; but it is not mentioned in accounts of any of the Highlanders' battles of the 1640s either. It may have been a later development or, perhaps more likely, it was a feature of these battles but contemporaries fail to describe it.

Thus, Alasdair MacColla has a good claim to have originated the 'Highland charge' at the battle of the Laney; and its origins thus lie as much in Ireland as in Scotland. It is possible that at least in part he was reviving tactics employed by the sword and buckler men of the north of Ireland in the civil wars and wars against the English in the late sixteenth century, but lack of detailed evidence of the tactics used in these wars makes certainty impossible.

Resistance to the Irish by the protestants in Coleraine grew daily more difficult after the defeat at the Laney. Losses in skirmishes and an increasing death toll from hunger and disease weakened the defenders. Salvation came from an unexpected source: not from the long-awaited army from Scotland but from the earl of Antrim. Late in April 1642 he at last returned to Dunluce Castle, and partially raised the siege of Coleraine by ordering his own tenants and followers to withdraw from it. He then sent food into the town, had the former protestant garrison of Oldstone released, and generally used all his influence against the rebels, though he did not actually take arms against them. Shortly afterwards protestant forces from western Ulster advanced to Coleraine and the Irish abandoned the siege altogether.[67]

Why had Antrim, after months of inactivity, suddenly returned to his estates and taken decisive action? Probably up to this point he had thought the best way to survive the rebellion which was tearing Ireland apart was to avoid involvement; such a stance was all the more attractive as he was experiencing a genuine conflict of loyalties, sympathising both with the Irish and with the king. But by April 1642 a Scottish army had begun to land in Ulster and the landing of Argyll's regiment on Antrim's own estates was imminent even though he had not joined the rebels. He therefore hurried back to Dunluce and made every effort to demonstrate that he was a loyal subject of the king.

Troops from Scotland first landed at Carrickfergus, commanded by Major General Robert Monro. Antrim wrote congratulating him on his arrival and hopefully recalling the traditional good relations in Scotland between the MacDonalds and the Monros. He offered to meet Monro to agree on measures for the good of the king's service, and apologised for the fact that in his absence 'my people were so unfortunate as to doe any hostile act, though in their own defence'.[68] Such reassurances from Antrim came far too late to be convincing — why had he allowed his men to fight for the rebels for three full months without intervening? Monro first led an expedition south to Newry, then on 25 May marched from Carrickfergus to subdue Antrim. His main force marched down the Bann, hoping to prevent rebels in Antrim escaping across the river. Antrim tried to placate Monro by laying on a 'mighty feast' in Dunluce Castle; Monro consumed the feast, then arrested his host. Men of Argyll's regiment had meanwhile reached Rathlin — where, according to tradition, they massacred many of the islanders — and now began to land in Antrim. Monro handed over all Antrim's estates to them except for Dunluce Castle. Probably he was alarmed by the way in which Argyll's men thought of themselves as an almost independent force with a right to Antrim's lands, and wished to assert his authority by denying them Dunluce. A further consideration was that Antrim himself was at first held prisoner at Dunluce; Monro may well have feared that if left in the custody of the Campbells his life might be short. After a few weeks Antrim was transferred by sea to Carrickfergus, 'hearing behind him the rocks and hills covered with the lamentations of his poor followers'. Dunluce then became the headquarters of Argyll's regiment under its colonel, Sir Duncan Campbell of Auchinbreck.

Although Monro's march to Dunluce had been outwardly a complete success — most of Antrim had been brought under his control with little bloodshed — in some ways the results of the expedition were disappointing. Numbers of Irish had been killed, but the great majority of the Antrim rebels had succeeded in fleeing to safety beyond the Bann. Others had withdrawn into the Glens of Antrim and Monro was reluctant to pursue them in such difficult terrain; only gradually were they hunted down and killed or forced to flee over the Bann. Among those who at first stayed in the Glens were, it was reported, 'Colonel Kittaghes sons' with five or seven hundred men and hundreds of plundered cattle; another source put the rebel strength in the Glens at 1000 men and relates that they burnt Glenarm.[69]

Alasdair's decision to try to remain in the Glens may have rested on more than just a determination not to abandon completely MacDonnell territory to the enemy; he may also have been influenced by the fact that he had fallen out with Sir Phelim O'Neill, the commander-in-chief of the Irish. The exact date of the incident is unknown, but it must have been some time between January and May 1642. Alasdair had evidently brought his men from Antrim to join the main Irish army under Sir Phelim. But Sir Phelim refused Alasdair the rank, and his men the precedence, that they thought was their due. Alasdair took offence, thinking he was being treated as a mere mercenary, and led his men back to Antrim. He still fought alongside the Irish, but insisted on being his own master.[70]

He can, however, only have held out in the Glens for a matter of days before retiring across the Bann and rejoining the other Antrim rebels who had linked up with the main Irish army. One of the first results of Monro's successes in driving the rebels from Antrim and Down was thus to reinforce Sir Phelim's army and enable him to advance against the protestant forces of western Ulster, the so called 'Lagan army' based on the area around Londonderry. The protestants, 'a handfull in comparison with their huge numbers' according to their commander Sir Robert Stewart, made contact with the Irish on 15 June and fell back before them. But during the following night they advanced to within half a mile of the Irish camp and began to prepare entrenched positions on a hill at Glenmaquin (a few miles from Raphoe, County Donegal). There they stood to arms till daylight on 16 June. Stewart claimed he had not more than 2000 foot and 300 horse, whereas the Irish had 6000 foot and 500 horse. This doubtless exaggerates the strength of the Irish (to whom another protestant source assigns 4000 men), but undoubtedly the protestants were greatly outnumbered; O'Mellan's Irish account does not give the Irish strength but confirms that their enemies had 2000 musketeers. 'Quiet and silent were the [British] during the night, but noisy and talkative were the Irish.' Dawn revealed the two armies occupying hillsides opposite each other, with low-lying ground in between them. Stewart hoped the Irish would attack him, relying on their superior numbers to cancel out the disadvantages of making an attack on prepared positions up a hill, but at first they stood firm. Stewart then sent forward a strong body of musketeers and horsemen to fire on the Irish and draw them down from their hill. This stratagem succeeded. The Irish evidently concluded that the entire protestant army was advancing, so they charged down hill to engage the enemy. They attacked in two bodies, one commanded by Sir Phelim O'Neill, the other by Alasdair MacColla. One account of the battle states that Sir Phelim and Alasdair 'did stryve for the van', each wishing his own men to have the honour of leading the attack. What we know of Alasdair's earlier dispute with Sir Phelim over precedence makes the story plausible. Another source informs us that in the battle Sir Phelim 'confided in the judgment of Alexander Macdanill commonly called Colkittagh'. Alasdair, it seems, demanded an immediate attack, and that he lead it. He got his way, though it may have been only by threatening otherwise to act on his own.

As the Irish charged, Stewart's advance party of musketeers and horsemen fired on them and then, as planned, retired hastily but in good order towards the main protestant force. This withdrawal evidently fooled Alasdair, as it was intended to, into thinking the battle was already won, the enemy in flight. Alasdair, 'a stoute brave Fellow . . . charged up alone to the [earth] work but was shot, and after a very smart skirmish the Irish fell back'. Stewart described how Alasdair's men 'come on with a furious and swift march, makeing a terrible outcry on their march according to their manner . . . Coll Kittaghs sonnes, cryed up for their valour as invincible champions, with their Highlanders and some others assaulted my brigade fircely in so much that they were not far from comeing to push of pike'. But Alasdair was now facing soldiers resolute and well trained enough to stand up to the fierce charge and howled war cries of his men. They were fought to a standstill by the musketeers and pikemen lining the earthworks. Seeing this, Sir Phelim's men who were supposed to be seconding the attack hesitated, then began to flee. Sir Phelim 'cried out to his own men saying that the [British] were retreating, but all in vain, for they would not come back to the charge'. The Irish advance quickly turned to flight and Alasdair's men, having suffered heavy casualties and there now being no hope of victory, soon followed them. Alasdair, though shot through the thigh, managed to escape with the help of his Irish friends; 'with much ado O'Cahan brought off MacDonnell in a Horse-Litter'. The fleeing Irish were pursued for several miles. Stewart estimated their losses at at least 500, perhaps 800, figures which would have been higher had the terrain allowed his cavalry to be used in the pursuit. Moreover, Stewart reported rather oddly, many of the Irish died on reaching safety 'being bursted with running'; many more were dangerously if not mortally ill.

Among these was Alasdair MacColla, and a report sent home by George Campbell (who had recently replaced his brother Colin as tutor of Calder and was serving in Argyll's regiment in Antrim) rejoiced at news that Alasdair had died of his wound eight days after the battle. The story was false, but George Campbell was justified in recording the decimation of 'Collis faction' and hoping that the supporters of the Campbells in Islay would be less afraid of them in future, for Alasdair had lost many of his friends and kinsmen at Glenmaquin, both Antrim MacDonnells (among them Donald Gorm), Irish, and Highlanders (MacDonald refugees from Scotland).[71]

Alasdair is said to have recovered from his wounds in the house of a priest called O'Crilly. This was, it seems, Patrick Crilly or Crelly, the Cistercian abbot of Newry, who was (or soon became) an agent of the earl of Antrim; he was said in 1644 to have been questioned 'for keeping Lord Antrim's cousin', the reference probably being to Alasdair.[72] Staunch Catholic though Alasdair was, spiritual consolation was not enough. His worldly hopes and ambitions had been shattered, though at least his material needs, and those of his brother and his men, were looked after; O'Cahan gave them £25 for clothing and assigned them 'coyne' on his 'creaghts' — that is, they were granted free quarters in the households of the men who accompanied and tended O'Cahan's herds of cattle.[73] But this did not hide the extent of the successive disasters which had struck Alasdair and his family. The ambitious plans of Antrim to revive the Clan Ian Mor under his own leadership by seizing its Scots lands in alliance with the king had come to nothing, and had brought imprisonment or banishment to Alasdair's family and to many other MacDonalds. Alliance with the Irish rebels, who had been carrying all before them, had seemed to offer some hope of a revival in his fortunes, but Alasdair joined them just as the rebellion ran out of steam and the initiative began to pass to the protestants in Ulster. Soon a Scottish army had landed and driven him from Antrim, placing all the lands of the MacDonnells of Antrim under Campbell control. His brave but ill-judged attack on the British at Glenmaquin had brought death to many of his own men and a further demoralising defeat to the rebels. In mid-July, when Alasdair may still have been recovering from his wound, the leaders of the Ulster Irish gloomily debated disbanding their forces and fleeing abroad. However, their morale was revived by the news that Owen Roe O'Neill, the most famous Irish soldier of the day through his long years of service with Spanish armies, had landed in Ulster. At the end of August he was elected general of the Irish forces, and began the work of trying to transform them from an enthusiastic but confused mass of armed men into a trained and disciplined army.

It was, however, some time before Owen Roe's reforms had any noticeable effect on the fortunes of the Irish, and Alasdair MacColla's mood continued to be one of despair. The Irish had failed to help the MacDonnells effectively, their rebellion might even be on the verge of complete collapse. It was time to leave the sinking ship, to desert the Irish while he could still gain concessions from his enemies by doing so. In August 1642 the earl of Leven, commander-in-chief of the covenanting armies which had humiliated Charles I in 1639-40, landed in Ulster to take command of the Scots army in Ireland, which had now reached its full strength of 10,000 men. How this affected the fortunes of Alasdair MacColla is related by Patrick Gordon of Ruthven.

'When generall Lesly [Leven] went ouer to Ireland, he fand that there was non of the Irishe commanderes so much to be feared as this man [Alasdair] for actiuitie and strenth of bodie. He was of such extraordinarie strenth and agilitie as there was non that equalled or came neire him. Hee was of a graue and sulled carriage, a capable and pregnant judgement, and in speciall in the art militarie, and for his wallour, all that knew him did relate wonders of his actiones in armes; wherfor generall Lesly, being well informed of his invincible courage, his great judgement in the art militarie, and happie successe which did euer accompany his interpryses ... lyke a craftie warriour sends to him, and dealles that he may serue his owne nation [Scotland], and takes vpon him to pacifie Ardgyll to releaue his father and brethren, and gett them restored to their ancient inheritance'.[74]

Patrick Gordon is not so well informed as he would like his readers to believe, and the tendency to hero-worship (he was writing after Alasdair's death) is obvious. His statement that Alasdair's enterprises were always successful indicates that he really knew nothing of his activities in Ireland in the past year. Nonetheless, it is possible that he is correct in his main point, that it was Leven who approached Alasdair in the first instance; but if this was so, Leven must have acted not because Alasdair was the most successful of the Irish leaders, but because he knew Alasdair had suffered defeat and demoralisation, and therefore might be ready to betray his allies.

In September 1642 a written agreement was reached between Leven and Alasdair; the recent rediscovery of this provides hard evidence to back up Patrick Gordon's story. Alasdair, his brother Ranald and all their men were, by the agreement, to receive a free pardon for their deeds. Their father, Coll Ciotach, their brothers and their friends held prisoner by Argyll would be freed. Coll and his children would have their lands and other property in Scotland restored to them, or would be given lands and goods to the same value. In return for these concessions Alasdair and Ranald were to recruit a company of men to serve against the Irish rebels, and would receive pay for their services. But they and their men 'shall before they cross the Bann instantly act and do some points of service against those rebels, both entering in their blood and spoiling of their goods and cattle, and use all other hostile courses and plots against them as shall clearly induce and prove their present fidelity'. Alasdair was to have to prove his sincerity before he gained any advantage from the agreement, so he would not be able to desert back to the Irish.[75] On 19 September Sir Duncan Campbell of Auchinbreck, colonel of Argyll's regiment, signed an undertaking to obtain Argyll's consent to the agreement.[76]

According to Patrick Gordon, Alasdair was 'so generous as he would in no termes take seruice against the Irishes, with whom he had once syded'.[77] Other evidence proves that Gordon is at least partly wrong. O'Mellan's Irish account of the wars states that Alasdair and Ranald gathered their men together and told them 'to take away the people of every house where they might be on coyne, their cows and their horses along with their household furniture, their sheep and their goats along with their accoutrements. They did so, and carried the plunder with them to Coleraine'.[78] A letter from Londonderry dated 7 October confirms that 'Col Kitto and divers rebels have submitted and brought in many cows for pledges'.[79] Alasdair and his men had suddenly turned on their O'Cahan hosts and kinsmen, and plundered them of their goods and livestock. But it may well be significant that there is no mention of Alasdair actually shedding the blood of the Irish, as his agreement with Leven had required. For all his treachery, he may have drawn the line at that.

Leven was not satisfied that Alasdair and Ranald had proved their sincerity convincingly. Therefore on 11 November he issued orders to them to choose 300 of 'those folk that came in with you' for service against the Irish — this is, incidentally, the only indication we have of the strength of the force Alasdair persuaded to desert the Irish. Some of Alasdair's men were to be sent into Irish-held areas to gather intelligence, and Auchinbreck was ordered to send Alasdair himself with some of the others 'for doing of some service against the enemy'.

Ranald and the rest of the men were to stay behind in Antrim; all the deserters from the rebels were to be maintained on the earl of Antrim's estates by his agent, Archibald Stewart of Ballintoy. As they had deserted him, massacring some of his men as they did so less than a year before, Stewart can hardly have done this with good grace.[80]

Quite what happened next is obscure, though the outcome is certain; Alasdair and Ranald MacColla succeeded in deserting back to the Irish again, in spite of the attempt of Leven to hold on to the latter as a guarantee of the former's loyalty. Patrick Gordon says Alasdair returned to Scotland with Leven but Argyll refused to release his father and brothers, whereupon Alasdair 'returnes to Ireland woueing to wreit his rewenge in blood, and did it indeed, as yee shall heire'.[81] This seems highly unlikely. It is hard to imagine that Alasdair would have trusted the covenanters sufficiently to have ventured back to Scotland with Leven, away from the protection given him by his devoted followers. In any case, Leven left Ireland on 30 November 1642,[82] soon after he had ordered Alasdair to be sent on an expedition against the Irish, so (unless the orders were cancelled) it is hard to see how Alasdair could have gone with him. It may well be true, however, that Argyll refused to release his prisoners and that this (perhaps combined with the failure of Alasdair actually to kill any Irishmen) led to the collapse of the agreement between Leven and Alasdair.

Tradition has a dramatic account of the break. Alasdair had joined Auchinbreck's regiment, it is related, and was preparing to attend a banquet (presumably in Dunluce Castle) with the officers of the regiment when a messenger arrived with a secret order to Auchinbreck that Alasdair was to be put to death. But the messenger did not know Auchinbreck personally, and had only been told that he was a big, dark man. Alasdair fitted this description, so the messenger delivered the order to him. After reading the message Alasdair told the messenger to give it to its intended recipient, but not to tell him of the mistake. Alasdair came to the banquet armed, and refused to surrender his sword as 'it is now in the bravest hand in Ireland'. Intrigued by this, Auchinbreck asked which was the next bravest hand; Alasdair transferred the sword to his left hand saying 'this one'. He then revealed that he knew of the treachery intended against him, and escaped with his men.

The tale is largely made up of common motifs: murder planned at a banquet, and messages ordering a man's death being delivered to him in error, thus saving him. And the story of the 'bravest hand' may have been intended to explain why Alasdair (through, in fact, confusion with his father) was sometimes referred to as 'ciotach', here taken to mean ambidextrous.[83] Nonetheless, it is quite possible that there is a basis of truth behind the tradition. Argyll certainly must have been tempted to have Alasdair killed to avoid further trouble, and in fact as well as fiction a banquet was a good time for treachery, as the victim could be caught unarmed and taken by surprise — as the earl of Antrim had discovered a few months before. And the tradition, recorded in the nineteenth century, does preserve accurately one important point about Alasdair's flirtation with the Scots army in Ireland which was otherwise unknown until the recent discovery of

Leven's agreement with, and orders to, Alasdair: the fact that Alasdair was put under Auchinbreck's command. If oral tradition could preserve this detail for over two centuries before being written down, then there is good reason for thinking there could be truth elsewhere in the story as well.

The agreement with the Scots army having broken down, Alasdair, Ranald, and their men escaped back over the Bann to Irish-held areas. Nothing is known of the welcome they received, but it can hardly have been an enthusiastic one and it seems they were not given employment in the Irish armies. Nothing whatever is known of their fortunes for a full year; they must have been distrusted and despised as men who had changed sides three times within a year. Alasdair no doubt argued that he had behaved with consistency; he had been seeking his own preservation and to help his father and his clan by whatever means were possible in fast-changing political and military circumstances. To others he might seem untrustworthy; to himself, his worst fault must have seemed to be that he had failed. All his trickery and treachery had failed to bring him any nearer achieving his ambitions, and had left him isolated and without allies.

There was only one small ray of hope on his horizon. In October 1642 his patron and kinsman the earl of Antrim had escaped from imprisonment in Carrickfergus and fled to England. There civil war had broken out between Charles I and the English parliament, and Antrim was soon deeply involved in royalist plots to enlist support in Scotland and Ireland for the king in order to bring him victory in England. And the price Antrim asked for this service was, through royal favour, the restoration of both the MacDonnells of Antrim and the MacDonalds of Kintyre and Islay to their former lands and powers.[84]

NOTES

1. *RPCS, 1625-7*, viii-x,xv,xciii-xcv, *1627-8*, xxiii-xxiv,xlv-xlvi, *1629-30,* xx-xxi,172-3; C. Rogers (ed), *The earl of Stirling's register of royal letters* (2 vols, Edinburgh 1885), i.75-6,386.

2. *RPCS, 1630-2*, xlvi-xlviii,389, *1633-5* xxxiv-xxxvi, *1635-7*, xxxviii-xl,xliii-xliv; Mathew, *Scotland under Charles I*, 187.

3. D. Stevenson, *The Scottish revolution, 1637-44. The triumph of the covenanters* (Newton Abbot 1973), 88-90; H. Guthry, *Memoirs* (2nd ed, Glasgow 1748), 36.

4. SRO, GD.14/19, Campbell of Stonefield papers, pp.135-7.

5. Macdonald, *Clan Donald*, iii.378.

6. S.R. Gardiner (ed), *The Hamilton papers* (Camden Society 1880), 11-13.

7. HMC 21: *Hamilton*, ii.50.

8. D. Dalrymple, Lord Hailes, *Memorials and letters relating to the history of Britain in the reign of Charles the First* (Glasgow 1766), 42-3.

9. R. Baillie, *Letters and Journals* (3 vols, Bannatyne Club 1841-2), i.93.

10. W. Knowler (ed), *The earl of Strafford's letters and dispatches* (2 vols, Dublin 1740), ii.187,210.

11. C. Innes (ed), *The black book of Taymouth* (Bannatyne Club 1855), 394-7.

12. Knowler, *Letters*, ii.184.

13. See D. Stevenson, *Scottish covenanters and Irish confederates* (forthcoming).

14. Knowler, *Letters*, ii.266.

15. Stevenson, *Scottish revolution*, 128.

16. Knowler, ii.302-3; *RPCS, 1638-43*, 185; McKerral, *Kintyre*, 38.

17. Knowler, *Letters*, ii.321.

18. Ibid, ii.339-40.

19. Ibid, ii.338,354,357; T. Carte, *Life of James duke of Ormond* (3 vols, London 1735-6), i.92.

20. W.D. Lamont, *The early history of Islay* (Dundee 1966), 60-1; Innes, *Cawdor*, xxviii-xxix.

21. Knowler, *Letters*, ii.361-2, partly reprinted in Hill, *Macdonnells of Antrim*, 57-8 and Loder, *Colonsay*, 134-6.

22. SRO, GD.112/39/776, Breadalbane muniments; Innes, *Cawdor*, 299.

23. SRO, GD.112/39/777.

24. Guthry, *Memoirs*, 199.

25. *RPCS, 1638-43*, 185.

26. Matheson, 'Traditions', *TGSG*, v.19,21.

27. W. Cobbet (ed), *State trials*, v (1810), 1391.

28. SRO, GD.112/39/777.

29. Innes, *Cawdor*, 298.

30. A.M. Mackintosh, *The Mackintoshes and the Clan Chattan* (Edinburgh 1903), 227-8.

31. Hill, *Macdonnells of Antrim*, 441-6.

32. Ibid, 254.

33. J. Lodge, *The peerage of Ireland*, ed. M. Archdall (7 vols, Dublin 1789), vii.115 cited in A. Mackenzie, *History of the Macdonalds and lords of the Isles* (Inverness 1881), 214-15. I assume the mysterious 'Punard' mentioned here to be Sunart, and 'Sir Dougall Campbell' to be Sir Donald.

34. Carte, *Ormond*, i.92; Knowler, *Letters*, ii.233.

35. HMC 8: *9th Report*, ii.255; N. Lamont, *Inventory of Lamont papers* (Scottish Record Society 1914), 180-1; H. McKechnie, *The Clan Lamont* (Edinburgh 1938), 155-8; Baillie, *Letters*, i.193.

36. Knowler, *Letters*, ii.422,426; HMC 23: *Cowper*, ii.162,233.

37. Knowler, *Letters*, ii.374.

38. J.R.N. Macphail (ed), 'Papers relating to the Macleans of Duart, 1670-80', *Highland Papers*, i (SHS 1914), 246; PRO, SP.16/475/95 (printed *CSPD, 1640-1*, 375).

39. Loder, *Colonsay*, 229 shows that the first year's feu duty was payable in November 1640.

40. Stevenson, *Scottish revolution*, 197-200.

41. SRO, GD.112/43/1, bundle marked 'state papers 1640-9'.

42. SRO, GD.112/39/823; *Com. Rin.*, i.460-1.

43. Eg, Innes, *Cawdor*, 298,301.

44. Hickson, *Ireland in the seventeenth century*, i.251-2.

45. James MacColl MacDonnell has often been confused with Sir James MacDonnell, another grandson of Sir James of Dunluce. In addition James MacColl has sometimes been taken to be Alasdair's brother. Both James MacColl and Ranald MacColla are sometimes said to have been captains in Stewart's regiment, but it seems they held more junior ranks. See Hill, *Macdonnells of Antrim*, 64-71,75,289,329;   Hickson,   *Ireland   in   the   seventeenth   century*,   i.112,145-6,234,236,237,243,254.

46. Ibid, i.148; G. Hill, 'The Stewarts of Ballintoy', *Ulster Journal of Archaeology*, new series vi (1900), 23.

47. Ibid, vi.14-15,79-80; Hickson, *Ireland in the seventeenth century*, i.148,234,235,237,238,239,242.

48. HMC 3: 4th *Report*, 108; *Journal of the house of lords*, iv.478; Carte, *Ormond*, i.188.

49. For the letter, and the evidence that it was addressed to Father Hegarty, see D. Stevenson, 'The Irish Franciscan mission to Scotland and the Irish rebellion of 1641', *Innes Review*, xxx, 54-61.

50. Hickson, *Ireland in the seventeenth century*, i.146-7,235-9,240-1,242-3; Hill, 'Stewarts', *UJA*, vi.78-9, 87,89-90, vii.14. Several sources state or imply that Alasdair and his men arrived from Scotland at this time to fight for the rebels. This is clearly wrong (though some other Highlanders may have come over to join the rebels), Gilbert, *Ir confed*, i.33; Shuckburgh, *Two biographies of William Bedell*, 173; *Com Rin*, i.460-1; Carte, *Ormond* , i.189. The story may have arisen through attempts to conceal Alasdair's service against the rebels at the start of the rebellion. Later writers have on several occasions sought to place Alasdair's conduct at Portnaw in the best light by distorting the facts. T. Fitzpatrick, *The bloody bridge and other papers relating to the insurrection of 1641* (Dublin 1903), xxiv-xxv does this by failing to mention that Alasdair ever served in Stewart's regiment, Hill, *Macdonnells of Antrim*, 62-3,75 by claiming that Alasdair served in Stewart's regiment before the rising began

(whereas in fact the regiment did not then exist) and that he left it as soon as the rising started.

51. Hickson, *Ireland in the seventeenth century*, i.145-8,236,345-6,348,ii.150-2,255-76; Hill, 'Stewarts', *UJA*, vi.78-80,87-8, vii.14-15; J. Hogan (ed), *Letters and papers relating to the Irish rebellion* (IMC 1936), 8; Gordon, *Britane's distemper*, 65.

52. The letter is printed in Hogan, *Letters*, 6-7; Hill, *Macdonnells of Antrim*, 64-8; Hill, 'Stewarts', *UJA*, vi.80-1; and Hickson, *Ireland in the seventeenth century*, i.48-50.

53. Hogan, *Letters*, 9-11.

54. Carte MSS, 2, f.321; *Journals of the house of commons* ii.417.

55. NLS, Wodrow MSS, Folio LXVI, ff.199-201.

56. *RPCS, 1638-43*, 185.

57. See D. Stevenson, 'The myth of the founding of the Scots Guards in 1642', *SHR*, lvi (1977), 114-18.

58. Shuckburgh, *Two biographies*, 173-4.

59. Hill, *Macdonnells of Antrim*, 69-70; E. Hogan (ed), *The history of the warr of Ireland . . . by a British officer* (Dublin 1873), 23-4; Gilbert, *Ir confed*, i.33; Hill, 'Stewarts', vi.82,87; Fitzpatrick, *Bloody bridge*, 222; T. O'Mellan, 'A narrative of the wars of 1641', in R.M. Young (ed), *Historical notices of Old Belfast* (Belfast 1896), 206-7. The translation in Young is untrustworthy at this point, and I am grateful to Dr Colm O Boyle for providing a more accurate translation from the Irish text printed in *Analecta Hibernica*, iii (1931), 7.

60. Hickson, *Ireland in the seventeenth century*, i.254; Hill, 'Stewarts', vi.85-6,88; Hill, *Macdonnells of Antrim*, 70-2.

61. K. Tomasson and F. Buist, *Battles of the '45* (London 1962), 105-6; J.T. Dunbar, *History of Highland dress* (Edinburgh and London 1962), 189-91.

62. Ibid, 190.

63. J.H. Burton, *History of Scotland* (8 vols, Edinburgh and London 1876), vi.366-7.

64. Kermack, *Scottish Highlands*, 132, notes the increase in mobility brought about by the change in the Highlanders' weapons. He further suggests that the new arms were cheaper than the old, enabling chiefs to arm more men; this may be true if only the substitution of sword and targe for claymore and armour is considered, but the adoption of the musket (expensive in itself and requiring continuing expenditure on powder and shot) must have cancelled out any such advantage.

65. Dunbar, *Highland dress*, 205-7.

66. Ibid, 205; H. Morley (ed), *Ireland under Elizabeth and James the First* (London 1890), 96; Nicholls, *Gaelic and Gaelicised Ireland*, 86; D.B. Quinn, *The Elizabethans and the Irish* (Ithaca, N.Y. 1966), 40; G.B. O'Connor, *Elizabethan Ireland. Native and English* (Dublin [1907]), 216,218-19; Hill, *Macdonnells of Antrim*, 162n.

67. Ibid, 72-4; Hogan, *History of the warr*, 23; Gilbert, *Ir confed*, i.33. Hickson, *Ireland in the seventeenth century*, i.246.

68. Gilbert, *Contemp hist*, i.425.

69. Stevenson, *Scottish covenanters and Irish confederates*, (forthcoming); Hill, *Macdonnells of Antrim*, 72-4; Young, *Historical notices*, 212; Carte MSS, 3, ff.239-40; *A true and exact relation of divers principall actions of a late expedition undertaken in the north of Ireland . . .* (London 1642).

70. Gilbert, *Ir confed*, i.33.

71. Hogan, *Letters*, 45-51; HMC 23: *Cowper*, ii.300-1; Hogan, *History of the warr*, 23-4; Hill, *Macdonnells of Antrim*, 74-5; Young, *Historical notices*, 213; *Analecta Hibernica*, iii.12; Innes, *Cawdor*, 287-8.

72. Hill, *Macdonnells of Antrim*, 79n, 277n,333; *Com Rin*, vi.225.

73. Young, *Historical notices*, 217; *Analecta Hibernica*, iii.16.

74. Gordon, *Britane's distemper*, 64.

75. Carte MSS, 4, f.230, printed in D. Stevenson, 'The desertion of the Irish by Coll Keitach's sons, 1642', *Irish Historical Studies*, xxi, no.81 (March 1978), 75-84, with spelling modernised.

76. Carte MSS, 4, f.231, printed Stevenson, 'Desertion'.

77. Gordon, *Britane's distemper*, 64.

78. Translation by Dr Colm O Boyle from *Analecta Hibernica*, iii.16-17, based on that in Young, *Historical notices*, 217.

79. T.W. Moody and J.G. Simms (eds), *The bishopric of Derry and the Irish Society of London*, i (IMC 1968), 245.

80. Carte MSS, 4, f.32, printed in Stevenson, 'Desertion'.

81. Gordon, *Britane's distemper*, 64.

82. Spalding, *Memorials*, ii.209.

83. Campbell, *Adventures in legend*, 212-13; Matheson, 'Traditions', *TGSG*, v.21-3. Dr Colm O Boyle points out a variant of the 'bravest hand' motif in J. Mackenzie, *Sar-obair* (1904 edition), 81-2n, where a Mackenzie of Applecross is said to have had the most, and the second most, 'liberal hand'. But though it may be a common motif, it would have been particularly appropriate when applied to someone thought to have been ambidextrous.

84. It is possible, though there is no evidence for it, that one of Alasdair's motives in submitting to Leven had been to try to help Antrim; Leven may have put pressure on him by hinting that Antrim would be severely treated if the MacDonnells of Antrim remained in rebellion under Alasdair's leadership. Alasdair's desertion back to the Irish would fit in neatly with this interpretation; he was free to act because Antrim had escaped.

4

Scotland's Veins Opened

BY the time that Alasdair MacColla's agreement with the Scottish army in Ireland broke down at the end of 1642, England had drifted into civil war between Charles I and parliament. This led in the following year to a re-shuffling of political alliances in Britain as a whole. In Scotland the covenanters received appeals for help from both the king and parliament. Since they had done much to stir up opposition to the king in England in previous years, they tended to favour parliament; and they feared that, if they stood aside and allowed the king to triumph in England, he would then use England's resources to subdue Scotland. But some moderate covenanters, though ready to fight for the covenant in Scotland, were not willing to fight in England in alliance with the king's enemies. They therefore drifted towards alliance with Scottish royalists, who advocated either non-intervention in England or intervention on the side of the king.

In Ireland responses to the English civil war complicated an already confused situation. Among the Catholic confederates some wished to ignore events in England and concentrate on conquering the parts of Ireland still in protestant hands. Others, who retained some vestiges of loyalty to Charles I, saw an opportunity for compromise: would not the king now grant the Irish the concessions they desired if in return they helped him in England? Arguments of expediency tended in the same direction: the English parliament was violently anti-Catholic and anti-Irish, and if it gained control of all England it would then turn to conquering Ireland and suppressing Catholicism. Protestants in Ireland were also divided over how to react to events in England. The regime in Dublin declared for the king, but many protestants were worried by his pro-Catholic tendencies and attracted by the English parliament's hatred of the Catholic Irish. Moreover the strongest protestant army in the kingdom, the Scottish army in Ulster, was controlled by the Scottish covenanters and was soon used by them to suppress royalism among the English and Scottish settlers in that province.

In these turbulent and murky waters the earl of Antrim set out to fish. After escaping from imprisonment by the Scottish army in Ireland in October 1642 he spent the winter in England, negotiating and plotting with English, Irish and Scottish royalists. His ambitious schemes received little encouragement from Charles I, and indeed he may not have revealed all his plans to the king for fear that he be ordered to abandon them; for though Antrim was genuine in his wish to serve Charles I, he was also anxious to recover his own Ulster estates and to forward the MacDonald cause in Scotland. Some of his plans to stir up the royalists of Scotland and Ireland owed more to such motives than to royalism.

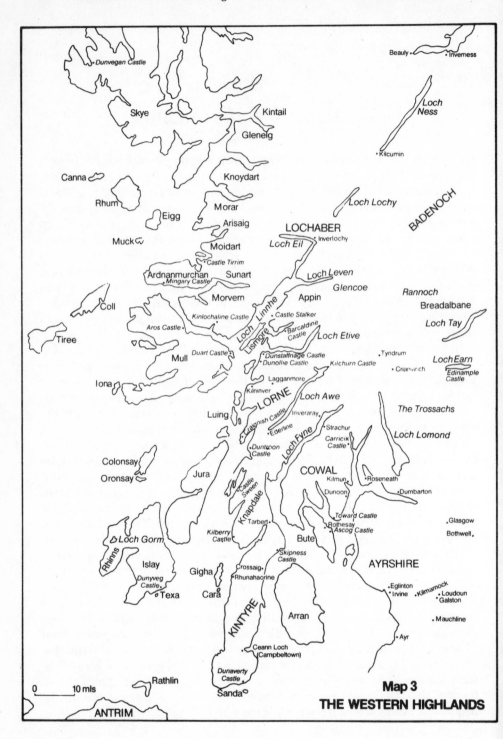

Map 3
THE WESTERN HIGHLANDS

They might be designed partly to help the king, but their political implications might well in the end do Charles more harm than good.

The essence of Antrim's plans was that he should preside over the combining of the linked but until now separate civil wars of England, Scotland and Ireland into a single war. English, Scottish and Irish royalists, Irish confederates, and the MacDonnells/MacDonalds and other Highlanders would combine to aid the king in defeating the English parliament, the task which was his first priority. After this the royalist alliance would turn to crushing any remaining enemies in the other two kingdoms — Scottish covenanters, the Scottish army in Ireland, Irish protestants who had sided with the English parliament, and extremists among the Irish confederates who refused to compromise with the king. The plan was impressive on paper, but the difficulties of implementing it were great. To co-ordinate the actions, and indeed even to reconcile the conflicting interests, of the various groups constituting such a royalist alliance was almost impossible. There was, moreover, one great danger inherent in the plan. Trying to arrange a grand alliance of the king's friends or potential friends in all three kingdoms would almost certainly provoke the king's enemies in all the kingdoms into a similar alliance. And recruiting Irish confederates and Highlanders to fight for the king would lose him the support of a great many protestants throughout his realms.

Nonetheless, Antrim found plenty of hot-headed royalists ready to plot with him, and even though the king favoured caution a semblance of royal approval could be claimed: Charles' Catholic wife, Queen Henrietta Maria, was ever ready to encourage plots which displayed more zeal than judgement.

The extent of Antrim's plots was revealed in mid-1643. In May, on landing at Newcastle in County Down on his way to negotiate with the confederate Irish, Antrim was captured for the second time by the Scottish army in Ireland. Letters found on him, and the interrogations of him and his servants provided news that was to echo round the three kingdoms in the months that followed. An army was to be recruited in Ireland to help the king in England. This was to be composed of both confederate Irish and royalists who had been holding Dublin against the Irish. If possible the Scottish army in Ireland was to be bribed into co-operating. Virtually all Ireland would then be in the hands of the king's allies, and an endless stream of reinforcements could be sent to his armies in England. Further reinforcements would come from Scotland. Royalists there with whom Antrim had been in touch — the marquis of Huntly and his son Lord Aboyne, the earls of Montrose, Airlie and Nithsdale, and Sir Donald Gorm MacDonald of Sleat — believed they could raise men and march them into England.

This much Antrim himself admitted, but under threat of torture and death his servants made further revelations. They testified that Antrim had also planned (if bribery failed) to drive the Scottish army from Ireland. A boatload of arms and ammunition was being sent to the north of Scotland for the use of Aboyne and Antrim's Highland allies, and another boat would take similar supplies to Nithsdale in the south-west. Antrim had said that he and his allies were 'resolved to do all the mischief they could by arms against the kingdom of Scotland'. Antrim strenuously denied this; the arms had been intended only for use in England, by the men he raised in Scotland — he himself had planned to raise a regiment in the Highlands and Isles — and no violence had been intended within Scotland. These denials are unconvincing. Clearly Antrim realised that there was no point in denying most of his plottings, as the evidence against him was strong; but he felt he had to deny the charges that his captors would be most likely to think would justify harsh action against him — trying to stir up civil war in Scotland, and to destroy the Scottish army in Ireland. But no matter how much he prevaricated and lied he was not believed. His own account of his plots implied that he had assumed that the covenanting regime in Scotland would sit back and allow him to raise forces for a royalist invasion of England. This was absurd; royalist forces could not possibly have been recruited and marched into England unless the covenanters were first overthrown, or at least so entangled in a civil war that they were powerless to prevent it. Moreover Antrim's version of his activities contains no mention of the MacDonnell/MacDonald cause, a highly implausible neglect. On this matter one of his servants provided a much more convincing story. Antrim had admitted that his brother, Alexander MacDonnell, had come to Ireland before him, but said he had only come to make arrangements with the Irish confederates for Antrim's visit. But his servant stated that Antrim had sent his brother with 'orders from him to deal with Coll Cittoch's sons to be of their party'; and before he had departed Alexander MacDonnell had told the servant 'that he would use his endeavours to draw over Coll Cittoch's sone before the Earl's coming'.[1] Alasdair MacColla, in disgrace since his attempt to desert to the Scottish army in Ireland, was to be offered employment; and any plan of Antrim involving Coll Ciotach's sons was almost certain to include a new attempt to seize former MacDonald lands in Scotland from the Campbells. Thus it seems that, as was only natural, Antrim's plans at this time included provision for the advancement of his own clan. That he had planned an invasion of Argyllshire soon became accepted as fact, and plausible embellishments were added to the story; Robert Baillie wrote that Antrim had plotted that 'Collkittoch's sones should waken our Isles', and that 'McClaine and Gorum [Sir Lachlan MacLean of Duart and Sir Donald Gorm MacDonald of Sleat], and other Clanes disaffected to the Campbells, should goe to arms' along with Lowland royalists.[2]

The revelation of Antrim's plots appalled most protestants, whether the king's friends or his enemies, by showing that he was willing to ally himself to Catholics; and not just Catholics, but Catholic Irish and Highlanders. The king's enemies were genuinely horrified, but also exploited the news skilfully for propaganda purposes; the fact that there was no real evidence that the king was behind Antrim's plots was conveniently ignored. In Scotland the news that Charles had been plotting civil war against the covenanters, even though up to this point they had refused to help his enemies in England, was decisive in precipitating them into an alliance with the English parliament. Those who had argued that the king would accept covenanting rule in Scotland provided Scotland did not intervene in England were shown to be wrong; their only safety therefore lay in ensuring that he did not triumph in England. In August 1643 a military, political and religious alliance, based on the solemn league and covenant, was agreed between a Scottish convention of estates and English commissioners. At least 21,000 covenanters were to march into England to aid parliament there. Thus Antrim's abortive plotting almost immediately proved disastrous for the king he served.

Only one small part of Antrim's plots of 1643 was put into practice: his plan to employ Alasdair and Ranald MacColla. In November they embarked on a prolonged raid through the Western Isles. There is, admittedly, no direct evidence that their venture was undertaken on Antrim's behalf, but the circumstantial evidence is strong. Antrim's brother had been sent to Ireland to recruit them, and it was doubtless he who helped them raise a force (probably largely refugee Irish and MacDonnells from Antrim and MacDonalds from the Isles). In allowing or even assisting this, the confederate Irish indicated a willingness to forgive Alasdair and Ranald their past treasons, probably because they hoped trouble in the Western Isles would weaken the position of their main enemy in Ireland, the Scottish army.

The fact that the expedition did not sail until November 1643 seems surprising; it was risky to commence such a campaign in winter. But the expedition may have been delayed by fear that reprisals would be taken against the captive earl of Antrim if his men invaded the Isles, this complication being removed in October when Antrim made a second escape from the Scottish army in Ireland.

News that Alasdair MacColla was in the Isles had reached Edinburgh by 24 November. On that day the privy council and the committee of estates combined to issue a commission of lieutenancy to the marquis of Argyll, as the committee of war of Argyll had reported that Alasdair and 300 armed and rebellious Irish, all papists, had landed in the Isles accompanied by two priests. Alasdair's brother Ranald was reported to be following with more ships laden with such 'godless and rebellious miscreants' resolved to trouble Scotland and pervert the king's subjects in religion and loyalty. The commission was at pains to stress that the covenanters were acting against Alasdair in the king's name, and that the invaders were aliens, 'Irish' who had sailed from Ireland; a report by the English commissioners in Edinburgh is more precise about the composition of the rebel force, referring to 'fifty Irish rebells accompanying the MacDonnalds who came lately out of Ireland'. An account of the careers of Alasdair and his followers is also included in the commission, carefully worded so as to bias all against them: since the beginning of the troubles they had been very wicked instruments by their disloyal attempts within Scotland and by invading the Isles with foreign forces; they had been chief actors in the Irish rebellion, committing many cruel murders and barbarous insolencies; fearing capture by the Scottish army in Ireland in 1642 they had submitted to it, but then had relapsed into rebellion. Argyll was therefore appointed king's lieutenant until 1 June 1644 to suppress them, with power to appoint deputies and levy 600 men.[3]

Alasdair appears to have made first for his old family home, Colonsay. His presence there was recorded by one Lauchton Campbell, a sailor who had been born on Islay and knew Alasdair by sight. He was one of the crew of fourteen men and boys aboard the ship *Paul* of London (180 tons) which had sailed from Londonderry on 22 November bound for London laden with salmon and hides.

With civil wars in both England and Ireland, trading on such routes was hazardous, so the ship was armed with six iron cannon. Almost as soon as the ship left Londonderry storms drove her towards the Hebrides, and on 23 November she anchored off Colonsay to ride out a gale. The wind was so high that no boat came out from the island for two days, but at last on 25 November six men approached in a boat, saying they had been sent by the tutor of Calder to discover what the ship was and whether it supported the king or the English parliament; the captain, Robert Paul, carefully replied that he was a merchant and intended harm to no man. The boat then left, saying the tutor would come out next day, Sunday, to confer with him. When the men in the boat reported back to their master on Colonsay he must have been vastly relieved by the news they brought; for he was not the tutor of Calder but Alasdair MacColla. He had evidently just seized the island, and seeing the *Paul* approach and anchor off shore he must have feared that it was a naval vessel, the presence of which indicated that his enemies had caught up with him. He had therefore tried to allay suspicions by pretending that the tutor of Calder still held Colonsay for the Campbells. Now that he knew the ship was a comparatively harmless merchantman, he prepared to capture it, using the fact, in order to achieve surprise, that a friendly visit from the tutor was expected.

On Sunday afternoon 'Alistar MacDonnald, son to Coile MacGillespicke, accompanied with fifty men, came into the ship, and the master, thinking it was the Tutor of Calder and his company let them all in purposing to make them welcome'. As soon as his men were on board Alasdair seized hold of Robert Paul, stating that he was arresting him in the king's name (though in fact he had no royal commission) and threw him over the side into his boat; the mate and one of the crewmen were dealt with in the same way. Some of Alasdair's men then threw back a hatch beneath which some of the crew were having a meal, and 'six of his Hagbutters shot down and deadly hurt one in the head and one in the arm'. But at this point, when capture of the ship by Alasdair seemed certain, it was saved by the quick thinking of one of the crew; the master gunner threatened to blow up the powder store. In fact since no attack had been expected he would not have been able to carry out this threat as a last resort to prevent the ship falling in enemy hands. But he did have a small amount of powder to hand, and this he dropped and set fire to. The bluff worked. Alasdair and his men fled precipitately to their boats to escape the expected explosion, leaving one of their number and one of the ship's crew dead behind them, but taking with them the captain, mate and another crewman. As they fled they cut the *Paul's* anchor cable, hoping the ship (or what was left of it, if it did blow up) would be blown ashore to be plundered. But the crew managed to put out another anchor, and early the next morning, fearing another attack, they weighed anchor and made sail. The wind was still against them, and eventually the *Paul* was driven ashore on the mainland, near Dunollie Castle. Here the crew found safety among the Campbells, but the misfortunes of the ship itself were not over: 'thunder and fire' broke its mainmast and left it unseaworthy.[4]

Meanwhile the preparations of the Campbells to expel the invaders were being completed. On 6 December Argyll commissioned James Campbell of Ardkinglas to act as his deputy lieutenant, and the same day he instructed the magistrates of the burgh of Irvine to deliver 1,000 pounds weight of gunpowder to Archibald Campbell of Kilmun for use on the expedition against the rebels.[5] The campaign which followed cannot be reconstructed in any detail from the fragments of evidence that survive — such as an item in the accounts of the tutor of Calder for £30:6:8 given to soldiers sent on an expedition against Alasdair in winter 1643.[6] However, Campbell of Ardkinglas wrote on 16 July 1644 a brief account of his activities as deputy lieutenant which reveals the main features of the campaign. He chased the rebels through the Isles until they escaped to Ireland, and then proceeded to Mull to punish the resetters (supporters and helpers) of the rebels, and gave them law — a bland phrase which no doubt means that he ordered their execution. Bonds of loyalty and obedience were then exacted from the rest of the MacLeans. The rebellion seemed over, but Ardkinglas now learned that the rebels were re-gathering on the 'Isle of Rachrie' — Rathlin Island — which they had evidently captured from the garrison established there by Argyll's regiment of the Scottish army in Ireland. Ardkinglas therefore led an attack on the island (sometime after mid-May 1644, as Alasdair's men still held Rathlin then)[7] and forced the rebels to flee to Islay and Jura. There, Ardkinglas related grimly, he had disposed of them by summary executions: 'I took them and causit cut of[f] above ane hundredth and ffyifteine of them and took some prisoners.'

Ardkinglas' campaign was completed sometime in June; Argyll's commission, due to expire on 1 June, was prolonged until 1 July on 30 May as the fighting was not yet over; but on 28 June Argyll reported to parliament in Edinburgh that all the rebels had been killed, hanged or captured except for thirteen who had fled to the 'North West Iles' — the Outer Hebrides. The enemies of the Campbells had been routed, but only at considerable trouble and expense; in addition to the 600 men Argyll had been instructed by his commission to levy, 500 more had been raised on his estates for the campaign, and his galley, boats and birlins had been employed to ferry these forces from island to island.[8] Nonetheless, this was the least important of the campaigns Argyll had been involved in during the first half of 1644. After arranging for Ardkinglas to suppress Alasdair MacColla in December 1643, he had in January 1644 entered England with the army of the solemn league and covenant, acting as president of the committee of estates which accompanied it. In April he had returned to Scotland to help deal with a royalist raid on Dumfries led by Montrose, and had personally led an expedition to Aberdeen to crush a royalist rising led by the marquis of Huntly. In the same months he had been closely involved in discussions about the future of the Scottish army in Ireland.

By the end of June 1644 all these crises had been settled satisfactorily from the point of view of Argyll and the covenanters. Most of the army in Ireland remained there; the army in England had made solid if unspectacular progress — and was about to make a major contribution to the great victory over the king at Marston Moor (2 July). Huntly's rising had collapsed, Montrose had fled ignominiously back into England, the rebels in the Western Isles had been exterminated.

Thus, both within Scotland and without, the covenanters had good reason for satisfaction at the progress of military affairs. Nonetheless, it was worrying that three revolts had taken place within Scotland, even if all had been defeated; and the leaders of all three risings had escaped capture. Huntly was no leader of men and posed no serious threat, having withdrawn to the far north to sulk in Strathnaver; but Montrose and Alasdair MacColla were soon to prove enemies of a very different calibre, especially when their talents were combined. Yet this, not surprisingly, was not something that the covenanters foresaw. Montrose was an isolated figure, distrusted even by many royalists because of his covenanting past, dismissed contemptuously by the covenanters as an opportunist turncoat. Many probably regarded him as a lesser threat than Alasdair MacColla. Montrose's incursion over the border had been defeated in a matter of days: it had taken months to clear the Isles of Alasdair's men. Montrose had not yet proved himself decisively as a leader of men in battle: Alasdair had. Montrose had the unswerving loyalty of a few friends and kinsmen, but he did not have any widespread support such as Alasdair possessed among the MacDonalds. Montrose had assembled no more than a few individual Scots royalists willing to cross the border with him, together with a small force of English royalists who accompanied him reluctantly: Alasdair could gather hundreds of MacDonalds and MacDonnells willing to fight under him — and many Irish were also ready to accept his command.

However, though the covenanters might fear a return to the Isles by Alasdair MacColla, they had for the moment defeated him decisively, killed most of the men he had brought to the Isles, and punished and cowed his supporters in the Isles.

Alasdair's escape from the fate of the men he left on Rathlin was a matter of luck; he had not been with his men but had returned to the Irish mainland.[9] He had been summoned, it seems, by Antrim to take over command of a new expeditionary force for a new campaign. It is, indeed, possible that he had not been driven out of the Isles as Argyll and Ardkinglas claimed, but had withdrawn to take up his new command, leaving men on Rathlin so he could use the island as a staging post when he brought his new force out of Ireland.

Antrim's recall of Alasdair signified that some of his plottings were at last bearing fruit. After his second escape from the Scottish army in Ireland in October 1643 Antrim had fled to the quarters of the Irish confederates. The previous month the marquis of Ormond's royalist regime in Dublin had concluded a cessation with the Irish, a truce designed by Ormond to enable him to send some of his forces to England to fight for the king, and by the Irish to enable them to concentrate their forces against the Scottish army in Ireland. In addition, the king hoped eventually to persuade the confederates to send part of their own army to England to help him. Thus the time seemed ripe for Antrim to revive his plans for a grand alliance and co-ordinated action by all who supported the king in the three kingdoms. But Antrim suffered from the disadvantage that few trusted him; even if his sincerity was admitted, his career seemed to prove that he was a deviser of over-ambitious plans which he was unable to implement. His first manoeuvres were therefore aimed at gaining credibility. He persuaded the Irish to give him the nominal title of lieutenant general, and then made his way to the king's headquarters at Oxford. There he claimed that he had been given real authority over the Irish armies, but this failed to impress the king and his advisers, who therefore ignored his request that the king ratify his position by appointing him commander of these armies. Thus Antrim failed in his main object, that of emerging by trickery with some generally recognised authority in Ireland which he could use to send Irish troops to England for the king. His plan for driving the Scottish army out of Ireland or bribing it to leave was also rejected, for fear that the covenanters would redeploy it in England. But two other suggestions by Antrim proved very attractive to the king: he offered to persuade the Irish confederates to send 10,000 men to fight for the king in England, and a further 3,000 to fight in Scotland.[10] Antrim might be generally thought to be 'a man of excessive pride and vanity, and of a marvellous weak and narrow understanding',[11] but there was an outside chance that he might be able to provide at least some of the men he so confidently offered the king, and the king was in no position to turn down such a possibility of gaining help. Charles therefore decided to encourage Antrim, even if he expected little from him.

On 20 January 1644 royal instructions were issued to Antrim. His first priority was to be persuading the Irish to send 10,000 men to England 'whereby we may be the better enabled to resist the Scotch invasion'; Scottish intervention in the English civil war on one side was to be balanced by Irish intervention on the other. Antrim was also to try to get the Irish to provide 2,000 men for Scotland, to serve under either Antrim himself or his brother Alexander, and to invade Argyll's estates. Antrim was to be joint justiciary of the Isles with the earl of Seaforth, and Sir James MacDonald of Sleat (who had recently succeeded his father Donald Gorm) was to have the rank of colonel. In arranging this expedition Antrim was to co-operate with Montrose, who was to be appointed royal lieutenant general in Scotland. Finally, Antrim was to try to bribe the Scottish army in Ireland to declare for the king.[12] The same day the king wrote to Ormond asking him to help Antrim,[13] and to William MacKintosh, chief of the Clan Chattan, requesting his assistance to Montrose and Antrim in raising Highland forces to attack Argyll's estates;[14] this latter letter was doubtless typical of others hopefully dispatched to all Highland chiefs who might be persuaded to support the royalist — or at least the anti-Campbell — cause.

Eight days later Antrim signed an agreement with Montrose. The latter had only been marginally involved in Antrim's plots which had been revealed in May 1643; probably he had little faith in Antrim's abilities, and he was not a man to be satisfied with a minor part in another man's ambitious schemes. In the agreement now signed Montrose is described as lieutenant general of Scotland, Antrim as general of the Highlands and Isles; thus Antrim had the more senior rank, but jurisdiction over only part of Scotland, while Montrose was lieutenant general of the whole country. In practice they seem to have negotiated with each other as equals. By the terms of the agreement Montrose undertook on behalf of Scots royalists to raise forces in the North-East and on the Borders; Antrim for his part would raise men in the Isles and try to invade Argyll's country from Ireland. All these risings were to take place by 1 April 1644.[15] Thus there were to be co-ordinated royalist risings in Scotland aided by an invasion from Ireland; while for the king the first priority in negotiations with the Irish confederates was to get troops for use in England, Antrim was giving priority to the Scottish venture. But, as was usual with Antrim's schemes, it proved impossible for him to keep his promises; and Montrose equally failed to keep his side of the bargain. The two men had set themselves an absurdly tight schedule — just two months in which to organise invasions of Scotland and royalist revolts there. Two attempts at royalist risings were made during April, Huntly's rising and Montrose's incursion over the border, but both were humiliating failures and nothing had yet come of Antrim's promised invasion; even the few men Alasdair MacColla had had in the Isles had been driven back to Rathlin.

Antrim had not abandoned his plans, however, though he had been unable to keep to the original schedule. On returning to Ireland after signing his agreement with Montrose, he had quickly won the support of the Irish confederates for his Scottish venture. They would not send men to help the king in England, as they saw no immediate benefit to themselves in doing so, but intervention in Scotland was a different matter. A successful invasion might well force the covenanters to withdraw the Scottish army in Ireland; if this happened the confederates would probably be able to complete their conquest of all Ireland. Therefore in February 1644 the supreme council of the confederates resolved to allow Antrim to recruit men and to provide him with 2,000 muskets, twenty-four hundredweight of gunpowder, some match and 200 barrels of oatmeal. These would be provided by 1 May — provided that the marquis of Ormond, who was to supply shipping to carry the men to Scotland, handed over an Ulster port, Greencastle (County Down) or Carlingford (County Louth, then regarded as part of Ulster), to the Irish so men and supplies could be assembled there. This demand led to long arguments, for Ormond refused to hand over a port, both through unwillingness to place a strategically placed port in the hands of the Irish and through fear that if Antrim was allowed to assemble his men in Ulster he would be tempted to use them to attack the Scottish army in Ireland in an attempt to recover his own County Antrim lands.[16]

Such fears and suspicions between Ormond and the Irish inevitably delayed Antrim's preparations. Not until late April did Ormond propose a compromise: arms, ammunition and provisions could be assembled at Carlingford, but the port would not be handed over to the Irish and Antrim's men must come there and board ship unarmed. For all his fears, Ormond had become an enthusiastic supporter of the venture, and was much encouraged by news of Huntly's rising in Scotland. He concluded that 'Now or never is the tyme to compleat the distraction of that fatall kingdom, and to returne into their bosome their own mischeefe.'[17] Antrim, too, suggested compromise and urged haste as the time was ripe to strike in Scotland. He suggested that to avoid the need for an Ulster port he would send his arms and provisions to Wexford or Waterford to be shipped directly to Mull, which was to be his expedition's rendezvous in the Isles. 'My Lord's friends in the Isles incourage him much to attempt something there, whyl those partes are disgusted with the present government of their country.'[18] Antrim still evidently intended to ship his men from Ulster, but it was soon agreed that they too should be shipped from Waterford or Wexford. To dispatch the men and their weapons from different ports would have added unnecessary hazards to an already risky venture; there would have been a good chance that they would fail to come together in the Isles as planned.

Now that plans were well advanced, Ormond revealed another of his worries about the expedition. On 22 April he wrote to Daniel O'Neill (a royalist agent who was working closely with Antrim) complaining that 'I must tell you, I feare the person to comand these men was not seasonably, nor sufficiently, thought of: It is a design of high importance, and would be governed by a provident, dilligent and discreet man.'[19] There was in fact no difficulty here. Antrim was of course in overall command of the venture and he intended that his brother, Alexander MacDonnell, should serve under him; apart from anything else the appointment was expedient because Alexander was said to be more trusted by the Irish than Antrim himself.[20] But neither man was actually expected to sail with the expedition (though if it was successful they might follow later). From the first, Antrim evidently intended that the man who made the initial landing in Scotland should be Alasdair MacColla. Tradition asserts that Alasdair was chosen by the warriors assembled for the expedition. It was proposed that the leader should be the man with the strongest arm, whereupon Alasdair raised his right arm, sword in hand, and declared 'This is it'; to the further question of who had the arm next in strength he raised his left arm.[21] As already seen, this story of Alasdair claiming the strongest arms is also told in connection with his desertion of the Scottish army in Ireland in 1642, and the claim may well have become attached to him simply through belief that he was ambidextrous, he being confused with his father. In any case, the story represents the ideal of how the leader of a warrior band ought to have been chosen rather than actual mid-seventeenth century practice.

On 25 March 1644 it was reported that 800 'Scotch Irish' (MacDonnells and Highlanders) had arrived at Portumna, County Galway, under the command of 'Collakitagh's Son'; Antrim was nearby at Loughreagh.[22] The son of Coll Ciotach referred to could have been Ranald, but it seems much more likely that it was Alasdair, by far the best known of the two brothers, and that at least some of his 800 men had recently returned with him from the raid on the Western Isles and now formed the nucleus of the force Antrim was assembling for Alasdair to lead back to Scotland. Alasdair's clan and family background, his fame as a warrior and his recent contacts with the Isles made him the natural choice as leader of the new expedition. As one source puts it, he was suitable 'because he was not only experienced in military discipline and endowed with special greatness of soul, but also he had long been well loved by and well known to his most noble fellow tribesmen . . . and so he was very well suited to raise them in a warlike alliance.'[23]

As the weeks passed, however, and the expedition was still not ready to sail, both Alasdair and Antrim grew increasingly frustrated. On 16 May Antrim wrote to Ormond complaining that he had maintained 2,000 men for three months; unless something was done quickly he would have to disband them, and 'I must discharge Alexander Mac Colle to go look after his own waies, whereby he may relieve his Soldiers and Raghlin he must be forced to abandon' unless food was sent to the island.[24] Ormond could spare no supplies for Antrim's men, but he sent Daniel O'Neill to let Antrim know 'what he hath done' concerning Alasdair MacColla.[25] What this meant was, it seems, that Ormond begged the Irish to help Alasdair, for on 24 May Daniel O'Neill reported that the Irish confederate supreme council at Kilkenny had at last after much debate agreed that Alasdair's men should march to Passage and Ballahack, two ports near Waterford, to be shipped to the Isles; they were to be there by 6 June. Moreover, the Irish agreed to provide food and arms for the men Alasdair had left on Rathlin, and he was to sail immediately with these supplies to relieve the island in a frigate commanded by a Captain Stafford.[26] At last, after months of argument and disappointment, it seemed that the departure of the expedition to Scotland was imminent.

The three ships provided for Antrim's men were hired through a Kilkenny merchant, Patrick Archer. The *Christopher* of Surdame and the *Angell Gabriell* were Flemish, and the *Jacob* of Ross was Irish and partly owned by Archer.[27] How many men boarded these ships in June bound for Scotland is uncertain. Antrim said at the time that he had sent 'hard on 1600' men, seven or eight hundred more having had to be disbanded through lack of ships; but in November he claimed he had sent 2,030 men plus officers; and Ormond claimed in July that 2,500 men had sailed for Scotland.[28] Presumably Antrim's figures are the more reliable, the discrepancy between the two totals he gives perhaps being accounted for by the fact that, at some time unknown between June and November, he managed to send a few hundred of the men he had had at first to disband to Scotland to reinforce the expedition.

Alasdair MacColla failed to save his men on Rathlin. By the time Captain Stafford's frigate reached the island the men had been driven back to the Hebrides by Campbell of Ardkinglas and killed. Alasdair therefore hastened back to Waterford to take over command of the new expeditionary force before it sailed; Antrim and his brother Alexander hoped eventually to follow him with more men.[29]

Something of the composition of the force that sailed under Alasdair can be gleaned from a list of officers Antrim sent to Ormond in November 1644.[30] The list names seventy-three officers; over two-thirds of them have Irish names, the rest names which are English, Lowland Scottish or Highland in origin, though some of these men came from families which had been settled in Ireland for generations. The Irish names mainly belong to families from County Antrim and northern County Londonderry, and there are of course many MacDonnells. Assuming that the men who served under them were similar in origin, it seems that there was much continuity of personnel between the forces Alasdair MacColla had commanded in Ulster in 1641-2 and the forces he led to Scotland in 1644, though there were now more refugees from the Highlands and men recruited from other parts of Ireland than before. Most of the officers and men had gained their military training in the wars in Ireland, but the discipline they were to show in battle may indicate that there was some truth in the allegation that some were veterans trained in the Spanish service in the Spanish Netherlands —

though it is perhaps more likely that the fact that some of the men landed from Flemish ships has here led to the false assumption that the men came from the Netherlands. Certainly Robert Baillie thought they had sailed 'from the Continent'.[31] Antrim's list divides the force sent into Scotland into three regiments, commanded by Lieutenant General MacDonnell, Colonel O'Cahan and Colonel James MacDermot. It has usually been assumed that the first of these is Alasdair MacColla, but elsewhere his rank while in Scotland is consistently said to have been major general, and Antrim's brother had a position in the force between Antrim (general) and Alasdair (major general); thus it was Antrim's brother Alexander who bore the nominal rank of lieutenant general. That this was so is confirmed by a statement that 'Thomas O'Lachnanus' commanded a regiment sent to Scotland in the name of Antrim's brother;[32] this is clearly the Sergeant Major (or Major in modern terms) 'Thomas Laghtnan' who appears on Antrim's list in Lieutenant General MacDonnell's regiment. This does however raise a further question: surely the command of the absent lieutenant general's regiment should have devolved on his lieutenant colonel, John MacDonnell? The answer is probably that he too was a close relative of Antrim's, holding a nominal rank through birth rather than ability. This Lieutenant Colonel John MacDonnell may well be the 'Young Colonel Macdonald' who quickly proved 'too young for the fatigues of the campaign, and became seriously ill'; he had to be carried on a litter, and there was thought to be little hope for his recovery until (according to a clerical source) he made a priest guardian of his body and soul, whereupon he recovered sufficiently to take part in the fighting![33] Thus Alasdair did not command a regiment, and therefore does not appear on Antrim's list of regimental officers — unless he be the Alexander MacColl listed as the captain of a company in the lieutenant general's regiment, for it was common for senior officers also to command companies in order to entitle themselves to extra pay.

The second of the three colonels was Manus O'Cahan who had, along with John Mortimer, led forces over the Bann into Antrim to join Alasdair when he had declared for the Irish rebels in January 1642; Mortimer now appears as a captain in O'Cahan's regiment.

The third regimental commander is listed as James MacDermot; this is an error for James MacDonnell, a son of Sorley MacDonnell who had been involved in Coll Ciotach's escapades in 1615. James wrote an account of the expedition's campaigns in Scotland; this has been lost, but the authors of the *Commentarius Rinuccinianus* made use of it in compiling their narrative.

Of·the five most senior officers of the expeditionary force, three (Antrim, his brother, and James MacDonnell) were MacDonnells of Antrim. One (Alasdair MacColla) was a MacDonald so closely linked to the MacDonnells as to be virtually a member of that clan, and one (Manus O'Cahan) was a member of the native Irish family most closely allied to the MacDonnells. The force might be Irish in name, and mainly Irish in personnel, but with such commanders there could be little doubt that it would be used in the interests of the Clan Donald. Members of the force not named in Antrim's list included three priests, one attached to each regiment,[34] and, according to tradition, Alasdair's two bodyguards, Dubhaltach MacPhee and Calum Mor MacInnes.[35]

For those who believed in omens, the first experience of the expedition on sailing on 24 June 1644 must have seemed threatening. Within twenty-four hours the ships were back in port, having barely escaped shipwreck in a sudden storm. Forty to sixty soldiers, it was reported, were taken out of the ships nearly dead from seasickness, and many others were in bad shape; good soldiers they might be, but they were no sailors. However, by 27 June they were sufficiently recovered for the ships to set sail again. Sailing from a southern Irish port meant that they had more than just the weather to fear; on the long voyage north they were in danger of encountering ships of the English parliament. But fortune was on their side. Liverpool had just fallen to the royalists, disrupting parliamentary naval operations in the Irish sea.[36] Alasdair's ships slipped through undetected, and on 3 July the frigate the *Harp* of Wexford (which was accompanying the three merchant ships, and probably had been the frigate which had previously taken Alasdair to Rathlin) captured a ship crossing from Ulster to Scotland. On board were about forty passengers. Most were allowed to go free, but eight were brought on board the *Harp* as captives, being regarded as men of sufficient status to be worth retaining for use in exchanges of prisoners. Two were Scottish parish ministers, returning from imposing the solemn league and covenant in Ulster: John Weir (Dalserf) and James Hamilton (Dumfries). David Watson (Hamilton's father-in-law) was a parish minister in Ulster, and Thomas Johnston was described as a preacher in Ulster; for reasons that are not clear he was soon released. Two of the captives were merchants, William Hamilton from Glasgow and William Irving from Dumfries. Archibald Bruce was a Lanarkshire man, and the final prisoner was John Weir's pregnant wife, Janet Cunningham.

Capture by Alasdair MacColla was to prove fatal to Weir; he was to die in captivity. But it is of great value to the historian, for Weir was a systematic man who kept both a brief diary of events and an odd sort of profit and loss account of providence's dealings with him, wherein sufferings and fears are balanced against mercies. These papers tell us much of the doings of Alasdair and his men in a period which is otherwise obscure.[37] Weir and his fellow prisoners remained in the *Harp* from 3 to 15 July. Actual sufferings he recorded included being robbed of money, clothes, books and horses, being parted from their servants, and poor food and accommodation. Weir's financial loss was substantial, for while in Ulster he had received 1,000 merks of his wife's tocher (dowry) from her brother, Lieutenant Colonel William Cunningham of the Scottish army in Ireland; Weir also lost horses and goods worth another 1,000 merks. He complained that he and his fellow prisoners were fed on the worst salt salmon and bacon, peas and a little bread 'and that sometime mouldie'. Drink was water and beer, which were sometimes rationed. The prisoners were given no chance to change their clothes, and almost suffocated at night when they were shut up below decks. Sick in mind and body, they were frequently searched; 'some of us wer buffeted and abused'; they were not allowed to write, and there was 'restraint of joynt worship' — their Catholic captors would not tolerate heretical worship. In addition Weir carefully listed their fears and uncertainties: fear of drowning, of the dangers of battle at sea, of being handed over to the royalists in Dublin, of 'the peril of taking our bibles from us' and of 'the frequent passions of the sea men' who were often drunk and threatening. But Weir was able to console himself with some mercies. There were no storms while they were on board and their health was reasonably good; they had the consolation of prayer, and the captain and some gentlemen showed them favour, preventing them being ill treated. Finally, 'It was a merci that kolcittagh was a prisoner before ws'; Weir evidently believed that it was only the fact that Alasdair wanted prisoners to exchange for his father that prevented him dealing harshly with the captives, handing them over to royalists for trial for treason, or perhaps even killing them.[38] This last fear must have been a very real one, for the racial and religious hatreds of English and Irish, protestant and Catholic were becoming increasingly bitter as the bloody war in Ireland dragged on, with atrocities on both sides.

Nonetheless, though Weir's situation was far from enviable, he was prone to exaggerate his own sufferings in the cause of God, to emphasise potential sufferings which never become actual in order to praise the Lord for sparing him from so much. The prisoners' food and living conditions on the *Harp* may have been poor, but they were probably little worse than those of the soldiers and crew crowded on board. To be robbed when captured was hardly unexpected. That presbyterian ministers, symbolising the covenants with their virulent hatred of Catholicism, should be insulted and manhandled by Irish and Highland Catholic soldiers and seamen was almost inevitable. What is surprising is that some gentlemen should have intervened to protect them. Alasdair himself is not mentioned in this context, but as commander of the expedition he probably had some part in the relatively civilised treatment of the prisoners; in Ulster in 1641-2 he had shown that though he gloried in battle, he could be merciful.

On 4 July Alasdair's ships anchored in the sound of Islay. There he heard of the fate of the men he had left in Rathlin but who had been driven back to the Hebrides: 'we heard of newes that five scor of Alasters men wer latli slain by the laird of Ardkinglass'. The four ships from Ireland at first pretended to be merchantmen seeking fish to buy, and local fishermen were invited on board to drink. Once on board — and exhilarated by wine — the fishermen were told the real identity of their hosts. Being supporters of the MacDonald cause, they rejoiced and told what they knew of the situation in Islay. Alasdair may have intended a landing in Islay, but news that his men from Rathlin were dead and the local population cowed into submission to Campbells and covenants decided him to sail on — encouraged, it is said, by the fishermen, who told him that two strong Campbell castles in the north were not adequately garrisoned.[39]

Next day, 5 July, the expedition anchored off Duart in Mull, but Sir Lachlan MacLean of Duart refused to join an enterprise which probably seemed to him little more than another raid on the Isles like those Alasdair had led previously. Such an expedition might be suited to desperate young men with nothing to lose, who could escape back to Ireland if things went wrong, but it was too dangerous a matter to be attractive to an established chief, especially to one who had found out the hard way in the Bishops' Wars the consequences of opposing the Campbells and the covenanting regime they represented.

However, on 6 July the expedition's spirits were raised by the capture off Duart of two English ships laden with wheat, rye, and sack (white wine), blown off course to the Isles while sailing from London to Londonderry. Alasdair now decided to begin action himself, instead of waiting hopefully for chiefs to declare for him and the king. On 7 July he landed part of his force, about 400 men under Manus O'Cahan, in Morvern (on the mainland opposite Mull) to attack Kinlochaline Castle, a small square keep dating from the fifteenth century which was now in Campbell hands. Alasdair himself sailed on, and the following day landed the rest of his army in Ardnamurchan to attack Mingary Castle.[40]

The landing of Alasdair MacColla and the Irish had been foreshadowed by portents, and was accompanied by further signs of great events to come. The royalist Patrick Gordon of Ruthven wrote of how visions and omens had shown God's wrath with the covenanters. Armed men and battles had been discerned in the air, along with the sound of drums, cannon and muskets. The sun had shone in the middle of the night. But even these events seemed ordinary compared to 'the warneing piece that was shot from heauin as the last and latter signall that should be giuen ws of our neir approaching punishment'. At the very moment that Alasdair set foot on Scottish soil this great explosive noise 'did ring in the eares of euerie man, woman, and child throughout the whole kingdome'. Thus was marked the arrival of Alasdair and the Irish 'who ware the first that begane the ware that afterward opened all the waines of the Kingdome, and drew forth oceanes of blood'.[41] James Gordon, minister of Rothiemay, later claimed that his own investigations had established that the great heavenly cannon shot at Alasdair's landing had been heard from at least as far south as Coldstream on the Tweed to at least as far north as Ross-shire. William Gordon, writing in the 1720s, recalled that he had in earlier years heard several gentlemen swear that they had been 'Ear-witnesses to the Truth of this story'; they themselves had heard the noise.[42] Father James MacBreck, a Catholic missionary at work in Scotland in the 1640s, confirms that such a supernatural occurrence took place, and adds another twist to the story: even Alasdair and his men were shaken by the explosion. 'Their landing was accompanied by some confusion arising from an extraordinary prodigy which occurred, for although the sky was cloudless and there was no sign of any disturbance of the atmosphere, there was suddenly heard a terrific explosion, so loud as to be heard in every part of Scotland, the effect of which was to make everyone feel as if his ears were stunned by a report from behind him, from an enormous brazen cannon of unheard-of dimensions.' As there were no flashes of lightning, clouds or rain at the time, 'There was an agreement among all persons who described the occurrence, that it was of an unusual character, and that it was absolutely impossible for human understanding to conjecture what it portended; when gradually the rumour everywhere spread that a cruel, savage, and foreign enemy had invaded the country'.[43]

In spite of Father MacBreck's denials, summer thunder seems the most likely explanation of this phenomenon, and since the significance of it was only decided on later it may be doubted whether, in an age of slow communications and bad timekeeping, it was really proved, rather than assumed, that the noise had really been heard throughout the land at the same moment — and that that was the moment of Alasdair's landing. But the wide acceptance of the story is in itself of interest; it shows that the landing of Alasdair and the Irish was later realised to have been so significant that it was appropriate it should have been accompanied by such a wonder.

Legend suggests that Alasdair himself was superstitious about the prospects of his expedition. He had been warned (in accordance with an old Highland belief) that when setting out he must kill the first living creature he met if he wished good fortune. In accordance with this he is credited by various versions of the tradition with killing a weaver while marching down to the harbour to embark from Ireland, with killing the weaver on landing in Kintyre (though in fact he did not land there) and with killing on Mull the son of one of his two sisters who lived on that island; he was sorry when he found the child was his nephew, but his subsequent good fortune persuaded him that he had been right to kill him![44]

Once landed, Alasdair prepared for the assault on Mingary Castle. This was a much more formidable fortification than Kinlochaline (which surrendered on the day that Alasdair landed). Built in a strategic position on a rocky headland commanding the north end of the sound of Mull and the entrance to Loch Sunart, it had formerly been the seat of the MacIans or MacDonalds of Ardnamuchan but was now held by a Campbell garrison established by Sir Donald Campbell of Ardnamurchan. In landing where he did Alasdair was doubtless influenced by the fact that this was former MacDonald territory — indeed it was the last major MacDonald possession to have fallen into Campbell hands, the MacIans having only been finally subdued in the mid-1620s. Alasdair could therefore hope that many of the local population would join him in attacking their Campbell masters. The castle itself consisted of a hexagonal curtain wall, about 200 feet long and twenty-five feet high. On four sides the wall stood on the top of cliffs which dropped sharply to the sea, while the one landward side was protected by a deep ditch cut across the promontory; here the wall was heightened to form one side of a strong keep. The only entrances to the castle were two small doors, one reached by steps cut in the cliff face, the other by a wooden bridge or drawbridge over the ditch.[45]

On 10 July Alasdair and his men, having ravaged part of Ardnamurchan, appeared before Mingary. His force (as O'Cahan had not yet returned from Kinlochaline) mustered perhaps 1,400 men, plus a few *excurrentes*, stragglers or camp followers, presumably local men who had joined Alasdair. Many cattle had been herded close to the castle walls to gain their protection, but on 12 July Alasdair's men drove them off. Next day the attack began in earnest. The main assault was on the landward gate, and in spite of continuous fire from the defenders, Alasdair's men managed to heap up wood and other combustible materials in the ditch and against the gate and set them on fire; tradition plausibly asserts that the roofs were torn off all the houses in the area and the materials — wood, thatch and turf — used in the assault, though it wrongly concludes that Alasdair failed to take the castle. After three hours the castle gate was on fire and the garrison half choked by the smoke; they had tried pouring barrels of ale over the castle walls, but had failed to extinguish the raging fire. At this point Alasdair broke off his attack to let the fire do its work and to give him time to get tools from his ships for the final assault on the gate. During this lull in the fighting a poor woman came out of the castle (presumably by the sea gate, since the other was on fire). When brought before Alasdair she revealed that the spring or well in the castle had dried up in the first hour of the siege, so the garrison would soon be forced to surrender for lack of water. That the garrison was short of water was probably true; why else waste good ale on the fire? But this alone could hardly have forced such a precipitate surrender as was now to take place. At noon the garrison surrendered on terms granted by Alasdair; the commander of the garrison and six of his men were to come out equipped with swords and guns, but the rest of the men were to leave their arms behind. All were to be allowed to depart freely.

This is the Irish account of the fall of Mingary: the castle was attacked and surrendered at noon the same day through shortage of water. But Patrick Gordon talks of the assault being continued night and day, and John Weir confirms that though the attack began on 13 July the castle did not surrender until the following day; Weir also notes that John MacKellor (evidently the commander of the garrison) and the other 'warders' of the castle were not freed as promised but seized and held prisoner. And when the garrison did surrender it was probably as much because it was a weak force neither expecting nor prepared for an attack as through lack of water. On 15 July Alasdair had the prisoners held on the *Harp* brought into the castle, along with the food from the two captured English ships. By this time Manus O'Cahan had arrived with his men from Kinlochaline Castle, which he had left well supplied and garrisoned. In the assaults on the two castles Alasdair had lost only nine men dead, with eight injured.[46]

His position was now much stronger than it had ever been on his previous raids to the Isles. Not only did he have many more men than before, but he now held two castles on the mainland, one of them (Mingary) being a major strength. All Ardnamurchan (and probably much of Morvern) was in his hands, and he now had direct authority from the king to summon men to join him and make war on his enemies, whereas his earlier ventures had been essentially private MacDonnell/MacDonald enterprises with royalist overtones.

Nonetheless, Alasdair knew his position was precarious. Up to this point he had had the advantage of surprise, but this was now lost and forces would soon be concentrated against him. If he failed to find allies to reinforce his little army, his expedition might soon end in defeat or ignominious flight back to Ireland. So far no chief had shown himself willing to join him, and there was no news of any force in arms under Huntly, Montrose or any other Scots royalist. Alasdair doubtless hoped that news of his success in Ardnamurchan and Morvern would change attitudes to his venture, and messengers were sent out to spread the good news. On 16 July Captain John Mortimer read out Alasdair's royal commission to those at Mingary; Colonel James MacDonnell was then sent with it to Sir James MacDonald of Sleat, while Mortimer and others were sent to try to persuade other chiefs — MacDonalds, MacLeans, MacLeods and the earl of Seaforth, chief of the MacKenzies, to rise in arms. Alasdair's main hopes lay in Sleat and Seaforth, but neither man was willing to put his expressions of support for the king into practice. Sir James MacDonald of Sleat was much less committed to the royalist cause than his father, Sir Donald Gorm, had been, and Seaforth was cautious and indecisive. Alasdair might have captured two castles, but these two men saw his fate as swift defeat, in which they had no wish to share.

To his failure to win Highland support was soon added another blow. On 17 July the Irish frigate left the anchorage off Mingary to pursue a ship that had been sighted; on 19 July the frigate re-appeared, hotly pursued by ships of the English parliament. By treaty the English had bound themselves to provide ships to protect the Scottish coast from landings from Ireland, but in spite of constant Scots complaints the numbers of ships agreed on had seldom been provided — and such ships had of course failed to prevent Alasdair from landing. Now at last the English navy had caught up with Alasdair. The usually accepted account of the fight that followed, that of Patrick Gordon, states that the two Flemish ships, being mercenaries, surrendered to the English at once, while the Irish ship fought till all her crew were dead and she was on fire. Thus Alasdair was left with no ships. But Alasdair had two Irish ships, the *Jacob* of Ross and the *Harp* frigate, not one, and John Weir's on the spot account states that no ships were destroyed, and that only one of the Flemish ships was captured in the fight on 20 July. The other Flemish ship and the Irish frigate reached safety by anchoring under the castle walls, and no mention is made of the second Irish ship. Not until 10 August were the second Flemish ship and one of the Irish (referred to as Captain Turner's ship) captured (Weir says by Argyll, but he had English help). The Gaelic history of the wars by Neil MacMhuirich adds further confusion by mentioning only one sea battle and placing it not off Mingary but in Loch Eishort in Skye. As neither Gordon nor MacMhuirich wrote while these events were taking place, and neither was present at them, Weir's evidence must be preferred to theirs. As will be seen shortly, the point is of some importance.

A further point noted by Weir made it doubly fortunate for Alasdair that the English had not caught up with his ships before he had landed his men: the English commander was Captain Swanley, the man responsible for the worst atrocity committed by parliamentary forces against the troops Ormond was trying to send from Dublin to England to fight for the king. In April 1644 Richard Swanley had captured a vessel laden with such troops, separated those he regarded as English from the Irish, and then had all the Irish tied in pairs back to back and thrown overboard. In all about seventy men and two women were drowned. Swanley's action was regarded as entirely justified by English parliamentarians, and was widely reported in the most revoltingly gloating terms. The Irish 'because they were good Swimmers, he caused to use their natural Art, and try whether they could tread the Seas as lightly as their Irish boggs and quagmires, and binding them backe to back, cast them overboard to swimme or drown, and to wash them to death, from the blood of the Protestants that was upon them'.[47] Alasdair's men would have found little mercy in such hands.

It is usually said (on the authority of Patrick Gordon and Neil MacMhuirich) that Alasdair had admitted defeat and was preparing to return to Ireland with his men when the arrival of the English and the destruction of his ships trapped him on the mainland, thus forcing him to undertake the march which was to result in his linking up with Montrose. This version of events makes a good story, and has proved attractive to royalists as it stresses the providential nature of the meeting of the two men, but three considerations cast serious doubt on it. John Weir's evidence indicates that at first Alasdair lost only one of his four ships. If Alasdair had really been trying desperately to escape to Ireland from the enemies closing in on him, attempted flight by sea would still have been his best policy. With the right winds and some luck, an attempted escape on his two blockaded ships, especially if undertaken at night, would have stood a good chance of success. Secondly, Alasdair can hardly have been resolved by 20 July (the day of the first sea fight) to abandon his expedition because no chiefs would join him, as he had only sent to many of these chiefs appealing for their help on 16 July; there had not been time for all of them to reply. Finally, there is the fact that nothing in Alasdair's career and character makes it plausible that he should behave in such a pusillanimous manner. Certainly he was meeting with difficulties and setbacks, but in such circumstances at all other points in his career he tended more towards the opposite fault — of advancing towards danger too eagerly. Now at last, in his third campaign in the Highlands, he had a sizeable force under his command and strong castles in his hands. Precipitate flight back to Ireland would have discredited him as a warrior and demoralised those who still sought to revive the fortunes of the Clan Donald. He had known from the start that the venture he was undertaking was one of great danger. If he was to abandon hope and flee at the first crisis there was no point in having come to the Highlands at all. The truth of the matter will never be known, but there does seem a strong presumption that Alasdair had no intention of fleeing. His enemies were gathering against him by sea and land; his natural response was to advance from his base at Mingary.

On 22 July Alasdair made his prisoners write to local parish ministers, Martin MacIlvory or MacIlvra (Iona) and Hector MacLean (Morvern), asking them to help to negotiate their release — in exchange, no doubt, for Alasdair's father and two brothers. Four days later one Archibald Campbell, a messenger from the marquis of Argyll, arrived and received a letter from the prisoners to him. Negotiations for the exchange of prisoners having started, Alasdair resolved to march in search of allies before the forces the Campbells were assembling against him reached Ardnamurchan. On the night of 29 July he left Mingary with his little army, being, in Patrick Gordon's words, as 'wise as ualiant, and neuer knoweing where fear duelt, [he] did looke alse cheirefullie as euer, and both by his wordes and courage did mightely incourage there deiected myndes'. First he marched east into Lochaber (a region in which Argyll was struggling to take over dominance from Huntly), in the hope of gaining support there and then continuing eastwards into Badenoch and other territories where Huntly's influence was strong. It is said that Alasdair still thought Huntly was in arms, not having heard of the defeat in April of his rising. This is hard to believe; it was now nearly three months since Huntly's defeat, and Alasdair must have heard of it on his arrival in the Isles — if indeed he had not known of it before he left Ireland. But it was Huntly whom

Alasdair, by his most recent instructions from the king, was supposed to join. It has usually been assumed that on landing Alasdair had expected to be able to put himself under Montrose's command. But after Montrose's attempt to march into Scotland from England had been ignominiously defeated in April, Charles I had hastily sent a new royal commission to Alasdair, ordering him to march his forces to join Huntly. Events had rendered these new royal orders as obsolete as the original ones, but though Huntly too had been defeated, Alasdair probably calculated that if he marched into the strongly royalist areas of Aberdeenshire and Banffshire his presence might spark off a new royalist revolt, which Huntly (who unlike Montrose was at least in Scotland) could return from exile in Strathnaver to lead.

It seems however that Alasdair was discouraged by his reception in Lochaber and by the lack of any indication that eastern royalists would join him, for instead of continuing eastwards he turned north to Kintail, MacKenzie territory, to make further attempts to persuade Seaforth and MacDonald of Sleat declare for the king.[48] Here Alasdair remained for some days, resting his men in safety; the Campbells would not advance so far out of their own lands in pursuit until they had recaptured Mingary and Kinlochaline, and though local clans would not join him they would not risk attacking him either. Seaforth, it is true, began to gather men on hearing that Alasdair 'is comeing in upon my bounds and my neighboures in the West Isles' and announced that he intended to march west to 'obviat any pejude [prejudice] could enshew by ye Eirishe incursions',[49] but these preparations were defensive rather than aggressive; and there was the possibility that though ostensibly raising men to oppose the Irish, he might end up by joining them if he decided this was expedient. At first he refused Alasdair's men permission to pass through his lands; when this was ignored he saved face by offering them free passage and food.

From Glenelg on 13 August Alasdair wrote to the marquis of Ormond in Dublin — spelling his name 'Wormott', which suggests a surprising vagueness as to the name of so prominent an individual. The tone of the letter is optimistic. The king's service was going very well and 'the Lords and other of the gentry of these Iles intrusted, are very ready to spend ther time, dedicatting themselves wholly to advaunce his Highness service' provided they were sent arms and ammunition from time to time, as these were not easy to procure in the Highlands. Ormond was asked to send such supplies and letters of encouragement to Seaforth and the rest. As to his own activities, Alasdair related how he had marched forty miles through Argyll's lands, 'burning, pilliging, killing, and spoyling all the way'. He had taken and garrisoned two 'very great castles' and was now going to march against Argyll's forces. With this letter he sent one Mr. Alexander MacDonnell and Colonel O'Cahan to explain the situation further to Ormond.[50]

Clearly Alasdair was not telling the truth — or not the whole truth. Seaforth and others may have asserted their loyalty to the king in general terms, but they were refusing to fight for him; and Alasdair's position was much more perilous than he admitted. There were two possible explanations for this. There was a risk that the letter might fall into enemy hands on its hazardous journey to Dublin, and he had no wish for them to learn of his weaknesses; but the messengers who carried it may have been instructed to explain the true situation to Ormond verbally. Alternatively Alasdair may have calculated that if he painted too gloomy a picture he would be ordered to cut his losses and return to Ireland; or at least that if his expedition seemed to be failing there would be no chance of reinforcements and supplies being sent to him. In fact, however Alasdair presented his case he had little hope of immediate help from Ireland. Ormond himself was short of supplies, and the Irish had no intention of committing further resources to the Scottish venture until they saw whether anything useful to them was being achieved by it; the main interest they showed in Alasdair's fortunes in August 1644 was to grumble at his failure to send back promptly to Ireland the ships that had carried his men to Scotland.[51]

Within a few days of writing to Ormond, Alasdair marched from Kintail. Though a few of the MacDonalds of Clanranald may have joined him, it had become clear that there was no point in lingering in the north in the hope of finding allies. Indeed the longer he waited the more likely he was to come into conflict with Seaforth, for the Irish were camped on this land and were exacting food and quarters from his clansmen. Alasdair's march was probably through Glen Sheil and Glen Moriston to the Great Glen and thence to Kilcumin (modern Fort Augustus) at the south-west end of Loch Ness. On the march he was probably joined by a few of the MacDonalds of Glengarry and Keppoch, including (according to Father MacBreck) one Donald MacRanald 'called the Fair', a veteran soldier who had fought in Flanders and Germany and who now acted as Alasdair's guide until he joined Montrose. Fearing that Alasdair intended to march on Inverness, the covenanters sent forces up Stratherrick to block his advance or, if he chose instead to break into Badenoch over the Corrieyiarack Pass, to follow him. Alasdair chose the latter route, sending ahead of him the traditional summons for all men to rise in arms under threat of drastic punishment if they failed to do so. This was the fiery cross, 'ane fyrie cross of tymber, quhairof everie point of the cross wes scamit [scorched] and brynt with fyre, commanding all maner of man within that countrie to ryse and follow the Kingis livtennand, the Lord Marquis of Montrose, under the pane of fyre and suord'. One such fiery cross was sent to the covenanting committee of war for Moray, sitting at Auldearn, with a message from Alasdair. This may indicate that his intention at this point was to march through Badenoch to the coastal plain of Moray and thence east to the Gordon country to raise Huntly's followers. But first he sought support among Huntly's Highland vassals and followers in Badenoch, especially among the confederation of MacKintoshes, MacPhersons and Farquharsons which formed the Clan Chattan. Alasdair must have been becoming increasingly desperate by this time at his failure to find recruits for his army, and this desperation was marked by a change in policy. Previously as he passed through the countryside he had treated the people well (apart from Campbell supporters in Ardnamurchan); he 'did no wrong, bot [except] took their meit'. He needed food for his men but otherwise treated the people as potential allies and waited for them to join him voluntarily. Now in Badenoch the threat implicit in the fiery cross was carried out. He took 'the cheife men and heades of the countray' prisoner and forced them to provide him with 500 men. MacPherson of Cluny's son Ewen Og brought Alasdair 300 men, though whether these were part of the 500 exacted under pressure is not clear. MacDonald of Keppoch now brought his men to Alasdair voluntarily. Others resisted and suffered for it. The committee of estates later awarded 600 merks as compensation to one Dougal MacPherson, who is described as the first man to have suffered at the hands of the Irish for his loyalty to the covenanters, his house and goods having been burnt. This appears to have been Dougal MacPherson of Ballachroan,[52] for it is recorded that on 22 August Alasdair camped at Ballachroan (near Kingussie). From this base he spent several days laying waste the country, burning the crops in the fields; and he 'carried away the choice young men, and pressed them into his service'.

Alasdair now at last had a substantial number of Highlanders to fight for him, but his delay in Badenoch to recruit men had given the covenanters time to assemble large forces to prevent him marching up Strathspey into Moray. To men raised in Moray had been joined levies of covenanting clans — Frasers, Grants, Rosses and Monros. Seaforth, anxious to avoid persecution by the covenanters, had brought his own men south to aid them, as had the covenanting earl of Sutherland. Alasdair was not strong enough to attack this formidable gathering to the north and east. The Campbells had mobilised to the west. Only one way out seemed left: Alasdair was virtually forced to march south through Glengarry into Atholl.

Royalist sympathies were strong in Atholl, but as elsewhere the population was cowed and demoralised by the seeming invincibility of the covenanters and by the ignominious collapse of all attempts at royalist resistance. Moreover the most powerful clan of the area, the Stewarts, were hampered in acting by the fact that their chief, the earl of Atholl, was a child. And to the Highlanders of the east Alasdair's venture had very much the character of an alien invasion. Cultural, social and political ties with Gaelic Ireland were weak, and Lowland influence much stronger than in the Western Highlands and Isles. The Irish were seen as foreigners; and leading them was an obscure, landless man, who might have an impressive genealogy but who had little else to recommend him. Alasdair was already a hero in the west; to eastern Highlanders he was a little-known adventurer trying to make them commit themselves to a lost cause. The men of Atholl therefore gathered their forces to resist Alasdair's advance, fearing that if they did not do so they would suffer the sort of plundering and destruction he had carried out in Badenoch.

The garrison of Blair Castle fled, leaving it to fall into Alasdair's hands, but he then had to draw up his forces opposite those of the Atholl men and prepare for battle — a battle with potential allies whom he did not want to have to fight. Some Badenoch men passed between the two forces trying to arrange a peaceful settlement, while Alasdair, 'as he hath related often since' (according to Patrick Gordon), stood a little apart from his men with his senior officers, and 'in a deepe contemplation and profound silence, lifts up his eyes to heavin, and with a short mental prayer ... invocates the aid of his Diuine Majesty'. He had sought help from all points of the compass with little success. Now it seemed he might have to fight the men of Atholl; and he might then be trapped in Atholl by covenanting forces advancing from both north and south. But imminent conflict and disaster were now to be averted in a way which must have greatly strengthened Alasdair's confidence that God was on his side.[53]

NOTES

1. HMC 29: *Portland*, i.120-2; *RPCS, 1638-43,* 436, 442-4; Spalding, *Memorials*, ii.242-50.

2. Baillie, *Letters*, ii.74.

3. SRO, PA.11/1, Register of the Committee of Estates, 1643-4, ff.64-6; HMC 3: *4th Report*, 490; *APS*, VI.i.61; C. McNeill (ed), *The Tanner Letters* (IMC 1943), 166.

4. Ibid, 165-9. The printed text refers nonsensically to the 'Rntor' of Calder, but the original (Bodleian Library, Oxford, Tanner MSS, vol.62b, ff.439-43) clearly reads 'Tutor'.

5. *Muniments of the royal burgh of Irvine* (2 vols, Ayrshire and Galloway Archaeological Association, 1890-1), i.101-2.

6. Innes, *Thanes of Cawdor*, 302.

7. Carte, *Ormond*, iii.300.

8. Inveraray Castle, Argyll Transcripts, xii.134; *APS*, VI.i.93; Sir James Balfour, *Historical Works* (4 vols, Edinburgh 1824-5), iii.198-9.

9. Carte, *Ormond*, iii.337.

10. J. Lowe, 'The earl of Antrim and Irish aid to Montrose in 1644', *Irish Sword*, iv (1959-60), 191-8.

11. Hyde, *History of the rebellion*, iii.510-24.

12. Gilbert, *Ir confed*, iii.89-90; R. Scrope and T. Monkhouse (eds), *State papers collected by Edward, earl of Clarendon* (3 vols, Oxford 1767-86), ii.165. Why Antrim's offer of 3,000 men for Scotland was reduced to 2,000 is not known. There is no foundation for the allegation (frequently made by supporters of Montrose) that Antrim had promised to send 10,000 to Scotland but in the end sent only about 2,000. Mention of Sir James MacDonald in the king's instructions shows that it was well known many months before Antrim's men reached Scotland that Sir Donald Gorm was dead; some sources claim that they thought he was still alive and expected his support.

13. Carte, *Ormond*, iii.235.

14. A.M. Mackintosh, *The Mackintoshes and the Clan Chattan* (Edinburgh 1903), 230-1.

15. Hill, *Macdonnells of Antrim*, 266-7.

16. Gilbert, *Ir confed*, iii.113, 125, 157, 158, v.1; *Com Rin*, i.454-65; Carte, *Ormond*, iii.261, 262, 273.

17. Gilbert, *Contemp hist*, i.582; Carte, *Ormond*, iii.281.

18. Gilbert, *Contemp hist*, i.583; Carte, *Ormond*, iii.284.

19. Ibid, iii.281; Gilbert, *Contemp hist*, i.582.

20. Hyde, *History of the rebellion*, iii.310.

21. *An Teachdaire Gaelach* (2 vols, Glasgow 1830-1), ii.61-2, cited in J.A. MacLean, The sources, particularly the Celtic sources, for the history of the Highlands in the seventeenth century (University of Aberdeen Ph.D. thesis 1939), 362; E.J. Cowan, *Montrose. For Covenant and King* (London 1977), 154.

22. Carte, *Ormond*, iii.268-9.

23. *Com Rin*, i.457, 461.

24. Carte, *Ormond*, iii.300.

25. Ibid, iii.300.

26. Gilbert, *Contemp hist*, i.584-5.

27. Gilbert, *Ir confed*, v.224-6; Gordon, *Britane's Distemper*, 64-5.

28. Hill, *MacDonnells of Antrim*, 80; Carte, *Ormond*, iii.318-19, 328.

29. *Com Rin*, i.457.

30. C. O'Danachair, 'Montrose's Irish Regiments', *Irish Sword* iv (1959-60), 61-7.

31. Spalding, *Memorials*, ii.385; Baillie, *Letters*, ii.233.

32. *Com Rin*, i.460.

33. W.F. Leith (ed), *Memoirs of Scottish Catholics during the XVIIth and XVIIIth centuries* (2 vols, London 1909), i.299, 324.

34. Ibid, i.281.

35. A. Matheson, 'Traditions of Alasdair MacColla', *TGSG*, v (1958), 23.

36. Hill, *MacDonnells of Antrim*, 80.

37. *Com Rin*, i.457-8; Carte, *Ormond*, i.482, ii.337; H. Guthry, *Memoirs* (2nd ed, Glasgow 1748), 161; J.S. Reid, *History of the presbyterian church in Ireland*, ed W.D. Killen (3 vols, Belfast 1867), i.459-62, 464, 555-9; Leith, *Memoirs*, i.281-2. *Com Rin* (followed by Carte) gives the number of Scots ministers captured as about fifty! R. Black, 'Colla Ciotach', *TGSI* xlviii (1972-4), 226 states that Alasdair's brother Ranald was to follow him to Scotland with reinforcements; but the source he cites is the commission to Argyll of November 1643, which refers to Alasdair's earlier expedition to the Isles. Weir's papers are at NLS, Wodrow MSS, Quarto XXIX, ff.63-8.

38. Ibid, ff.63-63v; *APS*, vi.i.324.

39. NLS, Wodrow MSS, Quarto XXIX, f.64v; *Com Rin*, i.460; Hill, *MacDonnells of Antrim*, 81. The editors of *Com Rin* wrongly identify the 'Ila' of their text as Iona (see the index) instead of Islay; this confusion was evidently shared by the authors, for they call 'Ila' St Columba's island.

40. NLS, Wodrow MSS, Quarto XXIX, f.64v; *Com Rin*, i.460,461; Gordon, *Britane's distemper*, 65.

41. Ibid, 62-3.

42. W. Gordon, *History of the family of Gordon* (2 vols, Edinburgh 1726-7), ii.424. William Gordon made use in his work of continuations (now lost) of both Spalding, *Memorials* and J. Gordon, *History of Scots affairs* (3 vols, Spalding Club 1841), though he refers to the latter as 'Straloch' as he believed it to be the work of James Gordon's father, Robert Gordon of Straloch — see *Scots Affairs*, i,preface, pp. 39-43.

43. Leith, *Memoirs*, i.287-8.

44. Campbell, *Adventures in legend*, 216-18; Matheson, 'Traditions', *TGSG*, v.23. See J.L. Campbell (ed), *A collection of Highland rites and customs* (Cambridge 1975), 41.

45. N. Tranter, *The fortified house in Scotland*, v (Edinburgh and London 1970), 35-7.

46. NLS, Wodrow MSS, Quarto XXIX, ff.64v, 65; *Com Rin*, i.460-2; Gordon, *Britane's Distemper*, 65-6; Leith, *Memoirs*, i.288; Campbell, *Adventures in legend*, 218; *Rel Celt*, ii.177.

47. S.R. Gardiner, *History of the great civil war* (4 vols, London 1893-4), i.337; J.R. Powell and E.K. Timings (eds), *Documents relating to the civil war*, 1642-6 (Navy Records Society 1963), 135-6, 138, 141, quoting J. Vicars, *Magnalia Dei Anglicana, or England's parliamentary chronicle* (London 1646), part 3, God's Arke, 224; *Mercurius Aulicus* (Oxford 1644), week 18, pp.965-6, week 19, pp.973-4, week 20, pp.983-4.

48. For Alasdair's activities from his capture of Mingary to his arrival in Kintail see Gordon, *Britane's distemper*, 65-7; Spalding, *Memorials*, ii.386; Sir Robert Gordon and Gilbert Gordon of Sallagh, *A genealogical history of the earldom of Sutherland* (Edinburgh 1813), 519-20; NLS, Wodrow MSS. Quarto XXIX, ff.64v-65; Leith, *Memoirs*, i.287-9; *Rel Celt*, ii.177. According to W. Gordon, *History of the family of Gordon*, ii.424, James Gordon, minister of Rothiemay (in the now lost continuation of his *History of Scots affairs* — see note 42 above), recorded the king's commission ordering Alasdair to join Huntly; James Gordon stated that he had himself seen the commission in the possession of Charles, 1st earl of Aboyne (the 4th son of the marquis of Huntly whom Alasdair was supposed to join).

49. W. MacGill (ed), *Old Ross-shire and Scotland* (2 vols, Inverness 1910-11), i.221-2.

50. Gilbert, *Contemp hist*, i.795-6, from Bodleian Library, Carte MSS, 12, f.62.

51. Gilbert, *Ir confed*, iii.256, 257, 258-9.

52. SRO, PA.11/3, f.135v. For MacPherson see also PA.11/4, f.117v.

53. Gordon, *Britane's distemper*, 66-72; Leith, *Memoirs*, i.290-1; Gordon, *Genealogical history*, 520; *Rel Celt*, ii.117-9; G. Wishart, *Memoirs of James Marquis of Montrose*, ed A.D. Murdoch and H.F.M. Simpson (London 1893), 54-6; J.C. Lees, *A history of the county of Inverness* (Edinburgh and London 1898), 66; *RMS, 1634-51*, no.1085; [J. Cant], *Memorabilia of the city of Perth* (Perth 1806), 166; *A true relation of the happy success of his majesties forces in Scotland* . . . ([Oxford] 1644), 6.

5

Alasdair and Montrose: An Alliance Formed

ALASDAIR's prayer on a hillside in Atholl was answered in a way that must have seemed miraculous to him. A man in Highland dress appeared and announced that he was the marquis of Montrose.

In mid-August Montrose, despairing of getting any support in England for a new invasion of Scotland, had crossed the border in disguise with only two companions to see if he could organise a new, entirely Scottish, royalist rising, or join the forces Antrim had sent from Ireland. When he entered Scotland he must have known that Alasdair and his men had sailed from Ireland nearly two months before; and he must also have known of the king's revised instructions to Alasdair not to try to join Montrose (as he had been driven out of Scotland) but to seek out his despised rival Huntly. In 1639 Montrose (then a covenanting general) had lured the royalist Huntly into his hands with guarantees for his safety, but had then treacherously arrested him and sent him to Edinburgh as a prisoner. From this event dated a bitter hostility between the two men which Montrose's subsequent conversion to royalism failed to remove. Now, as if to rub salt in the wounds caused by his failure to be in arms in Scotland, Montrose knew that the men he had been relying on from Ireland were to be diverted to Huntly; all he was left with was the grand title of lieutenant general of Scotland and, as if as a consolation prize, promotion by the king (in May) from earl to marquis.

It is indeed tempting to speculate that it was news that Alasdair's men had been told to seek out Huntly that led Montrose to cross the border and hasten northwards, believing that any risk was worth taking to avoid the humiliation of his own efforts failing while Huntly benefited from Alasdair's expedition. To motives of pride in taking such an attitude Montrose could add more rational justification: Huntly had repeatedly proved himself half-hearted and incompetent as a leader of men, so any royalist forces put in his hands would almost certainly achieve little or nothing.

By one account Montrose had, while riding northwards, the good fortune to intercept a letter which Alasdair had sent to him (believing him to be still in England) asking for orders (Huntly no longer being in arms). It is even possible that Montrose then succeeded in getting a message to Alasdair telling him to march to Atholl to meet him. But it seems more likely that the meeting was not thus arranged in advance, for when Alasdair entered Atholl Montrose was hiding in Methven Wood (to the north-west of Perth); had he arranged a rendezvous with Alasdair he would surely have moved on to Atholl to await him there. That he remained near Perth suggests that he was not certain which way the Irish were advancing and had therefore chosen a strategic point from which he could easily move north, east or west according to what news he received of Alasdair's movements. While in Methven Wood Montrose, it is said, saw a man bearing a fiery cross; when questioned, the man revealed that he was carrying it to Perth to raise forces to resist invasion; Alasdair MacColla and a great army of Irish were in Atholl threatening to lay waste the country if the people did not rise in arms under his command. Montrose and his two followers at once set out northwards, and reached Alasdair the next day just as he was finishing his prayer for guidance.

This account of the meeting of the two men is that of Patrick Gordon, who claimed that this 'I haue been the more bold to insert, because it came from the mouthes of both the authores'. When Montrose made himself known, Alasdair 'was much rejoysed therewith, and reuerently randered thankes vnto God, acknawledgeing evin with astonishment His divine bountie, when he most feared the event, and knoweing not what course to haue takin'. His men were equally enthusiastic, greeting Montrose with a mighty shout, throwing their caps in the air and firing their muskets. This nearly turned triumph to disaster, for the Atholl men had no idea what was going on in Alasdair's camp and naturally took the shouting and gunfire as the start of an attack on them. But bloodshed was avoided by the revelation to them that Montrose had arrived. They too then saluted him, and about seven hundred agreed to serve under him.[1] According to a royalist pamphlet, the Atholl men 'shouted and call'd out with one voyce, they would have no more of King Campbelles Government; they would either loose their lives, or have King Stuart to his owne place againe'.[2] This sounds fanciful, but many of the Atholl men were themselves Stewarts, and they doubtless recalled that when in 1640 Argyll had plundered Atholl to enforce submission to the covenant, his clansmen had boasted that 'they were King Campbells men, no more King Stewartis'.[3]

It was this meeting, more than the landing of Alasdair in Scotland, that deserved marking by portents and omens. Up to this point it had seemed likely that Alasdair would soon be defeated or driven from Scotland in spite of the success of his long march through the Highlands. Having failed to gain significant Highland support, he seemed to have little hope of successfully resisting the covenanting armies being gathered to move against him. Montrose too had been faced by ignominious failure, having failed to invade Scotland from England or to start a Scottish rising. The meeting in Atholl thus saved both men; and the way the meeting took place could not have been bettered dramatically had it been carefully planned and rehearsed.

Alasdair gave Montrose a formidable body of battle-hardened fighting men. The Irish and MacDonnells/MacDonalds who formed the great majority of his army might lack the finer points of formal military discipline and training, but they made up for this by love of, and skill in, fighting, by their zeal for the causes they fought for (for Ireland, for the Clan Donald, for Catholicism, and last and least, for the king), and by their ability to thrive in the harsh conditions of the Highlands. In return for all this, Montrose gave Alasdair and the Irish something they desperately needed — a veneer of respectability in the eyes of royalists (or at least in the eyes of those royalists willing to forgive Montrose his covenanting past). They now had at their head an eminent Scottish nobleman who held the king's commission as lieutenant general of Scotland. The character of the war they were fighting thus changed; it ceased to be so clearly as before a case of foreign invasion (though to many it remained that) and became at least for some essentially a Scottish royalist rising. And as Montrose was a protestant it could be denied that it was purely a Catholic venture which no protestant could in conscience join. Part of the importance of these changes lay in the fact that many royalists were to join 'Montrose's rising' who would never have joined the 'Irish invasion'. But it was even more significant perhaps that a much larger number of potential royalists who would have happily co-operated with the covenanters in crushing a foreign Catholic invasion now refused co-operation or gave it only half-heartedly since they did not wish to oppose the king's own representative. They would not, through fear of the consequences or through dislike of Montrose's covenanting past, fight for him; but they did their best to remain neutral or undertook passive resistance to the covenanting regime, thus gravely weakening its preparations for war.

The final gifts of the two men, Alasdair and Montrose, to each other were their gifts as military leaders. Both proved to be inspiring leaders of men. Both knew that they were engaged in a venture in which playing safe would almost certainly lead to defeat. Success depended on willingness to take great risks, though calculated ones, to fight unconventional campaigns to make up for their lack of numbers. They had to keep constantly on the move so as to retain the initiative, striking when they were ready, avoiding battle when they were not. To both Montrose and Alasdair expertise in this type of warfare seemed to come naturally. Yet from the start the seeds of the later quarrels between the two men were germinating. Montrose's leadership greatly widened the appeal and the significance of Alasdair's invasion, but such a widening also inevitably introduced diversity of ambition — or rather greatly increased a diversity already present.

Alasdair and his Highland allies fought primarily an anti-Campbell war, a Gaelic civil war which involved war on the covenanters as they were the Campbells' allies. The Irish had been sent to Scotland in the hope that they would force the covenanters to withdraw their army from Ireland, but they had strong sympathies with the ambitions of the Clan Donald and other enemies of the Campbells. In addition the Irish and most of the Highlanders who joined them shared religious motivation, seeing themselves as Catholic crusaders. But though to Montrose, a protestant fighting for a protestant king, Catholic allies were welcome, ultimately Catholicism was as unacceptable to him as covenanting presbyterianism. Moreover his first loyalty was to the king. His vision was of conquering all Scotland, establishing a royalist regime, and then leading an army into England to win the civil war there for the king. To neither Irish nor MacDonalds, on the other hand, would such an outcome be entirely satisfactory. The Stewart monarchy had only shown itself willing to make concessions to Catholic Gaels in Scotland and Ireland when it was under attack and needed their support. Would not the recent royal sympathy for both Irishman and Highlander evaporate overnight if the king was completely victorious in Britain as a whole and was restored to all his former powers — and indeed probably through victory more absolute than ever before? The Irish would at least go so far as to welcome Montrose's attempts to spread the war throughout Scotland; a Highland campaign alone would be unlikely to force the covenanters to remove their army from Ireland. But for Alasdair and many of his Highlanders even campaigning in the southern Lowlands was a distraction from the real war, the war against the Campbells.

At first, however, these potential tensions were submerged by general relief and rejoicing that Irish and royalists had come together at last, and by the knowledge that swift action was needed to avoid encirclement by the covenanters. Only in victory could the luxury of internal division be indulged in.

News of Alasdair MacColla's arrival from Ireland had reached the Scottish parliament in Edinburgh on 9 July 1644 in two letters. Hector MacNeill of Taynish (in Knapdale, to the north of Kintyre) had written to James Campbell of Ardkinglas on 4 July to report (erroneously) that some Dunkirk ships had arrived in the Isles. Dunkirk privateers, often acting in co-operation with the Irish confederates, were a frequent hazard to Scottish and English shipping, and Alasdair's ships, perhaps because they included two Flemish ships, had been wrongly identified as such raiders. The following day Sir Archibald Campbell, the captain of Dunstaffnage Castle, the great Campbell stronghold at the mouth of Loch Etive, got rather nearer the truth when he wrote to Argyll that four ships and a pinnace had come to the Isles and landed 200 of the Clanranald commanded by Antrim's brother. As often happened, Alasdair MacColla under a variant of his name, Alexander MacDonnell, is here confused with Antrim's brother of that name.

Garbled as these reports were, parliament took immediate action; Antrim's efforts to raise men to invade the Highlands were well known. Argyll's commission as king's lieutenant to act against Alasdair's previous incursion had only just expired, on 1 July, and it was now renewed; as before, Argyll himself was not to lead forces against the rebels, this task being deputed to Ardkinglas, who was to raise 500 men.[4] In addition three ships were ordered to sail for the Isles to attack rebel shipping. Two were vessels of the English parliamentary navy, the *Eighth Whelp* under Captain John Carse or Kerse and the *Globe* under Captain Richard Willoughby; they had recently brought arrears of the pay of the Scottish army in Ireland to Scotland, and had evidently remained as part of the guard the English parliament was supposed to provide on the Scottish coast. The third ship, the *Hopeful*, was a privately owned ship commanded by Captain James Jackson, who had hired it to the covenanters.[5] Surprisingly, for all the great armies they raised, they never attempted to establish a navy of their own.

In the days that followed, further reports made it clear that the invasion of the Isles was on a much larger scale than had been realised; the tendency was now for the size of the rebel force to be exaggerated. On 12 July the Scottish parliament was told that fifteen ships had landed 3,000 men under Antrim's brother and a son of Coll Ciotach. Three days later the number of rebel ships reported had dropped to nine; but the number of men had risen to nearly 4,000.[6] As a result of these new reports parliament on 16 July granted Argyll a fresh commission as king's lieutenant, giving him wider powers than before.[7]. But even now the covenanters expected no major civil war in Scotland. The easy defeat of earlier attempts at royalist risings had led to over-confidence. God had brought them victory after victory in Scotland, England and Ireland for seven years, demonstrating clearly that they had His favour. Surely He would not let 'them be troubled by so despicable an enemy as idolatrous Catholics and barbarous Gaels under that 'bloodthirsty monster' Alasdair MacColla?[8] Even once Alasdair and Montrose met the full danger was not seen. Robert Baillie remarked that to Montrose Alasdair was 'the smallest string in his bow, and a designe he least trusted in' — all his more important plots had failed. What was to be feared from 'some fifteen hundred naked Scots Irishes' hopping from island to island?[9] A more sympathetic observer, Gerolamo Agostini, the Venetian secretary in England, similarly believed Alasdair had no hope of success, lamenting to the doge and senate the defeat which would inevitably befall those 'poor folk' who had 'been so ill advised as to invade Scotland'.[10] The myth of the invincibility of the Scottish armies of the day was still powerful.

Argyll quickly got down to the work of trying to prove that this was no myth. By 22 July he had gathered 2,600 men at Dunstaffnage, divided into three regiments. This force proceeded to campaign in the Isles, Ardnamurchan, Morvern, Lochaber and surrounding areas until 2 September,[11] but apart from terrifying the countryside into submission it achieved little, for it found few enemies to engage. As the Campbell army advanced, Alasdair marched from Mingary (29 July), beginning the wanderings that were eventually to lead him into Atholl. Instead of pursuing him immediately the Campbells decided to concentrate first on regaining their castles of Mingary and Kinlochaline, so as to deprive the rebels of their bases.

On 3 August they drove off the plundered cattle Alasdair's men had gathered at Mingary. Four days later Argyll himself appeared, with five ships and many boats, and on 8 August he formally summoned the castle to surrender within twenty-four hours; if it failed to do so, then (as was common practice) the garrison could expect no quarter when it was stormed. When Alasdair's men remained defiant, pressure was exerted to persuade them to change their minds. The remaining Dutch ship and Captain Turner's ship (probably the *Jacob* of Ross) were attacked and captured; and on 14 August Mr Dougal Campbell was sent in to convey depressing news to the garrison. On 2 July a combined English and Scottish army had inflicted a crushing defeat on a royal army at Marston Moor, near York, and in Ireland Major General Robert Monro was leading the Scottish army there on a major offensive, penetrating deep into Leinster. But when this bad news failed to undermine the garrison's resolution, the Campbells began preparations for a long siege — they lacked the heavy guns and other equipment necessary for an immediate assault. Argyll himself soon departed. As chief of the Campbells his place might be at Mingary, but as the leading figure in the covenanting regime in Scotland he was badly needed in the south for consultation on the political and military situations in all three kingdoms. Moreover he probably knew by this time that Alasdair MacColla, after retreating on his approach to Mingary, was now daringly marching into Badenoch; Argyll was needed to co-ordinate action against him.

Argyll left Mingary on 20 August, handing over direction of the siege to Sir Donald Campbell of Ardnamurchan. Before he left he tried to encourage the covenanting prisoners in the castle by sending in to them linen, blankets, oatmeal and aquavite (brandy or whisky), and promising that Sir Donald would provide them with other necessities. Finally, he promised that when he returned 'he wold deliver Colkittoch and his sones'. He had decided to end the sufferings of the prisoners in Mingary by an exchange of prisoners.[12] But Argyll did not return, and the siege dragged on week after week without Sir Donald being reinforced or making an assault. Cut off from the outside world, reliant for news on whatever Sir Donald chose to tell them, the garrison and its prisoners did not know how Alasdair was faring. But as time passed and nothing happened the suspicion must have grown that all was not going well for the Campbells and the covenanters.

Once Argyll had been entrusted with defeating the rebels, the committee of estates in Edinburgh gave little further thought to Alasdair and his men. The fighting in England and Ireland was of much greater importance than obscure scuffles in a remote corner of the Highlands. But news that Alasdair and his men had advanced into Atholl and that Montrose had put himself at their head put a rather different complexion on the matter. Montrose might be hated as a traitor who had deserted the covenanters, but his daring and resolution were acknowledged and the rebels were now approaching the heart of the kingdom, while most of Argyll's forces were still in north-west Argyllshire and he himself had not yet returned to the Lowlands. On 28 August therefore the committee of estates began to assemble a new force to oppose the rebels. The Earl of Lothian was to march his men to Perth with all diligence, and Lord Burleigh's regiment was to march there from Fife. All fencible men (able-bodied men aged between sixteen and sixty) in Perthshire were to be levied. Next day orders were given for the establishment of a magazine of food at Perth, and a letter to Argyll informed him that all the forces of Angus, Perth, Stirling and Fife were gathering to pursue the Irish rebels; Lothian would command them until Argyll returned to take over. The hopeful assumption was that Lothian would drive the rebels north through Atholl into the hands of Argyll's men. Yet on 31 August the committee began to take precautions to protect Stirling, indicating a growing realisation that the rebels might advance rather than retreat.[13] These moves came just in time to save Stirling. But it was already too late to save Perth.

Knowing that forces were being assembled in Perth against him, Montrose marched quickly on the burgh to catch his enemies before their preparations were complete. From Atholl, where he had won the support of the Stewarts and the Robertsons (the latter led by Donald Robertson, tutor of Struan), Montrose marched to Aberfeldy, hoping to raise the Menzies; but old Sir Alexander Menzies of Weem refused to join the royalist Montrose — just as a few years before he had refused to join the covenanting Montrose. He is said to have maltreated a trumpeter sent to negotiate with him and then to have harassed the rearguard of Montrose's army as it marched through his lands. For this and his failure to rise for the king, Montrose ordered that his lands be laid waste and his crops burnt so 'that on the very threshold of the war he might terrify others'. Like Alasdair, Montrose had concluded that force was necessary to persuade men to fight for the king.[14]

The obvious route for an advance on Perth was down Strathtay, approaching the city from the north, but Montrose chose instead to lead his men south through Glen Cochill and the Sma' Glen, and then attack Perth from the west, perhaps hoping by this unusual approach to throw his enemies off balance. Purely by chance (or so it is said) this route brought him an unexpected bonus. Montrose's army intercepted a force of about 500 newly levied Highlanders commanded by Lord Kilpont, Sir John Drummond and the master of Maderty (the sons of the earls of Airth and Perth, and of Lord Maderty respectively). They were taking their men to join the covenanters in Perth as the regime had ordered, but all three were men with royalist sympathies. Lord Kilpont was a Graham, a kinsman of Montrose, and the master of Maderty was Montrose's brother-in-law. They had been prepared to serve the covenanters half-heartedly to avoid persecution, but now they found themselves facing annihilation by a greatly superior royalist force. Not surprisingly they decided to change sides and join Montrose. This is, as it were, the authorised royalist version of events; but there remains a strong suspicion that Montrose's new allies had been in touch with him in secret, and had cunningly contrived to have a free hand in raising men by pretending that they were recruiting for the covenanters. This may be the real reason for the route Montrose had chosen, to make rendezvous with his secret friends easy.

On the morning of 1 September 1644 Montrose resumed his march towards Perth. At Tippermuir or Tibbermore, a few miles west of the city, the covenanters hastily assembled their levies to bar his passage. As Montrose had calculated, the speed of his advance had taken the covenanters by surprise. Lothian had been supposed to command them in the absence of Argyll; but Lothian was in Edinburgh attending meetings of the committee of estates.[15] Lord Elcho therefore had the command thrust upon him. His army seemed, in numbers at least, adequate for the task committed to it: he had five or six thousand men, roughly twice as many as Montrose — though precision is impossible as figures of the numbers engaged, and of casualties incurred, in Montrose's battles differ greatly from source to source. The covenanters may also have been better armed than the rebels. Royalist sources may exaggerate in claiming the whole rebel army had only one barrel of gunpowder, but arms and ammunition were short enough for some of Montrose's men to be reduced to throwing stones at one point in the battle. But the deficiencies of the rebel army were greatly outweighed by two assets: high morale and skill in battle. As Gaels and (mainly) Catholics, the Irish and Highlanders of Montrose's army were determined on revenge on the presbyterian Lowlanders for past injuries. The Irish, the core of the army, were veteran soldiers, their Highland allies men brought up to regard skill in battle as an essential part of manhood. By contrast, the covenanters opposing them were hastily levied Lowland peasants and burghers, untrained and poorly led. The hundreds of professional mercenary officers, trained in the Thirty Years War, who formed the backbone of the covenanters' armies were nearly all already fighting in the Scottish armies in England and Ireland. The parishes of the Lowlands had already sent out to these armies all who felt any real zeal for fighting for the covenants. Thus many of those now rounded up to face Montrose would never have made first-rate soldiers; lacking competent officers and any training, they provided an ideal enemy for Montrose to test his men against.

Nonetheless, it took considerable daring on Montrose's part to attack an army so much larger than his own, and he could not have known quite how contemptible an enemy Lord Elcho's men were to prove. But he needed a quick victory to establish his credibility as a royalist leader and to hold together and gain recruits for his little army. Though the odds were against him, the longer he delayed the worse they would become, as more covenanting levies converged on Perth.

Conventional military practice, in drawing up an army for battle, placed infantry in the centre and cavalry on the wings. But Montrose lacked cavalry (apart from a few individual horsemen), and the most reliable troops he had, the Irish, lacked the long pikes regarded as essential if footmen were to defend themselves against cavalry; their weapons were musket, sword and dirk. He therefore placed the Irish in the centre of his line of battle, to oppose the covenanters' infantry, with the Highlanders from Atholl and Badenoch on the right wing, and Lord Kilpont's Highlanders on the left wing; both formations of Highlanders included many bowmen who (as bows had a much higher rate of fire than muskets) it was hoped could provide fairly successful protection against cavalry. For fear that the numerically superior enemy would outflank him, Montrose extended his wings as widely as possible by drawing up the Highlanders only three deep.

In this order the rebels advanced against the covenanters, led by Montrose and Alasdair; they 'marched with Pikes upon the head of the Battaile' by one account. Montrose commanded the right wing, Alasdair, it seems, the centre. Such an arrangement was unusual; if the general commanding a whole army took special responsibility for any particular part of the line, then he would normally command the centre. But in this case Montrose may have calculated that it was the Highlanders on the right wing who most needed his presence to steady them in battle; the left wing and the centre had their own trusted commanders, Lord Kilpont and Alasdair, to lead them. Moreover, from what followed it is clear that it had been decided in advance that Alasdair and the Irish should fight in their accustomed manner, a manner which must have been alien to Montrose. Instead of firing successive volleys of musket fire while steadily advancing on the enemy (or letting the enemy advance on them) until the two sides were close enough to come to 'push of pike' (hand-to-hand fighting with pikes), the Irish would fire one musket volley and then charge immediately to engage in hand-to-hand fighting with sword and dirk. To some extent this type of attack may have been, in this instance, forced on the Irish by their lack of pikes and gunpowder.

Credit for adopting this form of attack is often attributed to Montrose. While clearly he must be credited, as commander of the rebel army, with flexibility of mind sufficient for him to agree to the tactics of the Irish, it may be doubted whether he actually proposed them, or would have accepted them unless virtually forced to do so by the preferences of Alasdair and the Irish and by the lack of powder and pikes. Montrose doubtless had some knowledge of the qualities of Highland fighting men, but he had had no opportunity to see or hear of what was to become regarded as the typical wild Highland charge against a Lowland army. This was the first time for more than two centuries that Gael and Lowlander had faced each other in large-scale pitched battle. And while we have no evidence of Montrose's previous knowledge of this tactic, Alasdair had used it in Ireland at the battle of the Laney in February 1642. Montrose's centre at Tippermuir was to employ Alasdair's tactics; Montrose had the good judgement to let him and the Irish have their own way, and to see that as this was the case it was best to leave the command of the centre to Alasdair.

The battle commenced when the two armies were within musket shot of each other. The covenanters took the iniative by sending out a 'forlorn of horse', a small body of cavalry intended to draw the enemy's fire and perhaps to tempt some of them to break ranks in pursuit when the forlorn withdrew, thus giving the covenanters a chance to attack while the rebels were restoring order in their ranks and going through the elaborate process of reloading their muskets. But in this instance the forlorn provoked the enemy not just into skirmishing but into launching its main attack. The Irish fired their one volley and charged, determined to deny the covenanters the advantage of their superior firepower (they had a few small cannons as well as superiority in muskets) by coming to hand-to-hand conflict as soon as possible. What followed was not so much a battle as a rout. The lines of covenanting infantry began to collapse before the Irish, with the Highlanders on their wings, had even reached them, unnerved by the ferocity of the unexpected charge. Soon panic flight overtook almost the whole of the covenanting army.

The casualties it suffered on the battlefield were few, and were mainly incurred by the cavalry opposite Montrose's right wing who fought bravely before being overwhelmed. But many hundreds, perhaps well over a thousand, died in the pursuit that followed. Montrose tried to limit the pursuit and slaughter, probably both through dislike of such needless carnage and through fear that it might prove impossible to re-assemble his irregular, unpaid army once it had dispersed widely in undisciplined killing and plundering. But his efforts were largely unsuccessful, though the fact that the pursuit was not continued into Perth itself may have been his responsibility. His victorious men killed all the defeated enemies they could catch up with, the Irish trained in the terrible wars of their own country being particularly merciless. One Irish officer boasted that after the battle it was possible to walk the three miles from the battlefield to Perth without once touching the ground, treading on corpses the whole way. While obviously not literally true, the boast graphically conjures up a picture of the miles of fields outside Perth strewn with bodies on that sunny Sunday morning in the autumn of 1644.[16]

Either on the evening of the battle or the following morning — accounts vary —

Montrose demanded the surrender of Perth. This the provost, Robert Arnot, agreed to, as there were no forces in the burgh to resist and he wished to prevent bloodshed. The burgh's ministers later explained that there had been no hope of holding out, panic was spreading, and all dreaded that the town would be sacked. 'The hounds of hell were drawn up before our ports newly deeply bathed in blood' and demanding more with 'hideous cries'. Montrose granted generous terms, promising that their would be no plundering, no forcible enlistment of men into his army, and 'That no Irishes should get entry or passage through [the] town'; even Highlanders were regarded as civilised compared to the hated Irish. In granting these terms Montrose was trying to win support by showing mercy and moderation after the slaughter at Tippermuir. But though Perth itself was saved, 'the haill suburbis, for the most part' were plundered, and ammunition and cloth in the burgh were seized for the use of the rebels. Their other necessities were supplied in plenty by the dead covenanters — clothes, arms and ammunition in abundance; many of the corpses were left stripped naked.

Alasdair MacColla himself benefited financially from the battle; on Montrose's orders the burgh magistrates supplied £50 sterling for his use. Though his Irishmen were excluded, Alasdair entered the burgh along with Montrose. It was from the evidence of Perth citizens that the covenanters found out that Montrose was lieutenant general of the rebels, Alasdair being major general, though one ambiguity remained and was never cleared up. Montrose was lieutenant general of all Scotland, but Alasdair had been appointed by Antrim, who was only general of the Highlands and Isles; so was Alasdair's authority similarly limited geographically? Or was he just major general of the Irish? However, interesting as such points might be in theory, they mattered little in practice.[17]

Montrose stayed several days in Perth, resting his men and trying to recruit for his army; but though a handful of prominent individuals joined him there was no sign of popular support. He could not afford to wait long in Perth, for the covenanters were gathering a new army to advance against him. On 2 September eleven Lowland shires were ordered to raise all fencible men and march them to Stirling, and regiments of the Scottish army in England were summoned home to help deal with the rebels.[18] By 4 September Argyll had reached Stirling and taken over command, issuing orders to hasten military preparations and commence action against those who had shown support for the rebels. The cattle and other livestock of James Stewart of Ardvorlich, who had joined Montrose with Lord Kilpont, were ordered to be plundered, though Argyll showed himself against indiscriminate destruction and plundering. He ordered John Campbell younger of Glenorchy to punish by death any of his men found guilty of robbery, plundering or other disorders; robbing or destroying houses 'are thingis you kno I hate'.[19]

The covenanters believed that Montrose would be most likely to try to advance south by way of Stirling. But, daring as he was, he knew he could not face the full strength of his enemies. He therefore marched eastwards towards Dundee. Soon after he left Perth there took place the murder of one of his leading supporters, Lord Kilpont, by James Stewart of Ardvorlich. Patrick Gordon wrongly describes the murder as taking place in Perth; Lord Kilpont was walking by the river, and had a long talk with Stewart. He was heard to say that he would not meddle 'in that busines', whereupon Stewart drew a dagger, stabbed his friend through the heart, and fled to join the covenanters. Gordon assumed that Stewart, tempted by the covenanters' offer of a reward for Montrose dead or alive, had suggested that Kilpont join him in murdering Montrose. On his refusal Stewart killed him to avoid his treachery being exposed and fled. George Wishart's account is essentially similar, but he places the murder at Coupar Angus. Montrose had camped there and during the night Stewart (perhaps bribed by the covenanters) took Kilpont aside and suggested killing Montrose. When he objected, Stewart killed him and made good his escape after killing a guard. Henry Guthry offers a third site for the crime, Collace, a few miles north-east of Perth, where Montrose first camped after marching from the burgh. In this version of the story Stewart suggested killing both Montrose and Alasdair MacColla in order to win pardons for themselves from the covenanters. Stewart's own account is incorporated in the pardon he eventually received from the covenanters. This confirms Guthry in fixing Collace as the scene, and claims (with no mention of murdering Montrose or Alasdair) that Stewart had tried to persuade Kilpont to return to serving the covenanters; on Kilpont's refusal Stewart stabbed him to avoid betrayal and fled along with his son and four other relatives and followers, killing two Irish guards.[20]

From this confusion of stories some points can be settled with confidence. The murder took place at Collace. There had hardly been time for Stewart, after joining Montrose, to be bribed into killing him. Nor can he have plotted to kill him to obtain the price put on his head by the covenanters, as they did not offer this reward until later. The murder must have taken place a day or two before 8 September, when Stewart approached the covenanters seeking permission to see Argyll; it was not until 12 September that £20,000 Scots was offered for Montrose dead or alive as he had 'now joyned with ane Band of Irish Rebels, and Masse-Priests, who have thir two years by-gane, bathed themselves in the bloud of God's People in Ireland', and the same price was not put on Alasdair until 17 September, he having committed many murders in Ireland and now come to Scotland to continue to rob and murder.[21] More plausible than these royalist accounts is Stewart's own explanation of his actions, that he had simply tried to persuade Kilpont to desert to the covenanters. It would be surprising indeed if among Kilpont's men there were not some very reluctant royalists, since they had originally left home to fight for the covenanters, and Stewart might well have been in such a position. If so, it is probable that he would be bitterly resentful of having been virtually hijacked by Kilpont to serve Montrose — especially when he heard that Argyll had ordered the plundering of his estates. Yet it could also be argued that, though plausible, Stewart's story is suspect as it was told to earn himself a pardon and its account of his motives is ideally suited to doing this; he claimed to have been at heart a covenanter all along, and that he had tried to persuade Kilpont to change sides.

A rather different explanation is provided by a tradition which survived in Stewart's family until recorded by Sir Walter Scott. This version of events places

Alasdair MacColla at the centre of the affair. The Irish under Alasdair had committed some excesses while passing through Ardvorlich's estates to the south of Loch Earn; the tradition says that this was while they were marching from the west coast, which is clearly wrong, but it is quite possible that (either before or after Tippermuir) Alasdair had been sent up Strath Earn to ravage the lands of enemies and recruit men for Montrose, and by accident had plundered on Stewart's lands. Stewart demanded compensation for the damage from Montrose, but got no satisfaction. He then challenged Alasdair to a duel, but Montrose heard of this and parted the two men, insisting on a reconciliation. The antagonists shook hands, but Stewart 'took such a hold of Macdonald's hand as to make the blood start from his fingers'. He was still not satisfied, however, and at Collace furiously rebuked his friend Lord Kilpont for not supporting him against Alasdair and Montrose. Their argument culminated in a fight in which Kilpont was killed.[22]

The truth will never be known for certain, and it would be rash to give a tradition recorded in the early nineteenth century credence while rejecting seventeenth century written accounts. But it is notable that the latter all have obvious biases; royalists put Stewart's action in as bad a light as possible, the covenanters present his motives as idealistic. By contrast the tradition in his own family, which might have been expected to try to whitewash him, does not do so. It depicts Stewart as violent, hot-tempered, murdering a friend in a quarrel, prepared to desert the royalist cause not out of conviction but from a private grievance. The tradition cannot therefore be dismissed lightly. It may well provide the true explanation of a murder that contemporaries found both sensational and mysterious.

On leaving Perth Montrose made for Dundee. He camped near the city on 6 September and summoned it to surrender; but on its refusal he marched off northwards, not thinking his forces strong enough to attempt to storm it.[23] As Huntly's recent rising had indicated, royalist sentiments were still strong in parts of the north-east Lowlands, though they lacked competent leadership. But before Montrose could try to recruit his army there in safety he needed to deal with the covenanting forces based on Aberdeen, where a committee of estates was sitting supervising the imposition of the covenanters' authority in the area. In spite of Tippermuir, Montrose had far fewer men than he had had before that battle. Success had failed to bring him many recruits. Most of the Atholl men had returned home laden with loot after the victory, demonstrating that narrow clan loyalty and interest could prevail over national issues as easily in the East Highlands as in the West. Further, the death of Lord Kilpont had not just deprived Montrose of a promising officer; his men had insisted on returning home with his corpse to bury him.

In all Montrose had something of the order of 1,500 men as he approached Aberdeen, the covenanters in the burgh 2,500. But, as at Tippermuir, the covenanters were deficient in generalship. Lord Burleigh commanded their army simply because he was president of the committee of estates sitting in Aberdeen. His basic error was over-confidence. He decided not to remain within the burgh to defend it from assault but to draw up his army outside it (though still in a strong position) in the hope of tempting Montrose into attacking him so the royalists could be defeated in open battle. It is true that Aberdeen lacked formal defences, but Montrose, approaching along the north bank of the River Dee, would have found the burgh guarded by strong natural defences — the tidal mouth of the Dee on the south, the steep little valley of the Den Burn and the burgh loch on the west. To have marched round to attack from the north or east would have solved the problem of natural obstacles, but he would then have had to try to force an entry through the few gates or ports of the town, narrow and easily defensible. Montrose might well have hesitated in these circumstances, and then as at Dundee resolved not to risk his little army in attacking prepared town defences. But Burleigh obligingly drew up his forces outside the burgh to the west of the Den Burn, barring the Hardgate (the main route into Aberdeen from the west) at the top of a steep slope near the Justice Mills.

The men Burleigh commanded were mainly local levies raised by the leading covenanting families of Aberdeenshire — Forbeses, Frasers and Crichtons. While perhaps more warlike than the levies routed at Tippermuir, they still left much to be desired; it was said some of the Forbes horsemen took no part in the battle, not out of cowardice but simply because they did not know what to do! Moreover, the leaders of the local covenanters had greatly reduced the size of the covenanting army by refusing to fight alongside Huntly's eldest son Lord Gordon, who at this point was prepared to fight for the covenanters and had raised many of the Gordons in arms. Gordon had therefore been ordered not to march to Aberdeen and his forces eventually dispersed. To levies from the surrounding countryside were added citizens of Aberdeen; as royalism was strong in the burgh, many of them were reluctant to oppose the king's lieutenant general. Finally, there were some of the soldiers the covenanters had marched north against Huntly and had then stationed in the burgh as a garrison, and some remnants of the levies which had fought at Tippermuir. One suspects that the presence of these latter was hardly an asset. Their nerve had been shattered less than two weeks before, and they doubtless attempted to justify their flight by emphasising how irresistible the terrible onslaught of the Irish had been, thus spreading fear among their comrades.

The two armies drew themselves up facing each other in the usual way, with infantry concentrated in the centre and cavalry on the wings — though even now Montrose had fewer than a hundred horsemen and therefore had to strengthen his wings with infantry. Montrose sent a drummer boy with a summons demanding the surrender of the burgh in the king's name. If this was refused, then an opportunity would be given for old men, women and children to leave, but those who remained behind would be given no quarter if Montrose took the burgh.[24] Such terms were common in the warfare of the day, and it may be that Montrose's ultimata to Perth and Dundee had been similar in form, though details have not survived in these instances, and as Perth surrendered and Dundee was not captured there had been no opportunity for him to demonstrate how he intended to treat a city which defied him. It was bitterly ironic that it was to be Aberdeen, the largest centre of royalism in the country, which was first to discover his ruthlessness.

The covenanters rejected the summons to surrender, and as the drummer boy was carrying back their defiant message he was killed by a shot from the ranks of the covenanters; anger at this doubtless heightened the resolve of Montrose and his men to show no mercy that day. There is some confusion as to the details of the battle of Aberdeen, but the essentials are fairly clear. The engagement started when some of the covenanting cavalry indulged in the old-fashioned and increasingly discredited formal manoeuvre known as the caracole, whereby cavalry rode towards the enemy lines then wheeled away as they fired their pistols or carbines, retiring to reload without having made any attempt to break the enemy lines. This attack was totally ineffectual, and it was perhaps exasperation at this that led Sir William Forbes of Craigievar to give a demonstration of the cavalry tactic that was (largely through the influence of Gustavus Adolphus) fast replacing the caracole even in militarily backward Britain — the charge driven home with determination, aimed at crashing through and breaking the enemy lines. The demonstration proved disastrous, for when Forbes charged with his troop of horse, the rest of the covenanting cavalry failed to follow his example, either through ignorance of what he was trying to do, refusal to experiment with such new-fangled tactics, or because Forbes had hot-headedly charged without orders. Nonetheless Forbes' charge might have been successful if he had directed it against some of Montrose's Scottish soldiers, men relatively poorly disciplined and trained. But instead Forbes aimed for the centre of the enemy lines, where most of the Irish musketeers were stationed. Their response to the charge was a remarkable demonstration both of their discipline and of Alasdair MacColla's leadership and control over his men in battle. At Alasdair's command the Irish, 'being so well trained men as the world could afford no better' according to Patrick Gordon, opened their ranks and let Forbes charge deep into their formation. Had he been seconded by the rest of the covenanters' cavalry such a dangerous manoeuvre, the deliberate breaking of their lines, could not have been risked even by the Irish. As it was, once Forbes' troop had passed through the front line the Irish closed ranks behind it and the troop found itself surrounded, with fire being poured on it from all sides. Few if any of the troopers made their way back to their own army; Forbes himself was pulled from his horse and captured.

Meanwhile a general engagement between the two armies had begun. Montrose's right wing was twice charged by Lords Fraser and Crichton with infantry, but the cavalry failed to support the attacks and they were driven off. On Montrose's left wing the fighting was fiercer. A hundred Irish musketeers under Captain John Mortimer supported some of the few royalist horsemen and by their skill and discipline beat off a determined attack, but they were unable to advance to defeat an attempt by the covenanters at an outflanking movement until reinforced by a further hundred musketeers.

Hard fighting also took place in the centre, where the Irish charged after Montrose ordered 'Major Lachlan, an Irish Officer, to lay aside their Muskets and Pikes, and fall on with Sword and Durk', which they did, led by Montrose and Alasdair MacColla; 'Lachlan' was of course Sergeant Major Thomas Laghtnan who in practice commanded Antrim's brother's regiment. Thus as at Tippermuir the Irish attacked in their traditional manner, but they met much stiffer resistance than in the earlier battle. Fighting continued on the field for perhaps two hours, but then the covenanters broke and ran. Most of the cavalry made good their escape; the infantry were not so fortunate. Most fled back towards Aberdeen with the Irish in hot pursuit, and were cut down by the hundred. 'Thair wes littill slauchter in the fight, bot horribill wes the slauchter in the flight.' The last covenanters to remain on the battlefield were some of the Aberdeen garrison. They, 'lyke bold and weell trained souldioures, [made] there retreat in order', trying to escape over the Dee. But Alasdair saw what they were doing and led four hundred Irish in an attack which virtually exterminated them.[25]

Even more than Tippermuir, Aberdeen was an Irish victory; Montrose had far fewer Highlanders than before and few Lowlanders under his command. Tippermuir, though won over an enemy with great numerical superiority, had not really tested the Irish and Alasdair's leadership of them, for their charge had been so immediately successful that they had done little real fighting. But at Aberdeen they showed themselves able to resist fairly determined attacks — though admittedly these were unco-ordinated, through the incompetence of Lord Burleigh, who seems to have taken so little part in directing the battle that the covenanters were to all intents and purposes without a general. The prolonged fighting with sword and dirk after the charge of the Irish demonstrated that they were capable of pressing home their attack even after the initial impetus of the charge had failed to rout the enemy. And Alasdair's conduct suggests that he was not just an expert in personal combat but a leader whose qualities of generalship were rivalled among the royalists only by Montrose himself. He had skilfully destroyed Forbes of Craigievar's troop. After charging with his men he had sufficient control over himself and them to note the attempt of some of the covenanters to escape, and to gather together a strong enough body of his men, intent on pursuit and plunder, to thwart them.

For Aberdeen, Friday 13 September 1644 was indeed an unlucky day. The losses sustained by the covenanters outside the burgh were quickly followed by new horrors within it, as the Irish and other rebels burst in, pursuing their fleeing enemies, 'hewing and cutting down all maner of man thay could overtak within the toune'. The 'cruell Irishis', on seeing a well-dressed man, would make him undress before killing him, so as not to damage his clothes. Montrose had entered Aberdeen with his men but soon withdrew to establish a camp for his army; the Irish did not leave but continued the 'killing, robbing, and plundering of this toune at thair plesour'. Nothing was heard but 'Hovlling, crying, weiping, mvrning, throw all the streittis'. Some Aberdonians tried to protect themselves by wearing a bunch of oats, the royalist badge or identification mark (necessary when armies did not have uniforms), but few benefited from this.

Nightfall brought no relief, and intermittent plundering and killing continued on Saturday, Sunday and Monday. The corpses of the dead, stripped of clothes, lay in the streets, for the Irish would not allow them to be buried. 'The wyf durst not cry nor weip at her husbandis slauchter befoir hir eyes, nor the mother for the sone, nor dochter for the father', for if they wept they too were killed. The women raped and left in the burgh were well off compared with those herded out to the rebel camp to be enjoyed at leisure; a number of these latter unfortunates seem to have been carried off by the rebels as camp followers on their campaigns.

Not all the Irish took part in this work, for the day after the battle, 14 September, Montrose sent most of his army north to camp at Kintore and Inverurie. He himself spent the nights of the 14th and 15th in Aberdeen, on the former day having the king's letters patent appointing him lieutenant general and Alasdair MacColla major general formally proclaimed — though as a royalist Aberdonian noted, the letters had not been authenticated by any Scottish seals, the implication being that they were invalid. Another proclamation summoned all men to rise in arms for the king. Meanwhile 'the cruell Irishis [were] still killing and robbing all this whill that he is at this bussines'; Montrose could hardly claim ignorance of the atrocities being committed in his and the king's name. It may be that he had lost control of some of the Irish, but there is no evidence that he tried to control them, and his very dress was designed to indicate how closely he identified himself with the Irish. In Aberdeen, as in Atholl, at Tippermuir and in Perth, it was noted that he wore Highland or Irish dress, in an attempt to compliment the Gaels whose support he needed. But to Lowlanders the fact that Montrose presided over events in Aberdeen 'cled in cot and trewis as the Irishes wes cled' demonstrated the extent to which he had abandoned 'civilised' values and sold his soul to the savage Gael.

By this time Montrose knew that Argyll was advancing on Aberdeen from the south. He was tempted to stay and fight, but his leading supporters, especially Alasdair MacColla and the earl of Airlie, urged that he had not sufficient men to risk this.[26] Therefore on 16 September he marched to Kintore to join the rest of his army. The Irish still looting in Aberdeen were ordered to march with him on pain of death, but some remained behind and continued plundering and preventing burial of the dead.

All this account of the stay of Montrose and the Irish in Aberdeen has been taken from John Spalding's *Memorials*, he having been an eye-witness of some of what he described. He recorded the names of twenty covenanting townsmen who had been killed in the battle or later in Aberdeen; but he also listed the names of ninety-eight dead who had not been covenanters.[27] Gordon of Sallagh confirms Spalding's story in general terms; in Aberdeen Montrose's men 'killed the inhabitants, without distinction of age or of sex, to the number of eight score, which was done chiefly by the Irish and Scots Hylanders'.[28] The fate of Aberdeen was also very much in Patrick Gordon of Ruthven's mind when he denounced the excesses of the royalist army, and especially of the Irish. The latter, he claimed, everywhere killed all they could be master of, without pity or humanity. They seemed to kill their fellow men with the same sort of offhandedness with which they killed a chicken for supper. They were 'most brutishlie giuen to vncleannes and filthie lust', while as for their 'excessiue drinkeing, when they came where it might be had, there was no limites to there beastly appetites'. They plundered even poor labourers without mercy — though Gordon realistically added that as Montrose could not pay his forces it was hard for him to restrain them from plundering.[29]

These denunciations of the conduct of the Irish cannot be dismissed as hostile propaganda, for all were written by royalists, men who wished Montrose success but were horrified by the lengths to which he was prepared to go to achieve his ends. Many Lowland royalists would have been unhappy at the king's cause in Scotland being represented by Highlanders and (much worse) Irish, and covenanting propaganda skilfully exploited such racial prejudice by constantly referring to Montrose's men not as royalists but as Irish. To English and Scottish protestants the native Irish were the papist savages responsible for the massacre of hundreds of thousands of protestants in Ireland in 1641-2; in reality no such vast massacre had taken place, but that it had was widely believed. Even convinced royalists would hesitate to fight for the king if this meant fighting alongside such barbarians. This was one of the main reasons so few Lowlanders had joined Montrose, apart from men already bound to him by friendship or kinship, or living on the fringes of the Highlands and not sharing fully the general Lowland horror of all things Gaelic. It was therefore very much in Montrose's interests to try to change the image of the Irish, to present them as formidable fighting men who were well disciplined out of battle as well as in it. Instead, at Aberdeen he let the Irish confirm the worst suspicions of Lowlanders, both royalists and covenanters. It is true that the accounts of Spalding and others, though not intentionally biased, tend to give an exaggerated impression, so horrified were they at what had happened. There was no general massacre, for the total number killed was relatively small and most of the men killed had probably been in arms for the covenanters, though many had been royalist at heart and had thrown away their arms and fled into the burgh.

Compared to the worst excesses of, say, the Thirty Years War, Aberdeen had escaped very lightly. But so far the civil wars in England and Scotland had seldom been conducted with such indiscriminate ferocity as the Irish displayed in Aberdeen. The impact of the news from Aberdeen was therefore great. Montrose and the Irish under Alasdair MacColla had brought a new dimension to the civil wars of Great Britain. To the Irish, fresh from the terrible wars of their own country where the killing of civilians, women and children by both protestant and Catholic armies was commonplace, what happened in Aberdeen was not exceptional and the horror expressed at it must have seemed to them hypocritical; what they were doing was revenging the atrocities committed against the native Irish by, among others, the covenanters' own Scottish army in Ireland. But though the conduct of the Irish may be explicable, if hardly justifiable, for Montrose to have allowed them to indulge their lust for plunder and vengeance in a burgh generally known as outstanding for its support for the king was a miscalculation from which his campaigns never recovered. Quite apart from any moral considerations, it was simply inexpedient. He may have won Aberdeen; he may have ensured that in future his approach would cause terror; but he had finally lost hope of winning the active support of all but a tiny minority of Lowland Scotland's potential royalists. The double standard that allowed and even encouraged atrocities in Ireland but expressed revulsion at atrocities in Great Britain might be hypocritical, but it was a double standard that was generally accepted.

Alasdair MacColla must of course share responsibility with Montrose for events in Aberdeen, as the Irish were his men. But it may be significant that though Alasdair entered the burgh after the battle,[30] there is no mention of his spending two nights there like Montrose. It seems likely this is an indication that, as would be natural as he was Montrose's second in command, he marched the majority of the army to Kintore and commanded the camp there while Montrose remained in Aberdeen.

On leaving Kintore, Montrose and Alasdair moved north through the Gordon country, but persuaded only a handful of men to join them. They therefore retired into the Highlands, through Badenoch to Atholl, where the two men had first met. There they parted, for Alasdair moved back west to Ardnamurchan with perhaps 500 (though one account says 1,000) Irish musketeers and Highland bowmen. The rest of the army, about 300 Atholl and Badenoch men and 800 or 900 Irish, Montrose led eastwards again, then northwards past Aberdeen into the Gordon country. There were two reasons for Montrose dividing his forces in this manner. Having failed to get significant Lowland support, he was desperate for recruits, and the most likely place to find them was the West Highlands. The hesitant chiefs of the West and the Isles had failed to rally to Alasdair in July and August. But now he and his men had two victories behind them, were laden with plunder, and had Montrose to lead them, the chiefs might react differently.

It had been shown that the covenanters could be defeated; perhaps after all there was a chance of shaking the Campbell supremacy in the west. As Neil MacMhuirich put it, Tippermuir and Aberdeen 'raised the courage and spirit of the Gael from that forth, in so much that they did not turn their backs to the enemy, either on even terms or under a disadvantage'. The second reason for the division of the rebel army was that Alasdair wished to raise the sieges of Kinlochaline and Mingary, they being 'sore stressed by the Cambelles'.[31] In addition it may well be that he was anxious to get back to the West for a time; it was there, from his point of view, that the heart of the war lay, in MacDonald lands now in Campbell hands. The fact that Montrose did not decide to march his whole army west indicates his different outlook. He could see the sense of Alasdair relieving his castles, and he badly needed whatever recruits he could find, but he did not want to commit himself to a campaign in the West Highlands. If the Lowlands were to be recovered from the covenanters, then it was in the Lowlands that most of the fighting must take place. To have taken his whole army westwards would generally have been interpreted as a retreat or flight from the pursuing covenanters. Montrose therefore embarked on his second circuit of the Eastern Highlands to continue to make his presence felt. He had no intention of fighting any battles so had to keep constantly on the move to prevent his enemies catching up with him, in the process making them, toiling in endless ineffectual pursuit, look singularly foolish. At the same time his activities successfully diverted the attention of the covenanters from Alasdair MacColla, for once the rebel army divided the covenanters inevitably took Montrose, still threatening the Lowlands, to be a greater danger than Alasdair in a remote part of the Highlands. He was thus given a chance to recruit and consult with the chiefs.

To the covenanting regime in Edinburgh Alasdair when he marched west might be out of sight and mind, but the Campbells naturally saw things from a different viewpoint, and while still vainly pursuing Montrose in the east, Argyll also tried to direct his clan's military activities. The centre of Campbell preparations was Dunstaffnage Castle, the strongest and largest castle in their northern territories, situated conveniently close to Morvern and Ardnamurchan, as the first priority was recapturing Kinlochaline and Mingary. But Argyll also prepared for other eventualities; no major western chief had joined the rebels, but some might well be tempted to do so. Argyll therefore ordered that all food he had got sent from the Lowlands should be stored in Dunstaffnage; the Campbell forces besieging the two castles should be supplied from Lorne so the Lowland food could thus be stored in case of emergency. His orders were not fully obeyed, however. The captain of Dunstaffnage did use some of the Lowland food for present needs, thus earning himself a stinging rebuke from Argyll's wife at Inveraray.[32]

On 5 October Argyll, in pursuit of Montrose after the battle of Aberdeen, reached Ruthven in Badenoch. Three days later he heard that the rebels had divided themselves, and on 9 October he wrote from Ruthven to the captain of Dunstaffnage to warn him that Alasdair 'and his rebellious complices' were making for Ardnamurchan. Meal, bere (barley), biscuit, gunpowder and lead were to be sent at once to Inverlochy, Argyll's own galley and other boats being manned to transport these supplies. But Argyll warily warned the boats to be 'cairful to keep themselves in thair passadg from the treachari of the peopll thairabout'; he well knew how the Campbells were hated on the northern fringe of their empire.[33] Thus Campbell forces were to be concentrated at Inverlochy to intercept and defeat Alasdair before he reached Ardnamurchan.

Meanwhile the siege of Mingary dragged on. Sir Donald Campbell still attempted no assault, his main conflict with the garrison evidently being over who should feed the latter's prisoners; eventually he agreed to supply food for them after the garrison had threatened to provide no food themselves, cutting off the supplies of the hated presbyterian ministers first! Otherwise, however, the garrison showed itself ready to make concessions over some of the prisoners. On 3 September Mrs Weir, the birth of her child being imminent, was freed and sent to Inveraray; she was never to see her husband again. Fifteen days later the officers of the former Campbell garrison led by John MacKellor were given their freedom, the promise made to them when they had surrendered at last being honoured. This left only six prisoners, and Sir Donald secured the release of three of them on 20 September on promising to pay a money ransom for them. Only the three ministers now remained, and on 30 September it was agreed that they too would be set free as soon as Alasdair MacColla's father and two brothers were brought to Mingary and released with free passes to go where they wished. To further sustain the ministers' morale Sir Donald sent in carefully edited news bulletins — reports of Scottish and parliamentary victories in England, and the news that in Ireland Lord Inchiquin and his Munster army had changed sides, agreeing to support the English parliament rather than the king. This last piece of news was of more significance to Alasdair's supporters than they could have known at the time; three years later it was to be the war between Inchiquin and Irish confederates — which now began — which was to lead to Alasdair's death.

It seems that no news of the doings of Montrose and Alasdair was allowed to reach the garrison, and prolonged inactivity began to demoralise it. On 28 September John Weir noted that 'the people of the castle wer drinking al day and fought amongst themselves', three of them being wounded. The next day 'the like drinking was al day'. The suffering of the prisoners was not intense, but they were after all prisoners of a beleaguered garrison and had to put up with the discomforts that their captors were also experiencing. Their prison was 'a grim and nastie lodging' in which for the first month of their incarceration they had to sleep on boards in their clothes as they lacked proper nightclothes; but Sir Donald Campbell remedied this deficiency, and perhaps also supplied the ferns (bracken) and straw they got to lie on. Bread was short, sometimes entirely lacking, and their meat was 'starved milk kowes long keipt after killing, and after boyling putrified and stinking'. They had only water to drink — and one account graphically describes how the prisoners drank with their eyes shut so as not to see the green scum on the water, and with their teeth closed to try to filter out the mud! They were subjected to reproofs, lies, blasphemies and oaths. Even worse for good Calvinists, they had to put up with 'cursed masses, crucifixes, crossings and beads', the symbols of popery and idolatry, in their sight and hearing, while their own joint worship was sometimes interrupted and they were prevented from singing psalms (not surprisingly if, as one suspects, they tried to sing to drown the sounds of the hated mass!). Yet as usual John Weir, having listed the prisoners' sufferings, also found a number of mercies to be grateful for. 'We wer al togider in one roome the best Chamber in the Castle'; grim and nasty they might find it, but their captors were worse housed. They got much comfort from the scriptures, and soldiers and women of the castle 'conveniently served' them.[34]

The first real indication that those in Mingary Castle got that all was not going well for the Campbells and the covenanters was a startling one; on the night of 5-6 October Sir Donald Campbell suddenly struck camp and withdrew his men. News had reached him that Alasdair MacColla was marching west. Argyll's orders of 9 October for his forces to gather at Inverlochy to intercept him had come far too late.

On 7 October the garrison of Mingary heard for certain of Alasdair's approach, and sent out a force to meet him. Others took advantage of the lifting of the siege to sally out the next day to round up goats (the Campbells presumably having driven off all the cattle) for the garrison to feast on. And, significantly, the captain of Clanranald sent his son Donald to Mingary with forty cows. When Argyll had begun the siege of the castle he had summoned the captain to him and ordered him to raise the Clanranald against the rebels.[35] The captain had failed to do this, and now showed where his true sympathies lay.

For the three imprisoned ministers the lifting of the siege on Mingary was demoralising news, especially to Weir, who had fallen ill of a fever on 2 October and whose account of events was being continued by his colleague James Hamilton. But the end of the siege brought them some advantages: they were now allowed unlimited bread, meat, water and fire.

Alasdair went first to the relief of Kinlochaline. As much the smaller of his two castles it was probably in greater danger of capture than Mingary. When he got there he decided to abandon it; it was too vulnerable to attack and could not contain a large enough garrison to be of real use to him as a base. He therefore removed his garrison and burnt Kinlochaline before marching on to Mingary. At about 10 p.m. on 16 October the prisoners in Mingary heard musket fire. On asking what was happening, they were told that the triumphant Alasdair MacColla was approaching and guns were being fired in celebration. Shorly thereafter, just before Alasdair appeared, John Weir died, at the age of thirty-four. As James Hamilton explained, when Alasdair had left Mingary at the end of July, Weir had prayed to God that he might never see him again; the Lord had now granted him his wish — though hardly in the way Weir had intended.[36]

Weir's death left Hamilton and his father-in-law David Watson to spend 'a weirie winter' together in captivity, though they probably had the company of some new prisoners brought by Alasdair. In March 1645 Watson died, leaving Hamilton as the only prisoner left of those captured the previous July. Why Argyll had failed to arrange an exchange to release the imprisoned ministers is not clear. He must have been reluctant to free Coll Ciotach and his two sons, but he himself had promised to do so. He may have changed his mind after Tippermuir and Aberdeen, deciding that the family of so great a rebel as Alasdair had now become was too valuable to exchange for a few obscure ministers. The committee of estates did not share this view. At the end of October the committee sent £100 sterling to pay for the maintenance of Hamilton and Weir (it was not yet known that Weir was dead and Watson was evidently excluded from the committee's charity as he did not hold a Scottish parish), and it wrote to Argyll instructing him to arrange to exchange Coll and his sons for the ministers, but he seems to have done nothing. When in December Argyll returned to his estates, he and others were said to have gone 'to labor ffor relief of Mr James Hamiltoun, minister, furth of prison' but again nothing happened, in spite of increasing indignation among Hamilton's colleagues in the ministry of the kirk.[37]

Having arrived at Mingary, Alasdair spread the news of his victories and began again urging the local clans to rise against the Campbells. The Clanranald had set an example by rising even before he arrived; the captain of Clanranald had 'raised all the men of Uist, Eig, Moydart, and Arisaig, and the first thing they did was the spoiling of Sunart, leaving neither cow now sheep in it that they did not carry away to the plains of Castle Tirrim; and he sent his son Donald with a part of that prey to the garrison who were in Castle Mingarry'. On his arrival Alasdair met Donald and, after placing a fresh garrison in Mingary, they marched together to Castle Tirrim in Moidart, the seat of the captain of Clanranald. The captain then joined Alasdair in marching north to Arisaig and Morar, whence they summoned MacLeod of Dunvegan to join them. On his refusal they continued into Knoydart, where they met Angus or Aeneas MacDonald, the effective leader of the MacDonalds of Glengarry though he was not yet chief. Angus would not join them himself but evidently co-operated in raising the men of Knoydart and Glengarry under his uncle, Donald Gorm MacDonald of Scotus, to march with

Alasdair. Thus reinforced, Alasdair turned back into Lochaber; as he passed through the country Donald Glas MacDonald (the uncle of Angus MacDonald of Keppoch)[38] joined with the Keppoch men, and the Stewarts of Appin, the MacIans or MacDonalds of Glencoe and some of the Camerons flocked in to swell his ranks. The precise dating of these moves is uncertain. The commanders of the Campbell garrison of Castle Stalker (on a rock in Loch Linnhe at the mouth of the Great Glen) reported that he stayed the night of 20 October at Castle Tirrim; this must have been when he was on his way north to Arisaig, and Morar, so the claim in the same source that Alasdair was on the island of Lismore (close to Castle Stalker) on 22 October on his way to Lochaber must be erroneous — unless indeed it is Neil MacMhuirich, who describes Alasdair's journey through Arisaig, Morar and Knoydart, who is mistaken.[39]

Alasdair's journey west after leaving Montrose had been entirely successful. The Campbells had fled before him or withdrawn to their castles, Mingary had been relieved, and many clansmen had joined him — though it was notable that the more successful and powerful of the western clans still had not been convinced that it was in their interests to try to upset the status quo; the MacKenzies, the MacLeods, the MacLeans of Duart and the most powerful branch of the Clan Donald, the MacDonalds of Sleat, all preserved a watchful neutrality, trying to assess where their best interests lay. Moreover, Alasdair was probably disappointed by the lack of supplies or reinforcements from Ireland. Antrim and Ormond were doing their best, but neither had the resources to send aid. Charles I had praised Antrim's work in sending Alasdair to Scotland as a thing 'likely to prove soe much to the advantage of my affairs', and had hinted that Antrim himself should go to Scotland, but could offer no practical help. Antrim tried to buy a frigate for service in the Isles, but in the end could not pay for it. Ormond urged the Irish confederates to send help to Alasdair to 'keep life in the War of Scotland' but could do nothing himself; Alasdair's letter of 13 August had urged him to write to Seaforth and others and to promise them supplies, but Ormond would not make promises he could not keep and did not know what to write to them as he was ignorant of Scottish affairs and did not know their 'inclinations', their political stances.[40] Alasdair therefore had to do without further help from Ireland, just as Montrose had to do without the aid he always hoped for from England.

It was probably early or mid-November by the time Alasdair rejoined Montrose in Atholl. Montrose had led Argyll through the north-eastern Lowlands, evading contact except at Fyvie, where Argyll nearly caught him at the end of October and he escaped only after some fierce skirmishing. According to George Wishart, Colonel Manus O'Cahan distinguished himself in leading his Irish regiment at Fyvie, but apart from this reference there is no evidence that O'Cahan had yet returned from carrying Alasdair's letter of 13 August to Dublin. Thus it was probably his regiment rather than himself which won glory. Father MacBreck notes the death of the major of the regiment at Fyvie, but gives his name as Christopher — perhaps the christian name of the Sergeant Major Ledwitch recorded in the list of Alasdair's officers.[41] Montrose was at Strathbogie (Huntly)

Castle on 6 November, and from there he retired into Badenoch. He had led superior enemy forces on a long and fruitless march, but he cannot have been entirely happy with his progress. He had found few recruits; as Wishart remarked, apart from the Highlanders and Irish he had more officers than soldiers. A few nobles and gentlemen had joined him but there had been no popular response whatever to his repeated calls to arms. And as he moved back towards the Highlands many of his Lowland 'officers' left him, tempted by offers of pardon from Argyll and having no stomach for forced marches in the Highlands as winter approached.

The weather as Montrose's men moved from Badenoch into Atholl was enough to confirm fears of ordeals to come. Wishart simply records a long march through the snow, but Father MacBreck paints a melodramatic picture of the army forcing its way through snowdrifts, over hill after hill, some so steep that they had to crawl up them — and then roll down the other side! More credibly, he records that the guides leading them got lost and some, suspecting treachery, proposed killing them. But at last 'Colonel Thomas Lachlan' (Major Laghtnan), a man 'of ingenuity and dauntless courage', led them to safety at Blair Atholl.[42]

With winter now setting in it was generally taken for granted that the campaigning season was over. Argyll, for example, on 14 November sent 1,000 of his Highland followers home through Strathspey, Badenoch and Lochaber (plundering as they went) while he retired southwards.[43] Perhaps, having failed to intercept Alasdair on his march to Ardnamurchan, these Highlanders would catch him on his return. If so, Argyll was again too late. Alasdair reached Atholl without trouble, the recruits he brought more than doubling the size of Montrose's army. Estimates vary, but in all Montrose had now something like 3,000 men. The captain of Clanranald alone is said to have contributed 800 men, though this figure may well include the other MacDonalds (those of Glengarry, Glencoe and Keppoch), and in addition there were Stewarts, Camerons and the Irish.[44] Thanks to Alasdair's efforts Montrose now had a larger army than at Tippermuir or Aberdeen. But what was he to do with it? It was now winter, too late to begin a new campaign. And how was he to provide food and shelter for his men through a long winter? And how could he hold his army together through long months of demoralising inaction? The answer that was eventually agreed on to these questions was to bring Montrose one of his greatest victories, and was to win for Alasdair MacColla a major place in the history, literature and traditions of the Western Highlands.

NOTES

1. Gordon, *Britane's distemper*, 72-3; Spalding, *Memorials*, ii.402; Leith, *Memoirs*, i.291; Gordon, *Genealogical history*, 520; *Rel Celt*, ii.179; Wishart, *Memoirs*, 54-6; *A true relation of the happy success* . . ., 6.
2. Ibid, 6.
3. M. Napier (ed), *Memorials of Montrose and his times* (2 vols, Maitland Club, 1848-50), ii.477.
4. Balfour, *Historical works*, iii.208-9.

5. *APS*, VI.i.85, 86, 88, 141, 161; Powell and Timings, *Documents relating to the civil war*, 138,139.

6. Balfour, *Historical works*, iii.215,217.

7. Ibid, iii.220,221; *APS*, VI.i.159-60,167.

8. T. McCrie (ed), *The life of Mr Robert Blair* (Wodrow Society, 1848), 173.

9. Baillie, *Letters*, ii.214,217,262.

10. *CSPV, 1643-7*, 128,132.

11. Inveraray Castle, Argyll Transcripts, xii.139.

12. NLS, Wodrow MSS, Quarto XXIX, f.65.

13. SRO, PA.11/3, ff.34v,35v,36,37-v,38-v,39v-40.

14. Wishart, *Memoirs*, 56; Menzies, *Red and white book of Menzies*, 270-6; *APS*, VI.i.318; Spalding, *Memorials*, ii.434.

15. SRO, PA.11/3, ff.38v,40v; D. Laing (ed), *Correspondence of Sir Robert Kerr, first earl of Ancrum, and his son William, third earl of Lothian* (2 vols, Edinburgh 1875), i.171.

16. Wishart, *Memoirs*, 56-62; Gordon, *Britane's distemper*, 73-5; Napier, *Memorials*, ii.149-51; Baillie, *Letters*, ii.225,233,262; *A true relation of the happy success . . .*, 7-8; T. Carte (ed), *Collection of original letters and papers* (2 vols, London 1739), i.73-4. The account in Carte (printed from Bodleian Library, Oxford, Carte MSS, 14, f.36) is dated Inverlochy, 7 February 1645 and headed 'News from his Majesty's Army in Scotland'; in the published version Carte has added that it was written by an Irish officer, deducing this from the contents of the paper. Hill, *Macdonnells of Antrim*, 86 states that the report was written by Colonel James MacDonnell, but he cites no evidence to support this, and he may simply be assuming that the report is the same work as the narrative of the wars by the colonel mentioned in *Com Rin*, i.168,462, iii.295, iv.357, v.50. In fact the latter work, now lost, was clearly much more extensive than the report. It seems possible that the report was in fact composed by Alasdair MacColla himself, for it states that 'I was sent' to relieve Mingary Castle in October 1644, and other sources make it certain that Alasdair led that expedition. Admittedly the paper begins by referring to Alasdair in the third person, but it is possible that he began to dictate (the paper is not in his handwriting) an impersonal report in the third person but later lapsed into the first person — other examples of such changes in the course of documents can easily be found (e.g., Leven's orders to Alasdair of November 1641 mainly refer to him in the second person, but this changes to the third person at one point).

17. T.H. Marshall, *History of Perth* (Perth 1849), 188-94; Napier, *Memorials*, ii.152-61,165; Gordon, *Britane's distemper*, 75.

18. SRO, PA.11/3, 40v-41.

19. E.J. Cowan, *Montrose. For covenant and king* (London 1977), 162; SRO, GD.112/39/854,855,860, Breadalbane muniments.

20. Gordon, *Britane's distemper*, 75; Wishart, *Memoirs*, 64-5; Guthry, *Memoirs*, 165-6; SRO, PA.11/3, ff.127v-128v; *APS*, VI.i.359-60.

21. Napier, *Memorials*, ii.163-4; SRO, PA.11/3, ff.46-v, 50v-51; R.R. Steele (ed), *Bibliotheca Lindesiana. A bibliography of royal proclamations . . . 1485-1714* (2 vols, Oxford, 1910), ii.325-6; Laing, *Correspondence*, i.173.

22. Sir Walter Scott, *Legend of Montrose*, postscript to the Introduction.

23. Spalding, *Memorials*, ii.404; Napier, *Memorials*, ii.170.

24. L.B. Taylor (ed), *Aberdeen council letters*, ii (London 1950), 383.

25. Gordon, *Britane's distemper*, 80-3; Spalding, *Memorials*, ii.405-7; Wishart, *Memoirs*, 65-9; *A true relation of the happy success . . .*, 10-12; Carte, *Original letters*, i.74; Guthry, *Memoirs*, 167-8; Baillie, *Letters*, ii.234,262; Cowan, *Montrose*, 160-7; J. Stuart (ed), *Extracts from the council register of the burgh of Aberdeen, 1643-1747* (Scottish Burgh Record Society, 1872), 28-9.

26. Gordon, *Britane's distemper*, 85.

27. Spalding, *Memorials*, ii.407-13.

28. Gordon, *Genealogical history*, 521. The burgh register puts the total of dead at 'neir of aucht scoir', Stuart, *Extracts . . . 1643-1747*, 29.

29. Gordon, *Britane's distemper*, 161.

30. Napier, *Memorials*, ii.165,167.

31. Ibid, 89; Wishart, *Memoirs*, 72; Spalding, *Memorials*, ii.419; *A true relation of the happy success . . .*, 12; *Rel Celt*, ii.179; Carte, *Original letters*, i.74; Guthry, *Memoirs*, 168-9.

32. SRO, PA.11/3, ff.36v-37,38-v; *Joint print of documents in causa His Grace John Douglas Sutherland, duke of Argyll . . . against Angus John Campbell of Dunstaffnage . . . Court of Session, First Division May 12 1911* (Edinburgh 1911), 160,161,162-3.

33. Ibid, 163; Laing, *Correspondence*, i.174,175.

34. NLS, Wodrow MSS, Quarto XXIX, ff.63v-64v; Reid, *History of the presbyterian church in Ireland*, i.462-4.

35. *Rel Celt*, ii.179.

36. NLS, Wodrow MSS, Quarto XXIX, ff.64v,65v-67; Carte, *Original letters*, i.74.

37. SRO, PA.11/3, ff.85,89-90; Reid, *History of the presbyterian church in Ireland*, i.555-6; Sir Thomas Hope, *A diary . . . 1633-45* (Bannatyne Club, 1843), 210.

38. It is commonly held that Donald Glas was chief of the MacDonalds of Keppoch at this time, having succeeded his nephew Angus when the latter was killed in a fight after a cattle raid in 1640 (Eg, A.M. Mackenzie (ed), *Orain Iain Luim. Songs of John Macdonald, bard of Keppoch* (Scottish Gaelic Texts Society, 1964), 233-4). But the weight of the evidence points to 1646 as the true date of the raid and Angus's death (Eg, J. Mackechnie (ed), *The Dewar manuscript*, i (Glasgow 1964), 360-2; Thomson, *Introduction to Gaelic poetry*, 119,312 n.3; J. Macdiarmid, 'Folklore of Breadalbane', *TGSI*, xxvi (1904-7), 147-8; SRO, GD.112/43/1, bundle, state papers 1640-9), so Donald Glas must have commanded the Keppoch men under Alasdair either as a more experienced military leader than Angus or, if Angus was still a child, as his tutor. Many examples can be found of men other than the chief commanding clansmen in battle, so the fact that Donald Glas led the Keppoch men should not be used to support the argument that he was chief.

39. *Rel Celt*, ii.179-81; *Joint print of documents*, 164; Carte, *Original letters*, i.74-5.

40. Hill, *Macdonnells of Antrim*, 471; Carte, *Ormond*, iii.356, 358-9,364; Gilbert, *Ir confed*, iv.57-8; Gilbert, *Contemp hist*, i.89.

41. Gordon, *Britane's distemper*, 90-1; Spalding, *Memorials*, ii.426-7; Wishart, *Memoirs*, 73-5; Leith, *Memoirs*, i.297; O'Danachair, 'Montrose's Irish Regiments', *Irish Sword*, iv.64.

42. Gordon, *Britane's distemper*, 93; Spalding, *Memorials*, ii.428-9; Wishart, *Memoirs*, 77-9; Leith, *Memoirs*, i.299-301; Guthry, *Memoirs*, 171.

43. Spalding, *Memorials*, ii.430.

44. Ibid, ii.430; Gordon, *Britane's distemper*, 94; Wishart, *Memoirs*, 79; *APS*, VI.ii.461.

6

The Destroyer of Houses

'I WAS willing to let the world see that Argyle was not the man his Highlandmen believed him to be, and that it was possible to beat him in his own Highlands.'[1] Thus Montrose described to Charles I the background to his great victory at Inverlochy in February 1645, the culmination of his brilliantly successful invasion of Argyllshire. But this clear and forceful statement conceals a change of plan forced on Montrose by his men, for initially he had believed it impossible to keep an army together in the Highlands in winter. When his army assembled in Atholl in November 1644 he had therefore proposed seeking food and shelter in the Lowlands. According to Neil MacMhuirich, he put this proposal to his leading officers in a council of war at Blair Atholl, but 'the others thought that it would be safest for him that the army should be in the country of the Gael. Montrose consented to that, on the assurance that the army would get victuals and accommodation in it.' He consulted Angus MacAllan Dubh, a kinsman of MacDonald of Glencoe who was regarded as an expert on conditions in Argyllshire: could the army find supplies and shelter on Argyll's estates? Angus replied that 'if tight houses and fat cows as victuals to feed upon . . . would answer their purpose', then these lands could provide them. Montrose then agreed to enter Argyllshire, making the decision to do so unanimous.[2]

Patrick Gordon gives a much more detailed account of the debate, but one in which it may be suspected that his taste for heightening the drama of such turning-points has led to exaggeration, if not invention. On Montrose announcing that the army would move to the Lowlands for the winter, all the Clan Donald demanded that instead they march against the Campbells to gain revenge for past wrongs; if Montrose would not agree to this, they would leave him and return to their homes. Montrose saw so many difficulties in the proposal that he was reluctant to agree to it, but he consented to discuss the matter in a council of war, hoping that the votes of the Gordons and some of the Eastern Highlanders who had little sympathy for Clan Donald ambitions would ensure the rejection of the MacDonald plan. The debate was long. Montrose argued that Argyllshire was separated from the rest of Scotland by a continuous ridge of high inaccessible mountains, and the narrow passes through them could easily be kept by 500 men against 20,000. The Campbells could block these passes until they all starved in these 'desertes'. That this does in fact accurately represent Montrose's opinion is indicated by his letter to Charles I after Inverlochy; he there states that at some of the passes he would have been forced to turn back if opposed by a mere hundred men. Even if they reached the west coast, Montrose argued to his council of war, the endless alternations of peninsulas and long sea lochs meant the country was as serrated as a comb, easy to defend and hard to march through.

After Montrose had finished, Alasdair MacColla argued the opposite case. Routes into Argyll were known to some of those present. Their enemies had not the brains to foresee danger, nor the judgement to resist effectively. It was true that Argyllshire was considered impregnable, no enemy ever having been known to have entered it (clearly Alasdair was no historian), but this would make success all the more glorious, and the very fact that the Campbells were so smugly certain of their own safety had rendered them over-confident and careless. Through not having to fear invasion the Campbells had become 'stupid and doltish'. Here Alasdair is made by Gordon to typify the warrior who regards peace and security as things which inevitably lead to the decay of true manly virtues. In the light of Alasdair's background and career this may well be accurate. Turning to wider issues Alasdair stressed the importance of the marquis of Argyll, not just as an enemy of the MacDonalds but as the leading figure among the covenanters; to destroy his power would not just advance the interests of the Clan Donald, it would shake the covenanting regime in Edinburgh. And once freed from fear of the Campbells 'the whole highlanders with one consent would take armes for the king'.

This last argument was one which was doubtless intended to appeal to Montrose, but Alasdair's optimistic and speculative reasoning did not lead him to change his mind. The others on the council of war however were impressed by Alasdair's speech; his 'solid and subtill judgement was reuerenced with greatest authoritie' and Montrose was outvoted and forced to accept the decision with as good grace as he could muster.[3] Patrick Gordon's account may embellish and polish the truth, but the arguements he attributes to Montrose and Alasdair are plausible; and Gordon of Sallagh confirms that it was Alasdair (along with the captain of Clanranald) who played the leading part in persuading Montrose to march west.[4] Montrose may at first only have agreed to march as far as the west end of Loch Tay and there reconsider the matter, for Father MacBreck mentions further consultations held there. All the Catholics, he records, were determined to continue into Argyllshire, and they were encouraged by a priest who combined arguments about the need to spread the faith with optimistic predictions about the weather the army could expect.[5]

Montrose's doubts about the wisdom of a winter campaign in Argyllshire were eminently sensible. It was a venture even more risky that those he had already undertaken, and might well have proved disastrous had not the winter weather turned out to be unusually mild,[6] a point which added to the conviction of both Montrose and his Catholic allies that God was helping them. But though Argyllshire might seem wild and alien territory to Montrose, it held few fears for Alasdair MacColla and the MacDonalds, used to similar terrain. The main barrier they had to break through was not the physical one of mountains but the psychological one of belief that Argyllshire was impregnable. Montrose was demonstrating that the invincibility of covenanting armies was a myth; Alasdair wished to prove that the story of the inaccessibility of the Campbell lands was

equally mythical. Rightly, he saw that the myth had two effects: it discouraged the
enemies of the Campbells, but equally it fostered complacency among the
Campbells. The complete surprise achieved by the invasion of Argyllshire does
seem to indicate that it had never occurred to the Campbells that a rebel army
would try to march through their lands. The report that the marquis of Argyll
laughed when he heard of the attempted invasion[7] may be untrustworthy, but
incredulity at such convenient folly on the part of his enemies may well have been
his reaction to the news: by attempting the impossible they were making their own
defeat certain. The inaccessibility of Argyll (by land if not by sea) was an accepted
fact, backed up by proverbial sayings, such as that it was not possible to pursue
Campbell raiders returning to their homes laden with plunder further west than
Loch Tay,[8] and by the old Campbell taunt 'it's a far cry to Loch Awe', meaning
that enemies could never hope to penetrate to the lands around Loch Awe, the
heart of the Campbell empire. Not only Highlanders believed in the myth; Robert
Baillie was soon to write in bewilderment that 'The world believed, that Argyle
could have been maintained against the greatest armie, as a countrie unaccessible;
but we see there is no strength or refuge on earth against the Lord.'[9] The official
covenanting interpretation of the success of Montrose and Alasdair was that they
were God's enemies, but that He was using them to chastise His chosen people for
their sins.

The invasion of Argyllshire which now began had the national effects Alasdair
MacColla had predicted. The Clan Campbell as a whole was successfully
challenged for the first time in generations, and its reputation was shattered.
Through this, and through his own failings in resisting the invasion, the marquis
of Argyll was partially discredited; after December 1644 his supremacy among the
covenanters was never again to be as great as in the past. But the ravaging of
Argyllshire was aimed at more than simply inflicting humiliating military defeat
on the Campbells. It was, as far as Alasdair MacColla and his allies were
concerned, the first major success in a campaign designed to destroy the Clan
Campbell completely, reviving MacDonald power in its place. But military victory
in itself would not free land for restoration to its rightful owners, the Clan Donald
and other clans who had suffered at Campbell hands; therefore it was a brutal logic
as well as lust for revenge that dictated that all Campbell men who were captured
should be killed. As Neil MacMhuirich rejoiced, 'In short, all the territories of
MacCailin [Argyll] were spoiled and burnt on that occasion, and eight hundred
four score and fifteen men were killed in these countries without battle or skirmish
having taken place in them.'[10] The exact number of 895 killed may be open to
question, and doubtless some of them tried to resist the invaders and thus died
fighting, but there seems little doubt that a deliberate policy of exterminating
Campbell men went hand in hand with the complete destruction of their property,
though this was sometimes not mentioned or denied according to the needs of
propaganda.

The account of the campaign sent to Dublin, perhaps written by Alasdair
MacColla himself, relates with fierce joy that 'throughout all Argyle, we left
neither house nor hold unburned, nor corn nor cattle, that belonged to the whole

name of Campbell',[11] and Montrose reported that he had 'laid waste the whole country of Argyle',[12] but neither mentions any killing. Henry Guthry turned the implicit into the explicit, converting the lack of mention of bloodshed into the firm assertion that there had been none.[13] Other royalist sources however make no attempt to conceal the truth, though sometimes they argue that the plundering and killing that took place were just retaliation for similar actions by Argyll. MacMhuirich has already been quoted. George Wishart admits that all men fit to carry arms were put to the sword if they did not flee or hide as their houses and villages were burnt.[14] John Spalding wrote of Montrose burning and killing through all Argyll, leaving no house or castle unburnt except impregnable strongholds; the grain and goods of the people were carried off, their animals either driven off or, if this was impracticable, mutilated or killed.[15] Patrick Gordon explained that though Montrose (being generous and merciful) would have spared the people, the Clan Donald killed without mercy all able to carry arms wherever they found them. Before moving on from one part of the country to another they burnt and destroyed everything. Argyllshire was left 'lyke ane deserte'.[16] With their menfolk fled or dead, their houses destroyed, their food, goods and cattle carried off, the Campbell women and children must have suffered horribly in the winter months that followed.

It was in these weeks in December 1644 and January 1645 that Alasdair MacColla earned himself the terrible name by which he became widely known in Argyllshire — *fear thollaidh nan tighean*, 'the destroyer of houses', (or, more literally, the holer or piercer of houses).[17] Quite how widespread in Argyllshire this 'orgy of blood and plunder'[18] was is unclear. References to all Argyll suffering are frequent, but some remoter parts (including most of the islands) probably escaped, as did the lands of clans hostile, or potentially hostile, to the Campbells. Occasionally mercy was shown. A woman at Cromalt is said to have had her two cows returned to her by Alasdair when he heard she was a MacNaughton, not a Campbell; he may in reality have been rewarding the spirit with which she had at first driven off his men with her distaff, aided by the superstition which held that it was disgraceful and dangerous for a man to be wounded by such an object symbolic of womanhood.[19]

Traditionally, the invaders boasted that by the time they had done their work no cock crowed and no chimney smoked within twenty miles of Inveraray after they had passed.[20] When in 1649 (remarkably late in the day) the covenanters at last got round to forfeiting the captain of Clanranald for treason, they stated that he had 'mairchit in arms with [Montrose] through the countries of Breadalbane Argyll and lorne whair they brunt waistit and Distroyit Eightine parochis by burning the haill houses and corns and by robbing and Distroying and away taking of all the goods and geir they gott thairin;'[21] but alas for the historian, the eighteen parishes are not specified. A few estimates of local losses survive, indicating the devastation wrought on individual estates. The losses of Sir Robert Campbell of Glenorchy, the most powerful Campbell chieftain after Argyll, and his tenants are said to have exceeded 1,200,000 merks (over £66,000 sterling), and Glenorchy had to rebuild his tenants' houses and provide them with seed for their fields. In these civil wars of the mid-1640s he lost a son, a brother, six nephews and 'many considerable friends and Tennents'.[22] On the lands of a much lesser man, the captain of Dunstaffnage, buildings with a total of 207 couples (main roof beams rising from the walls to join at the apex of the roof) were destroyed. Oats which it was estimated would have made 190 bolls of meal were destroyed or carried off, as were 103 bolls of bere (barley) and 324 bolls of seed oats and grain for feeding horses. Ninety-seven cattle (forty-eight of them pregnant cows) were lost, along with 135 sheep and goats, seventeen horses and seventeen pigs.[23] In March 1645 Sir Dougal Campbell of Auchinbreck was awarded (though not paid) 10,000 merks as a first contribution towards his father's losses. To the death of his father at the hands of the rebels were added those of 'many of his kinsmen and Tennents'.[24]

The movements of the invaders cannot be followed in detail after they entered Argyll, though their route from Atholl through eastern Perthshire is clear. First they moved up Strathtay, plundering the lands of the Menzies for the second time. At Loch Tay the rebel army split into two parts, one of which advanced up each side of the loch plundering the lands of Campbell of Glenorchy and Sir Mungo Campbell of Lawers. By 11 December they were at the west end of Loch Tay. According to Neil MacMhuirich the captain of Clanranald, with his own men and those from the Braes of Lochaber, here split off from the rest of the army on a great plundering raid, only rejoining Montrose at Kilmartin in Glassary, where they brought him 1,000 cattle. But a glance at a map suggests that, unless the captain turned south to Loch Earn and thence into the Trossachs, which seems highly unlikely, this division did not take place until later in the march.

Castles and fortified houses held against the rebels were ignored; no time could be wasted on sieges if surprise was to be achieved in Argyllshire. Campbell of Glenorchy held on to six such islands of resistance to the rebel tide which swirled through his great estates. From Loch Tay the march continued up Glen Dochart, but at Loch Dochart the rebels received their first check. The castle on an island in the loch was close enough to the shore for its guns to command the only route through the glen, a narrow path along the shore. Montrose would risk heavy losses if he tried to hasten his men through while enemies held the castle, but he had neither the time nor the equipment for a siege; perhaps Argyll was impregnable after all. But, as was to happen so often in the years ahead, seeming Campbell strength was undermined by the resentment, concealed but still existing, of minor clans which had been forced to accept Campbell overlordship. The time had now come for the MacNabs to try to throw off former subjection. John (Ian) MacNab was effective leader of the clan though his father, Finlay, still lived and was chief.[25] John now came with his men and offered to help Montrose gain the island stronghold which had formerly belonged to them. Before dawn he and his leading clansmen went down to the loch shore and hailed the garrison; they had, they shouted, important letters from the marquis of Argyll for the garrison. The Campbell garrison, confident of the friendship of the MacNabs, sent a boat to bring them out to the castle. Once they had landed the MacNabs turned on the garrison and seized the castle. The way into Argyllshire now lay open. For this service John MacNab was given command of the new garrison Montrose placed in the castle, and a promise of ownership of the castle and its lands once the war was won.

In Argyllshire the rebel army divided (on 13 December) into three sections to spread death and destruction as widely as possible. The three divisions were commanded by Montrose, Alasdair MacColla, and the captain of Clanranald. The routes they followed are not known for certain, but the geography of the area limited the options open to them, and as they were evidently to reunite in Glassary, a reasonable supposition would be that one division left at Crianlarich to march south to Loch Lomond and thence west to the head of Loch Fyne while the other two continued by way of Tyndrum to Loch Awe. There one probably continued up Loch Awe towards Kilmartin while the other struck southwards to the Campbell headquarters at Inveraray on Loch Fyne. This last division was probably that commanded by Montrose himself, hoping to catch Argyll in his lair. If so, he was disappointed. As the rebels approached, Argyll took to his galley and escaped down Loch Fyne, coldly calculating that staying to defy the rebels from his castle would not help his demoralised and defeated clansmen. Cowardice his flight might look, but he could be employed more usefully helping assemble a new army than staying to be besieged in Inveraray.

The little town of Inveraray was burnt. Mass was celebrated in the heart of Argyll, on portable altars hung round with plaids to shelter them from the wind. But the triumphant rebels could not afford to linger long, for it was now late December and a new army was being formed to march against them. Montrose and his men therefore began to move away northwards through Lorne. This brought them new Campbell lands to plunder and removed them from the southern peninsulas of Argyllshire where they must have feared (as they lacked shipping) that they would be trapped. The move also brought the west Highlanders among the rebels towards their homes to deposit their plunder, and Montrose and Alasdair were also moving towards the northern fringes of the Campbell empire, where powerful clans which hated and feared the Campbells might now be persuaded to join the rebel cause.

The need for such new support was all the greater in that they had gained very few new recruits since leaving Blair Atholl. To the MacNabs had been joined the survivors of the MacGregors, the remnants of a clan almost exterminated, their very name technically illegal. Perhaps some among the population of Kintyre and Islay who still had dreams of reviving the Clan Donald's glory joined Montrose and Alasdair, but their numbers cannot have been significant, as no source mentions them. One surprising recruit was Patrick Campbell of Edinample, a brother of Campbell of Glenorchy, who had evidently decided that loyalty to king outweighed that to clan.

Whatever Campbell of Edinample's motives, his recruitment was no compensation to Montrose for the fact that so few members of other Argyllshire clans joined him. Many might secretly rejoice to see the Campbells humiliated; some might feel loyalty to the king. But most still believed that, in spite of Montrose's remarkable success, ultimate victory would lie with the Campbells.

They therefore remained neutral or accepted recruitment into Argyll's forces.

As he moved north, Montrose found things much the same in Lorne and Lochaber as further south; few would join him. The remnants of the once great Stewarts of Lorne swore loyalty to the king and were spared plundering, and about 150 Stewarts of Appin joined the rebel army. But most of those who made overtures to the rebels did so simply to avoid plundering. Alasdair MacColla consulted his priest about such offers, and agreed to show mercy to all who would abjure the covenants and join the royal army, but few of those who pleaded for mercy were willing to go so far; Father MacBreck explained that the Campbells were 'a crafty race, savage and tyrannical when in power, but abject and timid in defeat, and faithless even while they ask for mercy', trying to avoid commitment to the rebel cause. Campbell of Inverawe reached an agreement with Donald Farquharson, delegated by Montrose to deal with such negotiations, but then attacked a raiding party laden with plunder led by Farquharson. Inverawe was wounded and forced to flee to Dunstaffnage Castle for safety. Campbell of Ardchattan (whose mother was a MacDonald) succeeded in preserving his lands by providing a valuable service to the rebels. At the mouth of Loch Etive Montrose's army was brought to a halt by lack of boats, and a long detour of many miles round the loch seemed inevitable, justifying Montrose's fears about the difficulty of marching across the teeth of a comb. But Ardchattan, eager to hasten the rebels out of Argyll (and off his own lands), supplied boats to ferry them across the narrow mouth of the loch, their great herds of plundered animals swimming beside them. The ebbing tide carried some of the cattle down to the sea, where they were retrieved by the Campbell garrison of Dunstaffnage. A similar crisis delayed Montrose at Loch Leven, but again boats were eventually found. Now for the first time since leaving Blair Atholl his army was in lands where the majority of the population was friendly. The army's priests rejoiced in the support for Catholicism shown by the Stewarts of Appin and the MacDonalds of Glencoe, Glengarry and Keppoch, but found the Camerons a disappointment, being 'less civilised and less susceptible to piety'.

Once in Lochaber, Montrose moved north-east up the Great Glen, through Inverlochy (Fort William) to Kilcumin (Fort Augustus) at the south end of Loch Ness. Here he halted in the last days of January, undecided which way to turn next. The ravaging of Argyllshire was over. It had been immensely successful in killing, destruction and plundering, but far from easing his perennial problem of manpower it had made it worse. New recruits gained were outnumbered many times over by the clansmen who had now dispersed to deposit their plunder, to rest, and to tell of their deeds. Montrose had entered Argyll with perhaps 3,000 men. He had suffered no significant losses through battle or disease, but he had only 1,500 or 2,000 by the time he reached Kilcumin. In the long term the situation was reasonably encouraging; most of those who had left him would doubtless eventually return, bringing others with them attracted by tales of good fighting and easy plunder, and several chiefs came to consult with Montrose. Angus MacDonald, effective chief of Glengarry, now came to join the men he had previously sent out to serve Montrose, and Sir Lachlan MacLean of Duart and other MacLean chieftains arrived with a few men, having evidently left orders to raise their clan in arms. But Montrose's problem was short-term. He knew that a mainly Campbell army, bent on revenge, was hot on his tracks. Ahead of him at the north end of the Great Glen a large army of covenanters, perhaps 5,000 strong, had been levied in Ross and Moray to block his advance — though the fact that it was composed mainly of raw levies hastily swept together and that it was led by the eternally vacillating earl of Seaforth meant that it was a less formidable threat than it would otherwise have been.

As a place from which to watch the movements of these enemies and decide how to react to their approach, Kilcumin was well chosen. Montrose was between two enemies, but if he moved quickly he could attack one before the other could help it. Or if he decided that he was not strong enough to stand and fight, ways of escape were open to him; by marching up Glen Moriston or Glen Garry he could regain the west coast; or, by using the Corrieyairack Pass, he could take his army into Badenoch. But a quick decision was necessary if he was not to lose the initiative to his enemies.[26]

While at Kilcumin Montrose had a band or bond drawn up for signature, a bond of union and mutual defence to be signed by the king's loyal subjects who were now fighting for God, king and country. Some such equivalent to their enemies' covenants was badly needed to bind together the diverse interests which fought under Montrose, but it is doubtful if the bond now produced really served any useful purpose. In some ways it emphasised differences instead of disposing of them. The cause of God could not be defined in any but the vaguest terms, for it had to be acceptable to both Catholics and protestants, and Montrose felt it necessary to have it approved by a Catholic priest before it was signed.[27] Many of the signatures on the bond were only added later, after the battle of Inverlochy, and some of these simply represent token loyalty given to avoid plundering. Those who actually signed at Kilcumin doubtless include Montrose and Alasdair MacColla. Donald Glas MacDonald signed as representative of the MacDonalds of Keppoch, joining Angus MacDonald younger of Glengarry and the captain of Clanranald. Sir Lachlan MacLean of Duart and Murdoch MacLean of Lochbuie, Duncan Stewart of Appin, Donald Cameron tutor of Locheil, Donald Robertson tutor of Struan, and Patrick Roy MacGregor of that Ilk were the main representatives of Highland clans to sign, and they were joined by some of the handful of Lowland royalists who accompanied Montrose. But it is perhaps significant that no representative of Alasdair MacColla's Irish troops signed. Concessions to Catholic consciences might satisfy their religious doubts, but as representatives of the confederate Irish they could not swear loyalty to the king in the sweeping terms of the Kilcumin bond, even if they had been sent to fight under his lieutenant general. It could of course be argued that as Alasdair MacColla commanded the Irish he signed for them, but nonetheless the absence of the signatures of their leading officers serves to emphasise that not all Montrose's men were committed royalists. And it may well be that Montrose made no effort to get them to sign. Trying to create a united Scottish, Highland and Lowland, royalist movement was difficult enough without adding the further complication of the alien Irish.[28]

When Argyll had left Badenoch in mid-November 1644, thinking campaigning was over until the spring, he had journeyed to Edinburgh. By 27 November he had taken his seat on the committee of estates, and doubtless took part in debates on the failure of his forces to defeat the rebels. His services in leading the army against the rebels were approved, but he was relieved of command. This was hardly surprising; it was not just that he had failed, but that he had never really been intended to lead national armies in a major civil war. He had been commissioned to command against the rebels when it had been assumed that the rebellion was a fairly minor affair and that the fighting would be in a remote corner which was regarded as an exclusively Campbell responsibility. Now that a major campaign was necessary, and Argyll and other covenanting nobles such as Lothian and Burleigh had shown themselves incompetent as commanders, the natural thing to do was to recall one of the covenanters' prized professional soldiers with continental training from the army in England. William Baillie was therefore brought back to Scotland and given the command with the rank of lieutenant general; but Argyllshire and the Isles remained under Argyll's command, for only he could organise effective action in that difficult area. He was therefore to go west to organise action against the remaining rebels there — Montrose and Alasdair MacColla might be in Atholl but the Irish still held Mingary Castle in Ardnamurchan — and to prevent any further landings from Ireland. But before he left Edinburgh Argyll quarrelled with Baillie; he still hoped to exercise influence over the army Baillie now commanded, but Baillie refused to accept such interference.

Argyll evidently left Edinburgh by 13 December. He can barely have reached Inveraray before he heard the astonishing news that the rebels were advancing from Atholl into his lands. By 20 December the committee of estates in Edinburgh knew of the rebel move and ordered William Baillie to set off in pursuit through Breadalbane towards Inveraray. Six days later Baillie was again urged to march with all speed after the rebels who were on their way to Kintyre. The need for the second order probably reflects both the disorganisation of the covenanters' forces (they had not been expecting a winter campaign, and their new commander was only just taking over from Argyll) and the reluctance of Baillie with a Lowland army to try to emulate the Gaels in marching through supposedly impregnable passes in winter. He therefore marched by a more southerly route, taking his men westwards by way of Dumbarton. At Roseneath he met Argyll. The two men were already on bad terms and Argyll, now suffering from the added humiliation of his recent flight from Inveraray, was determined not to suffer the indignity of having to be restored to his lands by Baillie and a Lowland army. If his reputation was to survive in the Highlands, he needed to defeat the rebels himself. By the time Baillie reached Roseneath (early January 1645) Argyll knew the rebels were marching away northwards, and his need for military aid for his clansmen was not therefore so great as before. He was a member of the committee which had been set up by the committee of estates to advise Baillie while he campaigned in the west, and he persuaded the other members that Baillie's army was not needed, and that anyway it would be impossible to feed so many men in winter in a country already devastated. Baillie was therefore ordered back to Perth with most of his men; 1,100 of his best infantry were left behind to join the Campbells under Argyll in pursuing the rebels.[29]

To stiffen further the assembling Campbell levies Argyll had sent for Sir Duncan Campbell of Auchinbreck and most or all of his regiment of the Scottish army in Ireland. This quickly revealed that the loyalties of some members of the regiment were now divided. Ewen MacLean of Treshnish had served as a captain under Auchinbreck, but on reaching Scotland he changed sides and joined Montrose (along with Hector MacLean of Kinlochaline, who is said to have previously served under Auchinbreck).[30]. An additional setback to Campbell preparations was that Argyll dislocated his shoulder and injured his face in a fall from a horse.[31] Nonetheless he soon led his army north — though he may have commanded from his galley. By 22 January he was at Castle Stalker; by 31 January he, the Campbell levies, and the 1,100 Lowland infantry were at Inverlochy, whence he urged the hasty assembly of food and ammunition.[32]

In all, Argyll gathered about 3,000 men at Inverlochy. News of this quickly reached Montrose at Kilcumin. Tradition asserts that Ian Lom MacDonald, the poet of the MacDonalds of Keppoch, brought the vital message (to Alasdair rather than Montrose, by one account), which is at least more likely than the rival tradition that Allan Dubh Cameron of Lochiel, the chief of the Camerons, was the messenger, for he was a very old man. A convenient compromise asserts that Ian Lom brought the message, but that Lochiel sent him![33] Both Father MacBreck and Patrick Gordon attribute to Lochiel another role in the preparations for the coming battle. He had the reputation of being a seer or prophet, and predicted to Argyll that a decisive defeat would be suffered at Inverlochy by those who came there to seek battle. That Argyll laughed this off (as is claimed) is likely enough, though it has been asserted that it influenced his decision to remain on his galley and not command his army in person.[34] More likely Argyll, still not recovered from his fall and perhaps at last beginning to doubt his skill as a general, was happy to leave the command to a kinsman, Auchinbreck. Lochiel had little reason to love the Campbells, who were increasingly asserting their influence in Lochaber, but for the moment remained on good terms with Argyll — partly as Argyll had possession of his grandson, Ewen. Slyly undermining Campbell morale through gloomy prophecies may have been his way of supporting their enemies.[35]

The news that Argyll was at Inverlochy can hardly have come as a surprise to Montrose; he had marched north to avoid being trapped by the assembling Campbell forces. But now that he had drawn them out of their own lands into territories hostile to them, he decided to attack them before they were further reinforced and advanced further. The successful ravaging of Argyll might be dismissed as a fluke, achieved simply through good luck and the achievement of surprise. To defeat Argyll in battle in the heart of the Highlands would seem a much more decisive demonstration that the fortunes of the Campbells were, at last, in decline. Moreover, had Montrose tried to march off and avoid battle he would probably have suffered massive desertions from his already small army. Most of his Highlanders had been recruited from the west-central Highlands, the area centred on Inverlochy. The Campbells had already, on their march through Appin, begun to plunder and waste the lands of those who had joined Montrose. Faced with the choice of marching off with Montrose or returning to try to protect their lands and families from the vengeance of the Campbells, there is little doubt that most would have chosen the latter. Alasdair MacColla and the Irish would not have been persuaded easily to leave the Clan Donald and the Irish garrison in Mingary Castle to their fates.

Thus to march to defeat the Campbells at Inverlochy was obviously Montrose's first priority — if it was possible. The numerical odds against him were great, but he retained the willingness to take great risks without which the whole campaign would have been impossible. He did, however, conclude that to advance directly down the Great Glen on Inverlochy would be to invite disaster; his enemies would have good warning of his approach and plenty of time to deploy their forces to best advantage. And the very fact that moving down the glen was the only obvious way for him to advance on Inverlochy meant that, if another route could be found, his chances of surprising his enemies were good. Such a route was found, though it involved passing through the mountains by ways thought impassable in winter. Alasdair MacColla and his allies had argued that the mountain passes into Argyll were not impassable, and had been proved right; as if to outbid them in daring, Montrose resolved on an even more adventurous march. After the success of the march through Argyll he knew the physical endurance of which his men were capable; by using this to the full he might be able to surprise the Campbells at Inverlochy. Always an intensely competitive man, only content when his own leadership was undisputed, it is quite possible that he was determined on some decision which would win back for him the reputation with his men for leadership of unrivalled daring which he must to some extent have lost through his hesitation over the invasion of Argyll.

Montrose's extraordinary march took him and his army out of the Great Glen up Glen Tarff and thence over the mountains to Glen Roy and back into the Great Glen near Inverlochy. The march was through deep snow in places, but the weather again was with him; it was not so bitterly cold in the hills as might have been expected, as a thaw had set in — though this led to some difficulties as the rivers to be crossed were all in spate. Complete surprise was not achieved; some skirmishes with Campbell scouts and raiding parties were inevitable; and indeed, according to Patrick Gordon, Montrose, by advice of Alasdair and others, purposely sent forward a party to seek contact with the enemy, to draw the Campbells into battle and prevent them retreating. John Spalding supports the story, but it nonetheless seems highly implausible; what was the purpose of the epic march through the mountains if the only advantage it brought, surprise, was to be thrown away? It seems much more likely that Montrose sent forward a small party not so the Campbells would learn of his approach but to conceal it. This party would force any Campbells encountered into flight back towards Inverlochy before Montrose's army came in sight; they would therefore report only that they had come into contact with a small body of enemies, who would be assumed to be stragglers from Montrose's army or local men trying to protect their property or escape Campbell vengeance. Certainly this is what seems to have happened. It was not until the night of 1 — 2 February that the Campbells realised that what they had taken to be a series of sporadic and unrelated contacts with isolated and disorganised parties of enemies had concealed the approach of Montrose and his Highland-Irish army. The Campbells and their allies then hastily assembled for battle, fearing a night attack. But it was not until dawn that Montrose led his men forward to battle.

Sir Duncan Campbell of Auchinbreck commanded the Campbell-covenanter army: a stout soldier but a vicious man was Robert Baillie's judgement. He had helped conquer the estates of the MacDonnells of Antrim in 1642. He had now returned to Scotland to find his own lands laid waste by Montrose's men. Like Montrose, he had little in the way of cavalry, so the wings as well as the centre of his line of battle were formed of infantry. The leaders of the Lowland foot, Lieutenant Colonel John Cockburn and Lieutenant Colonel John Roch or Rough, commanded the wings, which were composed mainly of their 1,100 men but also included some Highlanders. In the centre the Campbells and their Highland allies were concentrated — 'all there pryme men', armed with muskets, swords, bows and arrows and axes, were there, supported by two small cannon. In this array the Campbells prepared for battle, their left wing resting on Inverlochy Castle in which some forty or fifty Lowland musketeers were stationed.

Montrose approached and drew up his battle line opposite them. His wings were composed mainly of Irish. Alasdair MacColla commanded the right wing, evidently with Antrim's brother's regiment (led for the moment by Ranald Og MacDonnell) under him. Alasdair's old friend Manus O'Cahan and his regiment formed the left wing. The centre was divided into three lines. The vanguard was composed of Stewarts of Appin and Atholl, MacDonalds of Glencoe and the men of Lochaber, the latter including 300 or 400 Camerons, though their chief, old Lochiel, was watching the battle from Argyll's galley in Loch Linnhe. Behind the vanguard came the main MacDonald strength, the captain of Clanranald and his men and the MacDonalds of Glengarry, supported (it is said) by all the leading MacLean chiefs — Duart, Coll, Kinlochaline, Treshnish and Ardgour — though few of their men were present. The third line of Montrose's centre was led by Colonel James MacDonnell and consisted of his Irish regiment and a few Highlanders. When they had all taken up their positions facing the enemy, Montrose's men fell on their knees, while behind them their priests prayed for the support of the Virgin Mary and two Irish saints, long venerated in the Highlands, St Patrick and St Brigid. Battle then commenced.

As usual the confusion of conflict ensured that no-one had a clear picture of the whole battle, or the precise order of events, but Spalding and Patrick Gordon agree that Manus O'Cahan charged first with Montrose's left wing, closely followed by Alasdair MacColla with the right wing. Orders had been given by Alasdair that the Irish were not to fire their muskets until they had almost reached the enemy. This is what was done; having fired a musket volley at point blank range, the Irish threw down their guns, 'leapeing in amongst them with there swords and targates'. In the face of this determined attack the Lowland infantry panicked and fled almost immediately. The Highlanders in the Campbell centre thus had their flanks laid bare to attack by the triumphant Irish almost as soon as the battle began. Montrose then ordered his centre to charge the shocked Campbells — though he himself (who should have known) stated that it was the leading Campbells of the centre who began the battle; with 'great bravery' they gave 'the first onset, as men that deserved to fight in a better cause'. These conflicting accounts suggest that fighting must have begun almost simultaneously along the whole line of battle. In the centre, as on the wings, Montrose's men closed for hand-to-hand fighting after a single round of musket fire, coming 'immediately to push of pike, and dint of sword'.

Attacked furiously in front and flanks, the front line of the Campbells was forced to give ground, throwing the lines behind into disorder. Soon all order collapsed, and after what must have been (judging by the Campbell death toll) fierce fighting they broke in a general flight. Some fled to the castle for safety (including the two Lowland lieutenant colonels) but this proved a trap. Inverlochy Castle was soon forced to surrender, and though the lives of Lowlanders in it were spared, 'of tuo hunder highlanders, none eschaped the clane Donald furie' according to Patrick Gordon — though these may be the same two hundred men who according to Spalding were killed after being prevented from entering the castle. The routed Campbells fled in all directions, the main pursuit continuing for eight or nine miles and only stopping then as Montrose's men were tired after their arduous march before the battle. The Campbells and their allies died by the hundred on the battlefield, cut down as they fled, or drowned as they tried to escape across rivers in spate or were driven into the sea. Argyll, seeing the battle was lost, was carried off by his galley. There was little else he could have done, but this flight while his clansmen were being butchered at Inverlochy, following so closely on his similar flight from Inveraray, completely discredited him in the eyes of many. Total losses among the covenanters may have reached the remarkable proportion of 50%: about 1,500 out of 3,000 men. Montrose protested that 'I would have hindered, if possible' this great slaughter; but to do so would hardly have been in his own interests.[36]

Tippermuir and Aberdeen had been Irish victories. Inverlochy was a joint Highland and Irish victory. The battle differed from the earlier ones in another important respect as well. In the first two battles the enemy had been Lowlanders, and the war had thus had a racial side to it. But Inverlochy was a battle in a Gaelic civil war, and (like the ravaging of Argyllshire which had preceded it) it demonstrated that, great as the hatred of Irish and anti-Campbell Highlanders for Lowlanders might be, the hatred of Gael for fellow Gael was even greater. The Lowlanders in Inverlochy Castle were spared, but the Campbells and other Highlanders were massacred. It was highly appropriate, almost symbolic , that at the start of the battle the Lowland infantry had been driven from the field; they were almost irrelevant, cleared aside so that the real business of the day, the slaughter of Campbells, could begin. Montrose himself, indeed, was almost an irrelevance in Gaelic eyes, and there was a strong tendency to ignore or deny his part in the battle. One of the earliest accounts of Inverlochy to reach Ireland stated that Alasdair MacColla had routed the Campbells and asserted that Montrose had been in a different part of the country at the time.[37] A tradition finds a different way, and a rather odd one, of depriving Montrose of credit for the victory: Alasdair MacColla began the battle without awaiting Montrose's orders, so he and not Montrose was the real commander of the victorious army![38] Religion also isolated Montrose. He might see Inverlochy as a victory won for a protestant king, but most of his men celebrated a victory for Catholicism against the heretic, all the greater as it had been won on the feast of the Purification. As Father MacBreck exulted (with a clerical joy in bloodshed and death rivalling that of the worst covenanting ministers), 'On the Festival of the Purification of the holy Virgin Mary, the enemy who blasphemed the Mother of God, were killed and cut off, almost to a man';[39] the better the day, the better the deed. Logically Montrose too should have been killed as a blaspheming heretic.

In the centre of the Highlands the most successful clan of recent generations had been routed utterly by fellow Gaels after its lands had suffered devastation. Argyll was discredited, many of his leading kinsmen were dead or captives. Auchinbreck was among the dead, accompanied by '16 or 17 of the chief Lords of Campbell'.[40] One measure of the impact of the battle in the Highlands is the remarkable quantity of Gaelic poetry, by both victors and (in one case) vanquished, that it inspired; and poets continued to refer to the battle throughout the coming century — with, of course, Alasdair MacColla rather than Montrose as the real hero.[41]

Greatest of all is Ian Lom MacDonald's hymn to heroic deeds, revenge and bloodshed — which completely ignores Montrose. 'Have you heard of the heroic countermarch made by the army that was at Kilcumin? Far has gone the fame of their play — they drove their enemies before them', he begins, and then tells of how he watched from a hill and saw the Clan Donald victorious. This was ample compensation for the devastation the Campbells had been causing on the lands of their enemies — even if the Braes of Lochaber were to remain uncultivated for seven years, the price would be worth paying. With glee Ian Lom rejoices in the naked corpses of Campbell warriors — the battered heads, the glazed eyes, the hacked and slashed bodies and limbs:

> You remember the place called the Tawny Field?
> It got a fine dose of manure;
> not the dung of sheep or goats,
> but Campbell blood well congealed.

Joy was not to be tempered by any remorse:

> To Hell with you if I care for your plight,
> as I listen to your children's distress,
> lamenting the band that went to battle,
> the howling of the women of Argyll.

For Ian Lom the heroes of the battle were the Clan Donald warriors led by 'Alasdair of the sharp cleaving blades'; for the poet not only ignores Montrose: he makes no mention of the Irish or of the other clans. The only reference to any clan apart from the MacDonalds and the Campbells is a rebuke aimed at the clans of Mull for not being present at the battle — the MacLeans of Duart had only sent a few men:

> Alasdair of the sharp, biting blades,
> if you had the heroes of Mull with you,
> you would have stopped those who got away
> as the dulse-eating rabble took to their heels.

Lowland participation in the battle is acknowledged only briefly — and contemptuously:

> Alasdair, son of handsome Colla,
> skilled hand at cleaving castles,
> you put to flight the Lowland pale-face:
> what kale they had taken came out again.

But of the wider issues implied by the presence of these despised cabbage-eaters at the battle, nothing is said. Ian Lom was well aware of such issues, and elsewhere wrote eloquently of the heroic Montrose and of the royalist cause; but here he is concerned only with the cause closest to his heart, the cause of the Clan Donald.[42]

Ian Lom records that one of the enemy dead at Inverlochy was 'the darling of the women of Kintyre'. The reference is evidently to Sir Duncan Campbell of Auchinbreck,[43] but it is surprising that the poet does not make more of his death, for it has a central place in the poetry and traditions which surround the battle. A song in praise of Alasdair MacColla claims that it was Alasdair himself who slew Auchinbreck.[44] Tradition, like the poem surviving in several different versions, adds further detail. Auchinbreck did not die in the battle, but was killed afterwards in cold blood by Alasdair MacColla. He had fought bravely, forcing back the MacDonalds a little wherever he appeared, but was eventually captured and brought before Alasdair. By one tradition he gave Alasdair information as to which clans had supported the Campbells in the battle, in return for a promise of mercy; but whatever passed between the two men, in the end all Alasdair would offer Auchinbreck was a choice of deaths: hanging or beheading (or, by another account, flaying or beheading). The doomed general replied, in a phrase which became proverbial, *dà dhiù gun aon roghainn*, 'two evils and no choice'. Alasdair then brought the debate to an end with one swing of his sword, but, messily, he misjudged his stroke; instead of cutting through his enemy's neck he sliced off his head above the ears.[45] These traditions of Auchinbreck's death are not confirmed by written historical sources, but they may well be true. Alasdair may have felt a special bitterness towards Auchinbreck as the man whose family had been granted the office of hereditary colonels of Argyll to reward their services in expelling the

MacDonalds from Kintyre;[46] as the man who had occupied the lands of the MacDonnells of Antrim in 1642; as the man who in the same year may have plotted to assassinate Alasdair when the latter tried to make his peace with the Scottish army in Ireland; and finally of course as the man who had commanded the Campbells at Inverlochy. Killing Auchinbreck helped compensate for the frustration felt at the escape of Argyll himself. It is known that when in 1647 Argyll was asked what he would do if Alasdair was captured, he replied that he would give him the choice of hanging or beheading, which suggests that the tradition of Auchinbreck's manner of death is true and that Argyll was determined to avenge his kinsman in the same way.

A fierce lament for Auchinbreck, ascribed to his sister Florence, brings out the divided loyalties of Gaeldom's civil war. The unfortunate woman was married to John (Ian) MacLean of Coll, and her husband and her son, Hector Roy, had fought for Montrose at Inverlochy. At heart she remained a Campbell: 'were I at Inverlochy, with a two-edged sword in my hand, and all the strength and skill I could desire, I would draw blood there, and I would tear asunder the Macleans and Macdonalds, and I would bring the Campbells back alive'. No woman on Coll shares her grief for Auchinbreck, but the women of Inveraray, Auchinbreck and Carnassary are lamenting. Florence complains that her rights have been taken from her, presumably because of her loyalty to the Campbells, and given to Janet (evidently her daughter). She therefore curses Janet and her own son Hector Roy. Tradition adds that soon after Inverlochy Florence went mad; whether or not this is true, the poem starkly portrays a woman in the first wild paroxysms of grief, torn between the conflicting claims to her loyalty of Campbells and MacLeans.[47]

The proportion of seventeenth century Scottish Gaelic poetry by women is surprisingly high — a feature which Gaelic culture shares with the cultures of many other 'heroic' warrior societies, though it is not easy to explain.[48] The works of two other woman poets lamenting their dead at Inverlochy survive. Duncan Campbell of Glenfeochan is said by tradition to have tried to flee across a river on horseback but to have been caught by Alasdair MacColla. The fight between the two men was going against Alasdair until he tricked Glenfeochan into thinking that he was about to be attacked from behind; when he looked round Alasdair managed to inflict a mortal wound on him, though with his dying blow he disabled Alasdair's horse.[49] There may have been some previous connection between the two men which had led to hatred or rivalry between them; yet another work by a woman poet, Dorothy Brown, puzzlingly assures Alasdair 'you are my loved one, and not Campbell of Glenfeochan, or any who came of his people'.[50] After Inverlochy there can have been few of Glenfeochan's people left, for in her poem his widow laments the deaths of her husband, her three sons, her four brothers and her nine foster-brothers. Such losses in one family seem at first incredible; but in an age when Highlanders still tended to fight in kin-based groups rather than in artificial military units it was quite possible for the killing of a group of enemies who had been surrounded to wipe out an entire family. Glenfeochan's widow, unlike Ian Lom, acknowledges the part of the Irish in the battle — and in the campaign in general; it was their arrival in Scotland which had given mettle to the

Clan Donald. Also included is a pointed reference to her menfolk's chief, the marquis of Argyll, in leaving his clan to its fate.[51] In the third poem written by a woman bereaved at Inverlochy, Mary Cameron (another of those who must have been torn by divided loyalties) laments her husband, Patrick Campbell younger of Inverawe, who had died of wounds after the battle.[52]

Poems name some of the leading Campbell dead. Others can be added from a rather garbled list given by John Spalding,[53] eked out by other sources. Archibald Campbell of Glencarradale (in Kintyre) and Archibald Campbell, provost of Kilmun, were both killed, as Neil MacMhuirich confirms.[54] John Campbell of Lochnell, his brother Colin and his eldest son John Gorm were all slaughtered. So were John Campbell of Ardchattan's brother, and Colin Campbell of Barbreck's eldest son.[55] The Highland allies of the Campbells also suffered; among the dead were the heir of MacDougall of Reray and a Major Menzies.

The list of prominent prisoners taken was also long. Colin Campbell of Barbreck is referred to by Ian Lom as the captain of Clanranald's prisoner.[56] Archibald Campbell of Glencarradale's eldest son survived the battle and thus succeeded him, but was captured, along with a son of Archibald Campbell of Dunstaffnage, Alexander Campbell of Pennymore and Colin Campbell of Inverliver. Allies of the Campbells captured were led by Sir James Lamont, chief of his clan, and Robert Lamont of Silvercraigs,[57] while the Lowland reinforcements were represented by the two lieutenant colonels, Cockburn and Rough, though both were soon released on swearing never again to serve in arms against Montrose. Rather surprisingly the covenanters respected, at least in part, the desire of the two men to adhere to their oaths, and they were found posts in which they were not directly serving against Montrose. Cockburn became governor of Stirling Castle, Rough governor of Perth.[58] Another prisoner was the captain of Skipness, if the story is true that he had been struck down by a Stewart who was about to finish him off when Ewen MacLean of Treshnish interposed to save him, being wounded himself in the process; until a few weeks before, Skipness and Treshnish had been serving together as captains in Auchinbreck's regiment in Ireland.[59] A final prisoner of note according to Spalding was 'the Laird of Sanct McDonald in Kintyre'. Is 'Sanct' perhaps a corruption of Sanda, indicating that Argyll had managed to force one MacDonald to fight for him, as if to balance Patrick Campbell of Edinample's incongruous presence among the rebels?

All these prisoners were spared, 'being men of quality';[60] they were given quarter as men of sufficient status to be valuable for ransom or exchange. A number of ordinary soldiers were also spared when they surrendered: the Lowlanders in Inverlochy castle, and probably many Highlanders who had reluctantly served the Campbells but were now ready to enlist in the ranks of the victors. Donald MacGregor had been 'foot-boy' to Captain Hew MacDougall who had been killed in the battle, but was afterwards taken on by Alasdair MacColla as his 'footman', his personal servant.[61]

A catalogue of corpses and captives hardly makes easy reading, but it does bring out the extent of the disaster which had struck the Clan Campbell. Members of many of its leading families had died or been captured. Only two clans of note had been persuaded to fight alongside the Campbells, the MacDougalls and the Lamonts, and they had shared in the losses and humiliation of defeat, shaking their belief that the best policy was to obey and serve the Campbells. Other clans crushed or greatly weakened by Campbell expansion had already proved hostile at heart — MacNabs, MacGregors, Stewarts of Appin. So too had most of the clans of the central west Highlands, who had watched the spread of Campbell domination and had seen it being gradually asserted over them — several branches of the MacDonalds, the MacLeans, the Camerons. The message of the ravaging of Argyll and of the battle of Inverlochy was clear: it might be a far cry to Loch Awe, but it was not far enough to make the Campbells invulnerable. Argyllshire was not inaccessible, the Campbells were not invincible in battle. The seemingly inexorable rise of the clan could be checked, and perhaps reversed. But however complete the victory, the process of destroying the Campbell empire had only just begun. If there is any truth in a hostile Argyllshire tradition, Alasdair MacColla himself realised the limitations of what had been achieved so far. On the day after the battle he is said to have mused, 'I am greatly pleased that the sixteen Campbell lairds were killed . . . But what is the good of that. Are not sixteen wives at home and the sixteen Campbells in their wombs?'[62]

For some, led by Montrose, Inverlochy had of course a much wider significance. Argyll, the great champion of the covenants, had had his men routed and had himself been discredited. Lowland royalists as well as Highlanders would not fear Argyll so much as in the past. With three great victories behind him, Montrose now felt that the complete overthrow of the covenanters was in sight. The day after Inverlochy he wrote to Charles I that 'I am in the fairest hopes of reducing this kingdom to your Majesty's obedience. And, if the measures I have concerted with your other loyal subjects fail me not, which they hardly can, I doubt not before the end of this summer I shall be able to come to your Majesty's assistance with a brave army' to make the king's English enemies as well as the Scots suffer the just rewards of rebellion.[63] Montrose may have exaggerated his own confidence — he was trying to hearten the king, to prevent him despairing and making concessions to his enemies — but undoubtedly Inverlochy was a great royalist victory in the war of the three kingdoms as well as a great MacDonald and Irish victory in the Gaelic civil war. But how was it to be followed up and exploited to the full? Many of his men would probably have liked to march back into Argyllshire to gain further revenge on the Campbells. But Montrose could argue that they had already suffered so greatly that it would be a long time before they were again a significant threat to their enemies; and to turn back into Argyll would look like flight before the army Seaforth had assembled at the north end of the Great Glen. Moreover victories in the Highlands, however sensational, would not in themselves destroy the regime of the covenanters. The decisive battles would be fought in the Lowlands, and it was time to return there before the absence of the rebels in the Highlands allowed the covenanters time to recover their balance and complete the preparation of Lieutenant General Baillie's army to march against them.

A few days after the battle Montrose therefore marched away from Inverlochy northwards up the Great Glen. Victory had brought him many new Highland recruits. Old Lochiel left Argyll and brought in a hundred well armed Camerons 'all dressed alike',[64] though these men and the other Camerons already with Montrose probably did not stay with him for long. MacLean of Duart had left his brother, Donald MacLean of Brolas, to raise his clan in arms, and after Inverlochy Donald brought out hundreds of men (though the estimate of 1,100 is probably greatly exaggerated) — MacLeans, MacNeills and MacQuarries. Alasdair MacColla is said to have been left behind at Inverlochy to await Donald MacLean's men, they then marching off together to catch up with Montrose.[65]

The covenanters' reaction to news of Inverlochy was a mixture of bewilderment and horror. The Scottish parliament was in session, and on 11 February it formally declared Montrose, Alasdair MacColla and some of their leading supporters to be forefaulted — being guilty of treason they had forfeited all rights to their lands, property, titles and lives.[66] Next day the general assembly of the kirk issued a solemn and seasonable warning on the state of affairs in all three kingdoms which included a passionate denunciation of the way in which 'the hellish crue under the conduct of the excommunicate and forefaulted Earle of Montrose, and of Alaster Mac-Donald, a Papist and an Outlaw, doth exercise such barbarous unnaturall, horrid, and unheard-of cruelty, as is above expression'.[67] A week later Argyll was present in parliament to give an account of his campaign against the rebels; to save face his wise and diligent conduct was approved.[68]

In his flight from Inverlochy Argyll had acted to ensure that Alasdair MacColla was deprived of one of the fruits of victory which he must have been hoping for. Coll Ciotach and his two sons Gillespie (Archibald) and Angus had been prisoners in Dunstaffnage Castle when Montrose and Alasdair had plundered their way past on the way to Inverlochy. Fearing that Alasdair would now return to attack the castle and free his father and brothers, Argyll had them hastened south to Dumbarton where they arrived before 13 February, perhaps even bringing them in his own galley. From there they were conveyed under heavy guard (Argyll's own horse troop) through Glasgow and Linlithgow to imprisonment in Edinburgh Castle, which they reached in late March.[69] Nonetheless, Inverlochy had in another way improved their chances of eventual freedom, as it provided the rebels with many prisoners. By 25 February the covenanters were considering a list of prisoners sent by Montrose with an offer to exchange them.[70] It was, however, to be over two months before any such exchange actually took place.

NOTES

1. Napier, *Memorials*, ii.176.

2. The translation quoted is from *Rel Celt*, ii.181, modified by MacLean, Sources, 14 and Dr. Colm O Boyle.

3. Gordon, *Britane's distemper*, 94-6; Napier, *Memorials*, ii.175-6. See also Wishart, *Memoirs*, 82.

4. Gordon, *Genealogical history*, 522.

5. Leith, *Memoirs*, i.303-8.

6. Ibid, i.310-11; Wishart, *Memoirs*, 82.

7. Leith, *Memoirs*, i.303.

8. Ibid, i.305.

9. Baillie, *Letters*, ii.262-3.

10. *Rel Celt*, ii.183.

11. Carte, *Original letters*, i.75.

12. Napier, *Memorials*, ii.175.

13. Guthry, *Memoirs*, 174.

14. Wishart, *Memoirs*, 81.

15. Spalding, *Memorials*, ii.442-3.

16. Gordon, *Britane's distemper*, 98.

17. Grieve, *Colonsay and Oronsay*, i.279; MacLean, Sources, 18; C. Fergusson, 'Sketches . . .of Strathardle, No. VI', *TGSI*, xxi (1896-7), 345-6; G. Gillies, *Netherlorn* (London 1909), 127.

18. Cowan, *Montrose*, 177.

19. Campbell, *Adventures in legend*, 219; Matheson, 'Traditions', *TGSG*, v.41, 43; 91.

20. Grieve, *Colonsay and Oronsay*, i.278.

21. *APS*, VI.ii.461.

22. Innes, *Black book of Taymouth*, 100-1, 103; *APS*, VI.ii.275.

23. *Joint print*, 165-7; Cowan, *Montrose*, 252.

24. *APS*, VI.i.361-2, 790-1, ii.275.

25. J. McNab, *The Clan McNab* (Edinburgh 1907), 14-15.

26. For the movements of Montrose's army in Argyll and incidents of the campaign see Gordon, *Britane's distemper*, 96-9; Spalding, *Memorials*, ii.434, 442-3; *Rel Celt*, ii.181-3; Wishart, *Memoirs*, 79-82; Leith, *Memoirs*, i.308-19, 322; Carte, *Original letters*, i.75; Baillie, *Letters*, ii.262; Guthry, *Memoirs*, 172-4; Innes, *Black book of Taymouth*, 101.

27. Leith, *Memoirs*, i.324-5.

28. Napier, *Memorials*, ii.72-4, original at SRO, GD.220/3/184.

29. SRO, PA.11/3, ff.118, 126-v, 129v, 148v, 158v, 166; Baillie, *Letters*, ii.262, 417.

30. Guthry, *Memoirs*, 175; *Rel Celt*, ii.183; [J.C. Sinclair], *Historical and genealogical account of the Clan Maclean* (London 1838), 124-5, 285, 331; A.M. Sinclair, *The Clan Gillean* (Charlottetown 1899), 332, 435; J.P. MacLean, *History of the Clan MacLean* (Cincinnati 1889), 276.

31. Balfour, *Historical works*, iii.256; Baillie, *Letters*, ii.263.

32. *Joint print*, 167, 168.

33. A.M. Mackenzie (ed), *Orain Iain Luim. Songs of John Macdonald, bard of Keppoch* (Scottish Gaelic Texts Society, 1964), xxviii, 239; A. Mackenzie, *History of the Camerons* (Inverness 1884), 92-3; Guthry, *Memoirs*, 178; Campbell, *Adventures in legend*, 221.

34. Leith, *Memoirs*, i.320-1; Gordon, *Britane's distemper*, 100-1.

35. Mackenzie, *Camerons*, 94-5; J. Stewart, *The Camerons* (1974), 44-8.

36. Napier, *Memorials*, ii.176-7; Gordon, *Britane's distemper*, 100-2; Spalding, *Memorials*, ii.444-5; Guthry, *Memoirs*, 179; Leith, *Memoirs*, i.321-2; Carte, *Original letters*, i.75-6; *Rel Celt*, ii.183-5; Wishart, *Memoirs*, 83-5; [J.C. Sinclair]. *Clan Maclean*, 124-5.

37. Bodleian Library, Oxford, Carte MSS, 14, f.121. See also Gillies, *Netherlorn*, 128.

38. Campbell, *Adventures in legend*, 222.

39. Leith, *Memoirs*, i.320.

40. Carte, *Original letters*, i.76.

41. MacLean, Sources, 32; Mackenzie, *Orain Iain Luim*, xxxv, 242.

42. Ibid, 20-5, 238-43 provides a text of the poem, a prose translation, and notes on it. D. Thomson, *An introduction to Gaelic poetry* (London 1974), 120-2 gives a verse translation of much of the poem which has been used for the four complete stanzas quoted above.

43. Mackenzie, *Orain Iain Luim*, 23, 241.

44. J.L. Campbell and F. Collinson (eds), *Hebridean folksongs*, ii. (Oxford 1977), 134-7, 239-41, 327-9.

45. W. Drummond-Norrie, 'Inverlochy 1431-1645', *Celtic Monthly*, v (1896-7), 84; MacLean, Sources, 28; Campbell, *Adventures in legend*, 222-4; Matheson, 'Traditions', *TGSG*, v.35; Mackenzie,

Orain Iain Luim, 241; A. Nicholson, *Gaelic proverbs* (2nd ed, Glasgow 1951). 161; Campbell, *Records of Argyll,* 210-11. See also Gillies, *Netherlorn,* 128-9.

46. J.R.N. Macphail (ed), 'The Campbells of Auchinbreck', *Highland Papers,* iv (SHS 1934), 60.

47. MacLean, Sources, 28 provides the translation for the lines of the poem quoted. Dr Colm OBoyle made a rough translation of the rest of the poem for me. The full text is in A.M. Sinclair, 'A collection of Gaelic poems', *TGSI,* xxvi (1904-7), 238-9. A.M. Sinclair, *Clan Gillean,* 373-4.

48. Chadwick, *The growth of literature,* iii.738-9.

49. Campbell, *Adventures in legend,* 223-4.

50. MacLean, Sources, 28.

51. A.M. Sinclair, *MacTalla nan tur* (Sydney 1901), 92, translated in MacLean, Sources, 26-7 and (by Dr John MacInnes) in Cowan, *Montrose,* 186.

52. Sinclair, 'A collection of Gaelic poems', *TGSI,* xxvi.240; MacLean, Sources, 26n.

53. Spalding, *Memorials,* ii.444-5.

54. *Rel Celt,* ii.185.

55. Napier, *Memorials,* ii.190.

56. Mackenzie, *Orain Iain Luim,* 25.

57. *APS,* VI.ii.419; H. McKechnie, *The Lamont Clan* (Edinburgh 1938), 167, 168, 462.

58. Guthry, *Memoirs,* 179; *APS,* VI.i.430, 461.

59. [J.C. Sinclair], *Clan Maclean,* 126.

60. Carte, *Original letters,* ii.76.

61. Napier, *Memorials,* ii.186.

62. Matheson, 'Traditions', *TGSG,* v.35.

63. Napier, *Memorials,* ii.178-9.

64. Leith, *Memoirs,* i.323; Mackenzie, *Camerons,* 95.

65. [J.C. Sinclair], *Clan Maclean,* 124, 127.

66. *APS,* VI.i.317-23.

67. A. Peterkin (ed), *Records of the kirk of Scotland* (Edinburgh 1838), 425. After his forefaulture the covenanters insisted on calling Montrose simply James Grahame, as he had been stripped of his titles, but the general assembly clearly had not realised that such a change followed logically on forefaulture.

68. *APS,* VI.i.327.

69. *APS,* VI.i.324, 327, 328; F. Roberts and I.M.M. Macphail (eds), *Dumbarton common good accounts, 1614-1660* (Dumbarton 1972), 142; Balfour, *Historical works,* iii.276, 288; J.D. Marwick (ed), *Extracts from the records of the burgh of Glasgow, 1630-1662* (Scottish Burgh Records Society 1881), 509; C.S. Terry (ed), 'Free quarters in Linlithgow, 1642-7', *SHR,* xiv (1916-17), 77, 78; Black, 'Colla Ciotach', *TGSI,* xlviii.226-7. It is not certain that Coll and his sons were only moved after Inverlochy but the timing of the move strongly suggests this. In Leith, *Memoirs,* i.323 Father MacBreck asserts that the prisoners had previously been held in a strong castle on an island in Loch Awe, rather than at Dunstaffnage. This suggests the possibility that Argyll had transferred his prisoners south into the heart of Argyll some time before Inverlochy, perhaps when Alasdair had landed in Ardnamurchan the previous summer. If this is so, then the ravaging of Argyll had shown that even Loch Awe was not safe, so the prisoners were sent to Edinburgh once the rebels had moved north out of Argyllshire.

70. Balfour, *Historical works,* iii.283.

7

Auldearn Refought

AS Montrose advanced up the Great Glen after Inverlochy, the news of his latest victory spread panic in the motley army the covenanters had assembled to oppose him. Seaforth and many of his men were not convinced supporters of the cause they were in arms for, and George Wishart dismissed most of his army as 'a mere rabble of new levies, peasants, drovers, shopmen, servants, and camp-followers, altogether raw and unfit for service'.[1] Seaforth himself therefore fled and his army scattered. James Fraser vividly describes the tension and uncertainty of the early months of 1645 when Montrose seemed free to range through the Highlands at will. 'There is nothing heard now up and down the kingdom but alarms and rumores, randevouses of clans, every chiften mustering his men . . . Montross and MacKoll in every manes mouth.' Even the children were terrified, and 'if a few goates be seen uppon the topps of hills in a twilight its concluded to be Coll Coll Mackoll' — Alasdair MacColla.[2]

At the head of the Great Glen Montrose bypassed Inverness, where the covenanters had a garrison, and moved into Badenoch. Before Inverlochy he had sent Donald Farquharson there to try to recruit men among Huntly's Highland tenants,[3] and he now went to join him. At the house of Raitbeg (just east of Tomatin) Montrose, Alasdair MacColla, the captain of Clanranald, Donald Farquharson and other rebel leaders dined with Angus MacQueen of Corrybrough, who was married to Farquharson's sister. Later, when a prisoner of the covenanters, MacQueen was to claim that he had at first refused to join Montrose, but changed his mind when his guest threatened to burn his house. In fact he probably joined the rebels willingly, and he marched with them to Ballachestell (later Castle Grant) to try to persuade the Grants to rise. James Grant of Freuchie signed the Kilcumin bond and raised 300 of his men, but apart from this the recruiting march into Badenoch seems to have been a failure; there is no evidence that Farquharson managed to bring in many men. Montrose therefore moved northwards to Elgin. Seaforth and local covenanting leaders had been meeting in the burgh but they fled on 17 February on news of his approach.

At Elgin Montrose received reinforcements which made up for his lack of success in Badenoch. At last he won significant support from the Gordons. Huntly's eldest son, Lord Gordon and his younger brother Lewis joined him, and the men they brought with them were doubly welcome as they were horsemen, vital if Montrose was to campaign successfully in the Lowlands. That there were only 200 Gordon horsemen was something of a disappointment; many of the Gordons still followed Huntly himself in refusing to have anything to do with

Montrose. Nonetheless, he now had more cavalry than ever before. He sought further reinforcements by ordering all the fencible men of Moray to join him, but very few obeyed. He therefore sent out his men to burn and plunder the property of the disobedient. Such tactics brought a few to heel; Seaforth, Mackenzie of Pluscardine, Sir Robert Gordon of Gordonstoun and others came in and signed the Kilcumin bond to escape plundering, but they had little intention of serving Montrose and faded away as soon as he marched off; even the Grants returned to their homes after enthusiastically joining in plundering.

On 4 March Montrose and Alasdair MacColla marched east to Bog of Gight (Gordon Castle) and Banff, plundering or exacting money from local covenanters. They then turned south towards Aberdeen, reinforced by about 500 Gordon footmen and some horsemen. The covenanters had intended to use Aberdeen as their base for operations against the rebels, but on 7 March, before advance parties of Lieutenant General Baillie's army could reach the burgh, the demoralised covenanting garrison fled on a rumour of Montrose's approach, leaving the burgh defenceless. When Montrose reached Turriff representatives of Aberdeen, mindful of his previous visitation, came to him to beg for mercy on this occasion; all the inhabitants, they related, were preparing to flee rather than await the arrival of the dreaded Irish. Judging that clemency would be more expedient than further bloodshed, Montrose promised that his infantry, which included the Irish, would not come within ten miles of Aberdeen. On 9 March Nathaniel Gordon and a few troopers entered the burgh to establish a royalist presence, and next day they were reinforced by 100 Irish dragoons; Montrose was content to observe his promise to the letter but to break it in spirit. The fears of the townsmen can have been little stilled by the fact that the hated Irish now occupying their burgh had been put on horses and called dragoons! But though the Irish were back in Aberdeen they behaved in a disciplined manner. All fencible men of the town were ordered to prepare to march out under Montrose, who was meanwhile moving south destroying covenanting property and summoning the countrymen to rise in arms. On 12 March he camped at Kintore.[4]

The long triumphant march since Inverlochy on which no opposition had been met with had, however, led Montrose's men to grow careless. On 12 March a party of them left Kintore to spend a few days in Aberdeen celebrating their victories — altogether about eighty officers led by Nathaniel Gordon, Donald Farquharson and Captain John Mortimer. They saw no need to post guards, and left the town gates open as they got down to enjoying themselves. By this time part of Baillie's army was camped just north of the burgh of Montrose led by his second-in-command, Major General John Hurry or Urry. Hurry's record did not inspire confidence in his loyalty; he had begun the English civil war fighting for parliament, had deserted to the royalists, and had now abandoned the king for the covenanters. But there was no doubt that he was an able and daring commander. On hearing of the careless confidence of the royalist revellers in Aberdeen, he led a raiding party northwards. After dark on the evening of 15 March Hurry posted guards at the burgh gates to intercept any fleeing royalists while he and the rest of his men burst into the town. John Spalding graphically describes the astonishment of the royalists, dispersed about the burgh drinking in their lodgings, at the sudden clatter of horses' hoofs. Most had the sense to lie low, hoping to escape detection, but Donald Farquharson, 'ane of the noblest capitans amongis all the hielanderis of Scotland', came out to see what was happening. On the raiders' demanding his name he gave it, and was at once shot. Others shared his fate or were captured, the latter including his brother-in-law Angus MacQueen and two Irishmen. With Montrose camped at Kintore, Hurry could not afford to remain long seeking further victims, and he soon withdrew with his prisoners and all the horses he could round up — including Huntly's best horse, which Lord Gordon had lent to Nathaniel Gordon. The remaining royalist officers, some on foot through lack of horses, then fled to Kintore to break to Montrose the news of the death of one of his closest friends and advisers. Next morning Farquharson's naked body, stripped of the fine clothes in which he had so recently been celebrating, was found lying in the street.

The killing of Donald Farquharson caused panic in the already tense burgh of Aberdeen. If the death of a drummer boy before the battle of Aberdeen the previous September was Montrose's excuse for sanctioning the rape of the burgh after the battle, what vengeance would he exact for the loss of a close friend? There were rumours that covenanters in the burgh had sent information to Hurry which had led to the raid, so representatives again hastened to Montrose, pleading the burgh's innocence and asking for mercy. Montrose sent them home without an answer, and then issued orders for Alasdair MacColla to march on Aberdeen with over a thousand of the Irish. The worst fears of the Aberdonians seemed to be confirmed, and many prepared for flight. But all was bluff. Alasdair and the Irish had been chosen to march on the burgh as those most likely to terrify the inhabitants with fear of imminent death and destruction, but it had been decided to limit their punishment to threat. At the last moment Alasdair stopped his 700 Irish infantry outside the burgh, and though he himself entered it with some hundred horsemen they were kept under tight control — though the plundering of the houses of prominent covenanters was allowed.

Alasdair remained in the burgh for two nights, royally entertained by citizens desperate to satisfy every whim of this barbarian of whose cruelty and bloodlust they had heard so much. On 17 March Alasdair buried Donald Farquharson, and the next day he marched off to join Montrose, who was now at Durris having recommenced his advance southwards. The relief of Aberdeen was great, but nonetheless it had suffered substantially from this second visitation by the Irish. According to John Spalding, Alasdair seized £10,000 Scots worth of cloth, gold and silver lace and other goods for himself and his men. By 1646 (and again in 1648) the burgh was claiming to have given £20,000 Scots worth of goods to avoid the burning of the burgh, and that it had also suffered 'great plundering', that the council house doors had been broken open and the burgh charter chest rifled. Yet when a tax was imposed on the burgh to compensate those who had, on the magistrates' orders, advanced money, clothes and other goods to Alasdair and his officers to avoid the sack of the burgh, the value of such advances was put at only £1,440 Scots! This provides a useful reminder that figures given for losses have to be used with care, especially when given by those seeking compensation, like the Aberdeen authorities in 1646 and 1648. They also took to claiming, doubtless to make their supposed huge losses seem more credible, that Alasdair MacColla had spent four nights in the burgh. In fact he arrived on 16 March and left on the 18th — though he had to return later on the latter day to round up some Irish who had remained behind to rob citizens of both clothes and money in the streets.[5]

At Durris Montrose lost his 500 recently recruited Gordon footmen; they had little interest in the war outside their own province, and now returned northwards to defend their lands from local covenanters. Montrose marched south by way of Stonehaven, Fettercairn and Brechin, destroying the property of enemies as he passed. But though he was still advancing, his movements were hampered by the forces of Baillie and Hurry. They contented themselves with skirmishing with outposts and stragglers, but Montrose did not feel strong enough to attack them. Baillie had received substantial reinforcements from both England and Ireland and the time was clearly not ripe for a royalist break-out into the southern Lowlands, so Montrose eventually marched off westwards to Dunkeld, to worry the covenanters by threatening to cross the Tay and march south while at the same time being close enough to the Highlands to seek refuge there if attacked. The problem of holding his army together was once again becoming acute; the further he moved south the more men he needed but the fewer he had, for few of those who served under him shared his ambition to wage war in the south, and many wished to return to their homes to rest after the rigours of campaign, to deposit their plunder and to protect their families. Many Highlanders now left him, including the men of Atholl, now conveniently near their homes, and most of his remaining Gordon and other recruits from the North-East were restless and sought permission to leave. Montrose decided that it would be best to give way to such pressures and divide his forces, but determined first to raise the morale of his men and dismay the covenanters by an exploit which would demonstrate that the initiative still lay with him.

Suddenly on the night of 3 — 4 April Montrose marched back eastwards from Dunkeld to attack Dundee with a force of about 150 cavalry and 600 foot; of the rest of his men some were sent into Atholl, while some moved to Brechin to rendezvous with him after the attack. Intelligence reports had indicated that Baillie and Hurry had retired south of the Tay, but nonetheless the risk involved in the venture was great. Montrose's appreciation of the need for haste is suggested by the fact that he summoned the burgh to surrender but then launched his assault without waiting for a reply. After fierce fighting his men broke into the burgh led by Lord Gordon and Alasdair MacColla; Montrose himself remained outside with a reserve force. Dundee was spared the indiscriminate killing Aberdeen had experienced the previous year, but considerable losses were suffered in the sporadic fighting which continued all day, parts of the town were burnt, and plundering was widespread; an official investigation later put total losses at £162,229:15:8 Scots, and the burgh complained that a great many of its inhabitants had been slaughtered. By late afternoon the entire burgh was in the hands of the rebels, many of whom were dispersed plundering and drinking. At this point Montrose heard that Baillie and Hurry (who had not moved south of the Tay as he had thought) were only a few miles away and advancing fast. That Montrose had not sent out scouts to give him longer notice of enemy movements seems remarkable, and he was lucky to escape total defeat for the sake of a dashing plundering raid which could bring him no advantage commensurate with the risks involved; it was indeed a 'misconceived and unnessary' venture[6] which perhaps had its origins partly in the hurt Montrose's pride had received when Dundee had refused to surrender to him in September 1644 after Tippermuir.

However, remarkably Montrose and his officers managed to round up most of their men, fear of the covenanters outweighing the attractions of drink and loot, and to lead them in a precipitate flight out of the burgh eastwards as the covenanters entered it from the west. In spit of hot pursuit the coming of night enabled the rebels to escape, slipping northwards into the hills and thence back to Dunkeld. Some rebels were killed or captured, however, and the covenanters, desperate for a success to restore their flagging reputation, publicised events at Dundee as a great victory. Four or five hundred, it was boasted, had been killed, and many of the Irish and Highlanders had thrown away their plaids and arms in order to run the faster, 'to the number of 6 or 700'. Two of the dead were leaders of the Irish 'for when they fell, there was a terrible houling among them, and they fought desperately to recover their bodies'. One of the corpses remained in the hands of the covenanters, but its face was too disfigured for it to be identified. Some hopefully claimed that this was 'Col. Kittoch', others that it was 'OCain, a man of great esteem amongst them', though in fact both Alasdair and Colonel O'Cahan escaped. An English writer celebrating the 'victory' at Dundee rejoiced in the defeat of Montrose and his 'Papist or rather Atheisticall co-partner in blood and villany, Mac ODonnel, an Irish caniball', thus adding a new epithet to those heaped on Alasdair by his enemies. Though he escaped with his life, Alasdair did suffer one loss at Dundee. Donald MacGregor, the footman he had acquired at Inverlochy, was captured, still carrying his master's hat, cloak and gloves; it sounds as if Alasdair had taken full advantage of the eagerness of the terrified burgesses of Aberdeen to press gifts upon him, and had equipped himself with fine clothes.[7]

Dundee was not the great victory that the covenanters claimed; Baillie was blamed for letting most of the rebels escape, and he in turn blamed Hurry, with whom he was on bad terms.[8] But it was more a covenanting victory than a royalist one, though royalist writers tend to gloss this over by concentrating attention on the brilliance with which Montrose conducted the retreat. At Kirriemuir on the way back to Dunkeld Montrose divided his army. Lord Gordon and his brother Lewis were sent north to help their kinsmen resist pressure from local covenanters, while Alasdair MacColla was sent (either from Kirriemuir or Dunkeld) to recruit in the Eastern Highlands. Montrose himself led the remainder of his men west into Menteith and the Trossachs. By remaining in the southern fringes of the Highlands he would still seem to the covenanters to be threatening to march south into the Lowlands. They would have to deploy forces to intercept such a move, and this would prevent them concentrating their army to reconquer the North-East. Moreover, Montrose's pleas for help from the king, especially for a body of cavalry, had at last been answered — at least on paper. Charles had promised to do his best to send 500 horsemen into Scotland, and Montrose was therefore anxious to remain as far south as possible so this cavalry force would have the best chance of linking up with him before the covenanters caught up with it.[9]

The wait in the Trossachs proved futile. The cavalry in the end were never sent, and the only recruits Montrose gained from south of the border were a few Scots royalists, including Huntly's second son, Lord Aboyne. From Doune on 20 April Montrose, harried by Baillie's forces and having to keep constantly on the move, wrote to the king in exasperation. If only he had had the use of the 500 horse for a single month he would have been able to march to the king in England with 20,000 men — a boast that shows Montrose at his most absurdly over-confident, ready to claim that he could have changed the entire military situation in Britain overnight if only some small but vital piece of help had been given to him; not enough help to detract from his own glory, but enough for the lack of it to be the only reason for his relative failure. For at heart Montrose was realist enough to know that though his victories had been sensational they had brought little or no practical advantage to the king he wished to serve.[10]

Meanwhile Alasdair MacColla was plundering and recruiting in Aberdeenshire, on Deeside and Donside — he is recorded in the Braes of Mar, in Cromar, and in Glen Tanner. On Lord Gordon's orders he was joined by Forbes of Skellater, 'a strong gentleman' with 200 men; Forbes had formerly been plundering royalist lands but now, to escape the revenge of the Gordons, was co-operating with them. Alasdair and Forbes marched south together and raided Coupar Angus; the estates of Lord Coupar were ravaged, a troop of covenanting horsemen was scattered, and the parish minister, Robert Lindsay, was murdered. According to Henry Guthry, Alasdair undertook this raid to try to help Montrose, whom he knew to be hard pressed by Baillie's army. As Alasdair had hoped, some of Baillie's forces hastened east to deal with him, allowing Montrose to escape northwards, first into Atholl and thence through the hills to Deeside. Either there or further north in the Gordon country he was rejoined by Lord Gordon and Alasdair.[11]

Montrose would doubtless have preferred that they came south to rejoin him in action against Baillie, but the situation in the North-East dictated that the rebel army should reunite there. The covenanters of the area had reassembled in arms once Montrose had passed southwards, and they had been joined in attacking the royalists by Major General Hurry; for after the raid on Dundee the covenanters as well as the royalists had divided their army. Baillie had stayed in the south to watch Montrose while Hurry had marched north to deal with the Gordons and their allies. This forced Montrose to come north as well; in spite of his difficulties with the Gordons they were still among his strongest potential allies, and he could not allow them to be totally crushed.

Montrose's own version of events gives a rather different explanation of these movements in April, an explanation which is typical of him in that it does not admit the pressures that in fact influenced his movements, and claims that all were really dancing to his tune. 'The Rebels being somewhat strong, they heaving brought five or sixe Regiments more from England and Ireland, I thought it not safe to hazard to deale with all their forces together, but resolved to make a fraction to devide my forces to make them doe the liken, which when I got them to doe and at a good distance one with another, I marched from Forth to Spey (night and day) with long marches, to force Urrey [Hurry] to feight, who was then lying at Spey to raise the North.'[12] Thus Montrose was in complete control of events. He sent Lord Gordon and Alasdair north to tempt the covenanters to divide their forces; they obliged, and Montrose then quickly reunited his army and defeated Hurry before Baillie could come to the latter's aid; a classic example of persuading an enemy to divide his forces then taking advantage of this to isolate and destroy one part of his army. But doubt is immediately cast on this by the other evidence. Montrose did not divide his army simply to tempt Baillie into similar action; the Gordons virtually insisted on moving north, while he was determined to remain in the south to link up with the cavalry he hoped for from England. Moreover Hurry cannot have marched north in pursuit of Lord Gordon and Alasdair, thus falling into Montrose's carefully planned trap, for Hurry moved north not after the rebel detachment but at the same time. Lieutenant General Baillie met with covenanting leaders who had come south from Aberdeenshire and Kincardine for consultations at Brechin on 5 April, the day after Montrose had been chased from Dundee. The northern covenanters had probably come to ask Baillie for help; certainly this is what they got, for at the meeting Baillie agreed to send Hurry northwards. It was evidently on the same day that Montrose, at Kirriemuir on his way back to Dunkeld, sent the Gordons northwards. Hurry thus was ordered north before he and Baillie could have known that the rebels had divided; Montrose and the covenanters resolved simultaneously that the bitter feuding for control of the North-East was important enough to justify intervention and the division of their armies. The decision was taken on 5 April. The local covenanting leaders were back in Aberdeen by 7 April. Lord Gordon crossed the Dee on 8 April. Hurry reached Aberdeen on 11 April but was then delayed in his advance by a mutiny in his forces.[13]

Montrose was to exploit with great skill and speed the fact that the two sections of the covenanting army were further apart than the sections of his own forces, but the situation was not one which he had created. Had the rebels really been concerned from the start to keep Baillie and Hurry as far apart as possible, Alasdair's raid on Coupar Angus would never have taken place, for it drew part of Baillie's army north-eastwards, much closer to Hurry than when it had been watching Montrose in Menteith.

Once Montrose, the Gordons and Alasdair had linked up, they set off in pursuit of Hurry's army. Hurry had about 1,200 foot and 160 horse,[14] and with them he fell back through Moray towards Inverness, for there he would be reinforced by the covenanting garrison and by forces raised by the covenanters of Ross-shire and Sutherland.

Montrose camped at Auldearn. Hurry attacked him on 9 May and was

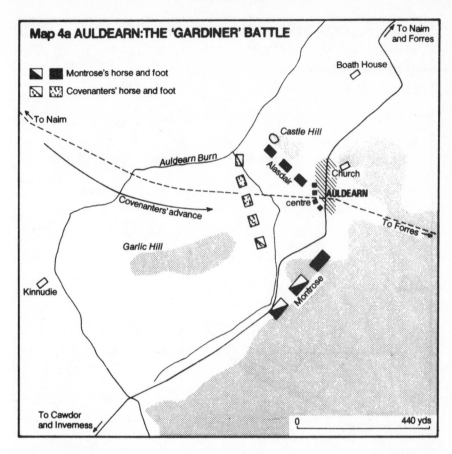

Map 4a AULDEARN: THE 'GARDINER' BATTLE

Montrose's horse and foot

Covenanters' horse and foot

To Nairn and Forres

Boath House

To Nairn

Auldearn Burn

Castle Hill

Alasdair

Church

AULDEARN

Covenanters' advance

centre

To Forres

Garlic Hill

Kinnudie

Montrose

To Cawdor and Inverness

0   440 yds

decisively defeated. This much is clear, but most other aspects of the battle are surrounded by confusion; Auldearn is by far the most difficult of Montrose's battles to reconstruct, and the reconstruction which is generally accepted is wildly misleading as it solves some problems by pure invention. All modern accounts of the battle are based, directly or indirectly, on the work of S.R. Gardiner, first published in 1886. According to this, Montrose carefully laid a trap for Hurry. The latter was tempted into attacking Aladair MacColla, thinking he was attacking the main rebel strength. In fact Montrose had drawn up most of his men out of sight ready to make an attack on Hurry's flank. The plan nearly failed either through Alasdair's force having been left too weak for the task entrusted to it, or because Alasdair stupidly nearly caused disaster by charging instead of fighting defensively; Gardiner favoured the former interpretation, ignoring George Wishart's charge that Alasdair, 'a brave man, but readier with his hands than his head', disobeyed orders, but modern biographers of Montrose have tended to favour Wishart — Alasdair 'made the dangerous mistake of leaving his position', he 'almost ruined everything'. But a great flank charge by Montrose came just in time to save Alasdair from the consequences of his own folly, and a major victory

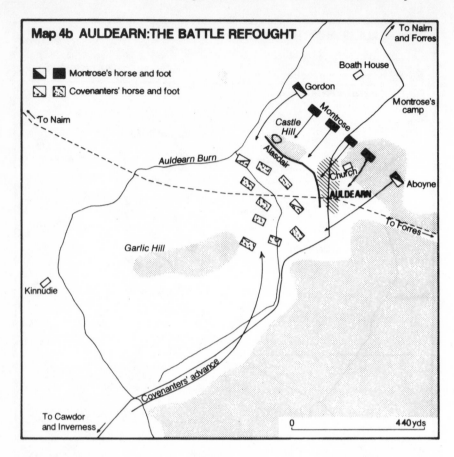

was won. Auldearn is thus crucial to the reputations of both Montrose and of Alasdair MacColla. In the accepted reconstruction Montrose displays outstanding tactical brilliance, unrivalled in the rest of his career; and Alasdair displays the characteristics which justify the judgement of him as 'brave but thick', showing his limitations by being too stupid to realise what Montrose was trying to do.[15]

Gardiner's reconstruction of Auldearn is, however, open to criticism on four main grounds. Firstly, having before him two main contemporary accounts of the battle, those of George Wishart and of Patrick Gordon of Ruthven, he chose virtually to ignore the latter (except for a few details) and put his faith in Wishart. But Wishart was, as usual, concerned to present Montrose as the consummate general, fully in command of the situation, and therefore was anxious to prove that if the battle nearly turned out to be a disaster for him, this must be someone else's fault — Alasdair MacColla's. Patrick Gordon on the other hand is an admirer of Montrose, but not a hypnotised hero-worshipper like Wishart. At times, as over Auldearn, he is prepared to criticise him severely. Such criticisms are not always trustworthy when he is dealing with the often strained relations between

Montrose and his own name, the Gordons; but in the essentials in which his account of Auldearn differs from Wishart's he has no Gordon axe to grind. Yet Patrick Gordon clearly regarded the near disaster at Auldearn as having been partly caused by Montrose's bungling. And Alasdair is not the man who nearly brought unnecessary defeat on the royalists; on the contrary, he was the man who saved the day when all seemed lost.

The second criticism of Gardiner's reconstruction is linked to the first. Like Wishart, he presents the battle as a matter of carefully drawn up forces, well thought out plans and logical decisions. Gordon by contrast tells of haste, muddle, confusion and improvisation that, taking all sources together, seems much more convincing. In his reconstruction Gardiner starts from the unquestioned assumption that Montrose planned the whole battle carefully. The disposition of forces he suggests is based on this assumption and on an examination of the ground, and he admits that it does not fit in with what Wishart says — and indeed that it is impossible to make complete sense of Wishart. Of the flank attack which he invents, Gardiner cheerfully assures his readers, 'The thing was so easy to do, and so advantageous, that Montrose can hardly have failed to do it.' This is a most extraordinary argument to find so great a historian resorting to, not only in the face of lack of evidence but of positively contrary evidence, and it turns his reconstruction into what ought to have happened rather than what the sources say happened. And in any case the underlying assumption that Montrose planned the battle in advance is almost certainly false; Montrose was taken by surprise by the enemy attack.

Thirdly, while Gardiner carefully studied the lie of the land at Auldearn itself, he assumed, again without question, that the covenanters approached Auldearn down the modern road from Nairn. But no source confirms this, and in fact the road was probably only a minor track in the seventeenth century. It seems the covenanters in fact approached from much further to the south — and if this is so, then Gardiner's own exposition of the topography of Auldearn makes his suggested flank attack an impossibility.

Finally, three major sources for the battle have come to light since Gardiner wrote. Some of Gardiner's followers have utilised details from them, but they have used them within the framework of Gardiner's reconstruction, failing to see that their evidence really demands a completely new look at the battle. Neil MacMhuirich's Gaelic account is little concerned with the overall shape of the battle, concentrating instead on detailed incidents, but on the whole it tends to support Patrick Gordon rather than Wishart. James Fraser's narrative is short but contains a few vital topographical clues, and the final new source is also tantalisingly brief: Montrose's own report of the battle to Charles I. This last is remarkable as much for what it does not say as for what it does, for it fails to provide a coherent picture of the battle, being so vague as to raise suspicions that it is purposely evasive. Not surprisingly, like Wishart it indicates that Montrose was in command of events; but its terse account of the battle does not sound entirely plausible, and it fits in with neither Patrick Gordon nor with Wishart. Of course it could be argued that Montrose was simply reporting the battle, not attempting a detailed description; and there is some truth in this. But had the great flank attack deduced by Gardiner ever taken place, it is remarkable that Montrose makes no mention of so brilliant a move on his part: false modesty was not among his failings. The impression remains that Montrose was not entirely happy with the battle, and had no wish to linger on the details of it. Thus the discovery of his own version of events in some ways creates more problems than it solves. Certainly this seems to have been the case where Wishart was concerned, for looking at his account and Montrose's together strongly suggests that Wishart had a copy of the letter before him as he wrote, but that he (understandably) failed to make sense of it; his misinterpretation of it evidently contributed much to the confusion apparent in his own account.[16]

According to Montrose, he pursued Hurry right up to Inverness. 'I pressed him so hard as I beat up his Rear for 14 miles, and put him to Invernesse.' Montrose then 'marched againe backe to Oldharne some 14 miles from him'; he had passed through Auldearn (in fact about eighteen miles, not fourteen, east of Inverness) earlier in his advance, and now returned there. Wishart confirms that Montrose pursued Hurry all the way to Inverness, also citing fourteen miles as the distance of the pursuit (doubtless taking these details from Montrose's letter), and he adds that Hurry reached Inverness under cover of darkness; next day Montrose marched back to Auldearn and camped. But Wishart's reference on its own is not entirely clear, and here Gardiner and his followers choose to accept Patrick Gordon's rather different story, which states that the same day that Hurry reached Inverness Montrose, in hot pursuit, was forced by nightfall to camp at Auldearn. It follows from this that if Hurry was only a few miles ahead of Montrose, it must have been much later by the time the former reached Inverness. Yet (according to Gordon) Hurry was back at Auldearn next morning and attacked Montrose. This is not merely implausible, it is virtually impossible. Hurry simply could not, in the darkness of one spring night, have reached Inverness, consulted local covenanting leaders, added their forces and the burgh garrison to his own men (already tired after a long march), and then marched them all back the eighteen or so miles to Auldearn.

Here, therefore, one must accept Montrose's own account, and Wishart's expansion of it. Hurry, with Montrose close behind him, reached Inverness on the evening of 7 May. That night or next day Montrose moved back to Auldearn while Hurry reorganised his forces in Inverness. James Fraser relates that Hurry crossed to North Kessock on what must have been the evening of 7 May (Fraser's dating is confused) to consult with the earl of Seaforth, and returned to Inverness the next morning. On the night of 8-9 May Hurry marched back to surprise Montrose and on the morning of 9 May the battle took place. This matter of Montrose's precise moves before the battle is of some importance, for if one accepts Patrick Gordon's version of events, Montrose had reached Auldearn for the first time as darkness was falling on 8 May, so he had no chance to study the terrain properly. His brilliant disposition of his forces for the battle next morning (on Gardiner's reconstruction) was therefore a remarkable testimony to his tactical genius, as at first light he was hastily positioning forces in an area he was seeing in daylight for the first time. But in reality Montrose had had plenty of time to move back to Auldearn (which he had already passed through) at leisure on 8 May, and he chose to camp there. Thus he fought the battle on ground he had chosen for his camp, not at a spot where he was forced to halt his advance by the coming of night; and in any case, it will be argued below that he made no brilliant dispositions before the battle.

As usual, the figures given for the strength of the forces engaged at Auldearn vary bewilderingly from source to source. Typically Montrose gives the lowest figure of any for his own force, 1,400 men, and a high figure for the covenanters, four to five thousand. Wishart awards him 1,750 men (including 250 horsemen) and Hurry 4,100. Patrick Gordon gives no total for Montrose's army but states that the covenanters had 4,000 infantry plus cavalry. He also cites some estimates that he had heard from covenanters; they thought Montrose had had not more than 2,000 foot and 300 horse, and the lowest figures they gave for their own strength were 3,000 foot and 700 horse. Only one source, John Spalding, ascribes as many as 3,000 men to Montrose; this is probably far too high, and the same may be true of his estimate of 4,500 covenanters. From this confusion one can only conclude tentatively that Montrose probably had something approaching 2,000 men, the covenanters about twice as many.

In composition Montrose's army differed considerably from those with which he had won his previous victories. For the first time he had a significant body of cavalry, several hundred men (mainly Gordons). And for the first time the army was not overwhelmingly Irish and Highland. Many of the Highlanders who had joined him after (or even before) Inverlochy had long since drifted away, and the numbers of the Irish had been depleted by casualties and desertion — the problem of Irish stragglers and deserters seems to have been growing, perhaps reflecting the increasing demoralisation of men long away from their own land and being marched endlessly on campaigns which seemed to be bringing little advantage to the Irish confederate cause. But in compensation for such losses Montrose now had the Gordons. According to Patrick Gordon, the men brought by Lord Gordon had more than doubled Montrose's strength, though this may be an exaggeration.

Hurry's forces at Auldearn were even more diverse than Montrose's. He had brought two infantry regiments, Loudoun's and Lothian's (or perhaps only part of the latter), with him on his march north, together with some troops of horse. Two further infantry regiments formed the garrison of Inverness, Lawers' and Buchanan's. Montrose refers to these four regiments as the best trained the covenanters had in the three kingdoms, but this is something of an exaggeration; certainly all was not well with Lothian's regiment, for it had formed the garrison of Aberdeen which had fled at the first rumour of Montrose's approach in March, and in April a mutiny in the regiment had delayed Hurry at Aberdeen for some days.[17] To these regular forces were added the levies of the north: the covenanters of Moray, led by the Inneses, Dunbars, Cummings and Roses, and of eastern Inverness and Ross-shire, led by the Frasers under Sir James Fraser (Lord Lovat's brother), the Rosses, Monros and some MacKintoshes. The earl of

Seaforth brought men of his own clan, the MacKenzies, and of the other clans of his vast estates — including MacAulays from Lewis in the far west. From the extreme north came the covenanters of Sutherland and Caithness under the earl of Sutherland. On paper this was a formidable roll call of names. But it is clear that not all the men available had come from the areas the names represented, and the covenanting zeal of many was doubtful; Seaforth in particular could hardly be trusted, though at last one side in the civil war had forced him to bring his men to battle.

In the middle of the night of 8-9 May Hurry marched with all his forces from Inverness, but he may not have known precisely where Montrose was camped, and may have found his march longer than he had expected. According to James Fraser, it was not until the River Nairn was reached (after about fifteen miles had been covered) that he heard for certain that Montrose was at Auldearn. He then hastened forward, anxious not to lose the advantage of surprise, though this meant that his men had to attack tired after a long march in pouring rain.

Two crucial questions now arise. How nearly was Montrose taken by surprise by the attack? And what direction did the covenanters attack from? The second question is not one which Gardiner ever seems to have asked. He simply assumed that the covenanters, approaching from Inverness, must have passed through Nairn and thence to Auldearn on roughly the line of the modern road. Yet one fact about the topography of Auldearn in the seventeenth century which has long been appreciated immediately casts doubt on this: Gardiner and his followers knew that in 1645 the main axis of the little village of Auldearn ran north — south, whereas the modern village's axis is at right angles to this, running east-west on the Nairn-Forres road. This was because the modern main road did not exist in the seventeenth century; it is an early nineteenth century turnpike.[18] The old road from Nairn to Forres ran well to the north of Auldearn, bypassing the village. But in the case of the old Inverness to Forres road it was Nairn which was bypassed; the road ran through Cawdor, passed some miles south of Nairn, and approached Auldearn from the south-west. This road, the only route of any significance to pass through Auldearn, then ran almost due north through the village, and joined the Nairn to Forres road north of the village.[19] Thus, taking the usual road eastwards from Inverness, Hurry would have marched his army roughly parallel to the present main road, but two or three miles inland, to the south of it, and would have crossed the River Nairn at least five miles above Nairn. He would then have moved north-east through Cawdor to Auldearn, attacking from the south-west rather than from the west. A few modern works have recognised that Hurry must have attacked from the south-west, but they have made this seem implausible by still assuming that he had somehow come through Nairn but then worked his way round to the south-west of the village; and it has not deterred them from continuing to believe in Gardiner's great flank charge by Montrose. They have simply swung the charge, like Hurry's approach, through an angle of 45°, having him charge due west instead of north-west as in Gardiner,[20] though this change in axis of the battle means that Montrose could not have hidden his men in what Gardiner had argued was the only spot in which they could have been concealed.

What do the sources for the battle have to say as to the direction of Hurry's approach? With one exception they say nothing, and this in itself strengthens the argument that he took the then usual route; had he made a detour through Nairn, this would surely have been mentioned. Such negative evidence cannot be pressed too far, but it receives confirmation from a clue given by James Fraser, the only contemporary to describe the battle who lived in the general area and who shows any knowledge of local place names. Fraser talks of the covenanters reaching the River Nairn; after leaving Inverness they made 'no stop till they came to Narden River'. It is highly improbable that he should refer to Hurry reaching the River Nairn if he meant that he had reached it in the royal burgh of Nairn — any more than he would have written of Hurry marching from the River Ness rather than from Inverness. The only reasonable deduction is that Hurry reached the Nairn well above the burgh. Another clue provided by Fraser only makes sense if one assumes that the covenanters approached Auldearn from the south-west; he states that there were very many covenanters killed among the banks and bushes around Kinnudie, Kinsteary and Brightmony. The covenanting dead at Kinnudie are explicable on the Gardiner-based reconstructions of the battle, for Kinnudie lies just south of west of Auldearn; but the dead at Kinsteary and Brightmony are not, for they both lie east of south of the village — almost directly behind the line of Montrose's supposed charge. On Gardiner's reconstruction the covenanters were driven back westwards and north-westwards; a few stray covenanters might have been killed to the south and east of the battlefield, but the many corpses reported there by James Fraser are an impossibility.

The evidence that the covenanters approached Auldearn from Cawdor and not from Nairn is thus strong. On the other of the crucial questions posed above, that of how nearly Montrose was taken by surprise, the problem is not that the sources are silent but that they contradict each other. Wishart assumes Montrose had time to make careful preparations to receive the covenanters' attack; he does not even indicate that Hurry was trying to surprise the rebels, though the night march from Inverness makes it clear that this was the case. Montrose similarly allows no hint that he had been surprised; he resolved to fight Hurry's superior army at Auldearn because he wanted to beat him before Baillie came north to join him. 'I resolved to feight, but chosed my posts and all advantages of ground, and to bide [await] them at the defence.' But Patrick Gordon presents a completely different picture, and one which fits in much better with what is known of the course of the battle. He states that Montrose was taken by surprise, and that this was in part his own fault. 'And indeid it canot be refuised but the generall was to blame, who, drawing so neir to his enemies, should not have bolded [built] his confidence wpon a generall report, but above all things should have bein cairfull of intelligence', sending out scouts and spies, capturing prisoners to interrogate about enemy movements and intentions; 'for want of which intelligence, if God had not prevented it beyond all expectation, all ther throates had bein cutt'.

The evidence provided by the rest of Montrose's career makes Gordon's charge plausible. His 'consistent neglect of adequate intelligence . . . was one of the most surprising, and potentially dangerous, aspects of his military career'.[21] At Fyvie, in the raid on Dundee, and now at Auldearn, his own leadership and the quality of his troops saved him from paying the full price of this extraordinary blind spot in his military virtues. But he was to fail to learn from these mistakes. His conduct leading up to his defeat at Philiphaugh, only a few months after Auldearn, displayed almost criminal negligence, and even his final defeat at Carbisdale in 1650 which led to his capture and execution owed much to inadequate intelligence.

Montrose had sent out some scouts and sentries on the night of 8-9 May, but they were not given adequate orders and were not properly supervised. The sentries 'had not gon far from the campe, being too confident that ther was no danger'. Some sought shelter from the rain 'which was very vehement all that night'. But it was one consequence of this rain that saved the rebels from surprise. When within four or five miles of the enemy Hurry, worried by the effects of the rain on the charges in his men's muskets, ordered them to fire and reload. To have unloaded without firing would have taken much longer, and Hurry wished to delay as little as possible in the hope of achieving surprise; it may also have been hoped that the heat generated by the firing would help to dry the guns. There was of course the fear that the firing would be heard by the enemy, so Hurry ordered his men to turn to face the sea, counting on the wind carrying the sound, already blanketed by the rain, away from the enemy.[22] This proved a miscalculation that ruined Hurry's otherwise daring and well executed plan for a surprise attack, for (still according to Patrick Gordon) a sudden change of wind carried 'the thundering report' of the volley to the ears of five or six scouts who had been sent out by Alasdair MacColla the day before.[23] They hastened back to camp to give the alarm and reported to Alasdair. He 'for all his dilligence' just managed to rouse two regiments, one Irish and one Gordon, from their beds by the time the enemy came in sight. In fact this force was not, it seems, two organised regiments but whatever men were first to arm and assemble; as well as Gordons and Irish it included Highlanders.

Neil MacMhuirich has a story that Lord Gordon and Alasdair, at the former's request, exchanged some men before the battle to symbolise the friendship of MacDonalds and Gordons. It seems likely that this incident has been invented to account for the fact that the force that Alasdair led into battle contained Gordons; normally the various groups among the royalists tended to fight under their own commanders. But the real reason was the confusion of a desperate attempt to stave off disaster at the last minute. Alasdair rushed whatever men he could collect forward to hold off the enemy until the rest of the army could be assembled. This too provides the only convincing explanation of why Alasdair was left alone for so long with a totally inadequate number of men — evidently only three or four hundred — to resist the full weight of the enemy attack. His lack of manpower was not a minor miscalculation by Montrose in an otherwise brilliant plan; had that been the case Montrose, already waiting to begin his surprise flank attack, would have intervened in the battle earlier. Rather Alasdair's weakness in numbers was the result of hasty improvisation in an emergency; the men he had were all that could be mustered to prevent the enemy bursting into the camp while Montrose, as Patrick Gordon puts it, 'gathered the rest of the foot'.

Alasdair advanced to meet the enemy just outside the village to the west. Here there was a marshy hollow studded with bushes where Alasdair's men could hope to hold the enemy infantry on broken ground, sodden from the night's rain, on which cavalry could not be deployed against them. It seems likely that, as Wishart asserts, the royal standard was hastily raised behind Alasdair's men, to ensure that Hurry believed that in attacking them he was attacking the main rebel force, though James Fraser refers only to Alasdair's own yellow banner. But if the royal standard was thus displayed it was not, as Wishart claims, so Hurry would overlook Montrose's main army, drawn up in hiding ready to attack him on the flank. It was done to divert attention from the royalist camp on the other side of Auldearn where confusion reigned. Hurry had to be tempted to advance to the west of the village rather than the east, for the royalist camp lay to the north-east of Auldearn, probably centring on Boath House, the obvious place for Montrose to have quartered himself. Thus Gordon says Montrose had 'the town and som little hiles' between himself and the enemy, the hills being those on which the village was built, Castle Hill (now the site of Boath Doocot) and the low hillocks running north-west from it. Alasdair's line was drawn up on the low ground to the west of the hills, probably stretching along the west side of the village, past Castle Hill and the other hillocks north to (according to James Fraser) Boath Wood. Hurry advanced, to attack the enemy he could see preparing to meet him, from the south-west, or perhaps from almost due south as his men turned off the Cawdor-Auldearn road to do battle in 'the bottom, westward of Aldern' as Fraser calls it.

Thus began the battle according to the dispositions suggested by Patrick Gordon (and supported by James Fraser). They fit the terrain and seem perfectly plausible. The same may be said of Gordon's description of the battle that followed. Yet extraordinarily Gardiner dismisses it. 'Gordon is vague where Wishart gives details', Gordon's account being 'too completely wanting in detail to inspire confidence'. In fact in most respects Gordon provides much more detail than Wishart. Why Gardiner really dismisses Gordon as worthless is that he fails to provide a coherent account of a logically planned and fought battle with Montrose in control throughout. Wishart at least tries to describe such a battle, and therefore wins Gardiner's support. Yet Gardiner admits that though Wishart tries, he fails. On the central point of when and where Montrose launched his attack he is forced to admit that Wishart is 'not very intelligible'. Nonetheless Gardiner then reconstructs the battle through a forced interpretation of 'Wishart's bungling statement' which creates a flank charge completely unknown until Gardiner wrote. Gardiner assumed that Wishart had bungled his attempt to give a clear account of the battle through having 'no knowledge of the formation of the ground'. In fact Wishart bungled because he was trying to create a carefully planned setpiece battle when no such battle had taken place. And Gardiner thus bungled even more in succeeding where Wishart had failed. He rejected Patrick Gordon because he describes confusion and improvisation instead of tactics and generalship; but this is not Gordon's fatal weakness, it is his main strength.

The men Alasdair MacColla hurried into position west of Auldearn early on the morning of 9 May at once came under attack by the leading elements of the covenanters' army — an infantry regiment and some horsemen. MacMhuirich identifies the foot as Lawers' regiment and some gentlemen from Lewis. After 'a brave and long maintained resistance' Alasdair was forced to give ground, partly through panic on the part of some of the Gordon levies mixed with his own men. Not surprisingly Patrick Gordon has nothing to say about this, but MacMhuirich claims to have known men who at this point killed some of the Gordons to prevent the panic spreading to all of these men 'who were not accustomed to skirmishing, hard conflict, or the loud, harsh noise of battle' and 'would not hear the sough of an arrow or the whistling of a ball without bowing their heads or fleeing'. Such propensitites to duck or flee having been harshly dealt with, Alasdair made good his retreat to the yards and dykes behind the village houses, which formed good defensive positions. But no further retreat could be made if disaster was to be averted, for he would have been forced back through the village into the men Montrose was still assembling.

The musket fire of Alasdair's men now checked the enemy; seeing this, he led a new advance. Whether this was wise or not is impossible to say. At first sight, to advance from a good defensive position against a vastly superior enemy seems folly, but Alasdair knew his men (or at least the Irish and Highlanders among them). They were not used to fighting from defensive positions; the fighting they knew and excelled in was the charge and hand-to-hand combat in the open. Even though their primary task was a defensive one, he may have calculated that it could best be achieved by a charge, even if his men would eventually be driven back again. There may also have been another reason which made an advance imperative if all was not to be lost. It seems from Patrick Gordon that this second advance by Alasdair took him further to his left than before. This may suggest that Hurry (more of whose men were pouring onto the battlefield all the time) was now beginning to outflank him on his left, round the south end of the village. Such a move would have had to be prevented, not just because Alasdair would soon be surrounded but because it would lead the covenanters into the area behind (to the east of) the village where Montrose was gathering his men.

Alasdair's new charge soon led him into difficulties; by this time there were two full foot regiments flanked by horse opposite him, and the boggy, bushy ground which had hindered the enemy advance now partly destroyed the impact of his charge. His men could not keep in order or find firm footing. The difficulty was especially great on Alasdair's left wing, the ground there being 'all quagmyre and bushes'. Nonetheless, on this ground Alasdair and his men held out obstinately, resisting charge after charge before at last being forced back in some disorder, Alasdair and others fighting a desperate rearguard action. Again he reached the safety of the dykes and yards, safe from attack by cavalry. But after 'he had done what was possible, or rather what was wnpossible to be don by any other but himselfe', all seemed of no avail. He seemed certain to be overwhelmed by the endless stream of enemy infantry massing before him. Gordon depicts Alasdair as being now 'for griefe . . . ready to burst' and exclaiming, 'Ach meseoures . . . sall our enemies by this on dayes work be able to wreast out of our hands all the glorie that we have formerly gained. Let it never be said that basse flight shall bear witnes of it, or that our actiones should seam to confesse so much; but let ws die bravely; let it never be thought that they have triumphed over our currage, nor the loayltie we ow to our soveraigne lord, and let ws hope the best. God is stronge eneugh.' But so close were the enemy that Alasdair whispered, so they would not hear him and be encouraged. It was perhaps this moment of decision, when Alasdair resolved to fight to the end rather than attempt a retreat or surrender that a Gaelic poet commemorates. 'Alastair . . . you were good that day at Auldearn, when you leapt amongst the pikes; and whether good or ill befell you, you would not shout "Relief".'[24]

Help arrived just in time to save Alasdair. The Gordon cavalry had had time to saddle and mount, and now came to his aid. Aboyne appeared with a hundred or so horsemen on Alasdair's left, where the enemy pressure was strongest and there was a danger that he would be outflanked. By a determined charge Aboyne broke up the enemy cavalry opposite him and pursued them so they had no chance to re-form; four of five of their colours were captured. On seeing the charge Alasdair is said to have shouted, 'Now . . . those ar indeid the vallient Gordones, and worthie of that name which fame hath caried abroad of them.' Now at long last Montrose 'having at lenth gotten the body of the foot togither' moved forward to join Alasdair 'to mak on body' with him. Thus Patrick Gordon clearly states that Montrose's men did not make a separate attack from Alasdair's, delivered from a different direction. They came forward through Alasdair's men to join and reinforce them, perhaps extending his line on the left, through the yards of the houses at the south end of the village and further south beyond the village.

Hurry's initial attack, when he had had full advantage of the partial surprise he had achieved, had failed to break through Alasdair's thin line of defenders. Some of the covenanters' horse had been driven from the field, and now they saw fresh forces pouring forward to reinforce an enemy who had already managed to halt their advance. At about the same time Lord Gordon with about a hundred horse charged on the royalist right, and like his brother on the opposite wing he drove back the covenanting horse.[25] Patrick Gordon noted that his men charged home with their swords, abandoning their ineffective pistols; like Forbes of Craigievar at Aberdeen, but with more success, Lord Gordon was experimenting with the charge carried through the enemy lines instead of relying on the old fashioned caracole.

With the horsemen on their wings routed and Alasdair MacColla being strongly reinforced by Montrose, the great mass of infantry in Hurry's centre 'began to stagger'. He had thrown his infantry into battle piecemeal as they reached the battlefield after their long night march from Inverness in the rain, his determination to take full advantage of surprise outweighing the need to allow his men to rest and regain the order which had probably been to some extent lost on the march. Even more important, by immediately throwing his men into battle against the obvious enemy, Alasdair's men, he deprived himself of the chance of discovering and raiding Montrose's camp while the majority of his newly awakened men were milling around in disorder. As it was, Hurry's own infantry was crammed together in a small area, already somewhat disordered and finding the sodden, scrubby ground difficult to fight in. This had not seemed to matter when the covenanters had held the initiative and had been confident that they would quickly break through the village onto open ground and destroy the enemy. But once the infantry had been halted, had been deprived of the cavalry screening its flanks, and was attacked by Montrose and Alasdair combined, it found it impossible to extricate itself and difficult to manoeuvre. Numerically the covenanters were still greatly superior to their enemies, but Hurry's ill-considered deployment of them meant that they were unable to take advantage of this; only the outer ranks of the mass of infantry crowded together could get at the enemy to fight. Montrose and Alasdair began to advance with their infantry, while their horse fell on the flanks and rear of the enemy. Hurry, Seaforth and Sutherland were forced to flee by Lord Gordon's horsemen, and those of Hurry's footmen who were not yet trapped on the battlefield soon followed their generals. Lord Gordon broke off his pursuit of these fugitives as he thought he saw a body of covenanting cavalry still undefeated, but this turned out to be Aboyne's men; they had failed to furl the enemy colours they had captured and thus appeared from a distance to be covenanters. However, this misunderstanding was probably to the royalists' advantage, for it brought Lord Gordon back to the battlefield to join in the slaughter of the enemy infantry, more profitable (if less exciting) than the pursuit of scattered fugitives.

The royalists granted no quarter as they got down to the business of destroying the now stationary and leaderless enemy they had surrounded. The covenanters' leading regiment was that of Lawers; as he was a Campbell, the Irish and Highlanders attacked it with special zeal. In addition the regiments of both Lawers and Lothian had previously formed part of the Scottish army in Ireland, giving the Irish another score to settle with them. Moreover all the royalists were determined to avenge two recent killings of royalists. Hurry's killing of Donald Farquharson was held to have been murder rather than a legitimate act of war. So too — and with much more justification — was the death of James Gordon, the son of George Gordon of Rhynie only a few days before the battle. He had been injured by Hurry's men as Montrose pursued them through Moray and had been left behind to recover from his wounds; but raiders from the covenanting garrison of Spynie Castle had murdered him in his bed.

The covenanters' foot were cut down 'even in rankes and fyles, as they stood'. Lawers himself was killed and his regiment almost exterminated. Most fought well as soon as they could get at the enemy, but eventually the butchery became almost a massacre. Some parties managed to break through the surrounding royalists, but they were pursued and killed as they fled west or south.

Some could only explain the disaster which had overcome a vastly superior covenanting army which had surprised the enemy in terms of treachery. Both Hurry and Seaforth had records which cast doubts on their dedication to the cause they fought for; and in the months ahead both were again to change sides, joining Montrose. One incident in particular inspired suspicion. A commander of the covenanters' horse, a Major or Captain Drummond, was court-martialled and shot in Inverness after the battle, for having wheeled his men left instead of right as Hurry had ordered at a critical moment. Instead of charging the enemy Drummond had ridden down some of the covenanters' own infantry. Did Drummond act thus through incompetence, cowardice, confusion in the heat of battle — or through treachery? Or — even more sinister — had Hurry purposely given him an order which would sow confusion in his own army, then had Drummond hastily shot so he could not reveal his treason? Strong as this last rumour was, it was hardly convincing. Had Hurry really planned to bring defeat to his own army, he could have done this much more simply, and with less risk to the royalists, than by staging a surprise attack which nearly succeeded and was only aborted by his treachery at the last minute. Moreover Hurry did not have Drummond executed at once, as though to close his mouth, as is often alleged. He referred the matter to the committee of estates in Edinburgh, which then ordered him (on 23 May) to try Drummond or, if there were insufficient senior officers in Inverness to form a court martial, to send him to Edinburgh for trial.[26] Certainly Drummond had given grounds for suspicion that he was guilty of more than just incompetence if it is true that, as Gordon of Sallagh states, he confessed that he had 'spoken with the enemie after the word and sign of battle was given'.

The general account of the battle of Auldearn given above is based on that of Patrick Gordon, aided by the compatible accounts of Neil MacMhuirich and James Fraser. They are unanimous in indicating that Alasdair MacColla bore the brunt of the battle for a considerable period before Montrose came to his aid, and they are supported in this by Gordon of Sallagh. But only Patrick Gordon gives any clear indication of the reason for this delay (though MacMhuirich seems to imply it at one point): Montrose had been taken by surprise. The other accounts simply leave this central question unanswered. Of the two accounts of the battle which provide any detail and are not compatible with Patrick Gordon, one (Montrose's own) ignores the question completely, the other (Wishart's) provides an answer which protects Montrose from the charge of having been surprised at the price of alleging actions on his part which are simply unbelievable.

As already noted, Montrose wrote to the king that he had carefully posted his army in defensive positions to receive Hurry's attack. The enemy arrived and 'fell hotly on', but were driven back. This 'seimd to coole of their fury, and [they] only intended to blocke us up (as it wer) till more number should come'. This in itself is odd; if Hurry had no advantage of surprise, then there was no reason for him to throw the first of his troops to arrive into battle without awaiting the rest. As the enemy clearly did not intend to retreat, he had plenty of time to draw up his full army in battle array and then launch an attack with his full strength. But Montrose, determined not to admit that he had been surprised, offers no explanation for Hurry's conveniently precipitate action. Seeing that Hurry, after his first attack, was awaiting fresh troops, Montrose 'divided my selfe in two wings, (which was all the ground would suffer) and marched upon them most unexpectedly, and after some hot salvyes [salvoes] of musket and a litell dealing with sword and pike, they tooke the chase', leaving 3,000 dead infantry on the field; and all their cavalry were killed or scattered. This really is a most extraordinarily offhand account of the battle. There is no doubt that Auldearn was the hardest fought of all Montrose's victories, and that the battle lasted longer than any of the others; in Edinburgh it was reported that fighting had continued for twelve hours.[27] Yet, according to Montrose, once the royalists advanced, all that took place was a few musket volleys and a little sword and pike work. Such a description hardly accounts for the 3,000 corpses which then, he claims, appeared on the field; with seventeenth century weapons they could only have been produced by prolonged fighting. And what were the two wings into which Montrose suddenly divided his army — in the middle of the battle? The only explanation consistent with other accounts is that the 'wings' are Alasdair's men, thrown into battle to prevent immediate disaster, and the bulk of the army later brought up by Montrose. That Montrose advanced as soon as he was ready, because the odds against him were increasing all the time as more and more of Hurry's men arrived, can well be believed; that they did not advance until the battle was nearly lost can only be because they were not ready earlier. Montrose, it seems, is concerned to conceal more about Auldearn than he reveals.

Finally, there is George Wishart's account of the battle. The only convincing explanation of his confused story seems to be that he was trying to conflate what he had heard of the battle from other sources with Montrose's letter, his first priority being not to contradict his hero in any way. The other accounts of the battle had therefore to be interpreted in terms of Montrose's version. Not surprisingly Wishart is confused; yet he is not quite so confused as Gardiner claims in order to justify his own reconstruction. Far from displaying ignorance of the terrain, Wishart begins with a clear and concise account of it; the village of Auldearn stands on a low ridge, and behind it and some hillocks was a hollow hidden by them. In this hollow (clearly the area around Boath House; by 'behind' Wishart means on the opposite side from the covenanters' attack), out of sight of the enemy, Montrose drew up his forces. Thus far his account is perfectly sound, but he is now led astray by Montrose's letter. He knew that Alasdair had begun the battle separately from Montrose, but did not know — or would not admit — why. Montrose must therefore have been stationed somewhere ready to attack the enemy. Moreover, Montrose speaks of two 'wings'; therefore, Wishart deduces, there must have been a left wing and a right wing. And if you have such wings, this implies a centre — yet Montrose does not mention this; the 'centre' filling the gap between the wings must therefore have been insignificant or nominal. Wishart now tries to apply this information to the terrain he has described. Alasdair was on the right wing with 400 men, on ground defended by dykes, ditches, bushes and rocks. Here he was told to remain at all cost fighting defensively. The centre, Wishart deduces, must have consisted of a few men stationed in the yards running along the west side of the village; in fact (as MacMhuirich and Patrick Gordon make clear) Alasdair fought here, but to make room for his 'centre' Wishart has pushed him north and west. Meanwhile Montrose concentrated his own men on the left wing. There seems little doubt that Wishart's 'centre' is pure invention. He has deduced it from Montrose's reference to two 'wings', but Montrose evidently meant simply that he divided his army into two parts or bodies. Why else does he say that this was all that the ground would allow? If he really meant that they were conventional left and right wings (with a centre between them), this explanation would be absurd, for only two wings would have been expected.

Having created a nominal centre consisting of only a few men, Wishart then has to explain this. He also has to account for the facts that Alasdair and not Montrose raised the royal standard, and that the enemy attack was at first directed solely against Alasdair. Answers to the three questions are combined by creating an ingenious battle-plan (mentioned by no other source). Giving Alasdair the standard was intended to tempt the enemy into attacking the royalist right and centre, assuming this to be the full royalist army. How raising the standard on the right would tempt the enemy to attack the largely nominal centre as well is not explained; nor are we told why Montrose wished Hurry to advance against this centre when it (on Wishart's account) consisted of only a few men the enemy would quickly have broken through. For Patrick Gordon the purpose of luring the enemy into attacking Alasdair was to prevent the rest of the royalist army being overwhelmed before it had armed and assembled. For Wishart the reason was that Montrose was ready to attack on the left wing, but wished the enemy to commit themselves against Alasdair so he could catch them off balance with the surprise attack. This meant that Montrose's men must have been hidden from the enemy — in the hollow behind the village where they had assembled. This is where Wishart's attempt to make sense of the battle loses touch with the topography of Auldearn, for in no way could Montrose's men in that hollow be regarded as a 'left wing' to Alasdair's right. To attack to the left of him — and of the imaginary 'centre' — Montrose's men would have had to march right down the east side of the village and then round the south of it westwards, and their attack could come as no surprise as they would have been partially in sight of the enemy.

Wishart was half right. Montrose did assemble his men in the hollow north-east of the village, but they did not form a left wing. Gardiner conceded that Wishart was half right — but chose the wrong half to believe in. Accepting that Montrose led a left wing, he argued (rightly) that it could not have assembled in that hollow. It must therefore have been in a hollow due south of the village; only there could it have remained hidden from the enemy and have delivered a left-wing attack. But this hollow brings Montrose's men so far round that they must have attacked not just on Alasdair's left, but almost at right angles to him. Hence they must have attacked the enemy's flank. In fact, as Hurry approached from the south-west (and not from the west as Gardiner thought), Montrose's men would not have been concealed from them had they lain in the hollow south of Auldearn.

Thus was created Montrose's great surprise flank attack at Auldearn, which has generally been hailed as the most brilliant tactical manoeuvre he ever carried out. Yet not a single source mentions a flank attack of any sort. Montrose did assemble his men behind Alasdair as Wishart says, but they did not then carry out a surprise attack on his left; he brought his men through Alasdair's to attack, though perhaps extending his line on the left. John Buchan compares the flank attack at Auldearn to Napoleon's manoeuvres at Austerlitz. For Colonel Rogers it makes Auldearn the most brilliant battle of the entire civil war period in Britain. But in reality it never took place; it is a nineteenth century fantasy.[28]

To return to Wishart: Montrose lay in wait until the moment was right to launch his surprise attack with the left wing. He was about to move when a messenger arrived to say that Alasdair and the 'right wing' were being routed; stupidly but bravely Alasdair had been goaded by the taunts of the enemy into charging forward from his defences and as a result now faced annihilation. To save the situation Montrose turned to Lord Gordon (commanding the horse) and said that Alasdair had routed the enemy; they should now charge if they wished a chance to share in the glory. Montrose's men charged, and the covenanters were overwhelmed. Thus Wishart ingeniously uses his argument that Montrose was hidden with his men to provide an answer to the awkward question of why, if Montrose (as is assumed) had had his men ready to charge since the beginning of the battle, he held them back for so long before attacking. Why did he nearly let Alasdair be defeated? Wishart's reply is that Alasdair only got into difficulties because he disobeyed orders, and that Montrose could not come to his relief earlier as he did not know what was happening; he was hidden with his men and did not know what was going on on the battlefield. It is this last point that strains credulity. If Montrose had really lured the enemy into attacking a few hundred of his men so he could then make a surprise attack, then the exact timing of his move was crucial; a few minutes too early and he would not catch the enemy off balance, a few minutes too late and the men with whom he had baited his trap would be overwhelmed. In this battle above all others it would have been necessary for him to see clearly what was happening. To wait calmly out of sight until inspiration told him the moment to charge had come would have been incredible stupidity. Thus Wishart has triumphantly rescued Montrose from one question about his conduct, but has raised one of equal difficulty in its place. And other sources directly contradict Wishart here. James Fraser says that Montrose and Lord Gordon, far from lurking in a hollow, observed the battle from Castle Hill, behind Alasdair. Neil MacMhuirich confirms that Montrose watched part of the battle from 'a high hill'. From there, seeing Alasdair hard pressed, he called out to his men to advance to join Alasdair in winning glory. That Montrose did thus try to encourage his men by telling them that Alasdair was winning may well be believed — James Fraser also records Montrose's action, but evidently thought that his words were true — for on being roused by news of the enemy attack many of them must have been inclined to flee rather than fight. But when Montrose thus encouraged them he was not hidden, but in full view of the battle.

At Auldearn as at Inverlochy the covenanters' losses may have totalled 50% or even more of their forces engaged. Montrose, Wishart and Fraser put their losses at 3,000, and though this is probably exaggerated, they evidently did lose over 2,000 men. Most of their senior officers made good their escape but Sir Mungo Campbell of Lawers was dead, his brother Captain Archibald Campbell a prisoner. Sir John Murray (son of Murray of Philiphaugh), Gideon Murray, Alexander Drummond of Medhope and Captain Bernard MacKenzie all fell and were buried in Auldearn churchyard (where memorials to them remain) along with a Captain Crichton. Lawers and four of his captains (Bruce, Cashore, Campbell and Shaw), five lieutenants and two hundred common soldiers were buried at Cawdor. But most of the dead, those scattered thickly on the low ground west of Auldearn, and around Kinnudie, Kinsteary and Brightmony, had to do without sanctified ground. The tendency of men to fight in kin groups and to command men raised from their own tenantry meant that as at Inverlochy some families and localities suffered frightful losses. Douglas of Cavers lost nine nephews at Auldearn, and two Gledstanes of Whitelaw died.[29] Old Lord Lovat lost many kinsmen, and was left with eighty-seven Fraser widows to support; he was often to rebuke his brother Sir James who had been so keen to march out the Frasers to fight for the covenants. 'Ever and anon the cry and grones of men and women for their lost friends were universally heard,' related their historian, James Fraser. Worst of all was the catastrophe which had overcome the Campbells of Lawers. Their estates had already been wasted by the rebels marching into Argyll the previous December, and after Auldearn the committee of estates ordered payment of 10,000 merks to support Sir Mungo's son and family. The surviving tenants on the estates were ordered to be drawn together in a company to protect each other from the enemies who would take advantage of the family's misfortunes. Three thousand bolls of meal were to be provided to support 300 women and old people who were starving.[30] Seaforth's clan, the MacKenzies, as well as those of his allies and followers, suffered severely. With Captain Bernard MacKenzie there died his company of men from Chanonry of Ross. Seaforth's chamberlain in Lewis and John MacKenzie of Kernsary died. Many of the men from Lochbroom and Lewis fought until they were killed. Rory (Roderick) MacLennan, chief of his name and 'the Bannerman of Kintail', refused offers of quarter from Lord Gordon and was shot. His brother Donald, Malcolm MacRae ('a pretty, young gentleman, bred at school and college') and Duncan MacIan Og MacRae died round him defending the banner. Tradition recounts that eighteen leading MacLennans fell at Auldearn, and that as a result the MacRaes, until then a subordinate clan, became the leading clan in Kintail through marriage to widows of the MacLennans.[31]

Wishart, Patrick Gordon and MacMhuirich combine to sing the praises of Alasdair MacColla as a warrior at Auldearn. It was the high point of his career as a swordsman. On other occasions his skill and strength are lauded in general terms; here we learn of them in detail. Wishart allows that he atoned for his rashness in advancing (thus supposedly nearly ruining Montrose's plan) by his 'splendid courage'. When his men were forced back he was the last to retreat. Time and time again the pikes of his enemies thudded into his targe but the sweep of his sword cut off the pike shafts. Patrick Gordon records that Alasdair performed 'wonderfull feats of armes for his fellowes to imitate'. He broke two swords, and when the enemy had fixed the points of enough pikes in his targe to force three or four ordinary men to the ground, Alasdair did not even have to kneel on one knee, but instead scythed through the pikes with one blow. It was doubtless this that broke his swords — or sword, for Neil MacMhuirich allows him only one broken weapon, and adds that it was replaced by one of his men giving up his own sword; some said it was his brother-in-law, MacKay or Davidson of Ardnacroish (married to his sister Jean), who thus left himself swordless, paying for his generosity with his life. But tradition asserts that it was MacKay's son who died at Auldearn, he himself being executed in Kintyre two years later.[32]

Alasdair's own valour was rivalled by those with him. MacMhuirich claims that several 'good gentlemen' were killed around him as they protected him on his retreat to the safety of the yards and dykes of Auldearn. One of the last to reach such safety was one Ranald MacKinnon. He was firing his pistol at the advancing enemy pikemen when a bowman shot an arrow which pierced both his cheeks and remained protruding on both sides of his face. Throwing down his pistol, Ranald now attempted to draw his sword, but it stuck in the scabbard. Only by bringing his left hand, which held his targe, down to grasp his scabbard could he tug his sword free; but this brief lowering of the shield brought him five superficial pike wounds in his neck and chest. Ranald then engaged himself in the task which had earlier occupied Alasdair, the hacking off of pikes embedded in his targe; until he had done this he could not move freely. As he neared safety he could hear Alasdair cursing the panic-stricken Gordons who had retreated with him and who were now unwilling to venture out of their defences to rescue Ranald. At last Ranald worked his way to the door into the garden which was sheltering Alasdair; but to get in he had to turn and stoop, thus exposing his back to the enemy. A daring pikeman tried to take advantage of this, running forward and thrusting through the doorway after Ranald; but Alasdair MacColla swung his sword and the pikeman's body fell in the doorway. Thus Ranald lived to fight another day.

'Many were the warlike feats performed on that battlefield by the MacDonalds and the Gordons,' concluded Neil MacMhuirich, and it is fitting to have ended an account of the battle by telling of some of the deeds of the warriors who fought there, for the remarkable result of the battle was achieved by warriors and their skill and bravery, not by generals and their tactics. Hurry throwing his regiments into battle in turn as they reached the field, and Montrose successively hastening forward Alasdair, the Gordon cavalry and then the bulk of his infantry as soon as they were ready, displayed no skills of generalship. The battle was won by the astonishing feats of arms of the Highlanders, Irish, and Gordons, who though taken by surprise by a greatly superior enemy snatched victory when defeat seemed certain. And the chief glory belongs to Alasdair MacColla and the few hundred men under him whose epic deeds checked the first onslaught of the enemy.[33]

In Gaelic tradition and poetry, and in the prose of Neil MacMhuirich, Auldearn stands second only to Inverlochy among the victories of the Montrose campaigns. Indeed so closely were the two battles linked in tradition that two anecdotes of Alasdair MacColla are told of both battles. Local tradition at Auldearn related that in the fighting Alasdair was hard pressed by Hay of Kinnudie, but tricked him by calling out, 'I'll not deceive you, my men are coming up behind you'; as Hay turned to protect himself from these new, imaginary enemies, Alasdair cut him down.[34] At Inverlochy Alasdair is said to have tricked Campbell of Glenfeochan in the same way. Similarly one tradition tells of how a blacksmith or tinker from Atholl called Robertson distinguished himself at Inverlochy, earning Alasdair's praise: ''Tis a pity we were not all tinkers today.'[35] The Auldearn version is more elaborate. Robertson the smith fought valiantly (wearing a frying pan under his bonnet as a helmet!), and Alasdair asked him how many men he had killed. On his replying nineteen, Alasdair exclaims, 'By Mary! I have killed only twenty-one myself . . . I wish that every man of mine was a tradesman like you.'[36]

A Lewis tradition, if it can be trusted, records a few incidents of the battle from the point of view of Gaels who fought for the covenanters under Seaforth. Among the Lewis bowmen were three sons of Donald Cam MacAulay from the parish of Uig — Angus, William and John. Angus had originally been ordered to remain behind to defend the area from attack in the absence of the men who had been levied, but on his wife remarking pointedly 'the men have left and the pigmies have stayed at home' he left to catch up with his brothers. At Auldearn William MacAulay was among those who were eventually surrounded. He held out for a long time, defending himself in a doorway with a sword in each hand after all the rest of the Lewismen had been killed, but eventually enemies got into a loft over his head and killed him. His brother John (and perhaps Angus as well) managed to escape from the battlefield, but were then pursued by a horseman who roared, 'I am Alister Ower, the Butcher.' Neither epithet is otherwise known for Alasdair MacColla, but evidently it was he. He may have called himself the butcher to terrify his foes, but it is strange that if he himself used the physically descriptive epithet *Odhar*, 'the Sallow', it does not occur in other sources. John MacAulay turned and shot his last arrow at Alasdair; he caught it on his targe but it had sufficient force behind it to knock him off his horse. Alasdair then hastily remounted and rode off, slinging his targe on his back to protect his retreat and shouting, 'Farewell, Lewis men, I have had as much of your shooting as will serve me this day.'[37] The incident has doubtless been exaggerated and elaborated in the telling, on the lines of 'how I once single-handed routed the greatest of warriors, Alasdair MacColla', but there may nonetheless be a basis of truth in it. For Alasdair to have mounted a horse to join in the pursuit of fugitives would have been natural, and for him to have decided to spare the few survivors of the men of Uig when they showed spirit enough to turn and fight is consistent with his similar small acts of mercy on other occasions.

Auldearn, like Inverlochy, was to be celebrated by Gaelic poets for a century.[38] Ian Lom proclaimed 'Health and joy to the valiant Alasdair who won the battle of Auldearn with his army', though after beginning thus he does at least acknowledge that Montrose had a contribution to make: 'Helmeted men with pikes in their hands were attacking you with all their might until you were relieved by Montrose.' Scorn is poured on the Highlanders who fought for the covenanters by mocking common christian names used by the MacKenzies (Duncan and Kenneth) and the Frasers (Thomas and Simon):

There was not a Dunky or Kenny in the land of MacKenzie who did not abandon his firearms on the moorland moss.

There was not a Tommie or Simmie in the lands of Lord Lovat who did not escape into hiding-holes everywhere.[39]

The unknown poet already quoted celebrated Alasdair in a memorable phrase leaping among the pikes at Auldearn. Another poem (existing in many versions) is said to have been composed by a woman who had fallen in love with a MacDonald on the march to Auldearn:

> My delight is the young man who left me yesterday evening: Alas, oh King and Son of Mary, but I found his visit short!

She hails the epic deeds of the Clan Donald and recalls how they 'took oaths on the Bible in the low strath of Auldearn that no sword would return to its sheath till King Charles would have the victory'.[40]

As there was hardly time for such pacts and ceremonies before the battle, this may refer to celebrations after it. It would have been an appropriate time for such oaths of loyalty, for more than any other battle Auldearn served to bring closer together the different groups and interests represented in Montrose's army. Irish and Highland foot with some Gordon support had fought off the initial enemy attack and thus saved the rest of the army. They in turn had been saved by the charges of the Gordon cavalry, and then by the arrival of the rest of the foot under Montrose. Alasdair had saved Montrose, then Montrose had saved Alasdair. All had shared in a most extraordinary victory, and their joy must have been accentuated by relief at disaster so narrowly averted.

NOTES

1. Wishart, *Memoirs*, 82-3.

2. J. Fraser, *Chronicles of the Frasers. The Wardlaw Manuscript* (SHS 1905), 289.

3. Gordon, *Britane's distemper*, 101.

4. Ibid, 109-10; Spalding, *memorials*, ii.447-54; Wishart, *Memoirs*, 87-8; Napier, *Memorials*, ii.186-7.

5. Spalding, *Memorials*, ii.454-8; Gordon, *Britane's distemper*, 110-12; *APS*, VI.i.470; Taylor, *Aberdeen council letters*, iii.45,116,119; Stuart, *Extracts from the council register of the burgh of Aberdeen, 1643-1747*, 48-9,97-8; Napier, *Memorials*, ii.187,190-1.

6. Cowan, *Montrose*, 198.

7. Spalding, *Memorials*, ii.458-63; Gordon, *Britane's distemper*, 112-17; Wishart, *Memoirs*, 88-95; Guthry, *Memoirs*, 183; *APS*, VI.i.519-21; Baillie, *Letters*, ii.264; *An extract of several letters from Scotland . . . concerning the defeat given to the rebels . . .* (London 1645), 4-6; J. Vicars, *Magnalia dei Anglicana*, The burning bush, 134-5; Napier, *Memorials*, ii.186.

8. Baillie, *Letters*, ii.418.

9. Guthry, *Memoirs*, 184; Spalding, *Memorials*, ii.164-5.

10. Montrose's letter of 20 April is printed in *Mercurius Aulicus*, 4-11 May 1645 (Oxford 1645), 1583-5; most of it is reprinted in Williams, *Montrose*, 233-4.

11. Spalding, *Memorials*, ii.468, 469; Gordon, *Britane's distemper*, 120-1; Guthry, *Memoirs*, 184-5; Wishart, *Memoirs*, 96-8; *APS*, VI.i.468,602.

12. *Mercurius Aulicus*, 25 May — 8 June 1645, 1611-12.

13. Spalding, *Memorials*, ii.463, 464-5, 466.

14. Baillie, *Letters*, ii.418.

15. S.R. Gardiner, *History of the great civil war* (2nd ed, 4 vols, London 1893-4), ii.223-7; Williams, *Montrose*, 242; Cowan, *Montrose*, 203.

16. Buchan, *Montrose*, 243n cites Montrose's letter but only uses a few details from it. Cowan,

Montrose, 204-5 quotes part of the letter but gives no reference to where it is to be found and does not allow it to modify his account of the battle derived from Gardiner.

17. Spalding, *Memorials*, ii.451,466.

18. G. Bain, *History of Nairnshire* (2nd ed, Nairn 1928), 202-3; *New statistical account of Scotland* (15 vols, Edinburgh 1845), xiii, 16.

19. See, eg, the description of the Forres-Inverness road in W. MacFarlane, *Geographical collections* (3 vols, SHS 1906-8), i.xli,231, and the 1797 plan of Auldearn at SRO, RHP.186. I am grateful to Miss Alice Kirkpatrick for letting me use her photocopy of this plan.

20. Williams, *Montrose*, 237 shows some realisation that the modern roads differ from those of 1645, in that he states that Hurry advanced by way of Culloden Moor and Kilravock House; but he then appears to assume (though his account is vague) that Hurry passed through Nairn. How he then managed to approach Auldearn from the south-west is not explained. Williams may have been influenced by the plan of the battle prepared for the National Trust for Scotland and displayed at Boath Doocot; certainly H.C.B. Rogers, *Battles and generals of the civil wars* (London 1968), 217-5 has been; he reproduces the plan. Rogers confuses matters by stating that Hurry was 'four miles west of Nairn' rather than at Inverness when he began his march to surprise Montrose. Hurry thus passed through Nairn. Rogers knew that the old Nairn-Auldearn road would have brought the covenanters into the village from the north; yet he gives no explanation of how Hurry managed to attack from the south-west. The vague assumption is that Hurry must have marched southwards, passing the village to the west, then swung round to attack from the south-west. Such a manoeuvre would have been pointless — and would have been guaranteed to ensure that surprise was not achieved.

21. Cowan, *Montrose*, 201. Napier, *Memoirs*, ii.500-1, realised that Montrose was 'almost caught napping' at Auldearn, but thought that he had still had time to make an 'admirable disposition' of his men.

22. Gordon actually says that Hurry resolved 'to turne down to the seasyd' for his men to discharge their guns out to sea. This is the only reference in any source that gives any support to the argument that Hurry advanced from Inverness to Nairn on roughly the line of the modern main road, for this route is much closer to the coast than the old inland route to Auldearn through Cawdor. But even on the former route, for Hurry to have marched his men down to the beach to fire off their guns would have involved a considerable diversion, lengthening the march of his already tired men, and delaying his march for longer than simply halting and unloading would have done. I have therefore assumed that Hurry turned his men towards the sea, rather than marched them down to it.

23. Surprisingly, while Patrick Gordon thus gives the credit for warning of the enemy approach to Alasdair's Highland or Irish scouts, MacMhuirich's account assigns this role to a Gordon, stating that Nathaniel Gordon brought the news from the advance guards.

24. 'Two Gaelic political songs of the seventeenth century', *Highland Monthly*, i(1889-90),281-2; I have modernised the translation given here. Another translation is in Mackenzie, *Orain Iain Luim*, 245.

25. Patrick Gordon states that Lord Gordon thus led a cavalry charge on Alasdair's right. But Gardiner, *Civil war*, ii.224-255n, rejects this on the grounds 1) that Wishart mentions Lord Gordon as being with Montrose on the left, and 2) that on Alasdair's right the hill was 'very steep' and the ground the cavalry would have charged into was too boggy and rocky for cavalry. But, 1) Wishart is wrong (as is argued later in this chapter) in placing Montrose and Lord Gordon on the left; in fact they were probably both on Castle Hill, close to the right end of Alasdair's line; from there Lord Gordon could easily have hurried down to lead his men in a charge on the right, and 2) the ground between Castle Hill and Boath house is almost flat, and Lord Gordon could thus perfectly easily have led a charge round the north of the hill to fall on Hurry's left wing. The 'very steep' hill here is a figment of Gardiner's imagination, perhaps arising from a confused memory of the hillocks lying north-west of Castle Hill but separated from it by level ground. As to whether or not the ground to the right of Alasdair's line was too boggy or rocky for cavalry in 1645, it is impossible to be certain; but it seems that the main boggy area lay to the south and east of Auldearn Burn, and a charge by Lord Gordon would have taken him across the burn to the firmer ground to its north and west. Moreover, though Gardiner refuses to have Lord Gordon's horse on this northerly side of the battlefield as the ground was unsuitable for cavalry, this has not deterred him from placing some of Hurry's cavalry here.

26. SRO, PA.11/4, f.93v.

27. Sir Thomas Hope, *A diary of public correspondence, 1633-45* (Bannatyne Club, 1843), 220.

28. Neil MacMhuirich adds confusion by referring to Montrose attacking the enemy from behind (*Rel Celt*, ii.190-3), having the royal standard with him, but on neither point is he supported by other sources.

29. Napier, *Memoirs*, ii.505n; Buchan, *Montrose*, 249.

30. SRO, PA.11/4, ff.102v-104.

31. A. Mackenzie, *History of the Mackenzies* (2nd ed, Inverness 1894), 189-90,326; A. MacRae, *History of the Clan MacRae* (Dingwall 1899), 68,187,336-7; J.R.N. Macphail (ed), 'Genealogy of the MacRaes', *Highland Papers*, i(SHS 1914),213.

32. Campbell, *Records of Argyll*, 226.

33. The contemporary or near-contemporary accounts of Auldearn are Gordon, *Britane's distemper*, 121-7; Gordon, *Genealogical history*, 524-5; Fraser, *Frasers*, 294-7; Spalding, *Memorials*, ii.272-4; *Rel Celt*, ii.184-93; Leith, *Memoirs*, ii.336-9; Wishart, *Memoirs*, 98-102, and Montrose's letter in *Mercurius Aulicus*, 25 May — 8 June 1645 (Oxford 1645), 1611-12. Gardiner's reconstruction is in *Civil war*, ii.223-7; the main accounts based on this are those in Buchan, *Montrose*, 244-50; C. O'Danachair, 'The battle of Auldearn, 1645', *Irish Sword*, i. (1949-53), 128-32; Cowan, *Montrose*, 200-6; Williams, *Montrose*, 236-45; Rogers, *Battles and generals*, 217-25. Accounts which pre-date Gardiner or ignore his work include Bain, *Nairnshire*, 202-9; G. Bain, *History of the parish of Auldearn* (Nairn 1898), 14-22,62; L. Shaw, *History of the province of Moray* (new ed., 3 vols, 1882), 259-62; C. Rampini, *History of Moray and Nairn* (Edinburgh and London 1897), 190-4; H. Rose, *A genealogical deduction of the family of Rose of Kilravock* (Spalding Club, 1848), 338-9; A. Mackenzie, *History of the Mackenzies*, 253-6; *New statistical account*, xiii, Nairnshire, 9-11.

34. Ibid, 10-11; Bain, *Nairnshire*, 205-6.

35. W. Drummond-Norie, 'Inverlochy 1431-1645', *Celtic Monthly*, v (1896-7), 84. See also C. Fergusson, 'Sketches . . . of Strathardle, No. vi', *TGSI*, xxi (1896-7), 348.

36. D. Cameron, 'Notes of Auldearn, Moy, and Culloden', *Highland Monthly*, v (1893), 178-9.

37. F.W.L. Thomas, 'Traditions of the Macaulays of Lewis', *Proceedings of the Society of Antiquaries of Scotland*, xiv (1879-80), 415-17; D. Morrison, *The Morrison Manuscript. Traditions of the Western Isles* (Stornoway 1975), 28-9.

38. MacLean, Sources, 38n, 41-3; Mackenzie, *Orain Iain Luim*, 244.

39. Ibid, 26-7,243-6.

40. Macdonald, *Macdonald collection of Gaelic poetry*, xiv,49-50. The translation quoted is that of Dr Colm O Boyle.

8

Alasdair and Montrose: An Alliance Broken

IT was probably just after Auldearn that Alasdair MacColla heard that the long imprisonment of his father and two brothers was over. Negotiations for an exchange of prisoners had at last borne fruit. On 24 April orders had arrived at Mingary Castle from Alasdair instructing the commander of his garrison there to march all but one of the prisoners held there to Lismore to be exchanged. The exception was James Hamilton, minister of Dumfries, who was not to be exchanged except on written orders from Montrose; as was soon to emerge, Montrose had decided that Hamilton should only be exchanged for his illegitimate half-brother, Harie Grahame. Alasdair had hoped to exchange Hamilton (whom he, after all, had captured) for his own relatives; whether or not he objected to Montrose appropriating his prize prisoner is unknown, but it may well be that he agreed to it as Inverlochy had provided him with enough Campbell prisoners to exchange for his own kin.

Hamilton must have watched in despair as his fellow prisoners — none of whom had been captive for as long as he — marched off rejoicing to be exchanged. But three days later they and their guards reappeared, weary from long marches over mountains and rocks. On reaching Lismore they had found no-one at the rendezvous, and so had returned. Thus providence, it seemed, was on Hamilton's side after all, for it was believed that in his weakened state the journey to Lismore and back would have killed him. Within an hour of the return of the dispirited prisoners to the fortress they had hoped never to see again, a letter arrived from William Stirling of Auchyle, Argyll's agent, to whom the covenanters had entrusted the exchange. Auchyle announced that he had now arrived at Dunstaffnage with prisoners for exchange, and a new meeting was hastily arranged; the two parties would assemble at Duart Castle on Mull at 10 a.m. on 1 May.

On 29 April the prisoners from Mingary were landed on Mull near Aros Castle and marched to Duart. Negotiations began but soon ran into difficulties. Auchyle's orders were that James Hamilton was to be the first to be freed — there was increasing indignation among his colleagues in the kirk at the failure to arrange his release — in exchange for Harie Grahame. But Auchyle had not brought Grahame with him, and Hamilton was not to be released without Montrose's orders — it is not clear whether he had been brought to Duart or again left at Mingary. Auchyle solemnly swore that orders had been given for Harie Grahame's release, and he vowed to bring Montrose's order for Hamilton's release within a month, binding himself to pay a financial penalty if he failed; but the commander of Mingary still refused to release Hamilton. Deadlock had been reached. But then Auchyle decided to break his orders, and went ahead with the other exchanges, including those of Coll Ciotach and his sons Gillespie and Angus. Eventually the commander of Mingary had only two prisoners left: James Hamilton, and Campbell of Glencarradale, captured at Inverlochy (where his father had been killed) and reserved for exchange with a Captain John MacDonald who (like Harie Grahame) had not been sent to Duart. But the covenanters also still had two prisoners in reserve: Coll, the eldest son of Gillespie MacColla, son of Coll Ciotach, and a brother of MacDonald of Largie who was married to a daughter of Coll Ciotach. Auchyle now offered both these men in exchange for Hamilton. The bargain was a tempting one — especially as Alasdair MacColla had probably entrusted command of Mingary to a fellow MacDonald. The commander was being offered two MacDonalds, both close kinsmen of Alasdair, for one minister of the kirk. This made more sense than holding on to Hamilton until he could be exchanged for one Grahame, so the commander accepted the offer. Thus Glencarradale returned to solitary captivity at Mingary while Hamilton was freed. The marquis of Argyll reported that he, 'blessed be God', was as well in mind and body as could be expected after his imprisonment, but he emphasised that 'To get him frie ther is a gentleman (my kinsman) yet lying in Misery'; efforts must now be made to get Glencarradale released.[1]

After Auldearn Montrose would have liked to follow the fleeing covenanters back to Inverness and capture the burgh. It was a major covenanting garrison in a strategic position on the edge of the Highlands, and its fall might have encouraged many Highlanders to join him. But he knew that Lieutenant General Baillie was hastening north and had to turn to face him — moving towards Inverness would look like flight. After burning the property of Campbell of Calder and other local covenanters, the rebel army therefore marched east to Elgin, arriving there on 11 May, two days after the battle. Here Montrose settled for some days. Wishart says he did this so that his wounded could be attended to,[2] but it seems that there was also another reason. While Montrose watched Baillie's advance, Alasdair MacColla had marched west to punish the covenanters of eastern Ross-shire for having fought at Auldearn. The only information about this episode comes from a passing reference by Ian Lom to Alasdair having at this time 'raised flames of fire in the land of Lovat', and from a rather confused passage in James Fraser's history. Fraser records that in May Alasdair's 'regiment' quartered around Beauly, while 'regiments' of MacKenzies and MacLeods quartered in neighbouring parishes. He then continues, 'True it is all were carrying on the same common cause and interest together.' This sounds absurd; the MacKenzies under Seaforth had just been fighting for the covenanters against Alasdair, and the MacLeods referred to had probably been raised by Seaforth in Lewis. All the same, sense can be made of Fraser's comment. Seaforth had probably hastened after Auldearn (as he had after Inverlochy) to make a nominal submission to the royalist cause to avoid the plundering of his estates; so his men were no longer enemies to Alasdair. However, the MacDonalds did not let the sudden feigned friendship of recent enemies deprive them entirely of the joys of plundering. They behaved according to Fraser 'like fiends and foes . . . with spullying and rapin up and down the cuntry, killing sheep, cowes, and oxen, to the shame of their profession in a civil country'. The Frasers were willing to submit but were first punished by plundering. Alexander Fraser of Foiness, who commanded the Fraser garrison at Lovat House, protested to Alasdair MacColla, boldly reminding him of an occasion in the past when the Frasers had forced the MacDonalds to flee. Alasdair, deciding the Frasers had suffered enough, came and apologised to Lord Lovat 'for his peoples misdemeanour and rudness', and Lovat assigned the MacDonalds quarters and food — thus he still had to support them, but at least their exactions were now orderly. To Alasdair Lovat sent wheat, bread, barrels of ale and beer, and bottles of 'aquavite'. Sometimes Alasdair dined at Lovat House.[3] Fraser is confused chronologically, and his account suggests a more extended stay by Alasdair in the Fraser country at this point than is possible. Fraser also records that at some unidentified point in the war forces commanded by Alexander Fraser of Foiness and Alasdair MacColla faced each other across the Spey. The two men developed great respect for each other, Foiness being 'a bold, daring man [who] feared no flesh' whose skill had won him military leadership of the Frasers. Alasdair remarked, 'truely there are not two such Alexanders in the Kings or Covenanters camp' as he himself and Foiness. Eventually they managed to meet; they 'stole an opportunity of a congress, and took their bottle of fraternity, and parted intimat friends, keeping closs correspondence ever after'; so at least Foiness told James Fraser.[4]

Exactly when and where Alasdair rejoined Montrose is unknown. After Montrose left Elgin, he and Baillie manoeuvred round each other in the Highlands of Aberdeen and Banff and on Speyside in bewildering marches, each seeking sufficient advantage to attack. But no occasion presented itself on which both generals were prepared to fight, and eventually Baillie withdrew to Inverness to supply his army. Montrose now again tried, as before both Inverlochy and Auldearn, to take advantage of his position between enemy armies to defeat them separately. When Baillie had come north (and been rejoined by the remnants of Hurry's army), a new covenanting army had been formed in the south under the earl of Crawford-Lindsay. Montrose now marched swiftly south to fall on this army. Presumably Alasdair and his men had rejoined him, for he needed all available men for such a venture. But the march, though spectacular, proved a failure. Montrose came as far south as Angus, but Crawford-Lindsay withdrew to a strong position and refused to be tempted out. Montrose then retired again northwards; he could not linger in the south, for as soon as he had turned his back on Baillie the latter had advanced from Inverness to attack the lands of the Gordons. As Baillie had doubtless calculated, this led the Gordons who formed a substantial part of Montrose's army to insist on returning to their homes, leaving Montrose so weak that he had to withdraw his whole army.[5]

In Cromar on Deeside Montrose halted for a few days early in June. While the Gordons continued homewards, he sent Alasdair MacColla on another recruiting expedition to the West Highlands. Doubtless Alasdair and his men pressed to be allowed to go, Alasdair wishing to celebrate with his father and brothers the end of their six years of captivity as well as to encourage the MacDonalds and their allies to continue to resist the Campbells. That Montrose had serious worries about the loyalty of at least some of the Highlanders to him and the king, or at least felt that they were demoralised and needed encouragement, is indicated by the fact that he now issued specific promises of reward once victory was won. On 7 June he promised Patrick Roy MacGregor of that Ilk that he and his friends would be restored to all their former lands in Glenlyon, Rannoch and Glenorchy which were in the hands of the king's enemies; further promises of reward to MacGregor were signed on 3 and 24 July, suggesting that difficulties in securing his services continued.[6] Similar undertakings were probably given to John MacNab, younger of that Ilk, for on 11 June MacNab agreed to share any rewards gained in the king's service which extended beyond his own or his predecessors' lands with his friends, provided they continued in the king's service.[7] Another problem Montrose dealt with from Cromar was that of Irish stragglers and deserters. Many such men had evidently gathered in Atholl, as a convenient base for plundering surrounding areas. Montrose now resolved on harsh action against them, instructing Robertson of Inver, who commanded his garrison in Blair Atholl Castle, to hunt down such Irish with fire and sword, burning the houses of all who gave shelter to them.[8]

From Cromar Montrose withdrew to remote Corgarff Castle on the upper Don, as if to wait there until Alasdair and the Gordons reinforced him; but he soon decided that he would be better employed in aiding the Gordons against Baillie. Defeating Baillie might be a poor second best to defeating Crawford-Lindsay to the south, but it was better than nothing. Moreover he may have been encouraged by what he heard of the state of Baillie's army. Baillie complained of lack of supplies and reinforcements, and he had been forced to send many of his veteran troops to Crawford-Lindsay in exchange for some ill-trained levies — though the loss was not so serious as he was later to make out, as many of the veterans were evidently mutinous.

Near Keith Montrose linked up with the Gordons, and then fell back before Baillie as if in flight. At Alford on 2 July on carefully chosen ground he awaited attack, giving Baillie an opportunity he could not afford to miss to win the victory his employers demanded. Alford was the only one of Montrose's six major victories at which Alasdair MacColla was not present, but many of his Irish were there along with some of his Western Highland allies. The Gordon horsemen under Lord Gordon and the earl of Aboyne formed the wings, though they in turn were flanked by parties of Irish musketeers; Montrose had evidently a high enough opinion of them to believe they could stand up to attack by enemy cavalry in such exposed positions. In the centre he massed his infantry — Gordons and Highlanders, those from the west being mainly MacDonalds under Angus MacDonald of Glengarry. For the first time Montrose faced in battle an enemy who was not greatly superior to him in numbers; both he and Baillie had something over 2,000 men, though Baillie probably had superiority in cavalry and Montrose may have had superiority in infantry. After a short but fierce fight the attacking covenanters were routed with heavy losses. The Irish again distinguished themselves; Patrick Gordon singles out 'corronell M'Lachlen' (Major Thomas Laghtnan), Manus O'Cahan and 'colonell M'Doniell' (Colonel James MacDonnell) for special praise (which indicates that all three Irish regiments were present), though he regrets that the Irish, in carrying out most of the killing, 'performed it with too litle compassion, and to much crueltie, no quarters being granted to any whom they could reach'. But the victory was marred by the death of Lord Gordon. Since he had joined Montrose after Inverlochy, the two men had become personal friends, and he had emerged as a daring and skilful leader of cavalry. It was not just his own men, or just the Scots, who lamented him: 'the forraineres, I meane the Irrishes' wept incessantly for him.[9]

Inverlochy had been fought on the feast of the Purification of the Virgin; Alford was won on the feast of the Visitation of the Virgin; and Montrose's next and final victory was to be won at Kilsyth on the feast of the Assumption of the Virgin.[10] Father MacBreck notes these remarkable coincidences, and he naturally took them as signs of the aid given by God and the Virgin in essentially Catholic victories; equally naturally, Montrose's protestant supporters found the coincidences embarrassing and therefore they fail to mention them.

The armies of Hurry and Baillie which the covenanters had sent north had been defeated at Auldearn and Alford. Montrose was at last free to turn south without leaving a covenanting army behind him which might force him to return north. Only Crawford-Lindsay now stood between him and the road to England; and Montrose's determination to take that road was strengthened by the fact that two weeks before Alford the king's army had suffered a crushing defeat at Naseby. Increasingly the royalist cause in England seemed on the verge of collapse; if Montrose did not intervene quickly he might be too late to serve his master. A circumstance that would make the final crushing of the covenanting regime in Scotland easier than it otherwise would have been was that in recent months an epidemic of bubonic plague had been spreading fast in southern Scotland, demoralising the covenanters and disrupting their military preparations. In May their regime had fled from Edinburgh; in July parliament met in Stirling and then, as plague approached, in Perth. Their forces now concentrated in the Perth area both to block Montrose's advance south and to protect the regime in the country's temporary capital.

At Fordoun in Kincardine Montrose was reinforced by Alasdair MacColla, who had returned from the west and had been plundering in Angus. The captain of Clanranald had given Alasdair all the young men of his clan who were not already with Montrose: over 500 men, it was said, commanded by his son Donald. Sir Lachlan MacLean of Duart brought out about 700 men. More MacDonalds of Glengarry came to join their chief. The Stewarts of Appin reappeared, as did the MacNabs and the MacGregors. In all Alasdair is said to have brought 1,400 men.[11]

Aboyne and many of the Gordons were still in the north raising new levies but, once rejoined by Alasdair, Montrose decided that he was strong enough to advance towards Perth to maintain pressure on the covenanters. He therefore marched to Dunkeld, crossed the Tay and moved within eight miles of Perth, camping at Methven and terrifying the burgh for some days with the threat of imminent attack. Eventually, however, his bluff was called; the covenanters sent out their cavalry against him and he was forced to retire to Dunkeld, leaving behind snipers to harry the advancing enemy. They took an easy revenge, if Wishart is to be believed, by murdering a party of Irish and Highland women captured in Methven Wood.

After about a week at Dunkeld Montrose was joined by about 800 infantry and three or four hundred horsemen under Aboyne, and by nearly a hundred Ogilvie horsemen. In all Montrose now had perhaps as many as 5,000 men (a tenth or more of them cavalry), more than ever before. Many Highlanders and Gordons had rallied to him, at last convinced by his repeated victories that it was worth taking the risk of fighting for him. Now ready to move, Montrose suddenly led his army south past Perth to Kinross, as if intent on marching into Fife. The primary purpose of this was doubtless to confuse the covenanters as to his intentions, but a subsidiary motive was to give his men an opportunity to ravage the marquis of Argyll's estates in the parishes of Muckhart and Dollar, his only major properties so far to have escaped destruction. At Kinross therefore Montrose turned west towards Stirling, marching through Argyll's lands, the ravaging of them being led by the MacLeans. As the army passed Alloa the earl of Mar invited Montrose and his leading officers to dine at Alloa House. Showing singular ill judgement at such a critical juncture, Montrose accepted and led his cavalry to Alloa, leaving Alasdair MacColla to march on with the infantry. Montrose had always complained that he could not move into the Lowlands in safety without cavalry; yet now, as soon as he had cavalry and had broken out southwards, he deprived his infantry of their cavalry screen and left Alasdair to march towards a major enemy garrison with footmen alone. Luckily his moves had taken the enemy by surprise, and they were unable to punish such folly as it deserved; having 'liberally feasted', Montrose caught up with his infantry.

Once past Stirling, Montrose turned south again. On 14 August he reached Kilsyth, where he camped. As he had hoped, the covenanters' army (with Baillie in command) was hastening after him, anxious to prevent him either escaping back to the Highlands or continuing southwards and ravaging Glasgow and the strongly covenanting south-west, where new forces were being raised. As in virtually all of Montrose's victories, he was now again to benefit from the misconceived eagerness of the covenanters to give battle.[12]

Baillie camped just a few miles from Kilsyth on 14 August. Discord reigned in the camp. Baillie was so discredited by his previous defeats — which he blamed on failure to support and supply him adequately — that he had little authority and felt unable to resist the advice of a committee parliament had attached to his army which included Argyll and other covenanting leaders who themselves had failed in battle against Montrose. The arguments among the covenanters culminated disastrously on the morning of 15 August. Baillie marched his men towards the enemy camp, and drew them up facing Montrose's army. But many of the covenanting nobles objected, favouring a different disposition. Baillie was directly east of Montrose's men, but it was argued that they would be in a far more advantageous position if they moved north and then a little to the west. This would place the covenanters on a hillside above Montrose; Montrose's flank would then be open to attack by them, and they would be in a good position to cut off any attempt by Montrose to flee back to the Highlands, either without fighting or after he had been defeated. In exasperation Baillie eventually gave way to such advice and began to move his army across the enemy front. Such a move inevitably led to some disorganisation and confusion which could be easily seen by the enemy drawn up opposite; an enemy which had time and again shown itself willing and able to exploit to the full any advantage offered to it by the covenanters' miscalculations.

It is impossible to reconstruct Montrose's battle array in detail, but as usual he had his infantry in the centre, cavalry on the wings. The front ranks of the infantry were Highlanders commanded by Alasdair MacColla. In front of the main lines a small party of men had been stationed in some cottages and gardens. MacLean tradition states that they were commanded by Ewen MacLean of Treshnish; MacMhuirich asserts they were a mixture of Irish and Highlanders under Major Laghtnan; perhaps Treshnish was there, but under Laghtnan's command.[13] The day was hot, and Montrose's Irish and Highlanders cast off their heavy plaids and fought in their white shirts (the long tails of which they tied between their legs) and barefoot. To give his army some approximation to a uniform to aid identification of friend from foe, Montrose had his cavalry wear white shirts over their other clothes.[14] Opposed to Montrose's 5,000 or so men the covenanters had perhaps 7,000. Kilsyth was thus by far the largest-scale battle Montrose ever fought; and once he had drawn up his men he largely lost control of events. The same is true of Baillie. The battle began before either general intended, with some of their officers acting on their own initiative.

As Baillie's men began awkwardly to turn away from the enemy to move north, some of his horsemen instead charged towards the enemy outposts, either disobeying orders in an excess of zeal to get to grips with the enemy or through confusion as to what they were meant to do. Montrose would doubtless have tried to take advantage of the stupidly dangerous move being attempted by the covenanters, but the attack on his outposts quickly escalated into a major engagement before he could intervene. The Highland and Irish outposts resisted the disorganised cavalry attack successfully, but the sight of the partial enemy advance tempted some of the Highlanders in Montrose's main infantry centre into charging 'without waiting for the word of command', at which, as Wishart puts it, Montrose was 'somewhat disconcerted'. It was evidently Alasdair MacColla, who commanded both Major Laghtnan's outposts and the main body of infantry, who decided to act without Montrose's orders and called on the Highlanders to charge to help the outposts. But at the last minute a typical, and potentially disastrous, inter-clan dispute over precedence arose: should the MacLeans, led by Donald MacLean of Brolas (Duart's brother) or the MacDonalds, led by the captain of Clanranald's son Donald, have the honour of leading the charge? The MacLeans were, it seems, drawn up nearest the fighting; but the MacDonalds (perhaps through Alasdair's favour) managed to get ahead of them and reached the enemy first. Montrose had not ordered the charge, but once it had been launched he was quick to see that he must support it; he therefore ordered a general advance.

The Highland charge burst through the disorganised attack of some of the enemy cavalry with little difficulty. The rest of the covenanters were still trying to move to new positions or were simply trying to find out what they were meant to be doing, confused by seeing some of their colleagues already engaging the enemy; officers were riding round seeking orders and trying to organise some concerted action as bewilderment and chaos grew. The milling mobs of confused covenanters put up little resistance when they suddenly found the white-shirted Highlanders charging into their midst with swords and targets, closely followed by the rest of Montrose's infantry and, on the wings, by his cavalry. A party of Gordons had been sent out on Montrose's left to try to occupy the hillside to the north that the covenanters had been trying to reach. Advancing too far after initial success, the Gordons got into difficulties, but were rescued by a cavalry charge led by Aboyne which routed the covenanters' right wing. The covenanters' whole army soon dissolved in confusion and panic flight, and the by now almost traditional slaughter of surrounded and fleeing covenanters by Irish and Highlanders began. And again half or more of the covenanters' total numbers were killed. Far from learning from past mistakes made in conducting armies against Montrose, the covenanters had redoubled them. Thus Montrose's final and greatest victory was by no means the hardest won; both Inverlochy and Auldearn had seen fiercer and more prolonged fighting.[15]

Five times Montrose had defeated covenanting armies, only to have new ones immediately appear before him. Now at last, after his sixth victory, no covenanting army remained in Scotland. Moreover the covenanting regime temporarily collapsed after Kilsyth as many leading covenanters (Argyll included) took refuge in flight to England or Ireland. Kilsyth was the culminating victory of royalist over covenanter. It was also the culminating victory of Gael, and especially the Clan Donald, over Lowlander. A poem in honour of Alasdair, composed in classical Gaelic (as opposed to the vernacular Gaelic of all the other poems about him), makes no mention of the cause of King Charles or of Montrose; the victors at Kilsyth are the Gaels led by the kindred of Colla Uais (one of the early, and doubtless mythical, heroes of the Clan Donald). Accompanying prose explanations do refer to the Gaels as forming the king's army, but this is almost incidental to the real, the essential, Gaelic character of the army. To some extent this is only natural in the context; the poem's purpose is to sing the praises of Alasdair and the Clan Donald. But the language used to describe the opponents of the Gaels emphasises the extent to which the war is being seen almost as one between different races or nations. There is no mention of the covenanters. The enemy is referred to either as the *Gall* (plural *Goill*) or as the men of *Alba*. The Word *Goill* was often used by Highlanders to denote Lowlanders; perhaps best translated as 'non-Gael', it had connotations of foreign-ness. Calling the covenanters the men of *Alba* emphasises the sense of alienation created by use of the word *Goill*, for *Alba* is Scotland; the poet does not, it seems, consider himself and other Gaelic Highlanders to be 'men of Scotland' — even though they are nominally fighting for the king of Scotland.

'The men of *Alba* are in panic rout because of Colla's kindred; many regions therein lack a chieftain; lords are heavy of spirit,' recounts the poet. The charter, written and sealed, that symbol of feudalism which had been used to legitimise the expansion of the Campbells and others at the expense of their neighbours, is contemptuously dismissed; but what overthrows its authority is not, for the poet, any vague traditional right to clan lands, but the sword. The hoped-for gains of the Clan Donald are to be based on right of conquest (though, ironically, doubtless then legitimised by feudal charter from the king). 'The broadsword's charter is the birthright of that bold people; often without seal's impression do they impose tax and tribute.' Underlying right of conquest is indeed the justice of the Clan Donald's cause. 'The men of *Alba* melt before them after every conflict, waged on behalf of right and justice.' But it is accepted that the Clan Donald's traditional 'rights' are themselves based on earlier conquest. 'By firmness of heart in waging combat came the better part of their heritage.' The enemy are not worthy of fighting the Clan Donald; the 'big paunched folk' are contrasted with 'the comely Gael', and 'No fit food for exploits by Gaelic nobles in fray of blue blades are the pithless rabble of the *Goill* who have not practised combat.' Time and again, the prose accompanying the poem relates, the men of *Alba* had collected great armies, but all were defeated by 'some few of the ancient noble lofty warlike stocks' of the Gaels. At Kilsyth the Gaels were filled with hatred at the sight of the enemy army 'by reason of their [the Gaels'] nobility and high descent as compared with the children of petty barons and churls'. The battle is won, and 'Bodies like clothes a-bleaching are stretched on hill-sides, ignoble of aspect; they have left foreign women wet of cheek and not joyful.' There was now no army of the *Goill* left to face the victorious Gaels.[16]

Montrose had always given the impression that, once he had finally defeated the covenanting armies in Scotland, he would at once raise a great army and march into England. But now that no army was left to oppose him he found that this was not practical. It would be folly to abandon Scotland, giving the covenanters a chance to recover, and in any case he had no great army, and few of the men he had got were interested in marching over the Border. Moreover, covenanting armies remained undefeated in England and Ireland, and would now doubtless hasten back to Scotland, and things were going so badly for the royalists in England that establishing a secure base for the king in Scotland might be the best service Montrose could perform for him at the moment; indeed the king himself might come to join him in Scotland. Montrose therefore settled to the work of establishing a royalist regime in Scotland and asserting his control of the Lowlands, filling the vacuum left by the collapse of the covenanters. Here the plague, which had so far helped Montrose, began to hinder him. Fear that the disease would spread to his army prevented him from occupying parts of the country — and Edinburgh above all. To have ruled from Edinburgh would not only have been convenient administratively, it would have helped to bring him legitimacy and credibility in the eyes of many.

As plague barred the capital to him, he decided to make Glasgow his headquarters. On the day of Kilsyth he wrote to the burgh magistrates ordering them to stop inhabitants fleeing at his advance and to have ready 'all sorts of provision' for his army.[17] After resting his men for two days at Kilsyth, Montrose marched them into Glasgow, which promised him a large sum of money for distribution among his troops to prevent plundering. But Montrose soon found it impossible to control his men, and sporadic looting began. The wealth of the burgh was an irresistible attraction to men who thought it the rightful reward for their victory. Montrose therefore hastily withdrew his army to Bothwell, where he camped. Emboldened by this, the citizens of Glasgow became less willing to indulge the conquerors than before. When on 19 August Montrose sent Murdoch MacLean of Lochbuie to get new clothes for his men, the provost refused to supply them without cash payment, which Lochbuie could not provide.[18]

The camp at Bothwell was soon thronged with prominent individuals and representatives of burghs and shires swearing loyalty to the king and undertaking to serve him and Montrose. The latter's status was enhanced by a commission the king had signed in July promoting him from lieutenant general to captain general and deputy governor of Scotland, with power to summon parliaments and create knights. He made prompt use of these new powers. On 18 August he summoned parliament to meet in Glasgow on 20 October; and Alasdair MacColla was knighted at Bothwell before the assembled army. This was the only knighthood bestowed by Montrose, a reward for and recognition of Alasdair's outstanding services, and a compliment to the Gaels he led and inspired.[19]

It is likely, however, that simple gratitude was not Montrose's only motive in knighting Alasdair. Already, within days of his greatest victory, Montrose was having difficulty holding his army together and maintaining its morale. He was faced with a problem common to any general or politician in his position. How do you reward and bind to you former neutrals and enemies who submit now that you are victorious, without simultaneously alienating those who have fought for you and thus made victory possible? It is expedient to show most favour to those whose loyalty is doubtful and needs to be bought, rather than to those whose loyalty is already certain. But to act thus, as Montrose (desperately trying to whip up support in the southern Lowlands) did, looks very like ingratitude. In encouraging waverers and new-found friends he seemed to be neglecting the men who had fought a long and bitter campaign for him and who despised those who suddenly discovered loyalty to the king once victory was won; surely such time-servers deserved punishment rather than reward? At the same time Montrose 'had to appear as a liberator and a statesman, where he had hitherto been known as a destroyer'.[20] His soldiers therefore were deprived of the plunder of Glasgow, and found him trying to control their conduct far more strictly than before. Almost inevitably, the result was disillusionment and demoralisation among his men.

Patrick Gordon expresses their outlook: Montrose now trusted in the 'faire promisses' of his new-found allies, and this led him 'to slight his old frindes, that had giuen him the best assistance for obtaineing so many wictories'.[21] Another Gordon historian, writing in the early eighteenth century but well informed, claimed that resentment among the Highlanders and Gordons who formed the bulk of Montrose's army at his attitude to them was not something new, appearing only after Kilsyth. In sending accounts of his victories to the king, Montrose never mentioned their services, and Alasdair MacColla in particular resented this.[22] This charge cannot entirely be dismissed as a biased attempt by a Gordon to justify the desertion of Montrose by the Gordons, for the charge is very specific and it is supported by the evidence referred to — by Montrose's own letters to the king. His reports on two of his victories, Inverlochy and Auldearn, survive, and they are remarkable for the extent to which those who fought for him are neglected. The impression is strong that none were to be allowed to share his glory by being singled out for praise. 'I' and not 'we' is the key word in these letters; they display a rampant egotism recalling that of Caesar's famous 'I came, I saw, I conquered'. This is consistent with Montrose's thirst for individual glory elsewhere in his career; but in this instance he might have pleaded one justification. The letters were in large part propaganda documents, intended for publication. It was therefore necessary to deliberately conceal the identity of most of the men who fought under him, to disguise the fact that the king had only been able to gather an army in Scotland by relying mainly on Irish and Highland Gaels, Catholics and barbarians. Yet, whatever his motives, Montrose seemed to be displaying gross ingratitude. At worst he seemed unwilling to attribute merit to any but himself; at best, he was ashamed of those who fought and died for him, so failed to mention them. Public recognition by Montrose of the part played by Alasdair and the Gaels in his campaigns was long overdue. Knighting Alasdair was thus probably in part an attempt to placate him, the Highlanders and the Irish. It was to prove too little and too late.

The part of the Lowlands slowest to demonstrate newly discovered loyalty to the king was the south-west, which had long been a covenanting stronghold. Levies being raised for the covenanters by the earl of Lanark had dispersed after Kilsyth, but there were fears that the earls of Cassillis and Eglinton would manage to raise new forces in Ayrshire. Montrose therefore now ordered Alasdair MacColla and John Drummond younger of Balloch into Ayrshire with half the Irish and many Highlanders to cow the countryside into submission and punish the recalcitrant.[23] At their approach the local covenanting leaders fled without offering any resistance. Establishing himself at Kilmarnock with 300 horsemen, Alasdair plundered the surrounding countryside for some days late in August. Then, judging that local landlords had learnt their lesson, he forbade further plundering and invited them to submit. Many came in and took protections. Where landlords had fled it was left to their friends or tenants to reach agreements with Alasdair, and in these instances at least he exacted financial penalties. The tenants of Sir William Mure of Rowallan agreed to pay 1,000 merks to avoid further plundering. Sir William Cunningham of Cunninghamhead's friends undertook to pay 1,200 merks, their lands having already suffered an estimated £10,000 Scots worth of damage. Loudoun House, home of the earl of Loudon, a Campbell and chancellor of Scotland, surrendered to Alasdair, and the countess agreed to pay 8,500 merks to save the parishes of Loudoun, Galston and Mauchline from devastation. In her anxiety to please Alasdair, she 'embraced him in her arms' and entertained him sumptuously — or so at least royalist gossip claimed. Neil Montgomery of Langshaw won a respite of four days for the earl of Eglinton's estates so the tenants could meet and agree on how much to offer Alasdair for his protection. Someone informed Alasdair that Langshaw had really sneaked off to Bothwell to get a protection from Montrose without paying. Alasdair came furiously to Eglinton Castle to demand an explanation, and Langshaw managed to persuade him that he had not sought to double-cross him. Agreement was reached that Eglinton's tenants should pay 4,000 merks, 600 at once and the rest at the end of September. As Alasdair's men withdrew they poached some deer from Eglinton's park and stole a few sheep, but apart from this his lands were now safe — three of his tenants had been killed before Langshaw had approached Alasdair.[24]

From Eglinton Alasdair moved on to Irvine. The burgh provost and most of the leading men fled by sea (mainly to Ireland) with their moveable goods when they heard of Alasdair's approach, but one of the baillies, John Dunlop, and a few others remained. They had sent away their wives and goods and were intending to follow, but Hew MacKaile (the parish minister) and the craftsmen and common people who could not escape persuaded them to stay behind to try to save the burgh from destruction. They got better terms from Alasdair than they had expected, 'some of us being in acquantance with him'. How the worthy burgesses had become acquainted with the dread Alasdair MacColla is a mystery; the most likely explanation is that they had met him while trading to Ulster or the Western Isles in the now distant days of peace. John Dunlop asserted that he had only acted to save the burgh, and that the magistrates of neighbouring burghs had behaved in similar ways; nonetheless he was later fined heavily for compliance with the rebels.[25] Other Ayrshire men guilty of dealings with Alasdair at this time were pursued in the church courts. The presbytery of Ayr heard Thomas Kennedy younger of Ardmillan confess 'that he had supped with Alaster M'Donald' in Kilmarnock — but only by accident! Fergusson of Kilkerran, Hugh Blair of Blairstone and others also admitted having met Alasdair in Kilmarnock.[26]

From Irvine Alasdair returned to the camp at Bothwell in the first days of September. Here he found a crisis had developed. In his absence (or possibly just after his return) many of the Clan Donald and other Highlanders had left Montrose. According to Patrick Gordon, discontent had come to a head because they claimed Montrose had promised them the plunder of Glasgow, but had then refused them this, promising them the money to be paid by the burgh instead. This promise too had been broken; presumably Montrose, trying to establish a government, had decided that other calls on the little cash available were more urgent. Instead he made a third promise: the Highlanders would be given some other, greater, reward. This was unsatisfactorily vague, so the MacDonalds 'shrunke all away' within two or three days. Their leaders remained behind with Montrose but explained that they could not stop their men reacting thus to broken promises. Montrose then made new promises which the Clan Donald leaders thought would give satisfaction, and they agreed to go and round up their men. Alasdair was sent to help them but 'he also being a male content stayed with them, and nether he nor they euer returned againe'. Thus Montrose lost nearly 2,000 of his best men; and Aboyne soon withdrew as well, marching his Gordons homeward.[27]

The reason given by Patrick Gordon for the withdrawal of the Highlanders does not provide a full explanation for their conduct. Wishart saw the incident as a recurrence of the old problem that the Highlanders expected to be allowed to return home from time to time to deposit plunder gained and look after their families. The latter consideration may have been particularly strong at this point; it was harvest time. And Wishart states that the Highlanders' leaders pressed to be allowed to go with their men, as it was necessary to provide food and shelter for their wives and children in devastated areas as winter was approaching; moreover, further action was needed against the Campbells, to prevent them from recovering and falling on their enemies. The Highland leaders therefore begged for leave of absence, but undertook to return within forty days, in greater numbers than before. Montrose was forced to agree, and sought to regain the initiative by actually ordering them to go and appointing Alasdair, 'who was only too forward in craving that office', to command them. Like the others, Alasdair swore to return, but in fact he had resolved not to do so. And he not only marched off with 3,000 Highlanders, he took 120 Irish without permission.[28]

Thus, for Wishart, what was taking place was one of the periodic withdrawals by the Highlanders to visit their families, pursue the feud with the Campbells, and then return with new recruits. But he then asserts that Alasdair (and by implication the others as well) had secretly determined not to return, though he gives no explanation for this. There is no other evidence to support the assertion, and it seems likely that Wishart has deduced that Alasdair and the Highlanders never intended to return merely from the fact that in the event they did not return, which is not entirely logical. Moreover Wishart implies that Alasdair was responsible for the withdrawal of all the Highlanders, and that their withdrawal was responsible for Montrose's subsequent defeat at Philiphaugh, and in this he is followed by many of Montrose's biographers. Mark Napier denounced Alasdair's 'faithless act', the 'mean and ruinous' conduct of a 'stupidly ungrateful' man.[29] John Buchan reached the odd conclusion that the Highland chiefs could not be blamed for their conduct because they knew no better! 'Alasdair alone desserves censure.'[30] Yet while the temporary withdrawal of the Highlanders was a major blow to Montrose, he had plenty of time to take account of it (as he had done in similar circumstances in the past) and avoid immediate defeat. Further, Alasdair was not responsible for the withdrawal of all, or even of most, of the Highlanders. Some had probably left before he returned from Ayrshire. According to Henry Guthry, it was not the Clan Donald, over whom Alasdair had most influence, who left first but the men of Atholl and the MacLeans; the pressures that they were putting on Montrose are probably indicated by letters of certification and assurance issued by Montrose to Alan MacLean of Ardgour on 1 September. This document relates how Ardgour had held his lands and barony direct from the king as a tenant in chief until the marquis of Argyll, by violent oppression, forced him to resign his lands and agree to hold them as his vassal. As Ardgour had served the king faithfully, Montrose swore that this wrong would be righted.[31] But in spite of this, Ardgour left with the rest of the MacLeans. Moreover, Alasdair did not lead most of the Highlanders who left Montrose; while he led a few hundred men into southern Argyllshire, the great majority dispersed to their homes in the north. In choosing to return to Argyll to attack the Campbells, Alasdair was undoubtedly motivated largely by his hatred of that clan. Guthry portrays Montrose trying to dissuade Alasdair from the venture, promising that he would join him in again falling on the Campbells at a later date, whereupon Alasdair details the wrongs Argyll had done him and his family which still called out for revenge. He then marched off with over 500 Highlanders and 'a strong party of Irish to be his life-guard'.[32] This figure certainly agrees much better with the number of men who are subsequently found fighting under Alasdair than the 2,000 or 3,000 men mentioned by Patrick Gordon and Wishart.

The expedition into southern Agyllshire was not only potentially of benefit to Alasdair himself; it was of great potential value to Montrose, as this was an area from which he had expected many recruits but so far had received almost none. While the other Highlanders recruited in the north, Alasdair's task included trying to persuade the Campbells' enemies in the south to rise. Indeed Sir James Lamont of that Ilk, sent by Montrose on just such a recruiting expedition, later claimed that he had asked Montrose to send Alasdair with him. Lamont had been commissioned by the king to rise against the covenanters in 1644 but had cautiously kept this secret; he feared the Campbells too much to act. He even agreed to fight for them, but this led to his capture at Inverlochy. How he regained his freedom is unknown, but Montrose may have treated him leniently in order to encourage his royalist leanings. After Kilsyth he summoned Lamont to Bothwell, and there on 26 August he gave him a commission to repair to Argyllshire and raise in arms all fencible men who would support the king. Fire and sword were to be used against the disobedient, and the men raised were to be brought to Montrose's army. According to Lamont, he agreed enthusiastically; in reality he probably — and very reasonably — was horrified at being thus ordered to march into the stronghold of the Campbells and summon them to fight for the king. Certainly he immediately asked for help. 'And that hee might have the better freedome for drawing together his owne freinds and followers and many others within that sheyre He desyred that his Excellence the Marquese of Montrose would be pleased to send Sir Alexander Makdonald who was Generall Major with some five or six hundred men to be assistants to him while hee gott his owne and others brought into a body.' This request, says Lamont, Montrose immediately granted.[33] It may be that Lamont exaggerates; he was concerned to prove that he had been acting as a loyal royalist. But he is the only person who was actually present at Bothwell who has left an account of why Alasdair marched west — and Lamont was not the man to take part in any wild Clan Donald venture in defiance of Montrose. It is likely that Alasdair urged that he be allowed to march into Argyllshire; but it does seem that Montrose agreed to the venture, and saw positive advantages in it in aiding Lamont. There also seems little doubt that, as on previous occasions, Alasdair intended to return, though the strongest argument in favour of this interpretation has been totally overlooked: Alasdair left the great majority of his remaining Irish troops with Montrose. It is very hard to believe that, if he really was cynically determined to leave Montrose to inevitable defeat, he would have thus abandoned his best troops, the men he had been given command of and had brought from Ireland, including old friends like Manus O'Cahan.

In leaving Montrose, Alasdair and the Highlanders probably thought that they were doing no more than they had done on previous occasions, but from Montrose's point of view this was far from being the case. He was no longer willing, as in the past, to withdraw to some place of safety, or to evade the enemy by keeping on the move, until Alasdair, the Highlanders and the Gordons returned. He was now for the first time determined to hold territory, instead of just defeating his enemies and moving on. He had summoned a parliament and was attempting to establish a government; to retreat now to the Highlands would emphasise his weakness and destroy his credibility, especially as such action would present such an extreme contrast to his own boasts. After Kilsyth, with a confidence that bore little relation to reality, he had informed the king that he would soon enter England at the head of 20,000 men. Yet retreat was, after the Highlanders and Gordons left him, the only course of action which made sense, for he found few Lowland recruits to replace them. Belief that providence was bound to bring him yet another victory blinded him to this. 'Montrose his ambition overswayed his judgement, ascrying all to himself, which was the occasion of his ruine and defeat at Philipshaugh' was Gordon of Sallagh's verdict.[34] Ascribing all to himself alienated his supporters; ambition drove him on regardless of rational argument.

The covenanters had large reserves of veteran troops already in arms in England and Ireland who could be brought home to deal with Montrose; Kilsyth, as it were, at last forced the covenanters to take Montrose seriously by making his defeat their first military priority, demoting the maintenance of the wars in England and Ireland to secondary considerations. To oppose them successfully, Montrose needed new recruits for his army by the thousand. But he soon found that even though he was now master of the Lowlands, very few Lowlanders would fight for him. Certainly the list of men who came to his camp at Bothwell, swore allegiance to the king, and received protections was impressive. But few of them were ready to stay and fight; and most of those nobles and lairds who would fight came alone or almost alone. Either they could not or they would not persuade their kinsmen, tenants and servants to fight for the king. Most who took protections did so simply to avoid plundering by the dreaded Irish and Highlanders, and had no intention of supporting Montrose in arms. Yet, in spite of the evidence Montrose retained a desperate faith in promises of support from men who were insincere or were loyal but incapable (through incompetence or opposition) of raising men.

The full extent of Montrose's failure to win new support was seen when the Highlanders and Gordons withdrew. At Kilsyth he had had 5,000 men; little more than two weeks later fewer than 1,000 of them remained, more than half being Irish infantry.[35] To replace those who had left, he had found perhaps 1,000 recruits; these were virtually entirely horsemen, which made them sound impressive, but in fact these mounted nobles, gentry and others were untrained, undisciplined — and many were even of doubtful loyalty. Montrose had longed for the day when, the power of the covenanters broken, he could recruit freely in the Lowlands. Now that day had come, and the full extent of the damage he had done the king's cause in Lowland eyes by employing Irish and Highlanders was seen. Exasperating as Montrose found the demands of the Highlanders and Gordons, they were virtually the only men in Scotland who would fight for him.

Montrose, however, refused to admit his failure and isolation. Leaving Bothwell on 4 September, he advanced to the Borders, having received assurances from the earls of Home, Roxburgh and Traquair that they would raise men for him. Reliance on these promises led directly to disaster, for within a few days of Montrose's leaving Bothwell, Lieutenant General David Leslie entered Scotland with over 6,000 veterans of the Scottish army in England, over 5,000 of them cavalry. The well-meaning but irresolute earls of Home and Roxburgh offered no resistance and were captured; there was now no hope of finding a significant number of recruits on the Borders. The only course of action left open to Montrose that was not suicidal was flight northwards. This is what Leslie expected, and he hastened towards Stirling to cut off such a retreat; but then he discovered that Montrose with a force so small that it hardly merited the name of an army was lingering on the Border. What Montrose's plans were is unknown; so passively did he await his fate that it may be that in his heart of hearts he knew that defeat was inevitable if he did not retreat, but perhaps after all his brave boasts his pride would not let him turn back. Better complete defeat than ignominious flight.

Montrose knew that David Leslie had crossed the Border with a formidable army. Yet on 12 September he camped his army at Philiphaugh while he himself took up quarters in Selkirk about four miles away. To the folly of thus separating himself from his army when he knew the enemy was seeking him, he then added the folly of refusing to believe reports during the night of 12-13 September that enemy forces were approaching. Early in the morning he was breakfasting in Selkirk when he heard that David Leslie was almost upon him. Hastening to Philiphaugh he found the day already lost. He led some desperate cavalry charges but only a few hundred of his 1,200 or so horsemen followed him; the rest of his 'new friends' dispersed without fighting. Eventually Montrose and the survivors of the horsemen who had charged with him recognised that they could do nothing to save the infantry, and so fled. The Irish infantry were then surrounded and virtually exterminated. Of the five to seven hundred Irish, over half died fighting. Others were captured on the field or while attempting to escape; some were promised quarter, but subsequently nearly all the prisoners were shot, and many of the wives and camp-followers of the Irish were massacred after the battle. Manus O'Cahan and Thomas Laghtnan were taken to Edinburgh and there hanged.[36]

Apart from the Irish who had marched with Alasdair and some small groups of Irish in garrisons or scattered in the north, the expeditionary force which had sailed from Ireland under Alasdair's command the previous year had ceased to exist. Montrose and a few supporters made good their escape back to the

Highlands, but they no longer had an army. Alasdair's reactions to the news of Philiphaugh are unknown, but it would be surprising if it did not lead him to blame Montrose for the loss of his Irish, both through his refusal to retreat when this became necessary and through his conduct just before the battle. Overweening pride and ambition had led to an unnecessary defeat and massacre. Montrose might have judged death preferable to retreat, but it would be easier to accept the nobility of this ideal if he had suffered the penalty of such a stance instead of fleeing at the last minute and leaving the Irish to pay the price. It is notable that Wishart feels the need to justify at considerable length the abandoning of the Irish to their fate.[37] The defeat had not even been the glorious defeat of a last charge against great odds; it had been an inglorious and unnecessary surprisal caused by incompetent leadership. How much Alasdair was to be influenced in the months ahead by bitterness at the death of the Irish he had left to serve Montrose is unknown; but it may well have been important in leading him to decide not to rejoin Montrose.

NOTES

1. Reid, *History of the presbyterian church in Ireland*, i.555-9 (this account of the exchange is convincing except for one major blunder; it asserts that Coll Ciotach had already been killed by Argyll); Black, 'Colla Ciotach', *TGSI*, xlviii.227; Spalding, *Memorials*, ii.478; SRO, PA.11/4, f.81; SRO, PA.7/23/2/33.

2. Wishart, *Memoirs*, 104; Spalding, *Memorials*, ii.474; W. Cramond (ed), *Records of Elgin* (2 vols, New Spalding Club, 1903-8), ii.251.

3. Mackenzie, *Orain Iain Luim*, 27 (the assertion in ibid, 246 that Ian Lom refers to Montrose's plundering of Fraser property in 1646 is not plausible, as the poem is concerned with the deeds of Alasdair, who was not with Montrose in 1646); Fraser, *Frasers*, 289-90.

4. Ibid, 328-9.

5. Baillie, *Letters*, ii.418; Wishart, *Memoirs*, 104-6; Gordon, *Britane's distemper*, 127-8; Spalding, *Memorials*, ii.474-6, 478-9.

6. A.G.M. MacGregor, *The history of the Clan Gregor* (2 vols, Edinburgh 1898-1901), ii.100-1, 104.

7. SRO, GD.112/40/2, bundle 'letters 1640-9'.

8. Napier, *Memorials*, ii.205-6.

9. Baillie, *Letters*, ii.418-9; Wishart, *Memoirs*, 106-12; Gordon, *Britane's distemper*, 129-33; *Rel Celt*, ii.192-5; Gordon, *Genealogical history*, 526; Fraser, *Frasers*, 299.

10. Leith, *Memoirs*, i.320, 343, 348.

11. *Rel Celt*, ii.194-7; Wishart, *Memoirs*, 114-15; Gordon, *Britane's distemper*, 135-6; *The true relation of the late and happie victorie . . . at Kilsyth* (1645), 3. Father MacBreck talks of Alasdair raising men from Kintyre, but this seems highly unlikely, Leith, *Memoirs*, i.347.

12. Wishart, *Memoirs*, 115-22; Gordon, *Britane's distemper*, 136-9; Baillie, *Letters*, ii.420; *True relation . . . of Kilsyth*, 4; *Rel Celt*, ii.196-9; Guthry, *Memoirs*, 191-2.

13. [J.C. Sinclair], *Historical and genealogical account of the Clan Maclean*, 134; *Rel Celt*, ii.200-1.

14. In Wishart, *Memoirs*, 123n it is asserted that the Highlanders 'never' fought wearing plaids. But if this is the case, how is it that no sources mention Montrose's men fighting in their shirts at any other battle, while four (Wishart, Gordon, MacMhuirich, *True relation*) mention them fighting thus at Kilsyth? Buchan, *Montrose*, 268 converts the white shirts into saffron ones simply because the latter, being the traditional colour of shirts for Irish and Highlanders, was what he thought they ought to have worn!

15. Wishart, *Memoirs*, 122-5; Gordon, *Britane's distemper*, 139-45; *Rel Celt*, ii.198-201; Baillie, *Letters*, ii.420-4; *True relation . . . of Kilsyth*, 4-6; Leith, *Memoirs*, i.348.

16. W.J. Watson (ed), 'Unpublished Gaelic poetry, III', *Scottish Gaelic Studies,* ii (1927), 75-91. Watson's rendering of *Gall* as 'Saxon' has nothing to recommend it, but otherwise I have used his translation.

17. Napier, *Memorials,* ii.222.

18. SRO, PA.7/23/2/36.

19. Gordon, *Britane's distemper,* 146; Guthry, *Memoirs,* 197; Wishart, *Memoirs,* 139-40; Leith, *Memoirs,* i.350; PA.7/23/2/34, 35. Wishart (followed by Guthry) states that Alasdair was knighted on 3 September, the day before Montrose left Bothwell and thus after Alasdair's march through Ayrshire; Sir Robert Spottiswoode did not reach Bothwell with the royal commission giving Montrose power to summon parliaments and create knights until 1 September (Napier, *Memorials,* ii.253), so it is assumed that he must have knighted Alasdair after that date. But Montrose must have known of the new commission at least as early as 18 August, as on that date he used his new powers to summon parliament. Thus he could have used these powers to knight Alasdair before the latter marched into Ayrshire, as Patrick Gordon claims. Certainty is impossible, but I have here followed Gordon rather than Wishart.

20. Gardiner, *Civil war,* ii.350.

21. Gordon, *Britane's distemper,* 145.

22. W. Gordon, *History of the family of Gordon* (2 vols, Edinburgh 1726-7), ii.483, 497.

23. Gordon, *Britane's distemper,* 146; Wishart, *Memoirs,* 134. Wishart states that John Drummond 'of Balloch' accompanied Alasdair into Ayrshire, rather than 'younger of Balloch'. This has led some historians to assume that it was really John's father George who fought with Montrose. But the almost contemporary family history confirms that it was John, 'esteemed a valiant gentleman', who 'was a chiefe officer' under Montrose, W. Drummond, Lord Strathallan, *The genealogy of the most noble and ancient house of Drummond* (Edinburgh 1831), 61, 264.

24. Gordon, *Britane's distemper,* 152; J. Paterson, *History of the county of Ayr* (2 vols, Ayr 1847-52), i.116-7; Hill, *Macdonnells of Antrim,* 99-101; Guthry, *Memoirs,* 195.

25. A.F. McJannet, *Royal burgh of Irvine* (Glasgow 1938), 163-4; *Muniments of the royal burgh of Irvine* (2 vols, Ayrshire and Galloway Archaeological Association, 1890-1), ii.58-9, 259-60.

26. Paterson, *History of the county of Ayr,* i.117-18; SRO, CH.2/532/1, Minutes of the presbytery of Ayr, 1642-51, entries for 3 Dec 1645, 14 Jan and 11 Feb 1646.

27. Gordon, *Britane's distemper,* 153-4.

28. Wishart, *Memoirs,* 137-8.

29. Napier, *Memoirs,* ii.569, 611.

30. Buchan, *Montrose,* 281.

31. J.R.N. Macphail (ed), 'Papers relating to the Macleans of Duart', *Highland papers,* i (SHS 1914), 333-4.

32. Guthry, *Memoirs,* 199.

33. H. McKechnie, *The Lamont Clan* (Edinburgh 1938), 168-9; N. Lamont (ed), *Inventory of Lamont papers* (SRS 1914), 430; NLS, MS 545, Lamont papers, f.1.

34. Gordon, *Genealogical history,* 529.

35. Guthry, *Memoirs,* 200; Gordon, *Britane's distemper,* 156.

36. Ibid, 156-60; Wishart, *Memoirs,* 142-8; Guthry, *Memoirs,* 202-4; *A more perfect relation of the late great victorie in Scotland* (London 1645); *Three great victories* (London 1645). For the order for the execution of O'Cahan and Laghtnan see SRO, PA.12/1, minute of 16 October 1645.

37. Wishart, *Memoirs,* 146.

9

The Second Ravaging of Argyll

IN the winter of 1644-5 Montrose and Alasdair had spent about two months in the lands of the Campbells. Now Alasdair and his allies had returned and were to spend more than twenty months savaging their hereditary enemies. For much of this period the surviving evidence is fragmentary. Rival Campbell and Lamont versions of events, prepared in connection with the trial of the marquis of Argyll in 1661, outline Alasdair's activities from September 1645 to February 1646, and much is known of events in May to June 1647 when Alasdair was finally driven out of Scotland. But trying to reconstruct his movements in the long interval between these two periods is largely a matter of trying to make sense of scattered scraps of evidence and traditional stories. These traditions have severe limitations as historical sources. They are not interested in dating events, or even in the order of events, and in some cases it is clear that they are confused, contradicting each other or other evidence. Many of the stories have usually been assumed to refer to the 1644-5 invasion of Argyll, simply because that is much better known than the later ravaging, but in fact most if not all refer to events in 1646. Another difficulty is that they are virtually all Campbell traditions, and therefore at times they may exaggerate Alasdair's brutality; but the fact that, surprisingly, they indicate a good deal of admiration for Alasdair's heroic qualities among his enemies suggests that any such distortion is limited.

Of conditions in Argyll in September 1645 little is known, but there is probably some truth in the claim made by some of Montrose's Highland troops that they were forced to leave him as the Campbells were recovering from Inverlochy and attacking the lands and families of those who supported Montrose. Orders issued by Argyll on 5 July 1645 (from Kilchurn Castle on Loch Awe) to some of the commanders of Campbell forces indicate that the Campbells had regained control of the heart of Argyll and were trying to assert their power on the fringes of their empire. Argyll ordered his commanders to draw together their companies and send out spies and watchers to the braes of Argyll and the borders of the shire to give warning of enemy movements. They were to oppose any attempted raids into Argyll, and were to try to feed their men with food taken from the enemy. 'Bot I desyre not that at this tyme thir be any great actis of hostilitie done againes nichbouris quho have joyned with the enemie unles you sie it for the good of the service.' The Campbells were not yet strong enough to revenge themselves on their neighbours, but were instead to try to persuade them to return to their allegiance to the Campbells by promising them that they would not be punished for having helped the enemy. On the day Argyll issued these orders, the synod of

Argyll assembled at Inveraray, its first meeting since May 1644. Many ministers and elders were absent, but the fact that the meeting took place confirms that Campbell and covenanting control was being re-established in Argyll.[1]

Alasdair led his Highland allies back into Argyll to thwart this Campbell recovery and destroy the power of that clan once and for all so the Clan Ian Mor could regain its lands and rights. He evidently left Montrose's camp at Bothwell on 3 September, the day before Montrose began moving eastwards. Alasdair is said to have camped at Cloverhill until 8 September, perhaps drawing together the Highlanders who had left Bothwell before him. It was this delay that led to reports reaching David Leslie that 'Colekintoe was sent away with 800 horse and foote' to Glasgow. Once Montrose had been routed at Philiphaugh, Leslie therefore determined to advance on Glasgow, but he soon found this was unnecessary. Alasdair had marched round the city towards Dumbarton. There the keeper of the castle, John Semple, refused to surrender. Alasdair was not prepared to waste time on a siege and therefore contented himself with ravaging Semple's lands so thoroughly that even four years later they were unprofitable.[2] The march west then continued. Sir James Lamont's brother, Archibald Lamont of Stillaig, provided boats to ferry Alasdair's men from Roseneath to Cowal. There Alasdair and Archibald Lamont marched north-west to Strachur on Loch Fyne, then swung south through Glendaruel to Auchinbreck. Old ties were abruptly broken now the Lamonts had deserted the Campbells. Sir James had been the tutor of Archibald Campbell, provost of Kilmun, but Kilmun was now forced to surrender his tower-house; quarter was promised, but some of his kinsmen and followers were nonetheless killed. Sir James was married to a sister of James Campbell of Ardkinglas, but when his wife's fourteen-year old brother Archibald fled to him for safety, Sir James handed the boy over to Alasdair Macolla with the recommendation (so Archibald later swore) that he be hanged or kept prisoner. Archibald was kept in Tarbert in irons for a month before being sent to join other Campbell prisoners in Mingary. There he remained, almost starving, for a year until an exchange was arranged.

In Cowal Sir James Lamont 'quickly drew together his ... friends and followers' and marched with Alasdair 'in good order' through Cowal, Argyll, Lorne and Kintyre for five weeks, 'none of their enemies dareing to stand in their way'. As they marched, Sir James went 'to the seaverall heads of the trybes, within the said bounds' (including MacLachlans, MacNeills and MacDougalls), all of whom agreed to help him in the king's cause. Soon he and Alasdair had 2,000 men in arms. The Lamont account claims that at first they did no harm to anyone, apart from taking the food they needed. But soon they heard that the Campbells had fallen on the Lamont lands in Cowal, 'killing all the poore people', men, women, and children, burning their houses and driving off their animals. News of this arrived when Sir James was in Lorne (urging Alexander MacDougall of Dunollie to join him), and as a result he 'burned all the Campbells their houses and cornes and killed all the ffenceible and armed men hee could overtake of them'. There was clearly no longer any hope of persuading the Campbells to submit or to fight for the king, so Sir James and Alasdair, reinforced by 500 MacDougalls, 'did with such courrage and resolution assaile and invade them where ever they could have notice of their being that in short tyme they extruded and expelled them out of the saids countries (Except some few who betook themselves to some castles and rocks within loghs and lakes) even as foxes when hunted hard doo to their holes'. But the old, women and children were spared.[3]

It is highly unlikely that Alasdair and Sir James really behaved so moderately and peacefully until suddenly provoked into slaughtering all men of military age by a Campbell attack on the lands of the Lamonts. From the start the policy of the invaders was probably to kill all Campbell men to destroy the military might of that clan, while encouraging all who resented Campbell domination to join them. Survivors of the Clan Ian Mor as well as men of lesser clans hastened to join Alasdair. In October Angus MacDonald of Largie, for example, joined Alasdair as captain of a company.[4] While Alasdair and the Lamonts assailed the Campbells from the south and east, other Highlanders who had left Montrose since Kilsyth attacked from the north and west. On 6 October Sir Robert Campbell of Glenorchy reported from Balloch Castle that 600 men of the Camerons, the Clanranald, and the MacDonalds of Glencoe and Glengarry had been robbing and plundering in Glendochart, Glenlochy and Glenfalloch for a week. In resisting this invasion the name of Campbell was getting no help from neighbours.[5]

From Inveraray on 19 October George Campbell, sheriff depute of Argyll, took up the same theme. 'It is not the enemies that entereit the countrey that is destroyeing the same, Bot everie neighbouris destroyeing another pairtlie throw not draweing to ane head, and pairtlie throw Joyneing with the enemie. So it is lyklie quhen forces comes that this countrey must be anew conqueist.' Now, as in 1644, invasion from outside Campbell territory might have been defeated if those the Campbells had confidently believed to be their friends and allies had remained loyal. George Campbell also refers to the MacLeans 'Allister' had sent to Islay, which suggests that the attack on Argyll from the north was part of a plan co-ordinated by Alasdair, rather than a completely separate enterprise.[6] In December 1645 the two main forces invading Argyll linked up in Lorne. Sir Lachlan MacLean of Duart met Alasdair at Kilmore and stayed there for three nights. With Duart was Martin MacIlvory, minister of Iona, who was later to confess to having shaken hands with Alasdair at Duart's insistence.[7]

It was probably at this December meeting that the triumphant enemies of the Campbells signed what the latter described as 'a most cruell horrid and bloody band' for 'rooting out the name of Campbell'. The band or bond of agreement has not survived, but Sir James Lamont admitted that it had existed; he had signed a band with the 'special men' of the clans 'bearing in plain Terms of combination among us for the ruin of the name of Campbell'.[8]

By the end of 1645 the Campbell presence in Argyll was limited to scattered garrisons, many of which were short of supplies. In October Inveraray could spare no provisions for other castles. By December Barcaldine Castle in the north had completely run out of grain, and the captain of Dunstaffnage was asked to send food there. Whether or not he was able to do so is unknown, but he did get meal to Sir Donald Campbell of Ardnamurchan, who was experiencing 'extreame necessitie' in Castle Stalker.[9] Petitions from the inhabitants of Argyll to parliament asking for food and military aid and 'shewing the furey of the enimey' brought promises that meal would be sent, but probably little ever arrived, and orders for levying a Highland regiment under Argyll brought no immediate help to the Campbells.[10] Indeed this last order evidently provided a new occasion for a further humiliation of the Campbells. James Campbell of Ardkinglas gathered many Campbell refugees and marched them towards the Lowlands, probably to be formed into the new regiment. On their march they recaptured the castle on the island in Loch Dochart from the MacNabs and besieged Edinample Castle on Loch Earn. They were joined by men loyal to the Campbells from the Menzies and the Stewarts of Balquhidder, and Ardkinglas reached Callander with about 1,200 men. There they were suddenly attacked and routed on 13 February by about 700 Highlanders from Atholl led by Patrick Grahame of Inchbrackie and John Drummond younger of Balloch. Refugees fleeing from this encounter met their chief, the marquis of Argyll, who was on his way to Ulster to try to persuade the Scottish army in Ireland to send men to help him against Alasdair MacColla.[11]

As Argyll's mission to Ireland suggests, the covenanting regime re-established after Philiphaugh was unable to give immediate aid to the Campbells. Its first priority was securing the Lowands and guarding against any attempt by Montrose and Alasdair to break out of the Highlands again. In fact such fears that the two rebel leaders would unite their forces were unfounded. Montrose is said to have sent repeated messages to Alasdair ordering him to rejoin his army as he had promised to do before Philiphaugh,[12] but Alasdair ignored these approaches. He was firmly established as master of much of Argyllshire, including the old lands of the Clan Ian Mor; surely it would be folly to abandon this and march his thousands of men to join Montrose's hundreds in the Eastern Highlands? In many ways it would have made more sense for Montrose to come west to join Alasdair, but there is no evidence that Alasdair ever suggested this. Bitterness at Montrose's tendency to take all the credit for victory for himself, anger at the way many of the Irish had been irresponsibly squandered at Philiphaugh, and determination now to give priority to Clan Donald ambitions, all must have combined to lead Alasdair to ignore his former commander. Montrose knew little of Alasdair's movements. On 23 October he instructed Robertson of Inver at Blair Castle in Atholl to 'let me be advertised what you can hear of Sir Alexander Macdonald, or where he is', and on 18 February 1646 he believed Alasdair had joined Inchbrakie and Balloch younger in an advance towards Glasgow. However, Montrose may have related this more because it was encouraging news than because he believed it, for he was writing to Huntly in an attempt to win the support of the Gordons.[13] To his approaches to Alasdair and Huntly, Montrose added negotiations with chiefs of the north and west Highlands. Seaforth, typically, proved hopelessly indecisive, but Sir James MacDonald of Sleat now at last undertook to help Montrose, and the response of the MacLeods and the MacDonalds of Glengarry was also hopeful.[14]

The covenanters were ignorant of the intentions of both Montrose and Alasdair. Late in October 1645 there was panic at a false report that the two men had merged their forces in Menteith and were about to advance south to join up with invading English royalists.[15] More justified were fears that Alasdair, having occupied Kintyre and Cowal, would turn back eastwards, overrun Bute and Arran, and raid Ayrshire. On 23 December the countess of Eglinton wrote to her husband of fears that Alasdair would 'com ouer and tak all that [he] can gett, and burne the rest'. She begged for advice, assuring the earl that the people of Arran and Bute were 'looking everi night for him in Arrane, for man, wyfe and bairne is coming ouer to this syde' (to Ayrshire) with all their goods, 'for he [Alasdair] is weri strong, and that I feir we find er it be long'.[16]

In January and February 1646 the rebels did indeed turn their attention to the west. According to a Campbell account, Sir James Lamont and 600 men returned to Cowal; at Strachur they killed thirty-three people (including women and children), destroyed 700 bolls of grain, and drove off 340 cattle and horses.[17] From Inveraray George Campbell reported that the rebels in Cowal 'Have beene in trysting with the bute men quho ar doeing all they can to put thame off till supplie come'. Such attempts to delay the rebels through negotiations failed, and in February Alasdair landed in Bute and quartered his men on the inhabitants for some time. Many houses were burnt and there was much plundering. But fears that he would continue west to the mainland proved unfounded; he eventually turned back east to Lorne and Kintyre. The Lamonts, however, remained in Cowal. Sir James said he parted from Alasdair on 12 February (perhaps the day the latter crossed to Bute) and that he stayed in Cowal to see to the welfare of the families of his men before marching with Alasdair to join Montrose. But instead of co-operating in this, Alasdair disappeared to 'the farr Isles of Loghaber'. This plan for the rebels in Argyll to join Montrose is almost certainly a figment of Sir James' imagination, one of his many attempts to prove that he was a good royalist whose best intentions were thwarted by others — in this case by Alasdair. Certainly he made no attempt to take his own men to Montrose.[18]

Of Alasdair's journey to the far isles of Lochaber nothing is known; it is not even clear which islands are referred to. Presumably he went to rally support from the local clans — MacDonalds, MacLeans, Stewarts and Camerons, perhaps helping them against local Campbell garrisons and persuading them to ignore Campbell threats that 'ther is nothing intendit for thame bot destructioune unless they submit in tyme'.[19] It may be that Alasdair was also concerned to ensure that the clansmen joined him and not Montrose.

Alasdair spent most of 1646 in Lorne, Knapdale and Kintyre, attempting to reduce the remaining enemy garrisons. The castle of Kilberry in Knapdale was besieged for a fortnight, but when the garrison sent out ale for Alasdair to drink, he is said to have taken the hint that the castle was well supplied and could hold out indefinitely, and marched off. His approach to Duntroon Castle provides one of several legends of a 'piper's warning' associated with Alasdair and his father. A piper in his forces played to warn the garrison that enemies were attacking. Alasdair therefore failed to surprise the castle and either killed the piper or cut his fingers off.[20]

At Craignish Castle Alasdair's luck was no better. An account of the siege is provided by an early eighteenth century family history of the Campbells of Craignish. The garrison was commanded by Archibald Campbell, tutor of Craignish or Barrichbeyan, 'the most generous, darring, strong bold man of his time'. He had 250 men in the castle or hiding in the surrounding countryside, while Alasdair had 1,500 men. The tutor, it is said, often challenged Alasdair to single combat. This Alasdair refused, but it caused him to be 'very revengeful' and to 'continue the siege much longer than he otherwise would, till at length he was necessitated to raise the siege and quit it having burnt all the country round and got most of the strongholds and places about there'. Tradition relates that Alasdair was wounded by an arrow at Craignish, and that he sent one of his men into the castle disguised as a beggar during the three-week siege to see if it was well supplied. The tutor saw through the disguise, so he gave the beggar plenty of food, telling him the castle could hold out for a year. Discouraged on hearing this, Alasdair abandoned the siege, observing bitterly, 'that is a sharp castle of whelks, the wind itself is the only thing that will keep up a constant fight with it. We will leave it.'[21]

None of the major Campbell strongholds fell to Alasdair, though some minor fortifications were captured or were abandoned as he advanced. It is said that he spared the lands of the MacCorquodales of Phantilands until their chief opened fire on his men from a fortified house on an island on Loch Tromlee. Alasdair then burnt the clan's houses, captured the island, and shot the chief and (perhaps) two of his sons.[22] At the home of the Campbells of Melfort, Ardanstur, the occupants fled leaving food on the tables. When Alasdair left after feasting he ordered that the house be spared, but one of his men set fire to it and was hanged for his pains.[23] A similar story is told of Alasdair eating a meal left by the fleeing occupants of a house in Cowal, but here it is Alasdair himself who then burns the house.[24]

The Campbells seldom stayed to resist Alasdair's advance. When they did, they were swiftly routed. The most important of such engagements was the battle fought at Lagganmore in Glen Euchar. The many traditions of this encounter vary in detail, but are consistent in essentials. Campbells assembled in Glen Euchar to oppose Alasdair, led by Donald Campbell 'the blue eyed' of Lochnell and John Campbell of Bragleen (also known as 'Little John of the Glen' and as Ian Beg MacIan), whose home was at the head of Loch Scammadale, from which the River Euchar flows. Alasdair was told that the Campbells were advancing and hastened to attack them, reinforced by the MacDougalls and the MacAulays of Ardincaple. Zachary Malcolm or MacCallum of Poltalloch is said to have been passing when the battle began, and to have joined in on the side of the Campbells, but it is more likely that he was already with their forces. Soon Malcolm was face to face with Alasdair, whose sword he is said to have broken, forcing Alasdair to flee until he got a new one. Eventually Malcolm was surrounded and died fighting. Lochnell and Bragleen fled when they saw that the Campbells had lost the day, but the latter was pursued and captured; he tried to pass himself off as a shoemaker but was betrayed by his incompetence at the craft. He and the other Campbell prisoners were then herded into a barn at Lagganmore, along with women and children rounded up in the neighbourhood. Alasdair, determined to terrify other

Campbells into submission by atrocity, then had the barn set alight. One of the women managed to escape through a hole in the roof, and the resourceful Bragleen burst out of the door with a peat creel over his head to protect himself both from the fire and from the swords of Alasdair's waiting men. All the others in the barn were burnt alive, the site becoming known as *Sabhal nan Cnàmh*, The Barn of the Bones. Bragleen was recaptured but Alasdair, impressed by his spirit, gave him a chance of life by letting him name his own fate. Any suggestion giving him too good a chance of escape would doubtless have been rejected, so Bragleen begged to be given a sword and allowed to fight his way out of a circle of armed men. This Alasdair agreed to. Bragleen soon found that it was impossible to break through the ring of enemies by conventional swordsmanship, but he hit on the expedient of suddenly throwing his sword high in the air. His disconcerted opponents naturally looked upwards, each fearing the sword would fall on him; taking advantage of this momentary confusion Bragleen was able to flee unarmed from the ring and made good his escape.[25]

Other accounts state that Malcolm of Poltalloch was not killed at Lagganmore. By one story Alasdair defeated Malcolm's forces at Ederline;[26] by another Malcolm was killed leading a dawn attack on Alasdair to recover plundered cattle in Glen Eurach, a few miles south-west of Ederline. Perhaps his death has been placed at Lagganmore through confusing Glen Eurach with its anagram, Glen Euchar. But wherever he died, Malcolm's bravery won him the admiration of Alasdair, expressed in a phrase which became almost proverbial — 'None remained loyal to Argyll but stone and lime and Malcolm.'[27] Only Malcolm, of all the Campbells' allies, had remained loyal to them, and now he was dead. But the problem presented to Alasdair by stone and lime, by Campbell-held castles, was to prove insoluble. And prophecy soon told him that he could not hope for success in future, for he accidentally came to a place called Gocam-Go or Goc-am-go.

In Alasdair's childhood a nurse had predicted that all would go well with him until he came to a place with this name. He would know when he reached it, for when he planted his standard in the ground it would twist or turn to the left, and a coin would jump from the ground. After this success would desert him. As to the location of Gocam-Go, accounts vary. One tradition says it was where Alasdair shot MacCorquodale of Phantilands, which presumably places it by Loch Tromlee. Another version has the pursuit of the Campbells after the battle at Lagganmore continuing to Gocam-Go, but this seems to reflect a further confusion of Glen Euchar, the site of the battle, with Glen Eurach, for the strongest tradition places Gocam-Go in the latter glen, near Ederline at the south-west end of Loch Awe. All traditions assert that Alasdair was upset when, on asking the name of the place where his standard had behaved so oddly, he was told that he had reached the Mill of Gocam-Go; and it is said that his luck did now desert him. A fuller form of the prophecy urged Alasdair to avoid meeting the 'Red Baron of Dunavich' or going to Gocam-Go or Aird na h-Eireir, as the combination of these three actions would lead him to disaster. He had already met the mysterious baron before reaching Gocam-Go, but nothing is said as to whether he ever came to Aird na h-Eireir. Indeed the only other mention of that place in these stories depicts Alasdair as eager to attack it but giving up after several attempts as he failed to discover how to get there, remarking 'well, well, let them be; it is not much if we leave one hamlet in Argyll unburnt'. Confusion has clearly crept in somewhere, so it is not surprising that most versions of the prophecy confine it to the dire consequences of Alasdair coming to Gocam-Go, though it is sometimes added that Alasdair at once confirmed that the prediction of disaster was true by throwing a magic stone over the heads of his men. In the past the stone had always been found easily after this ritual — a good omen. But at Gocam-Go the stone fell in a bog and was never recovered.[28]

Even if one has little faith in prophecies and omens, these tales are of interest as indicating once again Alasdair's high reputation. His ultimate failure and defeat have to be explained, even in the traditions of his enemies, in ways which will not undermine his heroic stature. Once he had by chance come to Gocam-Go, his failure was inevitable. In his striving his heroic qualities could no longer be of any avail, for he was fighting against fate, which no man can overcome.

The story of Alasdair's stay in Argyll in 1645-7 is primarily one of battle and skirmish, siege and plunder, destruction and atrocity. But time was also found for more personal matters. Alasdair had, at some time unknown, married a daughter of Hector MacAllister of Loup, thus taking a wife from a great Kintyre family which, though it had not taken the name of MacDonald, in fact represented the senior cadet line of the Clan Donald. So intense was the hero-worship that Alasdair inspired that his marriage must have disappointed many a Highland girl. 'My lyre, my harp and my violin, my music string wherever I might be; when I was a young girl your coming would lift my mind; you would get a kiss without a word,' sang Dorothy Brown of the island of Luing, 'you are my darling of all the men of the earth.' On a more martial note she dreamed of emulating his feats as a warrior: 'Alas that I am not as I would wish to be — Argyll's head under my arm, grey-haired Colin butchered and the Crowner captured'. 'Alasdair, my beloved darling, who did you see or leave in Ireland? You left thousands and hundreds, and you did not leave your own equal there. Rounded calf of light gait, leg for gathering the host together, no war will be waged without you and no peace will be made without your consent.'[29]

Even with generous allowance for poetic hyperbole,[30] the daughter of MacAllister of Loup must have been widely envied; but we do not even know her name. She bore Alasdair two sons, Coll, who was born about 1645, and Archibald (Gillespie), born about 1647. This suggests that Alasdair had married after his return to Scotland in 1644. Now, in 1646, he had reconquered the ancestral lands of his own and his wife's families, and doubtless hoped to raise his children on them.[31]

So far the fighting in Argyll after February 1646 has been related from local tradition, eked out with a few fragments from contemporary written sources. The existence of a contemporary pamphlet describing major sieges and battles therefore opens the welcome prospect of being able to discuss some of the fighting in a more satisfactory way, soundly based on a clear narrative of events. But unfortunately the contents of this pamphlet seem so extraordinarily at variance with both traditions and with other fragmentary sources that it seems at first sight that it must be dismissed as entirely fictitious. However, closer examination suggests there are elements of truth behind the lies though so distorted as to be almost unrecognisable.

The pamphlet in question was published in London in May 1646, and it claimed to be a report sent from Newcastle on 14 May, which had in turn been taken from a letter dispatched from Edinburgh on 10 May. A major Campbell offensive in Argyll which had met with brilliant success was detailed. The marquis of Argyll had sent 1,200 men into Argyll and 'Eilah' (Islay). They had found part of the rebel army besieging the castle of 'Eilah' (presumably Dunyveg) and attacked them. The rebels had fled after a sharp encounter, leaving 140 of their number dead including their leader, a brother of 'Colkiltoth', and the castle had been relieved. Argyll had also sent another 1,600 men to relieve 'Skipinoth' (Skipness) Castle where 'Colkiltoth' himself was leading the besieging forces. On hearing of the approach of Argyll's men, Alasdair had made a last desperate attempt to storm the castle, but after fierce fighting he was driven back with very heavy losses, his eldest brother and other rebel leaders being killed. Alasdair then fled with his remaining men to the hills, hotly pursued by the Campbells, so Argyllshire was 'now totally cleared of them'.[32]

Obviously the report is absurd: Alasdair remained in control of much of Argyll for another year. The report is simply propaganda. But like much of the best propaganda it is based partly on fact. The Campbells did make an attempt in April-May 1646 to reconquer their lands; but the attempt was a dismal failure. Apart from this distorted pamphlet account, only a few scraps of evidence survive of this Campbell venture. In 1649 Archibald MacAllister, minister of Kilchoman (Islay), in confessing his contacts with the rebels, mentioned that the captain of Skipness, Mathew Campbell, had come from Ireland to Islay; but then the captain of Clanranald also landed, and Skipness 'went away'. Clanranald stayed in Islay a long time, and the country people joined him.[33] That these events date from 1646 is confirmed by Neil MacMhuirich, who records that Clanranald, his son Donald and their forces came to Islay 'and they drove out of it all the clan Campbell that were in it'.[34] Finally Major General Robert Monro, the commander of the Scottish army in Ireland, refers to Argyll's regiment of that army landing in Ireland on 31 May 1646.[35] Thus what seems to have happened is that Argyll's regiment, having returned to Ireland after Inverlochy, undertook a landing in Islay (and perhaps also on Kintyre) in April or May 1646 under the command of Skipness. But Clanranald then also invaded Islay, and the Campbells hastily retreated to Ireland. It seems unlikely that Dunyveg Castle was held by the Campbells and that Skipness relieved it, as the pamphlet report suggests. Certainly by 1647 it was in rebel hands.

As for Skipness Castle in Kintyre, the pamphlet is correct in stating that the rebels besieged it in 1646. The Campbell garrison was led by Malcolm MacNaughton of Dundarave who withstood 'a long and hard seidge' which was raised some time before August 1646. He died soon afterwards, never having recovered from the hardships of the siege.[36] Moreover, Alasdair's eldest brother

Gillespie (Archibald) did evidently die at about this time, and it is said that his death took place at Skipness.[37] Thus the pamphlet may well be accurate in stating that the Campbells relieved Skipness in May and in the process killed Alasdair's brother. It may well also be right in claiming that this was the work of a different Campbell force from that which had landed in Islay, for a version of the pamphlet account which appeared in a contemporary newspaper adds the detail that the Campbell forces which relieved Skipness were led by 'Archbald and Arkinley'. The first of these names makes no sense (perhaps it is a confused reference to Archibald MacColla, who was killed there), but the second appears to be a corruption of Ardkinglas. In February he had commanded the Campbell refugees at Callander, and in June he was to lead a force recruited from such refugees in an invasion of Cowal. Ardkinglas thus clearly had a central part in Campbell plans to recover their lands, and he would therefore have been the natural leader of a force sent to Kintyre.

In May 1646 the Campbells probably relieved Skipness Castle and killed Alasdair's brother. They may also have relieved Dunyveg Castle. But such successes were only temporary, brief raids followed by hasty withdrawals. There were no major victories followed by complete expulsion of the rebels such as had confidently been narrated in London. Some indication of the true state of affairs in Kintyre and Knapdale is provided by a letter written by Alexander Campbell of Pennymore on 18 May. Pennymore had been captured at Inverlochy and held prisoner at Blair Castle, but had been freed in an exchange of prisoners.[38] He wrote from Castle Sween in Knapdale to the captain of Dunstaffnage, revealing that he had just arrived from Ulster where he had conferred with Argyll at Dunluce. Pennymore claimed that Argyll's negotiations for getting help from the Scottish army in Ireland were proceeding successfully. In fact the army refused to help Argyll, but it may have been accepted that he could use his own regiment in the army for raids on rebel-held lands (as the captain of Skipness' landing on Islay suggests). Pennymore assured Dunstaffnage that a party had already been sent to relieve the latter's daughter and son-in-law (perhaps George Campbell of Airds, who held Inveraray Castle), and that an army would soon land in Kintyre. From Ulster Pennymore had brought meal for this army and for the garrisons of Duntroon, Sween, Craignish and Dunstaffnage. But Pennymore's ship had had to retire hastily from Castle Sween because rebel boats were reported in the vicinity, so all the grain had had to be left there.[39] Thus in general terms his letter supports traditional accounts of conditions in Argyllshire. Campbell power was confined to garrisons, though as these were not all besieged continuously, supplies could sometimes be slipped in to them. Pennymore wrote after the invasions of Kintyre and Islay related in the London pamphlet had been repulsed by the rebels. He confidently expected another landing in Kintyre by Argyll's men from Ireland (perhaps intended to coincide with Ardkinglas' attack on Cowal), but this never took place. Early in June the Scottish army in Ireland was routed by the Irish at Benburb, and thereafter every man it could muster was needed as it tried to maintain a foothold in Ulster.

If the Campbells won no great victories in the spring of 1646, why were such triumphs reported in detail in London? The answer to this question lies not in events in Argyllshire, but in political developments in England. The English civil war was coming to an end. King Charles had been defeated. But there was increasing tension between the victors, between the English parliament and the Scottish covenanters, over who deserved most of the credit for victory and over what sort of peace settlement there should be. The covenanters' reputation in England had been seriously undermined by their long failure to defeat Montrose. Argyll's reputation as the most powerful man in Scotland through the military might of his clan had been shattered by the occupation of his lands and by defeat at Inverlochy. Disillusioned by what they saw as the ingratitude of the English parliament and worried by parliament's proposals for a peace settlement, the covenanters turned towards the defeated king. If they could reach agreement with him on a peace settlement which would protect Scotland's interests — and surely now that Charles had been defeated he would make all the necessary concessions — he and the covenanters could then combine to force such a settlement on the English parliament. But in thus conspiring secretly with the king the covenanters were taking a serious risk. When the English parliament discovered what had happened it might declare war on the covenanters; and it would be encouraged to do so by the military weakness the covenanters displayed by their inability to suppress the rebels in the supposed heartland of their military strength, Argyllshire. The covenanters desperately needed a great victory over the rebels; and some unknown propagandist provided it. On 5 May the king fled from his headquarters in Oxford and made his way to the Scottish army in England. The English parliament reacted with fury, and there was talk of military action against the Scots. The covenanters were anxious to persuade the English that such an attack would be dangerous, and that in any case it was unnecessary as the Scots were not allying themselves with the royalists. The report of victories in Argyll performed the first function by drawing attention to Scottish success in the field, while a declaration of the Scottish army in England sought to remove suspicions by forbidding officers and men to have any dealings with royalists who had fought against parliament, or to accept any gifts or favours from the king. It was thus no coincidence that the declaration and the story of victories in the Highlands were published together in the same pamphlet. The two disparate news items might seem to have nothing in common at first sight, but in fact they were meant to convey related propaganda messages.

Alasdair MacColla's reputed remark about stone and lime remaining loyal to the Campbells suggests that he was seriously worried by his failure to capture enemy strongholds. Without artillery, and with an unpaid and ill-disciplined army used to a war of movement and raids and unhappy at being tied down by long sieges, he had little chance of taking such castles. But he, like the Campbells, looked to Ireland for a solution to his problems. He was expecting reinforcements.

Ever since the earl of Antrim had dispatched Alasdair and his men to Scotland in June 1644, he had been working to persuade the Irish confederates to reinforce them. In this he was supported by both the king and by the lord lieutenant of Ireland, the marquis of Ormond. But at first the Irish were not willing to cooperate. From their point of view Alasdair's expedition to Scotland had not been entirely successful, for it had failed to force the complete withdrawal of the Scottish army in Ireland, though it was weakened by the withdrawal of men to Scotland to oppose Montrose and Alasdair. The Irish did not completely reject the idea of sending reinforcements to Alasdair, but they made it clear that they wanted major concessions from the king before they would thus help him.[40] After Philiphaugh Montrose himself appealed to Ireland for aid, concealing his true weakness by merely referring in passing to his affairs having received a minor setback caused by treachery rather than force. He needed more men, not to stave off defeat but to 'croune the game'.[41]

It might have been expected that news of Philiphaugh would have finally decided the Irish that their Scottish venture had failed and should be abandoned. But instead the supreme council of the confederates decided, in February 1646, to permit Antrim to raise 2,000 men from refugees driven from County Antrim. The confederates would then provide money to arm the men and transport them to Scotland. The reasons for this sudden change of heart by the Irish are not entirely clear, but it is likely that, now the king was facing complete defeat in both England and Scotland, the Irish feared that the united resources of those two kingdoms would be directed against them. Stirring up further trouble in Scotland would distract the covenanters' attention from Ireland. Moreover, late in 1645 intervention in Scotland gained a major ally in Ireland with the arrival of a papal nuncio, Giovanni Battista Rinuccini. The nuncio was already fascinated by Scotland. In 1644 he had published *Il Cappuccino Scozzese*, a work which soon proved a bestseller. It purported to detail the life of a Catholic missionary priest in Scotland, and though much of the narrative is wildly improbable it does indicate that he saw Scotland as a place of high drama and great danger in the fight against protestant heresy. Once he arrived in Ireland, he was in a position to help the Catholic cause in what he saw as a wild and romantic country to the north, and he was soon trying to divert some of Ireland's resources there. Rinuccini had specific instructions from the pope to maintain the Irish forces in Scotland; his existing interest in that country ensured that he carried out this order with zeal and tenacity in the years ahead.[42]

The Irish suggested that Antrim's brother, Alexander MacDonnell, should command the new expedition to Scotland, but Antrim in the end commanded in person. Success at last had come to his plans, after many months of argument and intrigue in Ireland, England, Flanders and France. Not all his followers favoured this frantic activity. 'We are worn spectre-thin by the Earl's oft frequenting of the wave,' grumbled one poet.[43] Others were more enthusiastic. A poem of 1645-6 invokes the protection of Jesus and Mary for Antrim, and gloats over the coming fate of the Campbells:

> His might shall overwhelm his foes, remnants of mockery shall they be, clan Campbell . . . shall suffer the extreme agony of disaster . . . Since thou hast been aiding to him at every season since the war began, protect to-day, O heavenly Lord, him and his company of warriors.

The poem can be dated to this period as it mentions Antrim's two frigates. In 1645 he managed to persuade the authorities in the Spanish Netherlands to provide him with arms and the two ships to carry men to Scotland. But, as was usual with Antrim's plans, all sorts of complications ensued. The French feared that Antrim was really trying to raise men in Ireland to fight for Spain against them, and French agents in Ireland therefore hampered him whenever possible. When one of the frigates put into Falmouth early in 1646 it was commandeered by local royalists.[44]

In spite of such setbacks Antrim landed in Kintyre in late May or early June 1646. How many men he managed to bring with him is unknown, but probably far fewer than the 2,000 hoped for. Some of those involved in getting men sent from Ireland had expected them to join Montrose, but not surprisingly Antrim chose to use them to reinforce Alasdair MacColla on the lands of the Clan Ian Mor. Wishart may be right in complaining that Antrim sought to persuade Highlanders to obey him rather than Montrose, whom he called in derision 'Governor of the Lowlands'. By his commission from the king Antrim was general of the Highlands and Islands, and this gave him a pretext for arguing that he was exempt from the jurisdiction granted to Montrose.[45]

Antrim's relationship to the royalist cause in general was becoming increasingly ambiguous. He was claiming to be the king's representative in the Highlands; but in Ireland he had supported the faction among the Irish confederates (led by Rinuccini) which was bitterly opposing a compromise peace treaty between the Irish and the king. In spite of this opposition the confederates resolved early in 1646 to accept this 'Ormond Peace'; and it was later said (admittedly by Antrim's enemies) that one of his reasons for accompanying his men to Kintyre was disillusionment with the peace.[46] Like Rinuccini he did want peace between the Irish and the king, but not the Ormond Peace, as it did not go far enough in protecting Catholicism. Perhaps (as was also alleged) he knew that Rinuccini was plotting to overthrow the Ormond Peace by force, and came to Scotland to avoid having to take part in an action so clearly contrary to the king's interests.

However, whatever politic motives influenced Antrim, they must have been outweighed by the joy of setting foot on the lands of the Clan Ian Mor. This was the high point of his and Alasdair's struggles to re-establish the clan on its ancestral territory. Alasdair had cleared out the Campbells, and now Antrim as chief of the Irish branch of the clan had joined him with reinforcements. The fort Argyll had built at Lochhead in 1639 to guard against invasion by the MacDonnells of Antrim now became Antrim's headquarters, armed with at least nine cannon.[47] A Highland poet greeted him with boasts of future glory which would come to the Clan Donald:

Welcome to Scotland to the Marquis and his army, as they march with martial strains to the lands of his ancestors, the royal people who were lordly.

Macdonalds of Isla were they, and kings of the Isles of heroes. May sovereignty over land and sea be to the royal company of the banners . . .

Great is the confidence of your friends, now that you have come to Scotland. You have been a great support to the King since the disorder began. Before the quarrel is ended, the rabble will be routed. Right will be uppermost, and slanderers will not have their way.

Every deceiver will get what he deserves, and every traitor will be laid low. We will not have a yoke to bear, and offenders will not have their will. The people of the wry mouths [the Campbells] will be trampled under our heels, and Clan Donald will be on top, as was usual for that people.[48]

The celebrations were short-lived. Within a matter of days of Antrim's landing news arrived which changed exaltation to despair. The king had given himself up to the Scottish army in England, and at the insistence of his new hosts — or captors — he sent orders on 19 May that all in arms in his name in Scotland were to disband their forces. Huntly obeyed immediately. Montrose followed suit after checking that the king really wished him to disband and making sure that his men were not punished; early in September he left for exile abroad. The immediate reactions of Antrim and Alasdair to orders to lay down arms and surrender all their hard-won gains are unknown, but can easily be imagined. And to natural reluctance to obey were soon added fears for their own safety if they did so, fears created by news from Cowal.

In the middle of May a large Campbell force under Ardkinglas landed in Cowal from Ayrshire. The Lamonts retired to their castles of Toward and Ascog. After about two weeks, on 1 June, the Campbells brought up artillery and began to bombard Toward. Two days later Sir James Lamont agreed on terms of surrender, though he may not have known of the king's order to lay down arms. Sir James, his family, and the soldiers of his garrison and their families, were to be allowed to retire under a safe conduct to Alasdair MacColla's quarters. Whether these were the terms Sir James had asked for is not clear, but it may be significant that the Campbells later argued that as Sir James was to go to another rebel-held area he was disobeying the king's orders to disband. This being the case, he could not claim to be fighting for the king, and therefore the Lamonts were not covered by the covenanters' assurance to the king that his supporters who disbanded would not be punished. Thus there is a suspicion that the Campbells tricked Sir James into surrendering by offering remarkably generous terms which were cunningly designed to demonstrate that he had not been fighting for the king. Certainly the terms of the surrender were not kept. At first the Lamont prisoners were well treated. Sir James was taken to Ascog and persuaded the garrison there to surrender on similar terms. But once Ascog had surrendered, the two castles were plundered and burnt, and the prisoners were taken to Dunoon. There in the kirkyard, perhaps after some mockery of a trial, the Campbells shot, stabbed or hacked to death over a hundred of their enemies. Thirty-six more, leaders of the Clan Lamont, were hanged — and by one account cut down before they were dead and buried alive — though Sir James was spared. The Lamont accounts of the terrible events in Dunoon may be exaggerated, but there is no doubt that a massacre of prisoners took place. The Campbells, themselves refugees driven from their lands with heavy losses, took a dreadful revenge on the Clan Lamont, for a special bitterness was felt against it. The Lamonts had been friends and allies of the Campbells until they had suddenly turned on them the previous September; and the Lamonts had provided the boats which had ferried the arch-rebel Alasdair MacColla and his men into Argyll.[49]

The horrifying news from Cowal must have strengthened any initial resolve Antrim and Alasdair had come to not to submit. They are recorded visiting Castle Tirrim and Duart Castle at about this time, which suggests that they may have visited other chiefs to try to persuade them to hold out as well.[50] In mid-June Lieutenant Colonel Robert Kerr (or Carr) arrived in Kintyre to order the rebels to disband in the king's name. He also brought a letter from Charles to Alasdair. The king had not known that Antrim had landed, but the covenanters had added a message to him stressing that the king wished all his supporters to disband. When Kerr reached Lochhead, Alasdair was away, in Islay, and this gave Antrim an excuse to delay replying; he had to wait until he could consult with him. But Antrim did agree that in the meantime he would commit no acts of hostility. This did not satisfy the covenanters, so Sir James Leslie was sent to Kintyre with new orders from the king to disband. Antrim's reply to Charles, written on 4 August, was sharp: 'I can not but admire how your Majestie should lay your commands upon a person whom you are pleased so much to slight.' The king had ordered him to disband but had not replied to his just desires (probably guarantees for his own and his men's safety, and promises of future reward for his services). 'When your Majestie is pleased to giue me the benefitt of the one, then you may to my power command me in the other', and if the Campbells tried to advance Antrim would resist. By 15 August Antrim had received an offer of terms for his submission, but rejected them as they contained insufficient guarantees for the safety of his men, who had advised him not to obey the king. On the same day Alasdair MacColla wrote to the king: since he had been ordered to withdraw from Scotland he presumed to say that he had hoped that his service to the king would have been better rewarded, and now asked the king to consider requiting him in some measure.

In the end, on a second message brought from Charles by Sir James Leslie, Antrim agreed to withdraw from Kintyre. The king had now given a secret verbal undertaking that Antrim would be given the lands in Kintyre that he claimed as soon as Argyll's estates could be forfeited. Considering that Charles was ordering the submission of his supporters in order to demonstrate to Argyll and the rest of the covenanters that he was sincere in his efforts to work in alliance with them, the promise was an odd one. Nonetheless, Antrim did now order his men to prepare to leave Kintyre. But at this (according to Leslie) they 'did mutiny highly to leave the Marquiss of Arguiles country, he being then possessed of a great deal of the said Marquiss of Antrims Estate in Ireland'. In the event, therefore, Antrim returned to Ireland late in 1646 with some of his men, but Alasdair and most of his followers remained in arms in Kintyre in defiance of both king and covenanters. The 'mutiny' may have been genuine, and may have had Alasdair's support, but it seems quite possible that it had been arranged by Antrim himself, being designed to demonstrate his obedience to the king while maintaining a MacDonald presence in Kintyre through the pretence that those who remained there did so against his orders.[51] Moreover events in Ireland may have encouraged Antrim to return there. In September Rinuccini and Owen Roe O'Neill, the general of the confederates' Ulster army, had staged a *coup d'état* and overthrown the Ormond Peace. The nuncio was then said to have sent a priest to Kintyre to urge Antrim to come back to Ireland to support the new regime among the confederates.[52]

Thus Alasdair retained for the moment the lands of the Clan Ian Mor, but he was now much more isolated than before. He was defying the king as well as the covenanters, and now that the former had joined the Scottish army in England, the Irish resolved to interfere no further in the war in Scotland.[53] Now that Alasdair could not claim to be fighting for the king it was much harder for him to find Highland allies; few believed the anti-Campbell cause could triumph on its own now that the king had disowned it and seemed to be moving towards alliance with the Campbells. Some clans had already left Alasdair, to look after their own affairs or to seek pardons from the covenanters. The Lamonts had left in February 1646. Two months later Murdoch MacLean of Lochbuie also had withdrawn, and the king's orders now persuaded some of the MacNeills, MacMillans and MacDougalls to leave him.[54] As autumn turned to winter the process continued, accelerated by the fact that the covenanters, anxious to restore peace in the Highlands, were now willing to offer pardons to nearly all rebels; only Montrose and Alasdair were declared to be exempted from any pardon. By the end of 1646 Seaforth and other leading MacKenzies, MacDonald of Sleat, MacDonald of Glengarry, MacLean of Duart and MacNab of that Ilk had all received pardons.[55]

The winter of 1646-7 must therefore have been a time of gloomy foreboding for Alasdair and his remaining supporters, as they awaited the next attempt to oust them from the territory remaining to them, centred on Kintyre and Islay. But for the moment it was the Campbells who continued to suffer. On 8 September 1646 the synod of Argyll was able to meet for the first time since July 1645, but only ten ministers were present and no elders. The reasons given for this graphically describe local conditions. Those absent were 'excused because of the troubles of the countrey and of their being scattered and chased fra their dwellings'. Members of the presbytery of Cowal (Dunoon) had 'gon for shelter to the Lowlands'. The presbytery of Kintyre was 'under the power of the rebels', and none were resident in the presbyteries of Argyll (Inveraray) and Lorne (Kilmore) 'but such as wer sheltered in garesons'.[56]

The synod wrote to the commission of the kirk in Edinburgh complaining that 'with the enemy there ar a number of freiris and seminarie priests, who are going about Kintyre and some of the Iles' seducing the people to popery. Many 'even of the better sort' were 'embraceing their superstition'. Famine was likely, 'there being no sowing in our countrey'. As for news of the rebels, they were said to be gathering in Islay 'quhair ther is a great feast prepared for them', after which they would move north to Ardnamurchan to meet Seaforth, Duart, Sleat and the captain of Clanranald. The news of this widespread support for Alasdair (which was of course in reality greatly exaggerated) was persuading many who had been ready to submit to remain in arms.[57]

In January 1647 petitions to the Scottish parliament revealed further details of the state of Argyllshire. Neither the marquis of Argyll nor Campbell of Calder had had any rents paid to them for three years. Such was the devastation that 'thair wilbe no labouring nor saweing for this ensueing yeir'. Parliament therefore ordered the payment of the huge sums of £15,000 sterling to Argyll and £30,000 sterling to the other heritors of the shire for the work of reconstruction, and a collection was ordered in churches throughout Scotland to provide for the refugees driven from their homes and now in danger of starving, and for the widows and orphans of Breadalbane. Argyll declared in March that two-thirds of the money raised by the collection should be given to the relatives of those killed and to the poor and aged, while the other third was used to buy seed corn for farmers. The collection evidently brought in large sums, for in 1649 the synod of Argyll was found guilty of misappropriation of funds for having spent 11,000 merks from it on the founding of schools.[58]

Of Alasdair's movements in late 1646 and early 1647 almost nothing is known. If the story that he captured Castle Sween is true, then he had one major success against stone and lime.[59] A report circulating in England in October reported that he was still doing much harm, making 'all the Herring Boats (that are there) Tributaries to him', presumably extorting money in return for protection.[60] In February 1647 it was said he had advanced to within thirty miles of Edinburgh, plundering and driving off many cattle. But Lieutenant General David Leslie had forced him to abandon most of his cattle, and Major General John Middleton had routed a party of 'Kilkettonians' and captured two or three of their garrisons, putting many to the sword. 'Kilketto' had about 4,000 well-armed men, but their morale was low and they had retreated to the mountains.[61] Here again victories over Alasdair are reported which in reality never occurred. The successes of the covenanters against rebels were real enough, but they had nothing to do with Alasdair. Presumably since Charles had ordered his Scottish supporters to submit it was assumed that all remaining rebels must be supporters of Alasdair, but in fact the rebels who were now being dispersed were remnants of Montrose's men and followers of the marquis of Huntly. The latter, after first obeying the king's orders to submit, had changed his mind and again risen against the covenanters; and he soon gained royal approval for his action, for in the end the king's attempts to reach agreement with the covenanters failed.

In January 1647 the covenanters withdrew their army from England, leaving the king behind to fall into the hands of the English parliament as he had refused to make some of the concessions they demanded. Released at last from military involvement in England, the covenanters could now concentrate their resources on crushing the remaining rebels in the north and west. A new army of veteran troops under professional officers was formed and sent north against Huntly. By the end of March most of Huntly's garrisons had fallen, all 'Irish' rebels, remnants of Alasdair's men, being executed without trial. At Wardhouse Castle fourteen Irish soldiers and one officer were executed. The commanders of the garrison at

Lesmore Castle surrendered on promise of their lives without any safeguards for their men, 'so I caused hang 27 Irish', as David Leslie grimly reported. One of the commanders who thus tried to win safety for himself was Alasdair's old colleague Captain John Mortimer; but though he was evidently a Scot, his association with the Irish was so close that he was judged to deserve death in spite of any promises given. He was sent to Edinburgh and executed.[62]

During this fighting in the north-east, Alasdair made some tentative approaches to the covenanters. Realising that his position was hopeless, he wished to save himself and his men. On 9 March the French agent in Edinburgh, Jean de Montereul, reported to Cardinal Mazarin that Alasdair had written to some members of the Scottish parliament saying that he was ready to leave Scotland provided that he was allowed to go to Spain and 'to take his people with him'; but Montereul (who had hoped the previous year to recruit Alasdair's men for the French service) did not think this would be allowed. On 27 March David Leslie wrote from Lesmore that Alexander MacDonald (presumably Alasdair) had written to him. Leslie had offered him a protection if he submitted, but now sought advice on how to deal with him. But nothing more is heard of these tentative approaches by Alasdair, for the covenanters were determined to make no concessions to him. On 4 March an act of parliament had confirmed that Alasdair was not to be pardoned or granted any terms.[63]

His overtures to the covenanters having been rejected, Alasdair now acted to hinder an advance by David Leslie's army by devastating the lands he would have to march through. Archibald MacDonald of Sanda and Duncan MacDougall led four or five hundred men through the parishes of Kilmartin, Kilmichael and Kilberry, burning all settlements and destroying 'all the people and guds' to deprive Leslie's men of food and shelter. Angus MacDonald of Largie with, it was said, about 1,000 men burnt the burgh of Inveraray. Alasdair MacColla himself was at Tarbert. He was reported to be in touch with Huntly (who had fled to the Western Highlands), Duart and Lochbuie. The MacDonalds of Sleat, Clanranald and Glencoe were coming together in the north, and both Cowal and Lorne feared new attacks by Alasdair.[64]

To military action Alasdair added verbal aggressiveness. In Edinburgh it was said that he had declared 'that he does not pretend to make war, either to support the authority of the King of Great Britain, or to overturn that of the Scottish parliament, but in order to recover his own and avenge himself on his enemies'. It was also said that Alasdair's father Coll Ciotach (in his first recorded action since his release from prison two years before) had tried to cause a rising in the Isles, but had failed because the people would not join him. Perhaps Alasdair had sent him north to try to persuade the MacLeans and MacDonalds to rejoin him.[65] However, one major island did accept Coll's authority. On 5 May 1647 Alasdair as major general of the king's forces in the Highlands (a title useful and impressive in some contexts, even if in others he asserted that he was not serving the king) commissioned his father to command in chief the lands of Islay and all other lands 'unto me belonging' in Scotland. With the assistance of Captain Daniel O'Neill (probably the lieutenant of that name recorded in James MacDonnell's regiment in 1644), he was to defend Dunyveg Castle until sent orders to the contrary by Alasdair or Antrim.[66]

This commission provides a badly needed key to Alasdair's position regarding the Clan Ian Mor's lands, and to his actions in the weeks that followed. Alasdair was now claiming Islay as 'his' land, but made no mention of Kintyre. This, combined with the fact that the king had given Antrim a verbal promise of Kintyre without mentioning Islay, strongly suggests that Antrim and Alasdair had agreed to divide the clan's Scottish lands between them. Indeed as the interests of the two men in these lands could obviously conflict, it may well be that such an understanding between them had been reached years before. Further, the commission probably indicates that Alasdair was intending to withdraw from Scotland to Ireland. Why else should he have suddenly decided to make his father (aged about seventy-six) commander-in-chief of 'his' lands? On this interpretation Alasdair had decided that it would be impossible to resist David Leslie's advance successfully (a decision also suggested by his approaches to the covenanters for negotiations). He therefore decided to withdraw temporarily, leaving his father to maintain a token MacDonald presence on Islay until he could return with reinforcements. Such an interpretation gains added plausibility from the fact that preparations to send such reinforcements were being made. Now that the king's attempt to form an alliance with the covenanters had failed, the Irish had reversed their former decision to send no further help to Scotland. The king had approved Huntly's renewal of resistance to the covenanters, and was doubtless prepared to give his blessing to Alasdair as well, whatever doubts there might be about his ultimate loyalties. By March 1647 it was well known in Scotland that the Irish were actively considering reinforcing Alasdair; a landing by 3,000 Irish was feared. Under the patronage of Rinuccini the confederates finally, in May and early June, agreed to raise 5,000 men jointly with Antrim and send them to Scotland.[67]

With the planning of such a new Irish invasion well under way, it made sense for Alasdair to withdraw temporarily to Ireland. It is even possible he was actually summoned there to take command of the new army; who was better qualified than he to lead it? But if Alasdair was encouraged to withdraw by news from Ireland, that same news encouraged the covenanters to attack him as soon as possible, before he was reinforced.

In mid-April David Leslie reached Dunblane with part of his army, having left Middleton in the north to pursue Huntly and his few remaining supporters. Argyll, learning from the disaster that had followed on his refusal in 1644 to allow Lieutenant General Baillie to command an army in Argyllshire (as honour demanded that that task be committed to a Campbell), agreed that David Leslie should lead the army against Alasdair, though he accompanied it both as the colonel of a regiment and as a member of a small committee attached to the army which Leslie was to consult.[68] Before Argyll left Edinburgh to join the army at Dunblane, Jean de Montereul tried to persuade him to let Alasdair and his men withdraw peacefully from Scotland; probably Montereul hoped then to recruit them for the French service. But at this request Argyll lost his temper, a rare event, saying that the only capitulation he would make with Alasdair would be 'as to whether they would make him shorter or longer than he was', whether he wished to be beheaded or hanged. Alasdair was to be offered the choice he himself had given to Sir Duncan Campbell of Auchinbreck after Inverlochy. Argyll also argued that if Alasdair left Scotland he would enter the Spanish, not the French, service, though this may have been simply an invention designed to deprive Alasdair of Montereul's sympathy.[69]

Considering the reputation of Alasdair as a soldier, the force Leslie marched against him was surprisingly small, perhaps only two or three thousand men. The composition of the force is uncertain, but it probably included Leslie's two 'Highland' regiments, led by Argyll and Ardkinglas. Though nominally containing 1,000 men each, they may well have been much weaker; Leslie complained that three of his Lowland regiments totalled only half their nominal strength. Robert Baillie called it 'a very small and ill-provided army', but Leslie may have been well informed as to Alasdair's weakness through the withdrawal of Antrim and the submission of many of his Highland allies. Estimates of the strength of the rebels in Kintyre range from 1,000 foot to 1,400 foot and two troops of horse.[70] Fear that Alasdair would soon be reinforced hastened Leslie westwards without waiting to gather more men; so too did bubonic plague which was spreading towards Dunblane and might destroy his army unless he moved.[71] Leslie left Dunblane on 17 May 'and made very long marches over the mountains, in stormy weather, without houses or tents . . . We had not so stormie a May these many years'.[72] He may have intended to surprise Alasdair by the speed of his advance; certainly he succeeded in doing so.

The outline of events after Leslie reached Kintyre is easy to establish, through his own dispatches and through the narrative provided by James Turner, who had just joined Leslie's army as adjutant general. But precisely why Leslie's victory was so easily won is harder to discover. Turner had strong views on this subject (as on most others), but these are not so reliable as is usually assumed, and unfortunately no evidence survives of events as seen from the point of view of Alasdair and his men except for a few traditional stories.

Leslie's own account is terse and factual. On 24 May he entered Kintyre. At sunset he charged 1,300 rebels and dispersed them. Sixty to eighty rebels were killed and three of their leaders captured, while Leslie's only casualties were nine men wounded.[73] To this Turner adds detail and explanation. Kintyre was easily defensible; 'there were such advantages of ground, that our foot, for mountains and marshes, could never have draune up one hundredth in a bodie, nor our horse above three in breast'. If Alasdair had positioned his men in such places 'I think he might have routed us, at least we sould not have entered Kintire bot by a miracle'. But Alasdair was 'ordained for destruction; for by a speadie march we made ourselves masters of these difficell passes, and got into a plaine countrey'. On this plain (the flat sandy land at Rhunahaorine Point) Leslie's cavalry advanced and Alasdair 'with little or no fighting' retired. But unfortunately Leslie had let his horsemen get far ahead of his footmen. Had they been present with their cannon to disorder the enemy 'I beleeve none of them had escaped from our horse'.

Turner's opinion of Alasdair was that in this campaign he behaved 'like a foole, (for no sojor he was, though stout enough)'. Turner provided a second account of these events in notes he wrote on Bishop Henry Guthry's *Memoirs*, which he furiously denounces for their unreliability. Guthry had related that Leslie reached Inveraray on 21 May and advanced into Kintyre on 24 May. Next day (a day later than Leslie indicates) he came into contact with the enemy and skirmished with them from morning to night. Here Turner corrects Guthry, asserting that he himself knew what had really happened 'as well as any man breathing' and wished to expose 'how the Bishop imposes lyes and contrived fables on his readers'. First, Alasdair had had 'good enough intelligence of Leslie's march into Kintire'. As Guthry had not claimed that Alasdair had been surprised, this attack on his veracity is simply irrelevant, but it is valuable in that it leads Turner on to further comments on Alasdair's conduct; 'if he had beene a soldier, and not excessivelie besotted with brandie and aquavitae, he sould have possessed the passes on this side of Kintire, where one hundred well armed and resolute foot might have done David Leslie mischiefe enough, and gone faire to have repelled his forces, especiallie his horse'. So Turner's two accounts agree that Alasdair MacColla was no soldier, and one adds that he was a fool, the other that he was a drunkard. What are we to make of these charges? The first is clearly ludicrous. Turner, a trained but conventional and pedestrian officer, assures us that one of the greatest of Highland warriors, whose deeds had made him known throughout Britain, was no soldier. What Turner presumably means is that Alasdair did not fit into the generally accepted Western European stereotype of a general, a man with experience in regular armies (preferably in the Thirty Years War) and learned in the military textbooks of the day. Alasdair the papist Irish barbarian belonged to a different world from Turner, who was unable to see how such an unconventional figure deserved the name of soldier.

As to Alasdair being a fool, it certainly looks at first sight as if he was one on this occasion. He knew Leslie was marching against him, yet allowed himself to be taken by surprise. There may well have been good reasons for this (as will be argued below), but they cannot excuse his miscalculation. The allegation that Alasdair was too befuddled by drink to organise the defence of Kintyre is harder to judge. Certainly tradition asserts that during the siege of Craignish Castle in 1646, at one point Alasdair had too much to drink, and that Alasdair was having a drink of ale when news was brought to him of Leslie's advance; but if Alasdair's drinking was really as notorious as Turner indicates, it is hard to understand why no other source mentions it. Lowlanders always tended to assume that much of the trouble with Highlanders stemmed from too much drinking, so it was the obvious charge to make when seeking to discredit Alasdair; and it is significant that the charge occurs only in Turner's rough notes on Guthry's *Memoirs*, and not in his formal memoir of his own life.

In writing about Alasdair and his men, Turner found himself faced with a major problem in justifying his own conduct. When Turner wrote he was a royalist; but previously he had served with the covenanters' armies in England and Ireland, and in 1647 he was, as we have seen, adjutant general in the covenanting army which was to drive Alasdair from Scotland and crush the remaining Highland rebels. He was thus acting against men who had some claim to be royalists. Turner wriggled out of this difficulty in a bold, if not entirely logical, way. In serving with the covenanters against Alasdair he was, he asserts self-righteously, acting on behalf of the king to punish Alasdair for his disloyalty to the royalist cause. In 1645 Alasdair had deserted Montrose, and was largely responsible for the disaster at Philiphaugh. In 1646 he had defied the king's orders to disband. Thus, claims this pious royalist, 'I thought it duetie to fight against these men', even though this meant acting as a senior officer in a covenanting army! There was therefore good reason for Turner to go out of his way to abuse Alasdair, to try to portray him as more of an enemy to the king than the covenanters were, and to make this argument acceptable to other royalists by portraying him in as unattractive a light as possible. As Turner's denunciations of Bishop Guthry suggest, he was in later years much given to vituperation of all with whom he disagreed — and, ironically, there is good evidence that he drank to excess.

On the encounter at Rhunahaorine Turner comments that Guthry's tale of skirmishing lasting all day 'is so false, that I beleeve that romance had its existence onlie in the Bishopes oune braine, and no where els'. Having gained the passes into Kintyre without meeting any opposition, crossing the narrow isthmus at Tarbert and down the western side of the peninsula where his route was constricted between sea and hills, Leslie 'very unadvisedlie' went several miles ahead of the foot with his horse. He met Alasdair hastening north to man the passes, and after a brief skirmish Alasdair retired, two of his men being captured. In his zeal to contradict Guthry, Turner thus denied that there was any 'battle' at Rhunahaorine worthy of the name, ignoring the sixty to eighty enemy dead reported by Leslie. Moreover Turner's criticism of Leslie's conduct is illogical. Clearly Leslie hastened ahead with his cavalry to secure the 'passes' before Alasdair could do so. If he met Alasdair at Rhunahaorine, then he only just prevented Alasdair reaching the point at which the hills nearly reach the sea, forcing an advancing army to move through these passes. That Leslie did not have his infantry with him when he met Alasdair doubtless (as he himself said) prevented him from winning a greater victory. But if he had held his cavalry back so the infantry could keep up there would probably have been no victory that day at all; the passes would have been held against him.[74]

If Turner's explanations of Alasdair's conduct (and of much more besides) are unconvincing, why was it that the latter was defeated so easily? Several reasons can be suggested, though there is danger in seeking too zealously for excuses for what may have been simple incompetence, a lapse in the constant vigilance that his position required. Alasdair may have been busy preparing to withdraw to Ireland, confident that he could do so before Leslie could reach Kintyre. But instead of advancing slowly, systematically securing the areas he advanced through and rounding up scattered bands of plunderers, Leslie made straight for the main concentration of rebels, his first priority being to defeat them. The parallel with Leslie's speedy approach and attack on Montrose at Philiphaugh is striking. Moreover the assumption that the obvious thing for Alasdair to do was concentrate all his forces on the narrow land crossing into Kintyre as an attack could only come there is invalid. Alasdair, eminent for his own raidings from the sea, must have feared Leslie would try to ship his men to some point on Kintyre's long coast. The sea was not a barrier cutting the peninsula off from the rest of the country; it was the main means of communication which rendered it accessible. Cowal had been attacked from the sea, and so might be Kintyre. Finally, traditions suggest last-minute difficulties which hampered Alasdair's attempts to secure the passes once it was known that the attack was by land and not sea. It is said that he ordered the MacAllisters of Loup to guard the passes but they refused to raise the siege of Skipness Castle to do so. A further tradition states that MacDougall scouts sent to discover if the enemy were approaching were captured and, after they had revealed the dispositions of Alasdair's forces, killed. This would help explain both why Alasdair was surprised and how it was that Leslie risked advancing into Kintyre so fast: he knew the passes were not held against him. An alternative traditional explanation of Alasdair's surprisal is that the rebels resorted to divination from the shoulder blade of an ox, but that the resulting intelligence of enemy movements was misinterpreted.

Alasdair is said to have spent the night before the battle of Rhunahaorine at Old Largie (or Rhunahaorine) Castle, the home of the MacDonalds of Largie. The tradition which depicts him drinking when news of Leslie's advance reached him places him at Tayinloan, but this may be the result of confusion between Old Largie Castle and the Largie Castle later built at Tayinloan.[75] The force hastened out to stop the enemy evidently included many of Alasdair's surviving Irish troops, as well as the MacDonalds of Largie. It is said the latter included fourteen (or fifteen) youths who had not yet shaved, and that all but one of them were killed.[76]

To the disgrace of being taken by surprise was added, according to some accounts, the shame of disorganised flight after the battle. Leslie could not press home his advantage immediately, for night was falling and he needed to wait for his infantry to catch up with him, but Alasdair decided on immediate flight to Islay and thence to Ireland. What orders were given to his supporters who remained (perhaps through lack of boats) in Kintyre is unknown. In the event many retreated to Dunaverty Castle. By one tradition a MacDonald laird remonstrated at Alasdair's desertion of them, at which he promised to return with reinforcements. The laird then said he could not stand siege at Dunaverty, to which Alasdair replied 'do as you like'. The haste, and even panic, of the flight is also suggested by the story that Alasdair fled in a boat he had found, and that when it was full he prevented it being swamped by those trying to get on board by hacking off the fingers of any who put their hands on the gunwale. After he had left, Archibald Og MacDonald of Sanda took over command (in fact his father Archibald Mor must be meant, for Archibald Og went to Ireland with Alasdair). He lit fires and left a piper playing near them so Leslie would think the rebels had camped for the night, and then continued the retreat to Dunaverty.[77]

These hostile Campbell traditions are, however, probably exaggerated. The picture of panic they paint is hard to reconcile with the large numbers of rebels who are known to have escaped. David Leslie himself was angry that his lack of ships enabled so many rebels to escape, and his secretary reported that 'In my opinion the better part of the Enemy that wes in kintyre at our coming heer, is quit out of' the peninsula.[78] Indeed the escape of so many within a single night raises the possibility that Alasdair's preparations to withdraw from Kintyre had been completed, and perhaps were even being put into effect, some of his men having already left. Perhaps Alasdair's encounter with Leslie at Rhunahaorine was simply a delaying operation, undertaken with only part of his forces and designed to cover the escape of most of the rest of his men.

On 25 May David Leslie heard that Alasdair and his father Coll had fled to Gigha. He at once dispatched Campbell of Inverawe with 300 men to pursue them, but delays in finding boats for the men enabled Alasdair to complete his escape to Islay. Many of the Kintyre country people came to Argyll and Leslie asking for pardon, but they were told that had their intentions been honest they would have tried to prevent the escape of Alasdair and the Irish from justice. Revenge and not pardon was the order of the day. Leslie advanced to Lochhead on 26 May, and found that the house of Lochhead and the fort had been abandoned by the rebels. By 31 May Leslie was lying before Dunaverty Castle.[79]

The massacre which took place a few days later has always been surrounded by controversy as to both the numbers killed and whether or not they had been promised quarter. Archibald Mor MacDonald of Sanda commanded three or four hundred men crowded into the small, ill-supplied castle. He refused David Leslie's summons to surrender on promise of quarter, whereupon Leslie immediately launched an attack. About forty rebels were killed and an outer ditch or defence was captured. The attackers lost only five or six men, but one of them was the major of Argyll's regiment, Mathew Campbell, captain of Skipness (though tradition claims that he was treacherously shot after negotiating with the rebels on Leslie's behalf). This preliminary attack sealed the castle's fate, for it cut the garrison off from its water supply. Sanda therefore agreed to surrender on the mercy of the kingdom: Leslie refused to let him surrender on his mercy. James Turner (who took part in the negotiations) claims that Leslie promised him that the prisoners would be spared, but that after a few days one of the regimental chaplains, John Nevoy, persuaded him to change his mind. From other sources it is clear that Argyll also had a part in inciting the massacre, and Thomas Henderson (Leslie's secretary) admitted that he had been involved, though he regretted it afterwards.

The massacre, as Turner stressed, was entirely justified by contemporary conventions of war. Once an offer of surrender on promise of quarter had been refused by a garrison it could expect no quarter. A surrender at mercy was an unconditional surrender coupled with a plea for mercy which might well be rejected. Whether MacDonald of Sanda and his men fully understood such conventions of 'civilised' warfare is another matter. Turner hypocritically argued that Alasdair's men did not deserve pity as 'that mad man and his cracke braind companie' had obstinately and rebelliously refused the king's orders to disband the previous year! According to the only truly contemporary account of the massacre by a covenanter who was present, Thomas Henderson, 300 prisoners were killed, but eighty of the men from the castle were spared and sent to serve in the French army. Turner says all the castle garrison, 300 men, were killed (forty of them in the attack before the surrender) except for 'one young man, Mackoull, whose life I begd, to be sent to France with a hundreth countrey fellows whom we had smoakd out of a cave, as they doe foxes', these presumably being identical with the eighty men Henderson says were part of the garrison.

'Mackoull' was, it seems, John MacDougall younger of Dunollie. A few other individuals escaped death with him. The infant grandson of MacDonald of Sanda is said to have been saved by his nurse, Flora MacCambridge, who fled with him to a cave in the Mull of Kintyre. MacDougall of Kilmun is said to have been rescued from the butchery by the marquis of Argyll after he had the presence of mind to shout in five languages 'Is there anyone here at all who will save a good scholar' — though by other accounts Argyll was not present when the killing took place. Angus MacEachran of Kilellan failed to save himself, but saved his family property rights by entrusting a small box of papers to James Turner before being killed. Turner gave the papers to Argyll, who in 1659 restored MacEachran's lands to his son.

Quite how the prisoners were killed is unknown. Turner says they were 'put to the sword', but this is no more than a conventional phrase. Probably they were shot, though a local tradition insists that they were thrown over a cliff. The killing is said to have been entrusted to relatives of the women and children Alasdair had had burnt in a barn at Lagganmore. Nearly a century later a visitor to Dunaverty saw 'the Sculls and Bones of these people lying above ground', and in 1822 some skeletons were exposed by an exceptionally high tide. Those who died were mainly men from Kintyre itself, like MacDonald of Sanda and Angus MacEachran, and from Lorne and central Argyll. The MacDougalls suffered particularly heavily; the only list to survive naming some of the dead includes forty-nine MacDougalls among ninety riames, the others named evidently being their tenants and followers.

Many royalist accounts exaggerated the size of the massacre, claiming that up to 500 had been killed, and claimed that promises of quarter had been given. Even without such embellishments the event was horrific enough, the Campbells taking a terrible revenge at Dunaverty as they had done at Dunoon in Cowal. To leave James Turner with the last word: 'yet I shall not deny bot heere was crueltie enough; for to kill men in cold blood, when they have submitted to mercie, hath no generosities at all in it.'[80]

After completing their bloody work at Dunaverty, the covenanters withdrew to Lochhead. There, at Whinny Hill, further killings took place. Hector MacAllister of Loup, evidently Alasdair's father-in-law, and two of his sons were executed, along with Alasdair's brother-in-law MacKay or Davidson of Ardnacroish and some of his men.[81]

David Leslie rested his forces for some time at Lochhead, complaining of lack of money, food and ships, but then moved back north to Loch Tarbert, where he would be better placed for crossing to Islay once ships arrived. He estimated that he had not even enough boats to carry half the footmen he wanted to take to Islay, and they could only carry 100 cavalry. To try to take Islay with so weak a force would be hazardous, 'committing all to God', especially as it was expected that forces would soon arrive from Ireland to reinforce the rebels.[82] Leslie sent ships to capture prisoners from Islay, to try to discover the strength of the enemy, but the island's shores were so well guarded that the ships had to return empty-handed. Reports that 2,000 Irish had landed (or were about to land) deterred Leslie from taking risks, but five or six days of waiting evidently decided him that the reports were false; there was no sign of the Irish. Few of the ships and boats Leslie was expecting had yet arrived, but on 19 June he managed to send an infantry force and 80 horsemen to Gigha. By 23 June he was on the island himself, intending to cross to Islay the next day, though he still complained of lack of cannon, ammunition and food.[83]

Leslie's impatience nearly led him to disaster. After writing to the committee of estates on 23 June, he decided the weather was good enough to risk sailing for Islay immediately, instead of waiting until the following day. But though most of his boats reached Jura by sunset, landing at the mouth of the sound of Islay, a storm prevented them crossing to Islay and some did not even get to Jura. Not until midday on 24 June did the covenanters finally land on Islay 'with great difficulties, not by opposition, but by reason of evil weather'. The landing was on the south coast, four miles from Dunyveg. That Leslie dared to land so close to the rebel stronghold suggests that he was by this time confident that there were few rebels left on the island. Some of his cavalry advanced to Dunyveg and surprised a party of rebels, killing four or five and taking some prisoners. From the latter it was learned that 'Alaster 16 days ago went to Ireland, carrying with him all the best of the gentilmen of this yle, with a number of the ablest of the cwntrie peopl, and the two commissioners sent to Coll fra Kintyre'. The commissioners were two gentlemen Argyll had sent to negotiate with the rebels. In Dunyveg, Leslie was told by the prisoners, Alasdair had left 100 Irish and as many local people, led by his father and his brother. In a fort on an island on Loch Gorm Alasdair had left 'the lyk number' under another of his brothers. Before leaving for Ireland Alasdair had sworn to his father 'as he was his son, or expected a blissing' to return shortly to relieve him; the rebels were now expecting 4,000 Irish to land soon, a prospect which naturally alarmed Leslie and his 'few foot, and handfull of horse', short of food, supplies and ships.

Nonetheless the covenanters advanced and demanded the surrender of Dunyveg. The garrison's answer convinced Leslie that 'there is nothing can be expected or had but by force of arms',[84] but he was soon proved wrong. If the brief siege of Dunaverty had ended in tragedy, that of Dunyveg was quickly reduced to farce by the conduct of Coll Ciotach. Without receiving any guarantee for his safety, Coll emerged from the castle and proposed some conditions for a surrender. These proved unacceptable to David Leslie, and his proposals were in turn rejected by Coll, who was allowed to return to the castle. On 29 June Coll announced that he wished to come out again, to talk with his old acquaintance the captain of Dunstaffnage, with whom he became friendly while imprisoned in

Dunstaffnage Castle. Again Coll failed to ask specifically for guarantees of his safety, and his request was followed by a letter asking for whisky! Leslie and his officers now discussed how to react to this extraordinary behaviour, and resolved to seize this notorious traitor if he again appeared. Coll obliged them on 1 July, coming out of the castle with a heavily armed escort. He was promptly made a prisoner. According to James Turner, this was done 'not without some staine' on David Leslie's honour; and certainly Coll must have believed himself to be protected in some way. Here again, it seems, Highlanders may have been acting according to different conventions of warfare from those accepted by the covenanters. But even if this is true, Coll's conduct was remarkable. Perhaps the most likely explanation is simply senility. At the age of about seventy-six he was no longer fit to act as commander of a garrison; and his request for whisky may suggest that it was he and not Alasdair who had a problem with drink. Did Coll perhaps hope, his mind wandering back to events of thirty years before, to negotiate a surrender which would save him at the expense of betraying his men, making his surrender of Dunyveg in 1647 a re-enactment of his surrender of the same castle in 1615?

After the capture of Coll there followed three days of what Leslie described as hard shooting. The castle garrison then asked for a parley. As a result of the negotiations that followed, articles of surrender were signed on 4 July by Argyll and Leslie on the one hand, Ranald MacColla MacDonald, Donald (Daniel) O'Neill and Donald Gorm MacDonnell on the other. The castle was to surrender on 5 July. Those in it were to leave without arms or baggage, but on swearing never to carry arms against Scotland again they were granted their lives. All the Irish and the three officers who signed the surrender were to go either to Ireland or to France. As many of the rest of the men as Leslie wished were to go along with his army, it evidently being intended they should now fight for the covenanters. These terms were very generous, but they were not kept in full. Though there was no massacre of the 176 fighting men who surrendered, two of the three garrison commanders (Ranald MacColla and Donald Gorm) are known to have been subsequently executed, though it may well be that Leslie had nothing to do with this, the two men being tried and executed in Argyll's court for crimes conveniently held not to be covered by the articles of surrender.

In writing to the committee of estates David Leslie clearly felt the need to justify his moderation at Dunyveg: 'what I did I was forced their to, which was contrar my desyre'. He had lacked food and all the materials necessary for a long siege. The castle had been well manned and would have been difficult to storm. Therefore he had been forced to grant generous terms, so 'that wherein I have done amisse cannot be impute to me it being none of my fault' but the fault of those who had not kept his army adequately supplied. James Turner later wrote that the garrison had been forced to surrender by lack of water, it having been another 'mad prank' of Alasdair's to leave a garrison in so stupid a place; but Leslie's account suggests Turner's memory was faulty.[85]

Islay was now entirely in Leslie's hands except for a 'little skurvie ile in the end of Yla . . . keepd by a bastard sonne of Coll Kittoch which we left to its fortune',

Campbell forces being left to besiege it.[86] The bastard son of Coll was almost certainly Angus. Writing from Edinburgh on 7 September, Montereul reported that the 'small castle in the middle of a lake' had not yet surrendered, though in an effort to force it to do so the covenanters had threatened to hang Coll Ciotach in sight of the castle. Angus is said to have replied 'that he would be glad to see his father receive what he had long ago deserved', and the threat was not carried out.[87] But at some time thereafter Angus was forced to surrender.

Meanwhile David Leslie and Argyll had turned their attention northwards. They first crossed to Jura, 'a horrid ile, and a habitation fit for deere and wild beasts' in Turner's opinion, and then crossed from isle to isle until Mull was reached. Sir Lachlan MacLean had submitted, in theory, in 1646, but Leslie now brought his army to demonstrate the covenanters' power and round up some stragglers from Alasdair's Irish forces. Duart hastened to surrender his castles, and, 'which was unchristian basenes in the lowest degree, he delivered up fourteene very prettie Irishmen, who had beene all along faithful to him'. Leslie had them all hanged. Old Sir Donald Campbell of Ardnamurchan, 'fleshd in blood from his very infancie', violently advocated a wholesale massacre of the MacLeans, only being reduced to silence by his chief, Argyll. Finally, before returning to the Lowlands, Leslie captured 'ane old castle in Knoggard or Moggart, I know not which', as Turner records with exasperating vagueness. This was evidently the captain of Clanranald's Castle Tirrim in Moidart; there is no sign that Mingary Castle was besieged at this time, which suggests that Alasdair had withdrawn his garrison from it.[88]

All the Western Highlands and Isles as far north as Mull were now under Campbell control, though the more remote isles to the north remained defiant under the influence of the captain of Clanranald. In 1648 a force of 600 men was sent against him, his associates, and some Irish in Skye, Uist, Barra, Rhum and Eigg, and in 1649 (peculiarly late in the day) his estates were declared forfeited.[89] Moreover the Western Highlands and Isles as a whole took years to recover from the systematic devastation and killing which had taken place. To make matters worse, bubonic plague followed Leslie's army into Kintyre.[90]

There was, however, one immediate pleasure to be enjoyed by the Campbells: the completion of their revenge on the kin of Alasdair MacColla. The families most closely related to him by marriage, the MacAllisters of Loup and the MacKays of Ardnacroish, had already suffered at Lochhead. But his father, brother and half-brother remained to be dealt with. At first it seemed that the luck which had so often aided Coll Ciotach's survival might still hold. On 27 July the committee of estates ordered David Leslie to send Coll to Edinburgh.[91] By 7 September he had arrived by ship, and it was said that the more moderate faction among the covenanters, which was growing in power at the expense of Argyll's faction, would spare his life. But Argyll acted hastily to prevent this, having him sent back to Argyllshire. There, in late September or early October, Coll was executed after being tried and sentenced by Argyll, acting as justice general of Argyll and the Isles, and George Campbell, his depute. He was hanged at Dunstaffnage, tradition says from the mast of his own galley. He is said to have been buried, at his own request, under one of the steps of Dunstaffnage Chapel, which stands near the castle. Donald Gorm MacDonnell from the Dunyveg garrison was executed the same day. He had served in the regiment of Colonel James MacDonnell which had come to Scotland in 1644, and was regarded as one of the leading warriors of these wars. One Alexander MacColl MacRanald MacAllister was also executed after surrendering at Dunyveg. Alasdair's brother Ranald was hanged at Inveraray, as was Ranald Og MacDonnell, who had commanded Alexander MacDonald's regiment at Inverlochy; he had been captured in Kintyre.[92] The fate of Alasdair's half-brother Angus is less certain, but he too was probably executed at this time.[93]

Alasdair MacColla had come to Scotland in 1644 to (among other things) restore the fortunes of the Clan Coll Ciotach, the MacDonalds of Colonsay. Now, just over three years later, his immediate family had been almost completely exterminated. But Alasdair may never have known of the full extent of the massacre of his kinsmen, for his career in Ireland was short.

NOTES

1. NLS, MS 1672, f.13; Mactavish, *Minutes of the synod of Argyll*, i.92-8.

2. J. Burns, 'Memoirs', 14, in J. Maidment, *Historical fragments* (Edinburgh 1833); *Three great victories*, [6]; *APS*, VI.ii.740.

3. Lamont, *Lamont papers*, 230-1; McKechnie, *Lamont clan*, 169-70, 172-4; SRO, GD.14/19, pp.114-15,127,129-30,133-4; *APS*, vii.338.

4. *APS*, VI.ii.461.

5. SRO, GD.112/40/2, in bundle of letters 1640-9.

6. *Joint print*, 171. I have assumed the 'Allister' who sent men to Islay to be Alasdair MacColla, but as the letter does not otherwise refer to him and does mention an Allister Stewart, this is not absolutely certain.

7. Mactavish, *Minutes of the synod of Argyll*, i.120.

8. SRO, GD.14/19, pp.113-15,130; McKechnie, *Lamont clan*, 171.

9. *Joint print*, 171,173-4,175.

10. Balfour, *Historical works*, iii.319,323,339,342,344; *APS*, VI.i.498-9.

11. Guthry, *Memoirs*, 213-14; Wishart, *Memoirs*, 165-6; *Joint print*, 174; Napier, *Memoirs*, ii.624,625; *APS*, VI.i.705.

12. Wishart, *Memoirs*, 148,180; Guthry, *Memoirs*, 204.

13. Napier, *Memorials*, ii.611,624.

14. Napier, *Memorials*, ii.260-2,264-6,268,270: SRO, PA.12/1, Col. Robert Home to Committee of Estates, c. March 1646.

15. H.W. Meikle (ed), *Correspondence of the Scots commissioners in London* (Roxburghe Club, 1917), 133; J.G. Fotheringham (ed), *The diplomatic correspondence of Jean de Montereul* (2 vols, SHS 1898-9), i.46-7.

16. HMC 10: *Eglinton*, 55-6; W. Fraser, *Memorials of the Montgomeries, earls of Eglinton* (2 vols, Edinburgh 1859), i.280-1.

17. SRO, GD.14/19, p.119.

18. *Joint print*, 174; J. Blair, *History of Bute* (Rothesay 1880), 213-14; Lamont, *Lamont papers*, 231; McKechnie, *Lamont clan*, 174-5.

19. *Joint print*, 174.

20. Campbell, *Adventures in legend*, 214-15; Matheson, 'Traditions', *TGSG*, v.25,75. For discussion of the 'piper's warning' legends see Black, 'Colla Ciotach', *TGSI*, xlviii.231-6.

21. A. Campbell, 'The manuscript history of Craignish', *Miscellany* iv (SHS 1926), 247; Matheson, 'Traditions', *TGSG*, v.47-51; Campbell, *Adventures in legend*, 220.

22. Ibid, 221-2; Matheson, 'Traditions', *TGSG*, v.31,33; *Argyll. An inventory of the ancient monuments*, vol ii, *Lorn* (Edinburgh 1975), 212. Family tradition gives the chief's name as Duncan, J.H. Macpherson, 'MacCorquodale of Phantilands and Tromlie. A pedigree orally transmitted', *Scottish Genealogist*, xi (1964), 14-15.

23. Campbell, *Records of Argyll*, 198-9; P.H. Gillies, *Netherlorn* (London 1909), 121-3.

24. Matheson, 'Traditions', *TGSG*, v.73.

25. Ibid, v.25-31,65-7; Campbell, *Adventures in legend*, 229-31; Campbell, *Records of Argyll*, 193-4,197,199; Gillies, *Netherlorn*, 123-5; Grieve, *Colonsay and Oronsay*, i.278.

26. Campbell, *Records of Argyll*, 198.

27. Campbell, *Adventures in legend*, 234; Matheson, 'Traditions', *TGSG*, v.55,57,71.

28. Ibid, 53-7,67-9,73; Campbell, *Adventures in legend*, 232-5; Campbell, *Records of Argyll*, 221-2.

29. P. Turner (ed), *Comhchruinneacha do dh'orain taghta Ghaidhealach* (Edinburgh 1813), 186-9. The translation quoted is by Colm O Boyle.

30. There is another poem in praise of Alasdair said to have been composed by a woman in D.A. Fergusson (ed), *From the farthest Hebrides* (London 1978), 98-9, but its authenticity is doubtful.

31. Macdonald, *Clan Donald*, iii.403-4; Hill, *Macdonnells of Antrim*, 114-15.

32. *A declaration published in the Scots army, proclaimed by order from Generall Leven at Durham, May 13, 1646 . . . with two victories against the enemy in Scotland. Two of Colkittoths brothers slaine* (London 1646), 13-14, cited in Black, 'Colla Ciotach', *TGSI*, xlviii.227-8. The report also appears in *Perfect Occurrences of both houses of parliament, and martiall affairs*, week ending 22 May 1646 (London 1646).

33. Mactavish, *Minutes of the synod of Argyll*, i.122.

34. *Rel Celt*, ii.203.

35. J. Rushworth (ed), *Historical collections* (8 vols, London 1659-1701), IV.i.399.

36. *APS*, VI.ii.412. The act refers to the house of Skipness, and this has been taken to mean a house MacNaughton owned in Skipness, A.I. Macnaghten, *The chiefs of Clan Macnachtan* (Windsor 1951), 38, but there is no evidence of any defensible building there except the castle. In 1642 Argyll had given the captain of Skipness a feu of the castle but had relieved him of the keepership of it, probably because Skipness was going to Ireland to serve as a captain in Argyll's regiment there, *Joint print*, 327-8.

37. It is sometimes asserted that Archibald was executed at Skipness in 1647, eg, Hill, *Macdonnells of Antrim*, 110-11n, Macdonald, *Clan Donald*, ii.402, but this seems to derive from a misreading and misdating of the pamphlet account of the 1646 siege of Skipness by Hill. Later seventeenth century sources which mention Archibald's death carefully distinguish between the deaths of Coll Ciotach and Archibald. The former was 'murdered', that is executed, while the latter was 'killed' in the king's service, Loder, *Colonsay*, 232,234.

38. Napier, *Memorials*, ii.276; *APS*, VI.ii.419,488-9.

39. *Joint print*, 176-7, and pedigree opposite p.386.

40. Carte, *Ormond*, ii.6,iii.380-1,384,386,389-90,395,399,403, 405; Bodleian Library, Oxford, Carte MSS, 14, f.259; Gilbert, *Ir confed*, iv.138-9; Hill, *Macdonnells of Antrim*, 269; D. Maclean, *The Counter-Reformation in Scotland* (London 1931), 122.

41. Gilbert, *Ir confed*, v.222,311-12; Napier, *Memorials*, ii.621.

42. Hill, *Macdonnells of Antrim*, 331,446-8; Gilbert, *Ir confed*, v.264,265,274,314,334,352; G. Aiazza (ed), *The embassy in Ireland of Monsignor G.B. Rinuccini* (Dublin 1873), liv, 149-50.

43. R. Flower (ed), 'An Irish-Gaelic poem on the Montrose wars', *Scottish Gaelic Studies*, i (1926), 115. Flower dates the poem to before January 1644 as it refers to Antrim as an earl and he became a marquis in that month. In fact Antrim's promotion dates from January 1645, so the poem may well refer to his efforts to send Alasdair to Scotland in 1644, and to early attempts to reinforce him.

44. Ibid, 113-14,117-18; Gilbert, *Contemp hist*, i.89-90 (this is confused as to dates); Gilbert, *Ir confed*, v.272,329,350.

45. Ibid, vi.50; Cary, *Memorials*, ii.40; Wishart, *Memoirs*, 184; *Com Rin*, ii.163-4.

46. Hill, *Macdonnells of Antrim*, 331.

47. NLS, MS 7194, f.2.

48. Macdonald, *The Macdonald collection*, 46-7, with translation from MacLean, Sources, 65-7.

49. McKechnie, *Lamont clan*, 187-93; Lamont, *Lamont papers*, 419-34; Cobbet, *State trials*, v.1379-87; SRO, GD.14/19, pp.91-2,102.

50. Mactavish, *Minutes of the synod of Argyll*, i.120-1.

51. HMC 21: *Hamilton*, i.112-13; Gilbert, *Ir confed*, v.1-2; Argyll transcripts, Inveraray, xii.149; *Rel Celt*, ii.203; Hill, *Macdonnells of Antrim*, 273. The precise date of Antrim's return to Ireland is not clear. *Com Rin*, ii.751 states that he reached Kilkenny from Scotland with his men on 17 January 1647; but Hill, 273n states that he had left Kintyre at the end of the previous September.

52. Ibid, 331.

53. Gilbert, *Ir confed*, v.353.

54. *APS*, VI.ii.545-6; SRO, GD.14/19, p.102.

55. SRO, PA.12/1, 17 June 1646; *APS*, VI.i.670-1; HMC 21: *Hamilton*, i.113.

56. Mactavish, *Minutes of the synod of Argyll*, i.99.

57. McKerral, *Kintyre*, 45-6; A.F. Mitchell and J. Christie (eds), *Records of the commission of the general assemblies of the church of Scotland* (3 vols; SHS 1892-1909), i. 66-8,70-2. Antrim had tried to persuade Abbot Patrick Crelly, who had cared for the injured Alasdair MacColla in 1642, to accompany him to Kintyre, Gilbert, *Ir confed*, v.334.

58. McKerral, *Kintyre*, 44-5; *APS*, VI.i.642-3,801-2; Mactavish, *Minutes of the synod of Argyll*, i.142; Mitchell and Christie, *Records*, i.173-4,219-22.

59. Eg, D. MacGibbon and T. Ross, *The castellated and domestic architecture of Scotland* (5 vols, Edinburgh 1887-92), iii.63.

60. *Perfect occurrences in both houses of parliament, and martiall affairs*, week ending 16 October 1646 (London 1646), under 12 October.

61. *Papers concerning the debates of the parliament of Scotland . . . and how Colkittoth is with his army within 30 miles of Edenburgh* (London 1647); *A declaration of the proceedings of the new moddel'd army in the kingdome of Scotland, against the Irish army under Generall Kilketto* (London 1647).

62. T. Birch (ed), *A collection of state papers of John Thurloe*, i (London 1742), i.89-90; W. Fraser, *The Melvilles, earls of Melville, and the Leslies, earls of Leslie* (3 vols, Edinburgh 1890), ii.96-8; SRO, PA.12/2, 16 April 1647, Leslie to the committee of estates; Gordon, *Britane's distemper*, 176,184,186,199; Rushworth, *Historical collections*, IV.i.455; J. Maidment (ed), *Analecta Scotica*, series i (Edinburgh 1834), 247.

63. Fotheringham, *Montereul correspondence*, i.193,199, ii.50; Birch, *State papers*, i.89-90; Fraser, *Melvilles*, ii.97; *APS*, VI.i.717,765.

64. SRO, GD.112/40/2, Glenorchy to his son John, 24 April 1647 in bundle of letters 1640-9; *APS*, VI.ii.462.

65. Fotheringham, *Montereul correspondence*, ii.120.

66. SRO, PA.7/23/2/49; O'Danachair, 'Montrose's Irish regiments', *Irish Sword*, iv.63.

67. Fotheringham, *Montereul correspondence*, ii.83; *CSPV, 1643-7*, 313; *APS*, VI.i.765; Aiazza, *Embassy*, 286; *CSPI, 1633-47*, 723.

68. Birch, *State papers*, i.90; SRO, PA.11/5, ff.17, 17v-18v.

69. Fotheringham, *Montereul correspondence*, ii.140.

70. McKerral, *Kintyre*, 49-50; SRO, PA.12/2, 16 April 1647, Leslie to the committee of estates; Baillie, *Letters*, iii.6; J. Turner, *Memoirs* (Bannatyne Club 1829), 45; Guthry, *Memoirs*, 243.

71. McKerral, *Kintyre*, 50-2.

72. Baillie, *Letters*, iii.6.

73. SRO, PA.7/23/2/50.

74. Turner, *Memoirs*, 45,238-9; Guthry, *Memoirs*, 243.

75. *Argyll. An inventory of the ancient monuments*, vol i, *Kintyre* (Edinburgh 1971), 160-1.

76. Campbell, *Records of Argyll*, 222; Campbell, *Adventures in legend*, 235-8; Matheson, 'Traditions', *TGSG*, v.75,77-81.

77. Ibid, 43-5,83; Campbell, *Adventures in legend*, 237-8; Cowan, *Montrose*, 254, citing SRO, GD.92/83.

78. D. Stevenson, 'The massacre at Dunaverty, 1647', *Scottish Studies*, xix (1975), 34.

79. SRO, PA.7/23/2/50; McKerral, *Kintyre*, 55-6.

80. Turner, *Memoirs*, 46-7,239-41; Guthry, *Memoirs*,243; Cobbet, *State trials*, v.1398,1410,1461-2; J.R.N. Macphail (ed), 'Documents relating to the massacre at Dunaverty', *Highland papers*, ii (SHS 1916), 248-60; Fotheringham, *Montereul correspondence*, ii.169; McKerral, *Kintyre*, 59-66; *APS*, vii.338-40; Campbell, *Adventures in legend*, 230,235-43; Campbell, *Records of Argyll*, 223-5; Gordon, *History of the family of Gordon*, ii.532; Stevenson, 'The massacre at Dunaverty', *Scottish Studies*, xix (1975), 27-37.

81. Campbell, *Records of Argyll*, 225-6; Cobbet, *State trials*, v.1391, 1410; SRO, GD.14/19, p.97; McKerral, *Kintyre*, 68-9; Fotheringham, *Montereul correspondence*, ii.151.

82. Birch, *State papers*, i.92.

83. SRO, PA.12/2, 23 June 1647, Leslie to the committee of estates.

84. Birch, *State papers*, i.91. This printed version of Leslie's letter gives 'cott' instead of Coll in the passage quoted above. This has been corrected from the original in SRO, PA.12/2.

85. SRO, PA.7/23/2/52,54; Turner, *Memoirs*, 47-8; Fotheringham, *Montereul correspondence*, ii.194; McKerral, *Kintyre*, 69-72; *Com Rin*, i.462.

86. Turner, *Memoirs*, 48.

87. Fotheringham, *Montereul correspondence*, ii.255. The mention in ibid, ii.194 of a bastard brother of Alasdair's in Dunyveg is doubtless a confused reference to Ranald.

88. Turner, *Memoirs*, 48-9; SRO, PA.7/23/2/54. See Hill, *Macdonnells of Antrim*, 111-13 for another account of the killing of the Irish in Mull. J. Drummond, *Memoirs of Sir Ewen Campbell of Locheill* (Abbotsford Club, 1842), 84.

89. *APS*, VI.ii.21-2,461.

90. McKerral, *Kintyre*, 77.

91. SRO, PA.11/5, ff.51-v.

92. Cobbet, *State trials*, v.1391-2,1396,1411,1461,1462-3; Fotheringham, *Montereul correspondence*, ii.255,261,281; W.D. Simpson, *Dunstaffnage Castle and the Stone of Destiny* (Edinburgh and London 1958), 41n; Campbell, *Adventures in legend*, 244; *Com Rin*, i.462; SRO, GD.14/19, pp.97-100,109; *Rel Celt*, ii.203-5; Turner, *Memoirs*, 48.

93. Black, 'Coll Ciotach', *TGSI*, xlviii.231,242 n.56. Black suggests that Angus escaped and settled in Antrim, but this is based on the identification of Angus as Coll's stepson Angus Mor, which is dubious.

10

Alasdair Has Departed From Us

WHEN David Leslie landed in Islay on 24 June 1647 he was told that Alasdair MacColla had left for Ireland some sixteen days before. This suggests that Alasdair has sailed on 8 June, but in fact he must have left some days earlier, for his landing in Ireland was known of in Dublin by 9 June. 'Kilketto' or 'Kolkitagh' had landed his men from fifteen (or, by another account, nineteen) vessels on the sands at Dundrum in the south of County Down. The strength of his force was put at seven or eight hundred men, and he had succeeded in marching them to the confederate Irish stronghold at Charlemont before the Ulster protestants could assemble to attack him. Only two of his men were captured, though he had to abandon his ships to the enemy.[1] Alasdair had evidently decided that to sail further south in search of an Irish-held port would be to risk capture by the English navy. Little is known of the precise composition of the force he had brought to temporary safety in Ireland, but it probably included the majority of the 'Irish' he had brought to Scotland in 1644 who had survived nearly three years of continuous campaigning, many MacDonalds (including Archibald Og of Sanda and Angus of Glengarry), and men of other clans which had joined him in arms.

That Alasdair had retreated from Islay to Ireland long before the advance of David Leslie rendered this necessary, and that he managed to bring so many men to Ireland in good·order, land them, and march them in good order to friendly territory, all again suggest that the story of Alasdair leaving Scotland in disorganised, panic flight is false — or at least greatly exaggerated. This looks much more like a planned withdrawal, though one greatly marred by miscalculations over how fast Leslie would advance, how long Dunyveg (and perhaps also Dunaverty) could hold out, and over how fit his father was to command a garrison.

On his arrival in Ireland Alasdair must immediately have discovered that there was no hope whatever of returning to Scotland almost at once with the 5,000 recruits promised by Antrim and the Irish, for the confederate Catholic movement was collapsing in a welter of intrigue and faction fighting. The main controversies continued to be over relations with royalists and obtaining a secure position for the Catholic church in any peace settlement. The 'Old English' among the confederates generally favoured a compromise settlement with the king. These were men who were Catholics but largely English in blood, descendants of pre-Reformation settlers in Ireland. As such they retained some feelings of loyalty towards the king. Opposed to them were the 'native Irish' faction, Gaels for whom any settlement with the crown would be a matter of political expediency rather than of loyalty. They were determined on full redress of their grievances against their English and protestant conquerors, and on guarantees for the free exercise and organisation of their religion. Not surprisingly the latter faction were led by Rinuccini, the papal nuncio, and had the support of most of the clergy. But however justifiable Rinuccini's attitude may have been from a purely religious point of view, he tended increasingly to ignore the political realities of the situation, the need for all enemies of the fanatically anti-Catholic English parliamentarians to unite to resist their attempt to reconquer Ireland and thus destroy both Irish and royalist causes. And now the English civil war was over, parliament could turn its attention to Ireland.

The Ormond Peace of 1646 had been an attempt at providing such unity between Irish and royalists, but Rinuccini had in September succeeded in overthrowing it. In the months that followed, Irish confederate politics were dominated by the efforts of Rinuccini to strengthen his position by purging from civil and military office all who had supported the Ormond Peace, the latter task being made more difficult by the fact that the confederates had four provincial armies with no strong central command. Owen Roe O'Neill's Ulster army was loyal to the nuncio. Through its great victory at Benburb in June 1646 it was superior in reputation to the other armies, and it had helped the nuncio seize power in Kilkenny. But O'Neill's men were hated in the other provinces for their plundering and brutality. The armies of these provinces were at best grudging in their support for Rinuccini. General Thomas Preston and his Leinster army had a particular hatred for O'Neill and the Ulster men, and therefore late in 1646 Rinuccini forced Preston (by threat of excommunication) to abandon a successful advance on Dublin, as he feared Preston might make a separate compromise peace with the marquis of Ormond and the royalists. In Munster Rinuccini's efforts to purge the provincial army collapsed in June 1647 when Lord Muskerry, a supporter of the Ormond Peace, fled from the supreme council at Kilkenny (fearing arrest or assassination) to the army and won control of it.

All this feuding between Irish factions inevitably led them to relax their pressure on their enemies. In Ulster protestant forces were allowed time to recover partially from disaster at Benburb. Even more important, Ormond was given time to negotiate the landing of English parliamentary troops in Dublin. He had decided that, as he could not hold the city for much longer against the Irish, he would hand it over to English protestants rather than Irish Catholics. Thus in June 1647 parliament gained a major bridgehead in Leinster without firing a shot. Parliament already had part of Munster (centred on Cork) at least nominally under its control. Murrough O'Brien, Lord Inchiquin, was a protestant who had originally defied the confederates in name of the king, but in 1644 he had switched his allegiance to the English parliament. In May 1647 he began a major offensive by capturing Dungarvan in County Waterford. By June he had turned north to ravage County Limerick. He then returned with most of his men to Cork to rest and reorganise, but part of his army based on Dungarvan raided parts of Tipperary and Limerick.

Thus when in mid-June Alasdair MacColla reached Irish quarters demanding

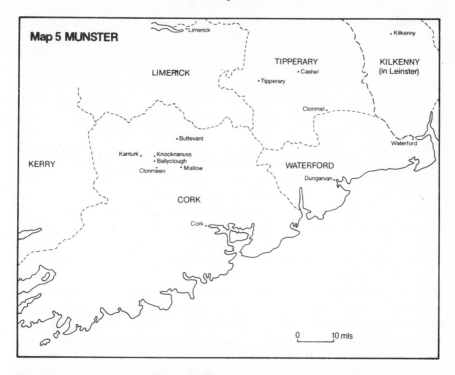

Map 5 MUNSTER

aid so that he could speedily return to Scotland, he found demoralisation, division and crisis. In Ulster victory at Benburb had been wasted. In Leinster parliamentary forces had just landed in Dublin. In Munster Inchiquin, the dread 'Murrough of the burnings', seemed to be carrying all before him. Alasdair turned naturally to Rinuccini's faction for aid; the nuncio favoured continuing the war in Scotland, and the marquis of Antrim supported his policies. In May Antrim had clarified his position by formally abduring heresy (though he had always been at heart a Catholic) and swearing the confederate oath. It is said that Alasdair asked that he and his men be attached to the Ulster army of O'Neill; most of his Irishmen were from Ulster, and service in Ulster would keep him as close as possible to the Highlands and Isles, ready to return there as soon as occasion offered. But Antrim was jealous of O'Neill; and Rinuccini, though reliant on O'Neill's support, hated him for discrediting the Catholic cause (through plundering by his men) and had no wish to increase his power. It was therefore decided that Alasdair should join the Munster army while Angus MacDonald of Glengarry was attached to Preston's Leinster army; the men who had come with them from Scotland were divided between them. It has been alleged that the men from Scotland were split up in this way as the result of some conspiracy by their enemies so that 'both should perish without the assistance of either', but it seems more probable that Rinuccini's party divided them so as to add forces faithful to him to both the armies which had shown hostility to his policies. Alasdair was appointed lieutenant general of the Munster army and governor of Clonmel, County

Tipperary, while Glengarry marched east under Preston to attack the parliamentary forces in Dublin.[2]

This Leinster army almost at once met disaster. At Dungan Hill on 8 August it was routed by English forces under Michael Jones. Many of the Irish fled soon after the confused battle began, but Glengarry's men, the redshanks 'whoe neuer yett experimented the arte of flight', stood firm and fought to the end: 'of 800 theire number, 100 was the most that excaped that furie', and most of these survivors were wounded. Rinuccini puts the strength of the 'Scots Irish' at Dungan Hill much lower, at 400 men, and adds that they were commanded by a Colonel Alexander MacDonnell who refused offers of quarter and was killed. Another account claims that 'The most of Preston's Foot [that] escaped were two or three hundred Irish, under the command of Major Huge Oge MacCormuck, who were in Mount Rose's service in Scotland.' Seeing that all was lost they charged and 'broke through those that charged them, with some loss' and thus escaped. Their commander was doubtless the 'Hugh MacCormocke' of O'Cahan's regiment sent to Scotland in 1644.[3]

Meanwhile Alasdair MacColla was busy with preparations for a campaign against Inchiquin under Lord Muskerry. But, as so often, political manoeuvres intervened to the detriment of military action. Lord Muskerry now decided that he would be able to oppose Rinuccini more effectively if he returned to Kilkenny and took his seat on the supreme council. To take over command of the Munster army in his absence he wanted someone whom he could rely on to continue to oppose Rinuccini and to demand a revival of the Ormond Peace. His choice fell on Lord Taaffe. Theobald, Lord Taaffe had been used by Ormond as both a military commander and an agent in negotiations with the confederates, but when Ormond left Ireland in July 1647 Taaffe had joined the confederates. Nonetheless, he remained at heart loyal to Ormond and the king. He was thus, from Muskerry's viewpoint, an ideal general for the Munster army; but his military experience was limited and his opposition to the nuncio must have strained relations between him and his lieutenant general, Alasdair MacColla.

In August Taaffe sent his army into County Cork; but he himself remained at Cashel, and Alasdair continued to serve as governor of Clonmel. As the latter's reputation was entirely that of a great fighting man, this deliberate failure to make use of his talents looks very much like a political decision, designed to exclude the nuncio's supporters from any glory that was to be won. If this was the case the plan misfired. Inchiquin feared the advancing Munster army so little that he slipped past it into County Tipperary. There he devastated the countryside and captured many castles, his campaign culminating in storming and sacking the rock of Cashel, killing about a thousand of those who had taken refuge there, and ransacking and desecrating the cathedral. From Cashel Inchiquin moved south, but when he heard that Alasdair and his men were holding Clonmel, he decided he could not afford the time for a siege. His supplies were running out and Owen Roe O'Neill was being sent south against him. He therefore withdrew to his garrisons in County Cork. Taaffe's Munster army meanwhile had hastened back to Tipperary to try to save the country from Inchiquin.[4]

Inchiquin's advance into Tipperary, following so soon after Michael Jones' victory at Dungan Hill, had led the Irish to fear that the two men had intended to link up, thus cutting confederate-held Ireland in two. This was why O'Neill was hastily summoned from Connaught (of which he had recently been given command) on Inchiquin's advance; but once it was seen that there was no great co-ordinated protestant offensive under way, O'Neill was sent to ravage the area around Dublin.[5]

Taaffe's first moves as a general had been disastrous, but though discredited he was not replaced, doubtless because of the delicate political situation; instead he was reinforced by three regiments from Connaught. The only commander on the Irish side to emerge with any credit from the campaign was Alasdair MacColla, whose reputation (combined with other circumstances) had deterred Inchiquin from attacking Clonmel. Later, with the benefit of hindsight, many were to come to believe that Taaffe began jealously to plot the deaths of Alasdair and the redshanks (now said to number 1,500, suggesting that since reaching Ireland Alasdair had been reinforced by Antrim), but this is unlikely. Taaffe was incompetent, not treacherous.[6]

Early in November Inchiquin concentrated his forces at Mallow for another advance eastwards. Taaffe decided to march against him and bring him to battle immediately, to put an end to stories (assiduously spread by the nuncio's supporters) that he had reached an understanding with Inchiquin. Moving westwards past Mallow, Taaffe forced Inchiquin to follow him to prevent the Irish ravaging his quarters. On 12 November Taaffe was at Kanturk, about twenty-seven miles north of Cork. Hearing that Inchiquin was moving in pursuit, Taaffe turned and marched back four miles eastwards and took up a strong position on the hill of Knocknanuss (Cnoc na nDos), otherwise known as Englishman's Hill. In preparing to fight there, Taaffe is said to have been encouraged by a prophecy that 'MacDonagh' would one day slaughter the English at that place; Taaffe owned some former MacDonagh lands, and held himself to represent that family.

Inchiquin came in sight of Taaffe on the afternoon of 12 November. By his own account he had 1,200 horse and nearly 4,000 foot, while Taaffe had 1,200 horse and 7,000 foot. Other accounts give rather different figures, but Inchiquin's seem as reliable as any, and there is no doubt about the main point, that he was greatly outnumbered. Not surprisingly he decided against an immediate attack on so strong an enemy, drawn up in a strong position, on a winter afternoon with the light already fading. He therefore camped for the night on a hill about a mile from the Irish position. Taaffe, fearing that the enemy would not fight, now dispatched an absurd letter to Inchiquin, stating that he was willing to forego his numerical advantage. He would send out one or two thousand men to fight a like number of Inchiquin's 'more for recreation that with a suspition that it might breake your Army', for he had heard Inchiquin's infantry were of good quality. A contemporary described Taaffe as 'a well-spoken man of both art and delivery, a fencer, a runner of a tilt, a brave, generous gamester, and an exceeding good potator in any liquor you please',[7] and the love of chivalric sports and the gambling instincts of this perfect gentleman are clearly seen in this ridiculous challenge.

Inchiquin's reply rejected the proposal with ominous sarcasm: 'you have performed as much as I desire in bringing your Army hither, I shall not desire you to loose any advantage you have in numbers of men, being your offer was only made for Recreation.' Even though outnumbered, he was eager to attack the enemy which had so conveniently marched up to him to be destroyed.

The following morning, however, Inchiquin decided to see if he could gain any advantage by playing on Taaffe's antiquated chivalry. He therefore wrote suggesting that both armies come down to the 'fair plain' to fight: 'we do stand upon no advantage of ground, and are willing to dispute our quarrel upon indifferent terms.' But though Inchiquin asserted that it would be he who made a sacrifice by moving off his hill, in reality the Irish would be making a greater one by giving up their stronger position. This even Taaffe could see, and he replied indignantly 'that he was not so little a soldier as to forego any advantage of ground he could gain'.

Nonetheless Taaffe was eager to fight, especially on ground where tradition prophesied victory; whether or not he believed the tradition, it was good for morale when spread among his men. Alasdair MacColla, it is said, did not want to fight that day 'upon a supersti[ti]ous observation; for that he was exceedingly afraid of Saturns malevolent influence, that day being to him criticall'. Alasdair may well, like many of his contemporaries, have believed in astrology, but the story (like that of his fate being sealed after he came to Gocam-go) is a little too neat, explaining the death of an otherwise invincible hero by showing that the stars were against him. But it would not be surprising if Alasdair and others hesitated to fight on the thirteenth of the month, and such irrational fears in him may have been grounded on estimates of the relative abilities of Taaffe and Inchiquin and of their men.

Taaffe drew up his army in two wings without a separate centre between them, perhaps because of the lie of the ground. He himself commanded about 4,000 foot on the left wing, while Alasdair commanded the right wing of about 3,000 foot, led by his Highlanders and Ulstermen. Two regiments of cavalry were attached to each wing. Inchiquin, in drawing up his army, placed (or so Rinuccini was later told) 'the best part' of his troops opposite Alasdair 'whom he greatly feared, and not without reason'. In both camps the word and the sign, essential if friend was to be distinguished from foe in armies without uniforms, were given. The word of Inchiquin's men was 'Victory', their sign a sprig of broom in their hats. Taaffe's men wore a straw rope around their hats and called for 'God and St Patrick'.

Neither side wanted to abandon its advantageous position, but eventually it was Inchiquin who took the initiative and forced an engagement by advancing and, by carefully calculated feints, forcing the Irish to move from positions which Inchiquin judged too strong to attack. He first moved his men as if concentrating his forces to attack and outflank the Irish right wing under Alasdair; and he positioned his two cannon to bombard that wing. All attention was now on the Irish right wing; it lacked cannon with which to reply to bombardment, and the men in it grew restive. Numerically it was the weaker of the two wings, and Taaffe seems to have begun hastily to try to transfer men from his left to Alasdair's right wing which was evidently about to be assaulted. But while all the noise and action on the right distracted the attention of the Irish, Inchiquin was quietly preparing forces for an attack on their left.

These preliminaries to the battle lasted about two hours, with sporadic cannon and musket fire, skirmishing as both sides sent out forlorns of horse to draw enemy fire, and deliberately confusing moves by Inchiquin's men. Then, suddenly, Inchiquin began to transfer men quickly from opposite the Irish right to their left. Taaffe, seeing at last that he had been misled as to the intentions of the enemy, ordered a general attack, hoping to catch Inchiquin off balance, before his transfer of forces was complete. But he was too late. The Irish left wing was by this time in some confusion, with many of its men demoralised by the long, tense wait watching the manoeuvres of the enemy. They advanced on Taaffe's orders, but their half-hearted attack was driven off by the musket fire of Inchiquin's men. Retreating Irish cavalry helped to disorganise the infantry by trying to retire through them, and soon the entire Irish left was streaming from the field in panic rout. The story that Taaffe, either through cowardice or treachery, purposely left Alasdair to his fate is false. He desperately tried to stop the rout, cutting down some of his own men with his sword when they refused to fight. Eventually he too fled, but when he did so he may well have believed that his whole army, right as well as left, had been overwhelmed. In fact, Alasdair MacColla and his men had just carried out their last 'Highland charge' with complete success.

Alasdair's charge on the right wing probably came at about the same time as the attempted advance of the Irish left, though communications between the two wings were poor, as the preliminary manoeuvres seem to have left them at least partially out of sight of each other. Alasdair's men advanced, fired one or two volleys of musket fire, and then threw down their muskets, drew their swords and charged. In the graphic words of one of Inchiquin's officers, they came 'routing downe like a Torrent impetuously on our foot'. A generally well-informed account written in the 1680s also described how 'MacDonell advanced with a select Band of targeteers, and Broad Swords' and charged Inchiquin's foot and 'being Seconded by his own Men, broke them clear, and put them to confusion, and was slaughtering them'. Inchiquin's cannon were overrun, and one of them turned on his own men. Most of his left wing, his best men, fled before the terrifying Highland charge with such alacrity that they suffered only light losses, perhaps only forty or fifty men, though Rinuccini, to bolster the reputation of his hero, absurdly asserted that 2,000 were killed. Several senior officers, 'divers of our galantest Commanders', refused to flee when their men did so and were killed, including Sir William Bridges and Colonel Gray. The triumphant redshanks soon reached Inchiquin's baggage train, and plundering this diverted them from a more prolonged pursuit.

Alasdair had carried all before him, but he was worried; he had no idea what had happened to Taaffe and his left wing. He therefore sent a messenger to seek news and, regathering his men from the joys of plunder, began to return with them towards the battlefield. His apprehension was fully justified. Not only had Taaffe and the left been routed but Inchiquin, advancing with his victorious men, had 'happened to look back that way and perceiving them [Alasdair's men] chasing our men' sent a strong cavalry force to the rescue. Alasdair, caught before his men had been fully restored to order after the earlier fighting, was overwhelmed by cavalry charges. Alasdair, Archibald Og MacDonald of Sanda (who held the rank of lieutenant colonel), nine of their captains and most of the rest of the redshanks were surrounded and slaughtered.

How precisely Alasdair died is uncertain. Inchiquin and two of his officers who wrote accounts of the battle all say simply that Alasdair was killed. But very soon accounts began to circulate attributing his death to treachery. Rinuccini related that Alasdair, 'who had separated himself a little from his troops to see after a messenger whom he had sent with an account of his proceedings to the other wing, met on his return fourteen of the enemy's horse, refusing quarter he killed four of them, and while parleying with their captain was treacherously stabbed from behind by a soldier and at once fell dead'. The Irish author of the 'Aphorismical discovery of treasonable faction' gave a rather different account. When Inchiquin's cavalry fell on the redshanks, 'then began the mortalitie on either side, the event doubtfull untill at length, the heroycke and valiant reddshanke, never yeldinge but rather gaininge grounde, were all for the most part slaughtered, theire warrlike chieftaine [Alasdair] behavinge himself like another Jonatha[n], that none durst aneere [come near] him, no such feates was seene by our progenitors acted by an ordinarie man (unlesse asisted by a higher Power) whoe could not be either killed, vanquished or taken prisoner.' Eventually Alasdair, seeing his men being slaughtered, 'yelded upon quarter of life and armes', a promise signed by Inchiquin. Alasdair, 'in restrainte' and riding behind an enemy horseman, was being taken from the field when 'one Foordone, a Captain of horse, cominge to him with a naked sworde, did t[h]rust him through, contrarie to all the lawes of both armes and nations'. The assertion that there was time in the heat of battle to send to Inchiquin to obtain a written promise of quarter is implausible, but otherwise there is nothing inherently improbable in this account, and another Irish author, Richard Bellings, also heard that Alasdair had been killed in cold blood by an officer after quarter had been promised to him.

Finally, the account written in the 1680s identifies Alasdair's killer as Major Purdon, the 'Foordone' of the 'Aphorismical discovery'. Alasdair had got quarter for himself and those about him from a cornet of horse (evidently named O'Grady). 'At which time comes up one Major Purdon, afterwards Baronetted, and demanded [of] the Coronet who it was he gave quarter to. On which he told him; on which Pourdon was in a fury, and shott MacDonell in the Head.' An odd story is added: that in revenge 'the Coronet for Seven Years fought Pourdon every year, but most commonly got the worse'.

Inchiquin's officers included a Major Nicholas Purdon (the surname was common in County Cork) who owned land at Ballyclough, near Knocknanuss. His name appears in records several times in the years that followed, and after the restoration of the monarchy in 1660 he appears as a lieutenant colonel, a commissioner for poll tax, a knight and a member of the Irish parliament. He died in 1676.[8] This, it seems, was the man who could boast of having killed the great

Alasdair MacColla — though only after Alasdair was already a prisoner. But the manner of Alasdair's death was not, perhaps, entirely inappropriate; in the past he had shown himself capable of treachery and ruthlessness, and had (less than three years before) killed Auchinbreck in similar circumstances.

But why did Purdon summarily kill so eminent a prisoner? Explanations are easy to suggest, but it is impossible to choose between them. Perhaps, indeed, as indiscriminate and cold-blooded killings were so common in the Irish wars of the 1640s, no special explanation is required to account for Alasdair's fate. Inchiquin's army had an especially bad reputation for mercilessness. Alasdair's reputation among Catholics was that of a great hero, but to protestants he was the archetypal bloodthirsty Gael and treacherous papist, a mass murderer of protestants in both Scotland and Ireland. And it could be argued that it was absurd to let so great a traitor escape punishment simply because he had found a junior officer willing to offer him quarter (this argument had been used by the covenanters after Philiphaugh to justify execution of prisoners who had been promised quarter). It is possible that Major Purdon, as his lands lay so close to Knocknanuss, had suffered loss at the hands of Alasdair's men during the Irish advance, and thus partly acted from personal motives.

A final explanation is provided by a tradition current in Lewis in the early nineteenth century, though the start of the tale does not inspire confidence. One day, the story runs, Alasdair was combing his hair, alone and unarmed, when a private soldier captured him. The soldier was taking his great prisoner to his commander when they met an officer who begged the soldier to give up the prisoner to him, so that he might have the credit for capturing so mighty a warrior. But Alasdair himself intervened, saying he would not let the honour justly due to the private for his bravery pass to another man. Infuriated, the officer drew his sword and stabbed Alasdair, killing him.[9] The background to the incident is obviously fictitious, but the suggestion that he was killed in a dispute over who should have credit for capturing him is not implausible. But the tale is too neat; it reads like, and probably is, a storyteller's answer to a question from a listener, 'But tell me, why was Alasdair killed after surrendering?' Indeed, all the accounts of Alasdair being killed while a prisoner raise doubts, as they seem designed to provide (like the legend of Gocam-go and astrological predictions of Saturn's malignant influence) explanations of his death which did not impair his reputation as the greatest of fighting men. So great a hero cannot have been killed in fair fight; therefore he must have died through treachery. Yet the accounts of Major Purdon's action are so circumstantial and widespread (though they differ in detail) that it is impossible to dismiss them completely. It seems Alasdair really did die in a way that seemed to confirm his invincibility in combat.

With Alasdair died most of the redshanks. So too did many of the Irish, who found no safety by flight. As Inchiquin laconically records, 'the execution ended not that day, for though we were killing till night as fast as we could, we found two or three hundred the next day in the woods, as we were viewing the bodies.' These too were killed, no quarter being offered them. Some claimed the Irish had lost 5,000 dead at Knocknanuss, but Inchiquin much more modestly claimed that only

3,000 had died. The Irish baggage and ammunition trains were captured, along with forty of their colours. Arms for up to 6,000 men were recovered on the battlefield and along the line of flight of the Irish. The remnants of Taaffe's army offered no resistance to Inchiquin's advance after the battle, and soon all Munster but a few garrisons was in his hands.[10]

To many commentators, however, it was the death of Alasdair MacColla above all else which rendered Knocknanuss memorable. For the Irish authors of the *Commentarius Rinuccinianus* he had been a second Judas Maccabaeus; like the great Jewish leader of the second century B.C. he had fought to reconquer his country and died in battle. The victories won in Scotland had owed much more to him than to Montrose, and all Ireland mourned his death except the spitefully jealous. Rinuccini himself related bitterly that 'This battle is rendered memorable by the ignominious flight of the Catholics and the loss of Macdonnell, who had fought thirty battles in Scotland, victorious always, in defence of religion and the King, and he would have been so now had not the Munster troops basely abandoned their brethren.'[11] The author of the *Warr of Ireland* in the 1680s lamented Alasdair's death, he 'being as stout and strong a Man as ever carried a Broad Sword and Targett of late days, and so vigorous in Fight, that had his conduct been equivalent to his Valour, he had been one of the best Generalls in Europe'.[12]

Patrick Gordon of Ruthven concluded that Alasdair had been 'one of the most braue and resolut gentlemen in all the highlands of Scotland'.[13] Father James MacBreck naturally stressed his religious as well as his martial qualities. He had been a man 'most respectful and reverential to priests', protecting them and their office, anxious to hear mass even in times of crisis, insisting on Latin benedictions by a priest at meals. He had been 'remarkable for zeal in the faith and strength and courage of mind and body, and it was thought that no man like him had lived for centuries'. His very name was a terror to his heretical enemies.[14]

Two anonymous verse epitaphs (one in English and one in Latin) for Alasdair survive, poor stuff as literature but emphasising his stature in the eyes of contemporaries. Both compare him to Judas Maccabaeus — and the Latin epitaph neatly contrasts him with the other Judas who had betrayed him: Taaffe was Judas Iscariot. In translation the Latin epitaph reads as follows:

> Epitaph of Alexander MacColla MacDonnell, General, who like a second Maccabaeus died gloriously, fighting for his faith and his country.

> > The hero conquered at Knocknanuss, and as victor he died,
> > Sold by his own allies, bought by the enemy.
> > The disastrous action of a Judas, no son of Mars,
> > Who in betraying his country sold his own general for money.
> > It was a perversion of fate that Taaffe should acquire fame
> > By turning a day of good fortune into one of disaster.[15]

The longer English epitaph is distinctly more flowery in language:

An Epitaph on Sir Alexander MacDonnell,
Lieutenant Generall of the Forces of Munster.

> Stout Machabee from whom the double ty
> Of zeale and of unbounded Loyalty,
> Too early for us, on too blacke a Day
> Inforced the tribut, which wee all must pay.
> Whyle thy sterne countenance and strong arme press'd
> The fates, but for a single interest.
> Like lightening captiv'd fortune shott her smyles
> To wayte on thee, through Scotland and her Iles.
> But when God added his, his cause and call
> Brought further merit to Mac-Donnells fall.
> And heere hee ends thus these two Kingdomes mourne
> That share the honor of his birth and borne.
> Great Prodigie of Valour sent to engage
> Men to beleeve that in some former age
> There have been Hero's to these threadde of thee
> Not clothed as yett in immortalitee.
> I heere do sacrifice these humble teares
> The embleme of the blacke my sad heart weares.[16]

No doubt more to Alasdair's taste than these epitaphs produced in Ireland would have been *Cumha Alasdair Mhic Cholla*, the Gaelic lament for him by Ian Lom:

> The spirited princely youth would rouse thousands, when he raised the pipe and the satin banner.
> There would rise with him unwearied men and young gallants from the small clumps of thicket where lies the mist.
> Your desire was to possess a backsword basket hilted, with its cleaving sharp blue edge of steel.
> You were not faint hearted or feeble as you rode up at the head of the brigade, on a high mettlesome steed well shod.
> You were not a coward in battle as you advanced to meet a squadron, to march to face them breast to breast was your wont.

Alasdair's death meant that the execution of Coll Ciotach would go unavenged:

> Often do I think before the break of day that you have not avenged your father; that is what has increased the unhealthy hue in my look.
> A grey-haired man who was in the rock, with iron shackles on his limbs, God will see that he was surety of a host . . .
> But my trust is in Christ that there will be a day for avenging all that before Thy great miracles cease.

I got news from Duncannon that has dimmed my eyesight, my utter woe
that Alasdair was dead ...
Sad to me is the dispersing of the men of Islay and the noblemen of Kintyre;
and no easier for me to bear was the loss of Ranald Og.[17]

Eachann Bacach MacLean joined his MacDonald colleague in lamenting:
'Alasdair also has departed from us — he fell at the hands of a baron in Ireland.'
The man who would have agreed neither to come to terms with 'the men of
Edinburgh' nor to submit to Argyll was dead.[18]

Alasdair did not go unremembered among the Gaels of Munster either. In the
mid-eighteenth century a local historian recorded that 'There is a very odd kind of
Irish musick, well known in Munster by the name of Mac-Allisdrum's march,
being a wild rhapsody made in honour of this commander, to this day much
esteemed by the Irish, and played at all their feasts.'[19] In the early nineteenth
century another writer drew attention to 'That wild and monstrous piece of music
known by the name of Ollistrum's March, so popular in the south of Ireland'. 'The
estimation in which it is held in Ireland is wonderful. I have heard this march, as it
is called, sung by hundreds of the Irish peasantry, who imitate the drone of the
bagpipe in their manner of singing it', and included with it were lamentations for
Alasdair by the women of Munster and Leinster. It has been claimed that this
work, with its 'impetuous energy and wild shrilly fervour', was 'undoubtedly the
same pibroch that they [Alasdair's men] marched to on the morning of their last
battle', but this, like the suggestion that the tune was played at Alasdair's funeral,
is no more than supposition.[20]

Alasdair MacColla was buried at Clonmeen, near Knocknanuss. The funeral
was arranged by Donough O'Callaghan, chief of his name and a member of the
confederate supreme council. O'Callaghan was a supporter of Rinuccini, whom he
had entertained shortly after his landing in Ireland in 1645, and his family burial
vault was at Clonmeen Church. He now agreed that Alasdair should be buried
among the O'Callaghans.[21] As the area was in Inchiquin's hands, O'Callaghan can
hardly have attended the funeral personally, and the Catholic rites Alasdair would
have wished for may well have been curtailed or omitted altogether. One imagines
a hasty, almost furtive, funeral, an attempt to give Alasdair an honourable burial
without attracting the attention of enemies.[22]

By the end of 1647 the Clan Coll Ciotach had been almost exterminated; and in
1650 an otherwise completely unknown son of Coll may have been killed by the
English, one Colonel 'Neal MacColkittagh' or 'Nice MacColleketagh'.[23] But there
were a few survivors of the family. Alasdair had evidently brought his two young
sons, Coll and Archibald, to Ireland with him in 1647, and they eventually settled
on the marquis of Antrim's estates in County Antrim. Coll, it is said, held lands
including Glasineerin Island on Lough Lynch, the birthplace of his grandfather
Coll Ciotach. Coll died in 1719 aged seventy-four, his brother Archibald in 1720
aged seventy-three, both leaving descendants.[24] In Scotland the family survived
for a time through Sarah, the daughter of Alasdair's eldest brother Archibald
(Gillespie). In 1661 Sarah, as Archibald's only surviving child and Coll Ciotach's

heir, was ordered to be restored to the family lands. She did evidently regain some lands in Colonsay and Oronsay, holding them from the earl of Argyll after he was restored to his lands in 1663. In 1686, the year after the earl's execution, James VII granted a feu charter to Sarah and her husband Aeneas MacDonald for Oronsay and Garvard on Colonsay. But after the revolution of 1689 and the restoration of the Campbells to favour nothing more is heard of the MacDonalds of Colonsay.[25]

With the death of Alasdair MacColla the already faint hopes of restoring the Clan Ian Mor disappeared. Even after he had been driven back to Ireland, Ian Lom had been able to dream of his return:

> When Alasdair crosses over to us with conflict in his train, nine thousand stout warriors will be ferried across the sea; may as many again be with him who would not betray him in his trust in them, of the men with the fair locks and red shield-bosses . . .

> Clan Donald famed for galleys and tall swift ships, though you stand as you do at this present crisis, the blood spilt must be paid for, it was not the sea that took it from us. God the Creator is strong; there is a tryst with victory.[26]

Once the death of Alasdair was added to his and Montrose's defeat and exile, however, all real hope of renewing the war in Scotland vanished. Antrim and Rinuccini, nevertheless, continued to work for such a renewal, but with the Irish cause crumbling around them their plans came to nothing. Early in 1648 Rinuccini was trying to arrange a new alliance between Montrose and Antrim, and urging that the best way to help Ireland was by causing a diversion in Scotland. Antrim's continued interest in a Scottish war is understandable, but Rinuccini's seems illogical. It was now clear that the greatest threat to the Irish confederates was that posed by the English parliament, not that of the weak and demoralised Scottish army in Ulster which might be forced to withdraw by Irish intervention in Scotland.[27]

In 1648 there arrived in Ireland men who might have formed the nucleus of a new expeditionary force to be sent to Scotland. After David Leslie's campaign in Kintyre and the Isles in 1647, the captain of Clanranald was the only major Isles chief who failed to submit to the covenanters, and refugees from other clans, 'the few that lived of the party on the King's side, were gathering round him'. The following year he sent his son Donald, Alasdair MacColla's old comrade, to Ireland with 'all those who remained with him of the men of Ireland, and some of his Scottish gentlemen along with them'. The captain had evidently decided that he could not renew the war in Scotland on his own, and therefore sent his men to fight for the Irish Catholic cause, perhaps on the suggestion of the marquis of Antrim. Whether he knew that once in Ireland the men would be used by Rinuccini's faction against the king's interests is uncertain.

Donald MacDonald sailed from Uist in 'a rigged low-country frigate which he had, and a long Gaelic ship' with about 300 warriors. In Ireland he and his men were assigned to Preston's Leinster army, joining 'those who lived of the Scots and

Irish of the MacDonnells and their friends who went over with Alaster son of Colla, to Ireland'. The new recruits and those redshanks who had survived Dungan Hill and Knocknanuss were concentrated in a single regiment, said to be 1,500 strong and commanded by Antrim's brother Alexander MacDonnell. Donald became lieutenant colonel, with Angus, a son of Alexander MacDonald of Largie, as the regiment's senior captain.[28] But by this time the dispute between the rival factions among the Irish had become so bitter that they were preparing for war with each other. The faction that held that peace with, and indeed alliance with, the king was the only course which would make resistance to the English parliament possible, managed to regain control of the supreme council. But Rinuccini, backed by Owen Roe O'Neill and Antrim, held that such an alliance betrayed the interests of the Catholic church. Antrim therefore withdrew his redshanks from the Leinster army to Wexford; but the supreme council sent Leinster forces after them to prevent a hostile army assembling. The redshanks were attacked (in October 1648) while trying to gain safety in a wood and were routed; most of their leading officers were captured and about sixty men killed. Antrim rallied the remainder of his men, four or five hundred, at Athy (County Kildare), but they too were attacked and dispersed and Antrim had to flee to Owen Roe O'Neill's army. Among the prisoners taken to Kilkenny by the triumphant forces of the supreme council were Donald MacDonald and Angus MacDonald of Glengarry. Antrim soon secured Glengarry's release and he (perhaps as a condition of his release) went to the continent to serve the exiled Charles II, whose father had been executed by the English a few months before. Donald MacDonald remained a prisoner until Antrim's wife, the duchess of Buckingham, raised a ranson for him. He then returned to his native Isles with many of his leading followers. The brief and unhappy career of the last of the redshanks, the last force of West Highland warriors to serve in Ireland, was over.[29]

Antrim still continued to try to launch a new Scottish venture, in alliance with Montrose and with papal help, but without success;[30] and when Montrose tried an invasion of Scotland on his own in 1650, without Irish or Highland support, he was promptly defeated and executed.

Alasdair MacColla was dead, and so were the causes he fought for. The Clan Ian Mor had finally disappeared from Scotland, and the collapse of the Irish confederate movement was swiftly followed by the brutal Cromwellian conquest. In both Scotland and Ireland the Catholic and Gaelic causes were lost. Thus Alasdair's career was ultimately one of failure. But how is one to assess his achievements in his moments of triumph, and the reputation his qualities won for him? On the one hand we have his great fame among his own people, the Gaels. On the other we have the very limited stature accorded to him by most English and Lowland Scots writers. At the centre of the problem of assessing the stature of the man lies his connection with Montrose. Most writers, contemporary and later, and all the most influential ones, who have considered Alasdair have done so in the context of Montrose's career. He has hardly ever been studied separately; and indeed the most widely understood way of identifying Alasdair is to refer to him as 'Montrose's major general'. For most biographers of Montrose their hero must have no rivals, and therefore Alasdair can be accorded only a limited role in his victories. His skill and valour as a fighter can only be safely acknowledged if it is hastily added that he was stupid, and useless except when Montrose was at his elbow to point the shambling giant at the enemy and tell him to charge.

Once this caricature has been imposed on Alasdair he becomes of great value to Montrose's supporters; not only is he no longer a threat to Montrose's unrivalled glory, he can be made a scapegoat for some of Montrose's weaknesses and failings. Alasdair thus becomes responsible for the disaster at Philiphaugh. He nearly ruins Montrose's supposedly brilliant trap at Auldearn. He is responsible for repeatedly hampering Montrose by withdrawing men from his army for expeditions to the west. Alasdair's own achievements both before and after his year with Montrose also tend to be denigrated, to ensure that he fits the caricature. We are told that 'there can be no reasonable doubt that Montrose could have done something for the royal cause without the Irish, whereas without Montrose Alistair was powerless to raise a man'.[31] This is a breathtaking piece of misrepresentation. By the time he had met Alasdair in 1644, Montrose had demonstrated clearly that hardly a man in Scotland would rise for him alone in the king's name. Alasdair, on the other hand had, through Antrim, at least managed to bring over 1,500 fighting men to Scotland and to recruit some (though admittedly disappointingly few) Highlanders. But such awkward facts can be played down by minimising the importance of the Irish contribution to the campaign, referring contemptuously to the men Alasdair brought to Scotland as 'a little band of Irish Macdonalds'.[32]

Similarly it is commonly asserted (rather than logically argued) that Alasdair was hopelessly incompetent in any independent command. The judgement that, although he did some service under Montrose as 'ane able and stout souldier' he 'was noe great head-piece',[33] is typical of many. In one sense the charge is hard to refute, since Alasdair had little chance to exercise independent command in his short career; but this should logically make the charge equally hard to prove. In fact his raids to the Isles in 1640-1 and 1643-4, his conduct in Ulster in 1642, and his movements in 1644 between landing in Scotland and joining Montrose, all suggest that he was a leader of very considerable energy, competence and initiative; there is no sign that he was lost without close supervision from above. And after leaving Montrose in 1645, Alasdair reconquered much of Argyllshire and held parts of it for nearly two years. Admittedly he was then forced to withdraw, but Alasdair was then facing the same problem that Montrose had faced (and failed to solve) after Kilsyth: how to turn from campaigns of constant movement to the much harder task of occupying and holding territory against attack. Yet Montrose's supporters have often delighted in portraying Alasdair's pathetic decline as soon as he left Montrose. To John Buchan 'The next four months of blundering in Argyll were to show how little of a general the Ulsterman was on his own account.' How Alasdair's successful occupation of most of the shire and his signing of a bond with other chiefs for the ruin of the whole name of Campbell is 'blundering' is not explained. In the same way the death of Alasdair in Ireland is often alleged to have been ignominious — with a smug undertone of 'and served him right'. He is said to have fallen 'obscurely in some unrecorded provincial quarrel' or in 'an obscure Irish foray'.[34] One would never guess from this that at Knocknanuss more men were engaged than in any of Montrose's battles except perhaps Kilsyth, and that much more is known of Knocknanuss than of any battles of the Scottish campaign.

Yet in spite of all such puzzles the stereotype has stuck. Alasdair was 'a man of herculean strength and proven courage; self indulgent and somewhat inclined to drunkenness; obtuse and incapable of forming or understanding any complex · strategy'.[35] He was an 'unusually strong man physically, and an expert swordsman, but of no great military talent'.[36] Never, it seems, do such writers ask themselves why a man with individual bravery but no other qualities of note was promoted to high rank. He lacked the usual prerequisites of the incompetent who wish to be generals, high rank and wealth.

Thus it is clear that in assessing Alasdair's true status as a soldier one must avoid being dazzled by the aura that has come to surround Montrose and has led to the denigration of all who might claim to share his glory. But equally, of course, it is necessary to guard against the opposite fault, that of inflating Alasdair simply by transferring Montrose's achievements to him wholesale, implicitly or explicitly. To Neil MacMhuirich the Gaels under Alasdair were 'the men who did all the service' in the 1644-5 campaigns. The *Commentarius Rinuccinianus* insists that the victories won then were much more those of Alasdair than of Montrose. And some later Highland and Irish writers have repeated such assertions — but have been content to leave them as assertions, believed in almost as articles of faith, without attempting to consider the evidence to see if they can survive such examination. To automatically belittle Montrose in the interests of Alasdair's reputation is as illogical — and as distasteful — as the opposite process.

Nonetheless, a fresh look at the 1644-5 campaigns does involve subtracting from Montrose some of the achievements usually attributed to him. Obviously if Alasdair saved the day at Auldearn amid near chaos, then that battle cannot be the greatest example of Montrose's tactical skill. But such reassessments will, it is hoped, contribute as much to the understanding of the real Montrose as of Alasdair. As Montrose's latest biographer has shown, Montrose warts and all is a much more fascinating character than the traditional Montrose the faultless hero.[37]

On Alasdair's ability as a strategist it is hard to pronounce for lack of evidence. That he did not always co-operate with Montrose's strategies does not prove (as is often assumed) that he was too stupid to understand them; usually it is an indication that his priorities, his war aims, differed from those of Montrose. Where one can see Alasdair's own strategic ideas in action there is no sign of incompetence. His decision in 1644 to land the Irish expeditionary force in Morvern and Ardnamurchan, at the northern edge of the Campbell empire, was well judged. He caught the Campbells off balance, for they had evidently expected his attack to be on Islay or Kintyre, as his long-term interests lay in seizing these lands. Having captured castles on landing, Alasdair avoided the danger of over-reliance on the security they represented by marching on before his enemies could blockade him in them. His march from Ardnamurchan to Atholl (where he met

Montrose), always on the move and keeping his enemies guessing as to which way he would turn next, is an example of precisely the type of warfare that Alasdair and Montrose were to practise together in the year that followed. The similarity suggests that Alasdair may have influenced Montrose's strategy from their first meeting; but this has been disguised by the common representation of Alasdair's march as a desperate and aimless blundering around seeking some superior to give him orders. On the other hand Montrose's similar marches are seen as purposeful and constructive. It is true that Alasdair's march owed much to improvisation, and that good fortune contributed to its ultimate success. But it is also true that Montrose's marches required constant improvisation, that such flexibility was essential to his success (though he tried to present the marches as carefully planned masterpieces of strategy); and Montrose's good luck as well as Alasdair's was remarkable.

Alasdair's determination to keep the war in the west alive after he had joined Montrose also made strategic sense, and involved more than just putting the interests of clan above those of the king. It prevented any significant Campbell forces being sent against Montrose, and encouraged the western clans to believe that their anti-Campbell interests as well as the cause of the king were being catered for by Montrose. The December 1644 invasion of Argyll, at first opposed by Montrose, again represented sound strategy by Alasdair — and led to one of Montrose's greatest victories. The campaign involved a sudden and daring move in a completely unexpected direction; and a recognition by Alasdair that the very fact that what he advocated doing was considered impossible by the enemy made it possible, as it led them to fail to take precautions against such an attack. This is hardly the argument of an obtuse man.

The principal example usually given of Alasdair's strategic incompetence, his defeat in and flight from Kintyre in 1647, takes on a new light when it is realised that he did not (as usually asserted) wait passively for attack but ravaged the country to the north to hinder any enemy advance; and that, moreover, he was evidently preparing a strategic withdrawal to Ireland if the strong reinforcements expected from there did not arrive in time to help him resist the army advancing against him. It is certainly true that he mistimed his withdrawal and was therefore surprised by David Leslie's remarkably fast advance; this blunder turned orderly withdrawal into humiliating and costly rout. But it was not the case that Alasdair was too stupid (or drunk) to have made any plans, but that a sound plan was not properly executed. The episode undoubtedly diminishes Alasdair's reputation as a general, but not nearly to so great an extent as is usually claimed.

Judgement on Alasdair's tactical skill is again rendered difficult by lack of detailed evidence. But if the argument is accepted that in Ulster in 1642 he devised what later became known as the Highland charge, and that he introduced it to Scotland in 1644, then his importance in British military history in the following century is much greater than has previously been realised. As well as playing a major role in the process that brought the Western Highlands and Isles back into national politics after generations of absence, Alasdair provided Highlanders with the tactic which enabled them to make this intervention effective by defeating their southern enemies in battle. Alasdair thus brought Montrose ideas as well as men.

In addition to leading his men in their devastating Highland charges, Alasdair proved able to keep control over them once the charge was made; a cool head prevented him from getting carried away in the exultation of combat. At Aberdeen, after victory was won, he was able to reorganise his men swiftly for a new attack (on a body of covenanters which was escaping). At Knocknanuss he was already bringing his men back from pursuing the enemy, and trying to discover what was happening elsewhere on the battlefield, when he was overwhelmed by a cavalry attack. But though Alasdair thus proved that he had the ability to remain aware of the battle as a whole even when he himself was engaged in combat or pursuit, it was his personal prowess as a fighter that made the deepest impression on his fellow Highlanders. To the members of a warrior society the individual skills and exploits of a warrior conferred greater fame than the skills of a general who directed battles rather than fought in them. Alasdair's physical strength and the recognition of him as the greatest of sword and targe men lie at the centre of his reputation among his own people.

Non-Highland commentators also often stress these qualities in Alasdair; but one can detect a difference in their attitude to them. Highlanders related Alasdair's martial skills with unalloyed admiration; outsiders temper admiration with wonder at the emergence of a general displaying such archaic characteristics. Those who stress that no man equal to Alasdair had been known for centuries are partly emphasising his outstanding qualities; but there is also a suggestion here that he was a man born out of his time.[38] In a Western Europe of professional armies, in which soldiers acquired military skills when they enlisted or were conscripted, in which generals were increasingly unlikely to lead their men into battle personally, there suddenly appeared from ages past what seemed a warrior band of fighting men trained from childhood, led by a tribal leader, the greatest warrior among them. These archaic warriors, strangely dressed, fought with archaic weapons. The use of bows and arrows was still common amongst them, and they deliberately threw away their muskets, the symbol of modern military technology, at the start of their battles, in favour of sword and targe. They favoured wild charges, howling their weird battle-cries, rather than disciplined formal military manoeuvres. And they prevailed over what were regarded as much more modern, civilised armies in spite of such primitiveness. No wonder the exploits of Alasdair and his men caught the imagination of many, even among enemies who loathed all that he stood for.

These archaic features of Alasdair as a soldier help to define his limitations. As a leader of his fellow Gaels of Ulster or the Highlands he was unrivalled. But how would he have fared as a leader of men not born to a warrior tradition? Moreover his own men expected him to charge with them, and though in doing so he strove to remain aware of what was going on in the battle as a whole, this nonetheless might have disqualified him from overall command of a large army in a major battle. In practice this limitation never hindered him, for he was always in a position to charge with his men without neglecting wider responsibilities. It may be that had such responsibilities been given to him he would have been able to adapt his style of command to meet them, but the opportunity to see whether or not this was so never arose. Nonetheless it was probably doubts on this score that led to the comment that Alasdair would have been one of the best generals in Europe had his 'conduct' equalled his valour; by conduct is meant leadership or command rather than personal behaviour.

Doubts as to Alasdair's conduct may also have extended to his trustworthiness in command. The main charge usually made against Alasdair on this score is of course that he deserted Montrose in 1645, though his actions in Ulster in 1642 really provide a better example, suggesting to many total unscrupulousness. But Alasdair was only one among many who found that the complicated civil wars of the three kingdoms presented them with conflicts of loyalty which led them to 'change sides' in the eyes of others while, in their own estimation, acting consistently. Montrose himself, once a leading covenanter, is of course a prime example of this. How was one to resolve conflicting claims to loyalty made by family, by locality, by country? How should loyalty to such causes be related to loyalty to political theory or religious conviction? And of course self-interest led many to desert or change sides to save or advance themselves. Alasdair's conduct in Ireland in 1641-2 suggests that his first loyalty was to his patron, kinsman and chief, Antrim; therefore he at first served against the Irish rebels though culture, religion and other ties of kin attracted him to the Irish side. The hostility of his protestant colleagues soon forced him, for self-preservation, to follow the logic of these ties and join the Irish; but soon the interests of his imprisoned father and brothers (and self-interest, as the Irish cause seemed to be collapsing) led him to submit to the Scots army in Ireland. Once it became clear this submission had failed to bring his family freedom, it was logical to turn back to the Irish. One may argue that Alasdair should not have put narrow interests of kin and clan before the great issues of politics and religion, but it is undeniable that there was consistency of a sort in his actions. Again in 1645 he had to balance loyalty to Montrose and the king against loyalty to clan, religion, and to the Irish. He did not initiate the withdrawal of Highlanders from Montrose after Kilsyth, and he left (with some of them) with Montrose's consent, reluctantly though it may have been given. Had it not been for Philiphaugh he might well have rejoined Montrose; after the battle there seemed little point in doing so. From the start there had been strains inherent in the co-operation between the two men. Alasdair and his Irish confederate troops were serving under a commission from a king against whom the confederates had revolted, and with whom they had made only a temporary truce. Alasdair was leading what he and the Irish saw as being, in part, a Catholic crusade, but they were serving under the heretic Montrose in name of a heretic king. Alasdair was working alongside royalists to revive a clan the monarchy had destroyed. As S.R. Gardiner put it, Alasdair 'was never a royalist in the sense in which Montrose was a royalist. He fought for his race and religion, not for any special form of government.'[39] Even if his clan loyalty be dismissed as narrow and parochial, through his devotion to Catholicism he could claim to be fighting for a cause a great deal wider than the insular divine right monarchy of Charles I.

However Alasdair has been neglected or derided by historians, there has never been any doubt about his fame among the Gaels — including even his enemies, the Campbells. 'No warrior in Gaelic history has captivated with greater force the imagination of the Highlanders, and there was none whose name and fame came down so vividly in popular tradition.'[40] Both by the real incidents that they record and by the mythical motifs that they weave into his life, the traditions affirm his stature. Both before and after his death Gaelic poem and prose emphasise his reputation. Even at the time of the 1745 rising his name was one to conjure with in inspiring Highlanders with martial fervour and confidence. The poet Alexander MacDonald then asked of the enemies of the Clan Donald:

> Have you ever forgotten that battle at Lochy,
> When we with our blades mowed you down like oats standing?
> And likewise Auldearn, where our mighty MacColla
> Left your hero from Lawers lying lifeless and silent,
> That rebel from hell with his regiment accurst!
> You scattered and fled like sheep from a martin,
> On the day of Kilsyth your panic was fearful . . .
> We left not alive a single survivor
> Of the breed of MacCailein we met in that battle;
> May they gain such a triumph every time that they meet us,
> In skirmish or battle, in the heat of pursuing,
> Ours the sword's victory, theirs but the pen's.[41]

NOTES

1. HMC 63: *Egmont*, I.ii.414-15; Rushworth, *Historical collections*, IV.i.561-2. Rushworth's 'Cumdrum' is clearly a corruption of Dundrum.

2. Gilbert, *Contemp hist*, i.151, 153; *Com Rin*, ii.755, 777. Confusingly, Irish sources usually refer to Alasdair in this period as Alexander MacDonnell, thus making him hard to distinguish from Antrim's brother of that name, and from two Colonels of the same name in the Irish armies; one (described as lately come from Scotland) was killed at Dungan Hill in August 1647. See, eg, ibid, ii.674, 755; Gilbert, *Contemp hist*, i.196; Aiazza, *Embassy*, 306-7.

3. Ibid, 306-7; Gilbert, *Contemp hist*, i.155-6; *Com Rin*, ii.755; Hogan, *Warr of Ireland*, 59; O'Danachair, 'Montrose's Irish regiments', *Irish Sword*, iv.63; Bagwell, *Stuarts*, ii.147-9; Rushworth, *Historical collections*, IV.ii.779-80.

4. Gilbert, *Contemp hist*, i.159; Carte, *Ormond*, ii.7; *Com Rin*, ii.777, 783. *Com Rin* states that Alasdair was made governor of Clonmel in September, but as Cashel was sacked on 4 September he was probably appointed the previous month (unless he was rushed to Clonmel at the last minute, as Inchiquin approached).

5. Bagwell, *Stuarts*, ii.152-6.

6. Gilbert, *Contemp hist*, i.173-4; *Com Rin*, ii.783-4.

7. Bagwell, *Stuarts*, ii.156-7.

8. *CSPI, 1647-60*, 16, 20, *1660-2*, 317, *1663-5*, 474; S. Pender (ed), *A census of Ireland, circa 1659* (IMC 1939), 242, 623, 642; *Burke's Irish family records* (London 1976), 975; W.A. Shaw (ed), *The knights of England* (2 vols, London 1906), ii.233; HMC 36; *Ormond* i.220, 245, 350, 353, ii.177, 194, New Series, iii.409, 413; R. Dunlop (ed), *Ireland under the Commonwealth*, ii.701.

9. D. Morrison, *The Morrison manuscript. Traditions of the Western Isles*, ed N. Macdonald (Stornoway 1975), 101.

10. Rinuccini's account of Knocknanuss is in *Com Rin*, ii.783-5, translated in Aiazza, *Embassy*, 335-7. Inchiquin's report to the English parliament is in *A true relation of a great victory obtained by the forces under the command of the Lord Inchiquine* (London 1647), reprinted in H. Cary (ed), *Memorials of the great civil war* (2 vols, London 1842), i.360-4 and McNeill, *Tanner letters*, 275-6. Two accounts by officers of Inchiquin's army appear in *A perfect narrative of the battell of Knocknones* (London 1647) and *A mighty victory in Ireland: obtained by the Lord Inchequin, neere English-mans-Hill* (London 1647). Two Irish accounts appear in Gilbert, *Ir Confed*, vii.35 (by Richard Bellings) and Gilbert, *Contemp hist*, i.174-5 (the 'aphorismical discovery'). Secondary accounts are in J. Buckley, 'The battle of Knocknanuss, 1647', *Journal of the Cork Historical and Archaeological Society*, v (1899), 109-32 (which includes a reprint of *A perfect narrative*), B. O'Brien, *Munster at war* (Cork 1971), 140-9, Bagwell, *Stuarts*, ii.156-8, Carte, *Ormond*, ii.9, and Hill, *Macdonnells of Antrim*, 113-14. For Sanda's death see SRO, GD.92/93. For traditions that Alasdair was killed by a sword-thrust under his back-plate after surrendering, see *Dublin University Magazine*, xxxi (1848), 220n and Buckley, 'Knocknanuss', 129-30. In the early nineteenth century local people would show visitors the spot where Alasdair was supposed to have been killed, and 'pretend to show the stains of his blood', T.C. Croker, *Researches in the south of Ireland* (London 1824), 116.

11. *Com Rin*, ii.784-6; Aiazza, *Embassy*, 337.

12. Hogan, *Warr of Ireland*, 74.

13. Gordon, *Britane's distemper*, 63.

14. Leith, *Memoirs*, i.292, 302, 350.

15. Gilbert, *Contemp hist*, i.176. My thanks to my wife and to Mr Thomas Pearce of the Department of Classics, University of Aberdeen, for their help in translating this epitaph.

16. *Com Rin*, ii.786.

17. Mackenzie, *Orain Iain Luim*, 34-9. Dr Mackenzie's translation refers to Coll as 'in Carrickfergus, with iron shackles on his limbs'; but *carraig* means simply 'rock', and there is no evidence that Coll was ever imprisoned at Carrickfergus. MacLean, *Sources*, 78 suggests that the rock on which Dunstaffnage Castle is built is meant; but much more plausible is Dr Colm O Boyle's suggestion that the reference to Coll being 'in the rock' in chains supports the tradition that he was hung in a cleft in a rock near Dunstaffnage. I have also altered Dr Mackenzie's translation of 'Dun Chanain' from Dungannon (County Tyrone) to Duncannon (County Wexford), as it seems more likely that news would have reached Ian Lom from the latter as it is a port, whereas Dungannon lies far inland. Dr O Boyle tells me that the alteration is in any case necessary on linguistic grounds.

18. This translation is partly from Mackenzie, *Orain Iain Luim*, 248, and partly the work of Dr O Boyle. See Fergusson, *From the farthest Hebrides*, 104-6 for an allegedly contemporary lament for Alasdair.

19. C. Smith, *The ancient and present state of the county and city of Cork* (2 vols, Cork 1893-4), 91n.

20. Buckley, 'Knocknanuss', 131-2; Croker, *Researches*, 116-117; E.W. Bunting, *The ancient music of Ireland* (collected ed, Dublin 1969), 1840 section, p.83 and introduction, p.92; *The Dublin Magazine*, April 1843, music section, 23-4.

21. *Com Rin*, ii.786. For O'Callaghan see ibid, ii.16-17, 192, 195, 197, 270, iii.169; *Burke's Irish family records*, 888-9; M.J. Hynes, *The mission of Rinuccini* (Dublin 1932), 32, 246; Gilbert, *Ir confed*, iii.216, iv.114, v.280, 283, 331, 332, 340, vi.238, vii.234, 235; *HMC 63: Egmont*, i.180, 191-250 passim. In the mid-nineteenth century it was believed that Alasdair had been buried at Buttevant Abbey (eight miles north of Mallow), and a skull of 'very large dimensions' was pointed out as 'that of the famous warrior, MacAllisdrum', C.B. Gibson, *The history of the county and city of Cork* (2 vols, London 1861), ii.474. In the early nineteenth century 'a large square pile of skulls and bones' of those killed in the battle was to be seen near the entrance to the Abbey, having been brought from a mass grave near the battlefield. They were later transferred to the crypt, Croker, *Researches*, 116, and Buckley, 'Knocknanuss', 123-4.

22. There was long preserved in Loughan Castle, County Tipperary, what was held to be Alasdair MacColla's sword. This was described as having a ten pound steel ball with a wheel through it running

along a groove (or 'open rod') in the blade, so that when the sword was swung the ball would run towards the tip of the blade to give added weight to the blow. But there is no real evidence that this ridiculous and useless curiosity had anything to do with him. See Buckley, 'Knocknanuss', 130-1, L. Duggan, 'The Irish brigade with Montrose', *Irish Ecclesiastical Record*, lxxxix (1958), 176,256, and *Dublin Magazine*, April 1843, music section, 25-6; Mackenzie, *Orain Iain Luim*, 249; Bunting, *Ancient music*, 1840 section, introduction, p.92; *Dublin University Magazine*, xxxi.220n. The sword was presumably a forerunner of the swords later made in Ireland with hollow blades partly filled with mercury, Hill, *Macdonnells of Antrim*, 117n.

23. Gilbert, *Contemp hist*, iii.150, 167.

24. Macdonald, *Clan Donald*, iii.403-8; Hill, *Macdonnells of Antrim*, 114-119; *Dublin University Magazine*, xxxi.220n.

25. Loder, *Colonsay*, 143-4, 232-5, *APS*, vii.232; J. Anderson, *Calendar of the Laing charters* (Edinburgh 1899), 599, 663, 666.

26. Mackenzie, *Orain Ian Luim*, 28-31.

27. Aiazza, *Embassy*, 367-9.

28. *Rel Celt*, ii.204-7.

29. Ibid, ii.207; Aiazza, *Embassy*, 419, 423, 441; Gilbert, *Ir confed*, vii.114-16, 277; Bagwell, *Stuarts*, ii.172-3; Hill, *Macdonnells of Antrim*, 333-4.

30. *Com Rin*, iv.274-6.

31. Cunningham, *Loyal clans*, 250.

32. Ibid, 249.

33. J. Somerville (11th Lord), *Memorie of the Somervilles* (2 vols, Edinburgh 1815), ii.359; Cunningham, *Loyal clans*, 251.

34. Buchan, *Montrose*, 277; Napier, *Memoirs*, ii.603.

35. Buchan, *Montrose*, 180.

36. Mackenzie, *The Highlands and Isles of Scotland*, 230.

37. E.J. Cowan, *Montrose. For covenant and king* (London 1977).

38. See Macdonald, *Clan Donald*, iii.596.

39. *DNB* under Macdonald or Macdonnell, Alexander or Alaster.

40. Macdonald, *Clan Donald*, iii.596.

41. J.L. Campbell (ed), *Highland songs of the Forty-Five* (Edinburgh 1933), 58-61. See also 150-1.

11

The Changing Highland Problem in the Later Seventeenth Century

THE campaigns fought by Montrose and Alasdair MacColla in Scotland in 1644-7 failed to achieve their objectives. They failed to destroy the power of the Campbells or the covenanters, or to advance the causes of the king, of the Irish confederates, or of the Clan Ian Mor. Nonetheless, the campaigns did have lasting effects of great significance. For the first time for many generations most of the clans of the Western Highlands and Isles had become involved in national political issues. The anti-Campbell clans had come, in resisting that clan and the policies of the covenanters' regime, to claim to be fighting for causes wider than that of the individual clan. Catholicism provided one such wider cause, but it was not shared by all the clans involved; of much greater importance in getting the clans concerned to work together was their fighting in name of the king. This 'royalism' might on occasion have been almost entirely nominal, a useful expedient rather than a genuine belief, but it was nonetheless significant. Fighting in a loose 'negative' alliance with the Stewart cause, an alliance based on hatred of common enemies, the clans were imperceptibly to develop sentiments of positive loyalty to the monarchy. If Highland Jacobitism was to be born in the 1680s, it had been conceived in the 1640s.

The Highlanders were thus launched on their remarkable century of periodic, violent irruption into national politics; the century began at Tippermuir in 1644 and ended at Culloden in 1746. In initiating this process (by resisting the alliance of Campbells and covenanters), the 'royalist' clans were greatly aided by a coincidental development which enabled them to make their voice in national affairs a major one: the appearance of the 'Highland charge' in its classic form. Montrose and Alasdair were eventually defeated, but the victories they had won had shown Highlanders what they could do. For a time the power of the Campbells and of the central government had been overthrown. If this had been done once, could it not be done again? Thus it has been said that 'in the long run the real significance of [Montrose's] wonderful campaign was its effect on the Highlanders. These astonishing victories put fresh heart in them.'[1] But though from one point of view the campaigns were fought in a war of Highland and Irish Gaels against Lowlanders, the Gaels fought in cooperation with Lowlanders — and under the leadership of one. And the covenanters had considerable Highland support — from the Campbells and (at least at Auldearn) from the MacKenzies and other clans of the north. Thus while it is true that in some senses Alasdair and

Montrose had 'done more than any others to widen the rift between Gaelic-speaking and Lowland Scotland. They unwittingly confirmed the portrait of [the Highlander as] the blood-thirsty savage',[2] it is also true that Highlanders and Lowlanders had in the campaigns worked together much more closely for shared political objectives than they had done for generations.

Political and military developments in 1648-55 hastened the development of the embryo conceived through the attempts of Charles I to find support in the Highlands in the preceding years. In 1647-8 the covenanting movement split into two factions. The Engagers (an alliance of moderate covenanters and royalists) claimed to uphold the covenants but in their treaty with the king, the Engagement, undertook to force the English parliament to restore to him at least some of his powers. Opposing the Engagers, the faction led by the marquis of Argyll (soon to be known as the kirk party) insisted that as the king had not sworn the covenants, the cause of God could not be advanced by helping him. In spite of opposition the Engagers succeeded in winning a majority in the Scottish parliament, and in raising an army to invade England.

Thus again the royalist and anti-Campbell causes came to be combined; and they won control of the covenanting regime. However, the political tactics adopted by the Engagers deprived them of the manpower of the anti-Campbell clans. To try to persuade the kirk of the sincerity of their claims to serve covenants as well as the king, the Engagers refused to accept the services of the leading 'malignants', men who had in the past opposed the covenanters in arms. The 'royalist' chiefs were therefore not allowed to raise their forces; and they were not likely to agree to others raising their clansmen. In June 1648 twenty-four leading MacKenzies and other leading supporters of the earl of Seaforth petitioned that their chief be allowed to lead them in support of the Engagement, claiming that the refusal to employ him (as he had for a time served Montrose) had so displeased the clansmen that they would not fight. They would not follow 'anie bot their native superiour'.[3]

The Engagers ignored such appeals on behalf of malignants; but the defeat of their army at Preston by Cromwell changed the situation. As the remnants of the Engagers' army fled back to Scotland, many Highland chiefs and royalists of the north-east began to raise men to support them and to resist English invasion. 'The Highlanders were ready to a man, Argyll alone excepted', and Seaforth was said (doubtless with some exaggeration) to have 'brought up 4000 choice men from the Hebrides and farthest parts of Ross and Caithness'. At this point, however, the extreme covenanters of the kirk party seized Edinburgh, established a new regime, and opened negotiations with the English. The forces of the Engagers reacted by withdrawing to Stirling to link up with the reinforcements they expected from the Highlands and the north.[4] The stage seemed set for a new civil war. Argyll suffered a new humiliation when 700 men he sent to support the kirk party regime were scattered by the Engagers near Stirling, and it was said that Highland captains and chiefs had 'combined themselves and entred into a Confederacy, to invade fall upon and destroy the Lord Marques of Argyles lands' and to lay waste other parts of the kingdom.[5] As in 1644-7, the chiefs who enlisted in the 'royalist' cause gave priority to the ruin of the Clan Campbell.

Civil war was, however, averted. In September 1648 the Engagers agreed to disband after Cromwell entered Scotland and made it clear that he would stay to support the kirk party regime until its enemies dispersed. But within a few months Highland 'royalism' again flared up and again threatened to initiate a civil war. Regional issues were as important as national ones. The first stages of the revolt evidently arose from the determination of local clans and landlords, led by the MacKenzies, to resist the establishment by the regime of a permanent garrison in Inverness. Even a normally staunch covenanter like John Monro of Lemlair was prepared to cooperate with royalists to resist this unwelcome central government presence in the area. Early in 1649, therefore, those concerned combined in arms under MacKenzie of Pluscardine (Seaforth's brother), seized Inverness and destroyed its fortifications. Perhaps encouraged by this news, the Robertsons and Stewarts of Atholl also rose in rebellion against the kirk party. The rebels had, however, no clear objectives and no plans for a major campaign, and they soon submitted when the kirk party offered them generous terms. The new regime had by this time fallen out with its English allies, who had just executed Charles I, abolished the monarchy and established a commonwealth. In these circumstances the kirk party was desperate to avoid a new war in the Highlands. But in spite of the generosity of its treatment of the rebels (or perhaps because of it), the rebellion soon revived in a more dangerous form. In April 1649 Pluscardine gathered his men and marched into Atholl. There he was joined by Lord Reay, who had long been feuding with the earl of Sutherland over the latter's claim to feudal superiority over the lands of Reay's clan, the MacKays. As Sutherland was a covenanter, Reay was a royalist. Soon the new marquis of Huntly (whose father had just been executed by the kirk party), Lord Ogilvie and Middleton (the former covenanting general) also rallied to the royalist cause. This alliance of eastern Highlanders and north-eastern Lowlanders looked formidable; but the rebels allowed themselves to be surprised and scattered by a few troops of covenanting horse at Balvenie and the rising collapsed.[6] Again the rebels seem to have lacked any objectives or strategy. They had risen through local grievances, hatred of the kirk party and anger at the execution of the king, but had no idea of what their new king, the exiled Charles II, wanted of them, or of what was in his best interests. Thus the efforts of some clans to cooperate with the royalist cause in 1648-9 were dismal and demoralising failures; nonetheless, they did serve to underline the emerging 'tradition' of shared interests of king and clans.

The problem of what action would be in the best interests of Charles II continued to perplex both Highland and Lowland royalists for the next year. They might hate the extreme presbyterian kirk party; but that party had at least proclaimed Charles king — of England as well as Scotland. The kirk party regime was thus a lesser evil than the regime of the English republicans; but on the other hand the kirk party would only admit the king to the exercise of his office if he swore the covenants and signed away almost all his powers. Should the young king reach some agreement with the kirk party out of expediency, as it controlled Scotland and could give him substantial help against the English republicans and regicides? Or should he work to overthrow the kirk party and establish a truly royalist regime in Edinburgh? Royalist exiles with the king in Holland argued endlessly over the issue.

Montrose favoured the destruction of the kirk party. Late in 1649 he sent forces to seize the Orkneys, and early the following year he joined them and landed in Caithness. His choice of landing place may suggest that he was determined that the royalist causes should not, as in 1644-5, be dependent on the fickle western clans. But though they had insisted on fighting for him on their own terms, they had at least been prepared to fight. The northern clans were not. Montrose had probably hoped for the support of the MacKenzies and the MacKays, but they showed no enthusiasm for his cause. Both lacked their chiefs (Seaforth was in exile in Holland and Reay was a prisoner in Edinburgh) and were demoralised by the failure of the Engagers and of Pluscardine's rising. In April 1650 Montrose's small army was surprised and routed at Carbisdale; shortly thereafter he was captured and executed.[7]

Montrose's last campaign did, however, help the king in one respect; it made the kirk party fear that Montrose would repeat his exploits of 1644-5, and therefore it agreed to some concessions in negotiating with the king. This helped Charles to reach agreement with the kirk party on 1 May (before news of Carbisdale had arrived). But though he now came to Scotland he was a puppet king, and the kirk party was so determined that he should remain one that he found himself almost a prisoner. Time, however, was on Charles' side. Many royalists (including Angus MacDonald of Glengarry) had returned to Scotland with him, and the gradual reaction in Scotland in favour of royalism which had been evident since the mid-1640s continued. The rule of the covenanters seemed to have brought nothing but confusion and years of civil war. The kirk party regime had only gained power with English help, and its policies of strict moral reform and its attacks on some of the powers of nobles and other great men alienated many. This royalist reaction was greatly strengthened by horror and fury at the action of the English in executing Charles I, king of Scotland as well as England and a member of Scotland's native dynasty. Such feelings were further intensified in 1650 when the arrival of Charles II in Scotland provoked English invasion led by Cromwell. The kirk party tried to insist that the war with the English was an ideological one, fought over religious issues; but to most Scots it came to be a national war against the old enemy, an extension of the long wars fought in earlier centuries to maintain Scotland's independence. And in this resistance to foreign invasion the Stewart dynasty was the symbol of national unity, of the cause of Scotland.

Nothing could have done more to unite Highlander and Lowlander than English invasion. Many Highlanders might resent alien Lowland rule, the attempts of Edinburgh regimes to make their claims to rule all Scotland mean something in practice as well as theory. But in hatred of the invading English enemy, Highlanders felt more identity with the idea of 'Scotland' than in anything else. Highlanders might call Lowlanders the *goill*, a word implying alienation and separateness; but the English were the *sasannaich*, the Saxons, traditional enemies of all Scots, the destroyers of the Irish Gaels, men so alien that some Highlanders shared the Irish belief that they had tails![8]

At first the kirk party succeeded in insisting that only those who truly upheld the cause of God should be allowed to fight in their ideological war. Like the Engagers they refused to employ 'malignant' royalists; and they also excluded the Engagers themselves. But after the catastrophic defeat of their godly army by Cromwell at Dunbar in September 1650, the kirk party regime began to collapse. Edinburgh was abandoned to the English and the regime fled to Stirling, hoping to hold the line of the River Forth. The furious demands of royalists to be allowed to share in resistance to the English grew ever louder; but at first the kirk party refused to alter its impractical policies. This provoked the king and royalists into plotting a *coup d'etat*, and a plan was agreed whereby Highlanders from Atholl were to seize Perth (where the king was staying) and the royalists of the north-east would rise in arms. As in late 1648 and early 1649, civil war between Highland and northern royalists on the one hand and the kirk party on the other seemed imminent. But incompetence and divided counsels wrecked the plot. Charles' English advisers persuaded him to cancel the rash venture and he, fearing the discovery of his plotting, then fled to join the royalists, who rose in arms to defend him and themselves. Charles was soon persuaded to return to Perth but the incident, known as 'the Start', emphasised the kirk party's weakness and forced it into concessions. The Atholl men and other royalists were granted indemnities for their conduct, and negotiations for allowing all willing to fight the English to do so began.[9]

Debate on the issue was bitter and prolonged, and disagreements on it led to a schism in the kirk, but eventually the more moderate wing of the kirk party abandoned the principle that only the godly could fight in God's cause. The result of this surrender appeared in a list of colonels appointed to raise forces in December 1650. As well as Lowland royalists, the new colonels included many Highland chiefs — Lord Kintail (Seaforth's son), Sir James MacDonald of Sleat, the tutor of Keppoch, the captain of Clanranald, the tutor of MacLean of Duart, Ewen Cameron of Lochiel, the chiefs of the MacKintoshes and the MacPhersons, and others.[10] A few weeks later the marquis of Argyll placed the crown on the king's head at his coronation; but he and the covenanters were being edged out of power by this flood of 'malignants' now being allowed places in the army and soon to be readmitted to parliament.

Some chiefs responded enthusiastically to the call to fight for king and country. At the battle of Inverkeithing, in July 1651, 500— or perhaps as many as 760 — MacLeans died fighting heroically. Their young chief, Sir Hector MacLean of Duart, died with them, and Alasdair MacColla's old comrades, Donald MacLean of Brolas and Ewen MacLean of Treshnish, were severely wounded. Some hinted darkly that those who hated Highlanders had somehow arranged for the MacLeans to be thus savaged by the English. The following September at Worcester the MacLeods suffered similar devastating losses. Lachlan, chief of the MacKinnons, was also present at Worcester, and Ian, chief of the MacNabs, died there. MacKenzies, MacKays, Frasers, MacGregors and other clansmen had reinforced Charles' army, and he is said to have called the Highlanders the flower of his forces.[11] But equally notable is the number of western clans which did not send forces to join the king. Various excuses have been put forward to explain this. The Glengarry MacDonalds and the Clanranald were engaged in war in Ireland, it is said, and so were not able to help the king.[12] But their intervention in Ireland had been in 1647-8, so it can hardly account for their lack of action in 1651. Lochiel is said to have raised 1,000 of his Camerons for the king, but not to have been able to reach Stirling with them before Charles started on the march south that led to disaster at Worcester.[13] But Lochiel had been ordered to levy men in December 1650 and Charles did not march from Stirling until the end of July 1651, which suggests that even if Lochiel did raise men he can hardly have treated coming to the king's aid as a matter of urgency. Vague assurances that 'the loyall clans' (by implication virtually all clans except the Campbells) were eagerly awaiting the opportunity to serve their king[14] are hardly convincing.

Why did some western clans fail to respond to the king's appeals? Exhaustion following the wars of the mid-1640s is doubtless part of the answer; but equally important is probably an order of priorities which put clan before king. Many chiefs felt their first duty was to defend their men and lands from enemies, and some were willing even to give offensive action against local enemies priority over action against the English. In April 1651 it was reported that the failure of Argyll to bring out men he was responsible for from Lochaber was greatly hindering the service; no neighbouring clan would send men to Stirling until the Lochaber men had left, for fear the latter would plunder their lands.[15] In the disturbed state of the Highlands after recent wars, few trusted their neighbours or wished to leave their lands unprotected. If, as seems likely, the men Argyll was held responsible for in Lochaber were (or included) the Camerons, then the fears of their neighbours are easy to understand. It was evidently in 1651 that the Camerons invaded the lands of MacDonald of Glengarry to force him to pay a feu duty due to Cameron of Lochiel as feudal superior of some of Glengarry's lands. Lochiel undertook a similar punitive expedition against MacDonald of Keppoch, to exact interest payments on a mortgage he had granted Keppoch. Ewen Cameron of Lochiel is usually, as the result of the work of an eighteenth century Jacobite biographer, regarded as the archetypal Highland Jacobite chief, ever zealous in the cause of the Stewarts though suffering from the effect of alien feudal superiorities which conflicted with patriarchal rights. Yet here he shows himself just as ready as any earl of Argyll to exploit feudal superiorities and the financial difficulties of neighbours in order to gain some hold over them. And Lochiel does this when the English are overrunning the country and the king is calling for his help.

Nonetheless, the English invasion and conquest of the Lowlands in 1650-1 did reinforce the growing alliance between many clans and the king, for even clans which did not get round to fighting for him nonetheless supported him. Perhaps some still thought of his cause as the lesser of two evils. Previously king had at least been preferable to covenanters; now he was preferable to the English. Absorption in local issues had prevented many coming to the aid of the king in the Lowlands; but when the English turned to the conquest of the Highlands, Highland zeal for the royal cause grew rapidly. Chiefs determined to fight to prevent their lands being occupied by the *sasannaich*; and in doing this they were willing to declare themselves to be fighting for the king, and they were ready to cooperate with Lowland royalists.

Active preparation for resistance to the English advance into the Highlands began in 1652 when Charles II appointed Middleton (who was in exile with him) to command his forces in Scotland. The king took this action after being approached by several chiefs (led, it seems, by Glengarry) and other royalists. Highland enthusiasm for this 'royalist' venture was doubtless increased by the submission of Argyll to the English. Now as in the 1640s fighting for the king conveniently entailed fighting against the Campbells. In March 1653, as Middleton had still not reached Scotland, the earl of Glencairn was appointed to command in his absence and open resistance to the English began. At first all went well; the English had not sufficient forces on the spot to attack the 'rebels' and therefore withdrew from much of the Highlands, concentrating on containing the rising until forces were assembled for an offensive. But long before the English were ready to attack, the rising began to fragment and collapse through poor leadership and internal dissension. Significantly, in this context, much of the trouble arose from friction between Highlanders and Lowlanders, and from inter-clan rivalries. According to an English report, the Lowland officers and nobles who led the rising were highly suspicious of their Gaelic allies, and were anxious to recruit as many Lowlanders as possible to protect themselves 'from the barbarous cruelty and treachery of the Highlanders' by keeping the latter 'in awe'.[16] After Middleton reached Scotland early in 1654, one of his officers, Sir George Monro, denounced the Highlanders serving under Glencairn as 'a pack of thieves and robbers', evidently referring in particular to Glengarry's men; in the duel that followed Glencairn wounded Monro.[17] Glengarry had to be prevented from fighting a duel with the earl of Atholl over precedence;[18] evidently the former was unwilling to accept Lowland rules of precedence that gave any man with a noble title automatic precedence over an untitled chief. Among the chiefs there was tension between Lochiel and Glengarry; and a reinforcement which soon proved a major complication was provided by the decision of Lord Lorne, Argyll's son, and a few Campbell lairds to defy their chief and join the royalist, national cause. Lorne and Glengarry promptly fell to quarrelling, the latter having 'an old grudge . . . since the great Montrose's wars' against the Campbells. They too had to be parted to prevent a duel; and Glengarry had to be dissuaded from leading an attack on Lorne's men.[19] Lorne led a march through Campbell territory into Kintyre, but then quarrelled with Lord Kenmure through refusing to let the latter attack the Lowland colonists Argyll had recently settled there to replace men killed or driven out in recent wars.[20] By preventing the rising developing into an anti-Campbell crusade, Lorne deprived those in arms of one of their strongest common interests.

Late in 1653 Glencairn did try to bring some unity to the Highland side of his chaotic rising by focusing it on hatred of the Campbells, ignoring Lorne's contribution to the cause. He urged Charles II that, above all else, he must declare Argyll a traitor; it would be easy to justify this as he had recently helped the English to capture Duart Castle. Denouncing Argyll would encourage all

Highlanders 'to engage against him', and in addition Charles should assure certain chiefs that he would free them from 'those bonds and yoakes which Argyle has purchased over their heads'. Their debts to Argyll and his feudal superiority over them should be cancelled. In urging the necessity for such encouragement of the chiefs, Glencairn also revealed his own bad relations with them; he asked the king not to believe any paper signed by Highland chiefs unless Glengarry was one of those who signed. Glengarry was showing himself the most loyal of the chiefs; but he was also demanding reward for his support. He claimed that Charles had promised him the title of earl of Ross and the lands of the former earldom, and was now pressing that the promise be honoured.[21]

Such attempts to unite the 'royalist' Highlanders by stressing commitment to the anti-Campbell cause failed, and when in 1654 the English moved large forces into the Highlands resistance was sporadic and fragmented. Many clans were mainly concerned with trying to keep the English out of their own lands, and this combined with endless squabbles among the royalist leaders to make victory easy for the English.[22] By mid-1655 the Highlands had begun a short period of peace and order unrivalled for centuries. Partly this was the peace of exhaustion and demoralisation. In the past decade many clans had suffered repeated heavy losses of men. Systematic devastations had laid waste many areas, culminating in the devastating of the lands of Seaforth, Glengarry, Lochiel and others by the English.[23] Moreover conquest had been carried out with a determination not seen before, backed by the seemingly endless resources of men and money of a regime which, after gaining power in England, had remorselessly conquered first Ireland and now Scotland. Resistance seemed hopeless, and the English showed themselves determined to treat any breach of the law as an offence against the new state, and able to punish such offences effectively by use of their army. Moreover, irksome as the rule of the conquerors was, it was also in some respects fair and practical.

At first it looked as if the English intended to adopt entirely traditional policies in the Highlands. The submission of Argyll to them made it seem likely that he would be, as in the past, used as central government's main agent in the Highlands; and in 1653 the English hopefully tried to revive the old policy of taming the chiefs by ordering them all to appear and find caution for keeping the peace and suppressing disorder.[24] The 1653-5 rising rendered this move useless in the short term, and when the rising collapsed the policy reappeared in a new form. As each chief in turn accepted the inevitable and agreed to lay down arms, he was bound by the terms of a written submission or treaty, and to help make defeat palatable concessions were sometimes included. The chiefs' authority was recognised by the very fact that the English were signing treaties with them, and they were made to find caution and to agree to be responsible for the behaviour of their own clansmen. They and their men were often given permission to carry arms to protect themselves from thieves and 'broken men'. Sometimes attempts were made to settle local problems which had led to disorder in the past. Lochiel, for example, was promised that the English would settle all payments of arrears (up to £500 sterling) due to William MacKintosh of Torcastle, who was feudal superior of some of Lochiel's lands. Moreover, arbitration was promised to reach a once and for all agreement between the two men. Rorie MacLeod of Dunvegan was promised help in collecting debts due to him.[25] Some chiefs may also have looked forward to benefiting from the general commitment of the English to abolishing remnants of 'feudalism', including feudal superiorities, though many chiefs would lose as well as gain from such a reform.

The English thus offered the chiefs positive benefits in return for their submission. They also made it clear that swift retribution would fall on chiefs who failed to take their responsibilities seriously; chiefs were no longer to get away with signing agreements with whatever regime was in power and then ignoring them. And a major government presence in the Highlands was to be maintained in the form of garrisons.

The greatest of the new Highland garrisons was that of Inverlochy, where a large fort was built. The first attempts of the English (in 1654) to establish such a garrison were furiously opposed by the Camerons, and in all about seventy English soldiers were killed. But the English persisted; Inverlochy was an excellent site for a garrison both because of its strategic importance at the end of the Great Glen, and because it lay at the centre of Lochaber, one of the most endemically unsettled areas of the Highlands. Eventually, in 1655 Lochiel submitted to the English; and he soon came to enjoy good relations both with the garrison and with the English authorities in general.[26] Lochiel is, indeed, the prime example of a chief who did very well out of English rule. The English paid off his arrears to the MacKintoshes, and tried hard to make the latter surrender their claims over Lochiel's lands, though in the end they failed. Not surprisingly, when monarchy was restored in 1660, MacKintosh denounced Lochiel for allying himself to the English usurpers for private gain.[27] Lochiel also profited from the troubles of his neighbour, MacDonald of Glengarry. The latter submitted to the English in June 1655, but by the following February was their prisoner. In March 1656 he found caution for his good behaviour, and in 1658 he was present (with Lochiel) at Inverlochy when Richard Cromwell was proclaimed Lord Protector on his father's death. But in 1659 the English commissioned Lochiel to act against Glengarry's men, who had risen in arms, robbing and plundering.[28] Thus Glengarry seems to have alternately submitted to the English and defied them, and at some point they confiscated his lands. The forfeiture was granted to Argyll, who in turn granted it to Lochiel. The latter's biographer insisted that he regarded himself as holding the land in trust for Glengarry; he wished 'to preserve it intire for the legall ouner'. But in the light of the bad relations previously existing between the two men this idealistic interpretation seems highly implausible; and Glengarry himself did not believe it, for after the Restoration he denounced Lochiel for having raised 7,500 merks in rent from his lands through the favour of the English.[29] Lochiel had in fact acted as virtually any chief would have done, taking full advantage of an opportunity to try to absorb a neighbouring clan.

Further, in the terms of his submission to the English Lochiel discovered a highly ingenious way of increasing his prestige and following as a chief. The only clan in the area with permission to carry arms was the Camerons. Lochiel exploited this by showing himself ready to certify that anyone found in arms (and therefore facing punishment by the English) was a Cameron, provided that they agreed to take that name, 'so that, in a short time, his name became so numerous as to spread itself over a great part of the Highlands'. Here again Lochiel is usually presented as acting selflessly, doing his best to help men who were in trouble,[30] but there was more to it than this. By asserting that these fictitious Camerons were his own men, and by their adoption of his name, Lochiel was getting them to admit dependence on him. It was a novel form of dependence in return for a specialised type of protection, but in essence it was no different from other methods employed by chiefs to create dependants and thus begin to absorb outsiders into their clans.

Finally, Lochiel probably did well out of English rule financially, benefiting from the presence at Inverlochy of a major garrison. To the officers and soldiers of the garrison were added their servants, wives and children. Others came to settle at Inverlochy attracted by the security offered by the garrison, 'so that this suburbs of the Garrison would have soon increased into a tolerable mercat town in these remote parts' had it not been for the Restoration of 1660.[31] This growing settlement must have created a thriving market for food, and the Camerons were best placed to supply it.

Lochiel thus benefited from English rule in several ways, and was soon on the best of terms with the conquerors, whose continuing favour to him indicates that they saw him as their loyal agent. He himself came to regard General Monck, the English commander in chief in Scotland, as his 'friend and protector'.[32] His enthusiasm for English rule has naturally been an embarrassment to those determined to present him as the unswerving Stewart loyalist, and two ways of explaining away his conduct have been suggested. The first is to point out that General Monck was eventually, in 1660, to bring about the Restoration, and to suggest that he had long been a secret royalist. Lochiel, it is claimed, had somehow discovered this; therefore in supporting the republican general Lochiel was actually upholding the interests of the Stewart dynasty.[33] Ingenious as this argument is, it is hardly plausible. The second type of defence of Lochiel has a valid point at its heart but is wildly illogical. His cooperation with the English, it has been claimed, is in itself proof of his devotion to monarchy. He supported the English because they provided the 'practical benefits of monarchical rule'. These were impartial government, law and order, and the suppression of feudal superiorities which put feudal lords between subject and government; it was 'the function of sovereignty to control or supercede' these superiorities.[34]

An argument which rests on a conflation of monarchical rule, good government and sovereignty hardly inspires confidence. If what Lochiel (and, it is claimed, other chiefs) saw as the essence of the 'monarchy' they are supposed to have craved was good government, and the English provided this much more effectively than Stewart kings had ever done, then their support for the Stewarts is puzzling. Moreover, obviously if one of the central points of the true monarchy the clans were supposed to have wanted was the abolition of intermediaries between subject and ruler, then the clans would have been seeking the abolition of clanship itself. Clan chief interposed between ruler and subject just as much as feudal superior.

It is true, however, that in some ways the English provided good government in the Highlands. Being outsiders, the English had no preconceived biases when it came to trying to settle inter-clan disputes, so even if the order they imposed through the vigilance of their garrisons was resented, it was at least recognised that the discipline was impartial. The English had welcomed Argyll's support, but carefully avoided using him as an intermediary in all Highland affairs. Yet the fairness of English rule and local enthusiasm for it should not be exaggerated. What Lochiel got from the English was not impartial rule but positive favour; he was their pet chief.

In the Highlands as in the Lowlands the Restoration of the monarchy in 1660 was almost universally welcomed. Whatever advantages English rule had brought had been outweighed by humiliation at conquest by the Saxons which had destroyed the semi-autonomy of many chiefs. Restoring the dynasty helped restore the national honour which it had come to symbolise. To a conservative society traditional monarchy was much more acceptable than the rule of English republican upstarts, revolutionaries as well as aliens. In religion the many Catholic or conservatively protestant 'episcopalian' clans expected more from restored monarchy than from presbyterian covenanters or Independent English. But in welcoming the Restoration it is likely that most chiefs were looking forward not to a continuance of strong central control on 'English' lines, to supposedly 'real' monarchy in this sense. On the contrary what they expected was the restoration of weak traditional government which would allow them to revert to 'the good old days' before the troubles when they had been semi-autonomous rulers.

This is certainly what the Highlands got after 1660, and with it came all the disadvantages of weak and inefficient government: the revival of old inter-clan feuds, of conflicting claims to actual possession of land, to feudal superiorities and to the loyalty of men. Worst of all, from the point of view of most clans, the weakness and cynicism of the restored monarchy was such that while the powers of the Campbells, who had served the covenanters, were soon restored to them, many clans which had served and suffered for the Stewarts were slighted or neglected, and found themselves still threatened by Campbell ambitions. Yet royal ingratitude was not in all instances as evident as those who claimed to have suffered from it argued. Again Lochiel is often regarded as the prime example of a general trend. At the Restoration, instead of 'enjoying the fruits of his loyalty', his 'troubles and difficulties multiplied'.[35] In reality his record as an active collaborator with the English, emphasised by the complaints of the MacDonalds of Glengarry and the MacKintoshes against him, could with some justice have been held to outweigh his services to the crown. Similarly, though Rorie MacLeod of Dunvegan is said to have resolved to fight for the Stewarts no more as the only reward the clan received was the knighting of two of his uncles,[36] it could well have been argued that the MacLeods had refused to fight for the king against either covenanters or Campbells; they had only risen in arms against the English invaders, and therefore deserved little reward.

Glengarry had much more genuine claims on royal favour, and these were acknowledged in 1660 when he was created Lord MacDonald (or MacDonnell) and Aros and granted a pension of £300 a year (raised to £500 in 1676). But he too was left dissatisfied, as he did not receive the earldom of Ross. Here, however, it was not just ingratitude which prevented his further promotion. The earldom of Ross had once been held by the lords of the Isles, and Glengarry evidently sought the title to support his assertion that he was the rightful chief of all branches of the Clan Donald. Was he dreaming of crushing the Campbells and re-establishing MacDonald supremacy in the west? Fear of such ultimate ambitions doubtless contributed to the refusal to make Glengarry earl of Ross. Moreover, even without that title his claims led to disputes among the branches of the Clan Donald; it was evidently his ambitions that provoked Sir James MacDonald of Sleat into gathering signatures to declarations of his own rights to chieftaincy of all the MacDonalds and to the earldom of Ross. In the later sixteenth century the MacDonalds of Sleat had regarded themselves as *de jure* lords of the Isles, and though in the seventeenth century they had abandoned open claims to this title, they were hostile to what looked like the first moves by the MacDonalds of Glengarry to establish their right to the title. Undeterred by such opposition, the new Lord MacDonald referred to himself as 'Cheeffe and principall man' of 'the name and Clan of McDonalds', and he managed on occasion to get such designations of himself inserted in official documents.[37]

At first it at least seemed that those Highlanders who had fought for the king would have the satisfaction of seeing the power of the Clan Campbell broken at the Restoration. The marquis of Argyll was convicted of treason and executed in 1661 (to the fierce joy of the poet Ian Lom), and his titles, lands and offices were forfeited to the crown. The following year his son and heir, Lord Lorne, was sentenced to death by parliament (instigated by his enemies) on a trumped up charge. Briefly it seemed that there was hope of a real revolution in the distribution of power in the Highlands following on the fall of the Campbells. But those who ruled in Charles II's name in Scotland had little interest in the Highlands; their main concern was that the natives should be kept quiet with as little trouble as possible, and ensuring this was of course, so far as the Western Highlands were concerned, the traditional task of the house of Argyll. Lord Lorne had emphasised this in pleading for his father's life. Many 'horrid insurrections and rebellions of Islanders, and remote mountinous men' had been crushed by the Campbells. They had brought 'many notorious malefactors and cruell oppressors' from their 'strong holds and inaccessible places, otherwayes hardly to be overtaken without great blood shead and expence'. The Campbells had always been willing to put down the insolence of 'the remote rebellious lawless men' who lived in distant places, 'the horror of rocks, woods and mountains'.[38]

Lorne's plea did not win pardon for his father, but the argument that Campbell power must be maintained if the Highlands were to be kept in control was widely accepted. Moreover, it was argued that the destruction of the house of Argyll would be unjust as well as inexpedient. Even if the marquis of Argyll deserved forfeiture and death, his son Lord Lorne had served the king faithfully in the 1650s; why should he share in his father's disgrace? Such reasoning had the support of the king's secretary, the earl of Lauderdale, and eventually prevailed.

In 1663 the death sentence on Lorne was remitted; he was restored to the title of earl (though not of marquis) of Argyll, and he was granted a gift of his father's forfeited lands and offices.[39] As a great feudal landholder, a clan chief, sheriff of Argyll and justice general of Argyll and the Isles, the new earl immediately became the dominant figure in the Highlands. But one complication in the restoration of his family's property was to lead to endless trouble.

When, in the 1640s, the covenanters had forfeited the marquis of Huntly's estates they had granted them to the marquis of Argyll to help to compensate him for his losses. To strengthen this title granted by a revolutionary government, Argyll had proceeded to buy up the right to many debts owed by Huntly, granting the creditors instead the right to seek payment from him. Thus, Argyll hoped, even if his right to Huntly's lands by gift of the covenanters' regime was overturned, he would still have a good claim to the lands in payment of the Huntly debts now owed to him. When the marquis of Argyll was forfeited in 1661, Huntly's family lands were restored to him; but his responsibility for those debts of his family which were owed to Argyll was denied. Thus when Lord Lorne was restored to his father's property in 1663 he was held to be responsible for the debts due to Huntly's former creditors even though he was not given the Huntly lands, out of the revenues of which his father had intended to pay off the debts.

This arrangement was no doubt justified on the grounds that it would punish the Campbells financially for their past sins even while restoring them to most of their powers. Some such sop to the enemies of the Campbells was badly needed, for there was strong opposition to renewed favour to the new earl of Argyll: ratification of his restoration in the Scottish parliament in 1669 was not put to a vote for fear that it would be rejected.[40] But however it was justified, the decision to saddle the earl of Argyll with the Huntly debts proved disastrous. The only way Argyll could hope to satisfy his creditors was by being ruthless in collecting all debts due to him. His position in the years after his restoration was bound to be difficult. He was the government's main agent in the West Highlands and Isles and was expected to exact obedience to the law. But he was also the son of a traitor whose every move was watched with suspicion for any sign of disloyalty. Thus in 1664 he complained to Lauderdale that every time he acted in the interests of the peace of the Highlands there were complaints that he was serving his own interests. Everything he did was misinterpreted and reported to Edinburgh by Lord MacDonald and other resentful royalists. As peace and order were in his own interests, in serving the state he inevitably served himself as well. He had been urged to settle differences between himself and the earl of Seaforth, and was trying to do so; but he feared to do this in the normal way, by signing a bond of friendship with Seaforth, for his enemies would assert that he had drafted a new covenant.[41]

To the inevitable resentment of many clans towards Argyll there was now added hostility to his determination to force payment of all debts owing to him. The largest of such debts, and the ones which caused most controversy, were those owed by MacLean of Duart. Argyll offered to assign his MacLean debts directly to his creditors, who would then collect the money themselves, but the MacLeans ill-advisedly refused to agree to such an arrangement. Argyll was thus left caught between his creditors and debtors in a financial morass from which it proved impossible to escape.[42]

Even before the troubles of the 1640s and 1650s the MacLeans had been deeply in debt, and the wars which followed had greatly increased their indebtedness. Argyll had bought up the right to many of these debts, and in 1650 Sir Hector MacLean of Duart had admitted owing Argyll £60,000 Scots. The MacLeans claimed to have paid off some of the debts in the 1650s, but the clan's affairs appear to have been badly managed during two successive minorities following the deaths of Sir Hector in 1651 and Sir Allan in 1674, and the debt to Argyll mounted steadily. By the 1660s Argyll was claiming over £100,000 Scots, and in the following decade this rose to over £200,000. The MacLeans argued that this was far more than was really due from them, and it may well be that Argyll, exasperated by repeated failures to get satisfaction from them, ended by demanding more than his pound of flesh. But the law was on his side in what became the main issue; the debts were sufficient to give Argyll a claim to the MacLean lands in Morvern, Mull and Tiree unless they were paid. In 1674 Argyll launched an armed invasion to gain possession of the lands he claimed, but the MacLeans soon drove out most of the intruders and the Campbells did not regain full possession until a new invasion in 1679.[43]

The progress of this, the greatest feud and clan war of the Restoration period, caused increasing tension and disorder in the West Highlands, with large-scale raids and counter-raids. Other clans were drawn into the conflict, and hatred and distrust of Argyll grew. His ruthless pursuit of his legal rights was 'forced upon him by dire necessity'.[44] The government had forced him into an impossible financial situation while simultaneously granting him wide responsibilities for the peace of the Highlands. His conduct in pursuing the MacLeans soon won him an unenviable reputation as a man who was defrauding his own creditors by failing to pay them while viciously oppressing his debtors. Inevitably this reputation and his concentration on his financial difficulties reduced his effectiveness as the representative of central government in the west.

The Campbell-MacLean feud was outstanding in its scale and its culmination in open warfare, but in another sense it was typical of the period in that one side (the Campbells) had full official support for its actions. Warfare in which neither side could claim the positive approval of government or law had largely disappeared from the Highlands after 1600, and even after the turmoil of 1637-60 it did not revive. Battles, therefore, seldom took place unless one party — usually the aggressor — had some official sanction for its conduct. Thus in the conflict at Mulroy in 1688 (usually regarded as the last inter-clan battle) the MacKintoshes had been reinforced by government troops in trying (unsuccessfully) to subdue the MacDonalds of Keppoch. Raiding and small-scale violence between clans were still common, but such major battles were rare. Increasingly it seems that feuds once largely pursued by violence were instead forwarded primarily by resort to the intricacies of the laws of landholding and debt. Violence arising from the traditional aggressiveness of chiefs towards each other was partly sublimated into endless legal claims and processes. Of course resort to such methods of aggrandisement at the expense of others had been used in the Highlands for generations by the more successful clans; but now they appear to become general. It was symptomatic of such changes that when (in 1672) the earl of Seaforth and Lord Reay signed a bond of friendship a new clause was added to older promises of mutual good will and support: 'none of us shall buy pleas or debts, nor have wee bought any against other.'[45] Guarantees were now needed against your neighbour's lawyer as well as against his sword.

Quite why this development was taking place is not clear, but obviously the growing indebtedness of Highland chiefs, already detectable before 1637 and greatly increased by the ruinous wars that followed, had a central part in the process. The growing confusion of debts owed by and to chiefs combined with military conquests and political forfeitures to throw land and financial rights into confusion. Further, growing (if intermittent) government interference in the Highlands since the beginning of the century indicated to chiefs than when undertaking aggression it was increasingly wise to gain official approval by ensuring that you had some legal pretext — however far-fetched or unscrupulously exploited — on your side. It may also be true that increasing involvement in national affairs under the covenanters and the English was changing the attitude of chiefs more effectually than the statutes of Iona had done. For many chiefs attachment to the monarchy (and to the idea of Scotland that it symbolised) had become much more real than in the past. Chiefs who had fought for the king had come into more frequent contact with Lowland and English officials and politicians than their predecessors. After 1660 most leading chiefs paid at least occasional visits to court in London. In this new, wider world of national politics in which such chiefs were beginning to move, hesitantly at first, clan warfare (like many other features of clan life) was regarded as a sign of barbarism; and it appears that gradually chiefs came to accept and to adopt this attitude, or at least to understand that involvement in private war would lead to their exile from this new world they were entering. The ideals of a warrior society were in decay, being subverted from the top as chiefs adopted new outlooks and loyalties. Aggression must be confined to the legal forms developed and exploited by Lowland landlords, making use of the absurdities and complexities of the law, except in extreme cases. When chiefs did openly resort to violence they first gained the sanction of law and government. If they turned to violence without such support, their own part in instigating it had to be disguised.

Many chiefs seemed, outwardly at least, to have lost the taste for plundering raids and wars with neighbours. But violence did not disappear, or even decrease. Instead other forms of violence now come to predominate. After 1660, 'the Highlands were in a state of wild lawlessness. The scale of operations was smaller than in the sixteenth century and the manpower of the clans was seldom called out in private quarrels, but it was the heyday of the caterans and sporadic raiding was constant.'[46]

Already in the early seventeenth century in the Eastern Highlands the main problem of disorder had not been clan war and raid, openly inspired by chiefs, but the activities of bands of caterans or robbers, often giving allegiance to no chief or landlord. These bandits were frequently 'broken men' who were outside any recognised form of social order, Highland or Lowland. Living by plunder, sorning (forcible exaction of food and shelter) and blackmail (extortion of protection money), such gangs had proved impossible to control. They raided widely, often into Lowland areas bordering the Highlands on the south and east, but melted away into the hills or dispersed when pursued. With the decline in clan warfare this form of lawlessness had begun to emerge as a major problem in the west as well as the east even before 1637; and after 1660 the problem of broken men became acute throughout the Highlands on a much larger scale than before. The preceding quarter of a century of turmoil had torn many Highlanders loose from a settled place in clan society. Many had been driven from the land they had farmed. Communities and families had been broken up. Some, after years of war for clan, king, country or covenanters, had become addicted to lives of violence and lawlessness and had no wish to return to more settled ways. Others were unable to obtain any land to farm or graze, or to find any chief ready to take responsibility for them, and were thus forced into the life of broken men. If the troubles of 1637-60 had in some ways hastened the decay of the ideals of a warrior society among chiefs, they had also served to revive such ideals (though in a debased form) among many ordinary Highlanders.

One of the most important economic developments in Scotland after 1660 helped those who led lives of lawlessness. In the Highlands as in the Lowlands the cattle trade, and especially cattle exports to England, expanded rapidly.[47] Ever greater numbers of cattle being moved long distances through the Highlands proved tempting and easy prey for broken men to 'lift'. The busy movements of drovers through the Highlands also provided excellent cover for the movements of broken men. If asked to explain themselves, they could often plausibly claim to be drovers going about lawful business. Recognition of the connection between the booming cattle trade and the broken men is indicated by attempts by the privy council to introduce a system of licensing all drovers.[48]

Another guise under which broken men and other robbers moved through the Highlands was as members of the retinues of chiefs and other legitimate travellers. Chiefs and others were therefore forbidden to travel accompanied by any but their own domestic servants. This order suggests that many chiefs and other clan leaders were willing to aid thieves. They might no longer lead, or openly approve, cattle raids themselves, but they were not necessarily adverse to allowing bands of their clansmen to raid, or to acting as patrons of broken men. Their motives were probably mixed. They doubtless profited from such ventures, taking part of the proceeds in return for their help, or at least for their willingness to turn a blind eye. Giving occasional aid to broken men might be the only way a chief could prevent them raiding his own lands. Such men could also be used to raid neighbours and other enemies, thus allowing a chief to pursue a feud while denying any involvement. Finally, some chiefs may have allowed their own men to raid because clansmen regarded the raid as part of their birthright; too strict an insistence on rigid law and order might strain clan loyalties to breaking point. In 1663 Alexander MacDonald of Keppoch and his brother were murdered, evidently because the young chief had tried to bring unruly elements within the clan under control and prevent raiding and other lawlessness. One of those involved in the murder soon emerged as the new chief.[49] This late example of the replacement of a chief held to be unsatisfactory by leading clansmen may well have led other chiefs to hesitate before disciplining their subjects for causing disorder.

Chiefs proved incapable of preventing cattle raiding and its attendant violence and disorder. Government action proved equally ineffectual. Ordinary Highlanders seem to have celebrated the Restoration in 1660 with an orgy of robbery and violence, bursting free from the constraints of English military rule. Throughout the Highlands 'the law was set at nought with an audacity which seems at times to have filled the Council with despair'. Some urged that the garrisons established by the English at Inverness and Inverlochy should be maintained, but national sentiment insisted that all such symbols of English rule be removed — greatly to the advantage of the caterans. All the privy council could think of doing to deal with the situation was piously to restore the policies of James VI and summon all chiefs to appear. Only a handful did so, yet in the succeeding years the council repeatedly reinforced failure by renewed orders for chiefs to appear annually, orders which were ignored with equal monotony. Rather half-hearted attempts at additional policies proved equally ineffectual. Planting garrisons at strategic points (1664) failed because they were not properly maintained and were too small. Raising watches or Highland companies had no noticeable effects. The issuing of commissions to a few individuals to raise such forces represented an admission (1667) that insisting that all chiefs and landholders in the Highlands had a duty to suppress disorders was pointless. The duty lay 'upon many persons in generall, and no person doeth make it his work and is interested and employed in speciall to that effect' and therefore disorders 'doe abound and increase daylie'. Yet when the companies or watches failed to bring about any improvement the council simply reverted to the old discredited policy, summoning all chiefs to stamp out lawlessness.[50]

Difficulties which arose in trying to implement council policy in 1669 illustrate problems which recur throughout the period. Several nobles with Eastern Highland interests refused to be made responsible for maintaining the peace in the whole area. Optimism had been aroused by a decrease in disorder in the Highlands in the previous year, but now it was found that 'the theefes were only quiet because they were imployed to keep the rest from stealing; and for that hade great liberties allowed them', which clearly illustrates one difficulty in attempting to establish armed bodies of Highland police. Further, making certain great men specifically responsible for the depredations of thieves had led to a drop in the numbers of crimes reported, but it turned out that there had been no drop in the crime rate. All that had happened was that victims feared to complain of their losses for fear of arousing the wrath of the great men who would be legally bound to compensate them.[51]

The failure of the Restoration government to take more effective action to root out Highland lawlessness seems remarkable at first sight, but the explanation for it is simple. The Highlands were no longer the area which presented the most direct and dangerous challenge to the regime. It was the problem of how to crush opposition to the Restoration religious settlement that obsessed the king's ministers. Resistance was concentrated in the Western Lowlands, but support for the 'conventiclers' who refused to worship in the episcopalian state church and held their own conventicles instead was also strong in parts of the east. Alternating policies of repression and concession failed to restore religious unity to protestantism in Scotland, and resistance culminated in major rebellions in 1666 and 1679. Persecution drove the more extreme conventiclers into denying the legitimacy of the whole regime, even of the monarchy itself. The conventicler problem was thus clearly a far greater threat to the regime than Highland lawlessness directed almost entirely towards private gain. Suppression of crime must take second place to suppression of rebellion. It is true that when in 1667 (during the Second Anglo-Dutch War) a Dutch landing in Scotland was feared, Argyll reported that 'if, as God forbid, we should see any invasion, I feare the disorders [in the Highlands] would prove as great a retardment to his Majesties affaires, as the phanatiks [the conventiclers]'.[52] But Argyll exaggerated in order to provoke action for 'setling the Highlands'; and also, no doubt, in order to underline his own loyalty to the crown. The 1666 Pentland Rising by the conventiclers had led to fears that Argyll, with his family's presbyterian traditions, might sympathise with the rebels, and that his father's Lowland colony in Kintyre might support them. In an ostentatious display of loyalty Argyll had led a small expedition into Kintyre to root out any conventiclers.[53]

Lawlessness and violence might be endemic in the Highlands, but the loyalty of Highlanders and their chiefs (apart from occasional doubts about Argyll) to the crown was no longer questioned. If the chiefs had to choose in a crisis between the crown and the crown's main enemies, rebellious presbyterians, the regime was confident that most would choose the former. It was no longer feared that Highlanders would intrigue with foreign powers (as some had done in the previous century). The military and political links between the Highlands and Gaelic Ireland, which had survived the plantation of Ulster and revived strongly in the 1640s, had been finally broken in the 1650s (though some cultural links lingered on). The MacDonnells of Antrim had abandoned their Scottish ambitions. Thus fears that Highland lawlessness would aggravate the perennial Irish problem of the crown had disappeared. Highland disorder was accepted because there were more urgent matters which were given priority by the regime.

A startling demonstration of the growth of the tendency, present since the 1640s, to regard the Highlands as a centre of support for the crown came in 1678. In a desperate attempt to terrorise the conventiclers of the south-west into submission, all other expedients having failed, the regime raised the so-called Highland Host. About a third of this 8,000-strong force consisted of Lowland militia, but the rest were Highlanders. Recruitment was limited to the more 'civilised' Eastern Highlands, and the men raised there were led by respectable nobles, the marquis of Atholl and the earls of Perth, Mar, Moray and Caithness; but nonetheless the regime's reliance on such Gaels in a crisis was remarkable. The Highland Host terrorised the conventiclers for about a month and then was disbanded. The swift withdrawal of the Host was surprising, but was in part forced by the determination of the Highlanders themselves to return home. Many chieftains feared that in their absence their lands and homes would be open to attack by their neighbours and others, and were unwilling to give the king's interests priority over the clan's for long; and the clansmen were anxious to carry home the rich booty they had plundered in the name of the king. The government may indeed have been glad of an excuse to disperse the Host so quickly, for though it had been successful in cowing the conventiclers for the moment, it was a propaganda and public relations liability, providing the conventiclers and their sympathisers with plentiful ammunition. 'From the wild Highlands a host of Savages ... more terrible than Turks or Tartars, men who feared not God nor regarded man' had been sent against poor Godly 'civilised' protestants. The gentlemen of Ayrshire protested at the approach of 'so inhuman and barbarous a crew'. In spite of the services of many Highlanders to the crown during the troubles, many royalist Lowlanders joined opponents of the regime in regarding them as savages, and were dismayed that the crown should employ them. In the horrified reaction to the Host few seem to have noticed that though the Highlanders had plundered widely, they had been responsible for very little violence.[54]

The employment of the Highland Host had been, nonetheless, partly successful, and this combined with several other developments in the late 1670s to bring about far-reaching changes in official policy towards the Highlands. The Host, and its desire to disperse promptly, indicated both that the Highlands formed a potential bastion of support for the crown, and that the full potential of this loyalty could not be realised until disorder was suppressed and men could march out for the king without fearing their neighbours. To this was added the argument that the activities of the earl of Argyll were endangering the precarious *status quo* in the Western Highlands, and that (as he had government approval for his actions) his conduct in harrying the MacLeans might undermine the loyalty of some chiefs. As the Campbell-MacLean struggle approached its climax other clans began to fear for their own future; once the MacLeans were destroyed would any clan be able to withstand the relentless march northwards of Campbell power? Other chiefs, and some nobles with Highland interests, therefore began moves to support the MacLeans and undermine Argyll.

In the late 1660s the MacDonalds of Keppoch and Glengarry, the MacIans of Glencoe and the Camerons all sent men to Mull to help the MacLeans resist any attempt at a Campbell takeover. Lochiel led forces to Mull each summer for several years, encouraged by payments from the MacLeans, who in thus buying support from their neighbours increased their own financial problems.[55] Argyll's first invasion of Mull, in 1674, provoked a revival of support for the MacLeans by Lord MacDonald, who was soon joined by the Camerons. In 1675 Argyll, as feudal superior of some of the Camerons' lands, managed to persuade Lochiel to sign a contract undertaking to give token assistance to the Campbells in Mull; but Lord MacDonald remained defiant and many Camerons remained in arms. 'It is lyk they will pretend, it is to keep the cows,' remarked Argyll sarcastically; and he was was soon proved right in thus thinking the Camerons were concerned to do more than just defend their cattle.[56]

It was reported in 1676 that the 'ambitious grasping' of Argyll at mastery of the Western Highlands and Isles had led Seaforth, Atholl, Lord MacDonald, MacLeod of Dunvegan and others into 'a combination for bearing him down'.[57] The anti-Campbell alliance may not have been quite as extensive as this suggests, but it is clear that in the Lowlands as well as the Highlands the feeling was growing that though Argyll's actions were strictly legal they were oppressive and potentially dangerous. Yet the privy council at first continued to see the resistance of the MacLeans and their allies to Argyll as simply rebellious lawbreaking which must be suppressed. In October 1678 a new order for chiefs to appear in Edinburgh and give caution for keeping the peace was issued, and it was said that this was designed primarily to break up the combination against Argyll. Orders had already been given for the raising of two Highland companies of 150 men each, which were to be joined by 100 men from the army in suppressing disorder. Special responsibility for punishing criminals was given to the commanders of the two companies, and to the earls of Argyll, Caithness and Moray, and MacKintosh of Torcastle.[58]

Any doubts about the wisdom of granting Argyll such official support were temporarily swept aside by news of events in England. Panic was raised by the revelation of the alleged 'Popish Plot' (which in reality never existed) to murder the king and replace him by his Catholic brother and heir, James, duke of York. Leading protestants would be massacred and a papist tyranny established. By November 1678 the Scottish privy council was sending urgent orders for the disarming of all Highland papists. The following January a proclamation against all Scottish Catholics was issued, again ordering that they be disarmed. Lord MacDonald, Keppoch and several leading MacLeans were all regarded as Catholics (how justly it is impossible to say). Therefore when they failed to give up their arms and continued to defy Argyll it was feared thay they might not be concerned only with local issues; they might be involved in some great Catholic plot.

To try to prove their loyalty Lord MacDonald and the MacLeans wrote to the council claiming that they were only resisting Argyll to avoid being 'forever ruined and enslaved to him'; and they offered to provide forces to help to suppress the rebellious conventiclers of the south-west. The offer was ill-judged; to men terrified of cunning and devious Catholic machinations it sounded like an attempt to march armed Catholics into the Lowlands to further their own ends. The approaches of the Highland 'papists' were therefore rejected as insolent and threatening. Thus the fact that the culmination of the Argyll-MacLean feud coincided with panic over the 'Popish Plot' encouraged the council to continue to give enthusiastic support to Argyll's plans for a new invasion of Mull, providing him with troops and ammunition to second his own resources.

Argyll had succeeded in buying the neutrality of Lochiel (who since 1675 had reverted to open support for the MacLeans) by cancelling some debts due by him, a transaction which gave rise to the saying that 'Ewen has lost his God, and Argyle his money.' But the MacDonalds of Glengarry and Keppoch still aided the MacLeans, and the allies tried to divert attention from Mull by widespread plundering of Campbell lands on the mainland. It seemed, briefly, that the outbreak of open rebellion by the conventiclers in 1679 might save the MacLeans. In June the council wrote ordering Argyll to 'disentangle yourself from the expedition . . . against the rebellious people in the Highlands' and march his forces south to attack the conventiclers instead. But the Lowland rebels were promptly defeated without Argyll's help, and he proceeded to overrun Mull and the rest of the MacLean lands, crushing all resistance.[59]

This major clan war in the west increased fear, tension and disorder throughout the Highlands. In September 1679 the privy council was driven into a virtual admission that it had lost control. Plans to send substantial regular forces into the Highlands had had to be cancelled as the men were needed to serve against the conventiclers, and the council now temporarily abandoned any attempt to impose order within the Highlands by assigning 400 men to guard the passes which led from the Highlands into the Lowlands, to try at least to prevent broken men spreading disorder into the Lowlands.[60]

Argyll had triumphed over the MacLeans; but his very triumph was to make a major contribution to his downfall. It drew attention to his oppressions, to the aggrandisement of the son of the arch-traitor the marquis of Argyll at the expense of clans which had fought for the king in the 1640s and 1650s, just at the moment that the power of Argyll's great protector, the duke of Lauderdale, collapsed. Lauderdale had dominated Scottish politics since the early 1660s, government of the country being largely entrusted to him. Opposition to the increasing corruption and selfishness of his regime, and to the inadequacy of his policies, finally brought about his downfall in 1679 when the complete failure of his policies for dealing with the conventiclers and the Highlands was revealed. The conventiclers had revolted, and reliance on Argyll in the Western Highlands had led to a major upheaval instead of stability.

The vacuum created by Lauderdale's fall was filled by James, duke of York, the king's brother. Charles sent James to Scotland in 1679 mainly because his presence in England was an embarrassment. James' open Catholicism and the Popish Plot were provoking attempts to secure his exclusion from succession to the crown. For the rest of Charles II's reign James was to have a major influence on government policy for Scotland, and his main concern was to ensure as far as possible that, when the time came, Scotland would support his claim to the throne. Looking at Highland policy from this point of view, it seemed folly to allow the advance of Argyll and the destruction of clans which had served the crown in battle — and some of which had Catholic sympathies. In the 1660s it had seemed expedient to ignore the grievances of such clans, for in the general enthusiasm for the Restoration of monarchy there had seemed no need to seek their positive support for the dynasty. Now, in the 1680s, the dynasty (in the person of the Catholic James) needed to rally all the support it could find to counter those who opposed it, or might later oppose it, on account of James' religion. The concentration of so much power in the hands of the Campbells looked dangerous in the light of their former support for the covenanters; and even if Argyll's basic loyalty to the regime was accepted, his rigid and tyrannical insistence on his legal rights, backed up by misuse of his own judicial powers, was damaging to the crown's interests. Personally James was on good terms with Argyll; but he decided that it was necessary to curb the earl's power.

Already by February 1680 James had worked out a 'scheme' aimed against Argyll which he revealed to his advisers.[61] This was probably the plan which he outlined in a letter of advice on the government of Scotland which he sent to the king. Charles should, his brother advised, depend on 'Loyal familys'. The 'extraordinary favours and partialities formerly shewn to the Lord Argile, could neither be answer'd nor without much difficulty amended, since that family had been so much advanced and so much power put imprudently into their hands'. Though it was admitted to be a matter of 'much difficulty', there is implicit here a determination to deprive Argyll of at least some of his judicial powers and feudal superiorities. As to the MacLean problem, James suggested that 'if the King would pleas to pay what was due to My Lord Argile, he might preserue that antient and Loyal Clan of the MacLanes.' The clan would then, in gratitude, become a great support to royal interests in the Highlands, whereas if 'the Earle of Argile haue the MacLanes estate, he would be greater than it were fit for a subject to be'.

Though deprived of some of his powers and of the MacLean lands (compensation being given for the latter), Argyll was to be allowed to remain one of the government's main agents in the Highlands. This is made clear by further suggestions made by James as to Highland policy. He complained that the two Highland companies supposedly employed to suppress Highland thieves were useless, and indeed in reality hardly existed, as the captains kept few men in arms so they could pocket the excess pay. James therefore proposed that the money used to pay the companies should instead be used to pay the four great men of the Highlands, Huntly, Atholl, Argyll and Seaforth. Each would get about £700 sterling a year in return for making himself responsible for any thefts by men from his quarter of the Highlands. Payment would depend on their carrying out their duties zealously, and would make them more dependent on the crown than in the past.

There is no sign in all this advice of James having (at this point, at least) any general commitment to the destruction of the dependence of many clans on feudal lords, so as to make all chiefs directly dependent on the crown, although this is sometimes alleged. Argyll's dangerous pre-eminence was to be removed. The loyal MacLeans were to be saved from ruin. But, more comprehensively and systematically than before, the Highlands were to be carved up into four areas under the overall control of great 'feudal' nobles with Highland interests.

These plans of James' are usually dated to 1681,[62] but two pieces of evidence suggest early 1680 as the correct date. Firstly, in February 1680 the privy council issued a commission for keeping the peace of the Highlands to the four nobles named by James; and as his plan had suggested, they were to be paid substantial salaries, £500 sterling each *per annum*.[63] Secondly, in mid-1680 Charles II intervened to save the MacLeans of Duart from complete ruin, stating that on the ending of the Argyll-MacLean feud 'the settlement of the peace of the Highlands doth very much depend'. Argyll was eventually ordered to see that Duart was left with an income of £300 sterling a year, part at least of this being provided by the rents of the island of Tiree, which was to be restored to Duart.[64]

Argyll appears to have accepted, reluctantly, responsibility for saving Duart, but he evidently resisted attempts to persuade him to reach some general agreement with his own creditors and to surrender some superiorities and judicial powers. Pressure to force him to do so continued to grow. By early 1681 the duchess of Lauderdale knew enough of the offensive against Argyll being mounted by James (in alliance with the earl's creditors, debtors and other enemies) to write that 'I wish the Earl of Argyll would sell his estates, so as his family may not be a prey to his enemies, who are too many, and may be too powerful, if he take not good and speedy heed.'[65] When parliament met in Edinburgh in 1681, moves were made towards starting an inquiry into Argyll's exercise of his jurisdictions. These moves had been approved by James; but suddenly he insisted that parliament drop the matter. His motives are not clear. He may have decided that to encourage Argyll's personal enemies to savage him in parliament would seem unjust, and thus arouse sympathy for him. Or he may have staged events in the hope of demonstrating to Argyll how strong opposition to him in parliament was, and thus persuade him to make the concessions James was demanding as the price of further protection against parliament. The reason James himself gave for his action was that he had decided that Argyll, as a servant of the king whose powers had been granted to him by the king, should not be answerable to parliament for his exercise of these powers, as that would undermine royal prerogative.[66]

Argyll's own subsequent conduct suggests that he may have put yet another interpretation on James' actions, concluding that they indicated that James was afraid to go ahead with action against him. Certainly Argyll now showed the foolhardy and provocative arrogance of a man who believed himself invulnerable. Parliament had passed the Test Act introducing an oath designed to bind men as strongly as possible to acceptance of the true hereditary succession to the crown, thus ratifying James' right to succeed his brother. To make the oath palatable, and still fears about the consequences of accepting a Catholic as king, the oath also bound signatories to the established protestant church. While the act was being debated in parliament, Argyll suggested that each king's sons and brothers should be required to swear the oath, and thus bind themselves to protestantism. The amendment was defeated, and Argyll had been willing that an exception should be made for James, freeing him of the oath. But nonetheless Argyll's suggestion must have reinforced James' fears that the over-great house of Argyll would again emerge as a champion of extreme protestantism and oppose a Catholic succession.

As if determined to display his immunity from attack, Argyll then proceeded to add insult to injury by declaring that he himself would only take the rather confused oath as far as it was consistent with itself. Such open contempt for the oath, imposition of which had become central to royal policy in Scotland, threatened to reduce it to absurdity. Argyll's enemies urged that such defiance must be punished. Argyll was arrested, tried, and condemned to death for treason. Yet even now, it seems, there was no intention of ruining him completely. His life and lands were to be spared, but he was to be taught a lesson by showing that he could easily be convicted and his life put in jeopardy if he went too far; and it was resolved to 'make use of this occasion to get him more into their [Charles' and James'] power, and forfeit certain Jurisdictions and superiorities which he and his predecessors had surreptitiously acquir'd, and most tyranicaly exercised'. Charles therefore consulted James over how best to dispose of Argyll's superiorities and jurisdictions 'which he thought too much for any one Subject, and was glad (he sayd) he had got them out of so ill hands'.[67]

There seems no reason to doubt this account of the intentions of the royal brothers. Argyll's wings were to be clipped, more severely than had been planned before his trial, but his neck was not to be wrung. But they had blundered. The Test Act oath itself turned out to be a miscalculation, as it served to display how many opposed a Catholic succession instead of emphasising general acceptance of it. And the conviction of Argyll on what seemed so trifling a pretext immediately turned him into a protestant martyr in the eyes of many. James doubtless saw the conviction as following on a long series of actions by Argyll, but legally the conviction rested on a single remark, reckless but justifiable, about the oath. To most Scots, therefore, the conviction seemed unjust and tyrannical. To make matters worse, Argyll escaped from Edinburgh Castle before indignation at his conviction could be dispersed by the intended royal pardon. He fled first to London, then to Holland, where protestant enemies of James were gathering. It was too late to think of pardoning him. Now that he had joined the regime's enemies the forfeiture of his title and lands, which followed on his conviction, had to be implemented.

Thus more by accident than design Charles II forfeited a head of the house of Argyll for the second time in twenty years. He soon followed precedent again by restoring a second Lord Lorne, to avoid visiting the sins of the father on the son. The earl's son had married Lauderdale's step-daughter, and now Lauderdale's influence (though declining) again contributed to the preservation of the Campbell chiefs. But the restoration was very partial this time. Charles II was well aware that he had 'not been well informed when he raised Argyl so high last time he was in this condition'. Therefore, in spite of Lorne's pleas, his father's jurisdictions and superiorities were not returned to him. Not only did he not get his father's title, his own title of Lord Lorne was forfeited (though for convenience it will be used here). Even lands of which the earls had had actual possession (as opposed to holding superiorities over them) were not fully restored. Inveraray was confiscated. Lorne was to retain land worth £15,000 Scots a year, and allowances were to be made to other members of the family. But the rest of the estates were to be used to pay off, at last, his father's and grandfather's debts, and to give some compensation to families ruined by his grandfather when they had served the king in the 1640s. Only after these calls on the estate revenues had been met was any surplus to revert to Lorne.[68] News of this humiliation of the Campbells must have brought joy to the anti-Campbell clans, though it is doubtful that any in fact benefited materially through compensation for past sufferings in the few years before political revolution restored the Campbells to power.

James' hopes that the Highlands could be settled by assigning the task to Argyll and three other nobles had proved unfounded even before Argyll's disgrace. Therefore in March 1681 he got the privy council to agree to raise two new Highland companies; but they were to be composed of Lowlanders. Such 'neutrall and disinterested persons' would, he argued, 'receaue more universal obedience from and be more terrible to all of them [the clans] than any natives can be'. The companies were to be self-supporting, it was hoped, living off the lands of law-breakers, and the men were to be recruited from the regular army. However, this new initiative was combined with yet another repetition of the tired old summonses to chiefs to appear annually in Edinburgh. And, as usual, all these orders, new and old, proved ineffectual in practice. Late in 1681 the council ordered the establishment of a garrison at Inverlochy, but early the following year Lochiel captured and drove out the soldiers with contemptuous ease.[69]

Such outrages inspired another commission for securing the peace of the Highlands. Commissioners for the pacification were appointed and were to move through the Highlands accompanied by armed forces and hold justice courts. Surprisingly, for once the commissioners entrusted with such duties soon actually began to meet and take action, though why they should have shown a zeal lacked by their many predecessors is not clear. Their records show them moving from place to place taking bonds from chiefs and others, trying cases, executing the guilty. In gaining at least partial obedience from some chiefs, they may have benefited to some extent by reactions to the fall of Argyll: if the government could ruin the greatest man in the Highlands, then lesser chiefs would hesitate before openly defying it. However, the success of the commissioners was largely confined to the east. When in August 1683 they ventured to Inverlochy in the more turbulent west, Lochiel soon rid himself of their unwelcome presence. First he stirred up a mock riot evidently aimed against the commissioners, and then he intervened to 'protect' them by escorting them out of Lochaber to safety!

Perhaps as a result of this debacle, a professional soldier, Lieutenant General Drummond, was ordered to join the commissioners to strengthen their nerve. By mid-1684 he was reporting remarkable achievements. As a result of his efforts, areas bordering on the Highlands had 'never bein in such quyet and security for above 20 yeirs befor'; the task of preventing theft was not so great as had previously been thought. Crimes formerly complained of were no longer being committed; only a few fugitives from justice remained to be rounded up. Unfortunately this was a great exaggeration. Drummond was probably fooled by Highland lawbreakers dispersing, and crime ceasing, in an area on the approach of the commissioners; but they reassembled to continue their lawless lives once the commissioners had moved on. Nonetheless, under Drummond and his successor the earl of Breadalbane (formerly John Campbell of Glenorchy), the commissioners did have greater success in suppressing raiding and violence in the Highlands than any other body since the Restoration.[70]

In 1685, however, this progress in the Highlands was abruptly halted. Charles II died in February, and the commission for the peace of the Highlands lapsed. The duke of York succeeded as James VII of Scotland and II of England but his right to the throne was challenged by Charles II's illegitimate son, the duke of Monmouth; and when Monmouth led a rebellion in England, the exiled earl of Argyll landed in the Highlands to support his cause.

Argyll's venture was hopeless from the start. Many in Scotland were deeply troubled by having a Catholic king but very few were ready to rebel against him. The earl was no inspiring leader of men, and he received only limited support even from his own clansmen, as his financial difficulties had made him a harsh landlord. Moreover, rumours of Argyll's plottings had led in 1684 to the marquis of Atholl being created lieutenant of Argyllshire. He had then led 1,000 of his own men from the Eastern Highlands into the Campbell lands, disarming the population, arresting those whose loyalty was suspect and establishing a garrison at Inveraray.[71] Nonetheless, the arrival of Argyll led the government to summon men from many parts of the Highlands to converge on their old Campbell enemies. Nearly all the clans which had fought the Campbells in the 1640s under Montrose and Alasdair MacColla now contributed to ravaging their lands in 1685. The men of Atholl, the Stewarts of Appin, the MacIans of Glencoe, the MacDonalds of Glengarry, Keppoch and Clanranald, the MacDougalls of Lorne, the Camerons, the MacKintoshes and a few surviving MacAllisters from Kintyre all hastened to join the enterprise. As these forces concentrated against the earl of Argyll, the secret committee of the privy council (which was coordinating action against him) issued orders to Atholl, who was commanding the forces, which by their severity indicate the panic of the government at the prospect of a new Campbell-led protestant rebellion against the crown. All rebels who did not submit at once 'are to be killed, or disabled ever from fighting again; And burn all houses except honest men's, and destroy Inverarra and all the Castles . . . Let the women and children be Transported to remote Isles.'[72]

Execution of these draconian policies of massacre or mutilation of all rebels and banishment of their families was happily rendered unnecessary by events. The rebellion quickly collapsed, and Argyll was captured and (in accordance with his conviction in 1681) executed. Nonetheless the order is of interest as an indication of official attitudes. Highlanders were still regarded, through their barbarity, as meriting harsher punishment for their actions than Lowlanders. Lowland conventiclers had been in intermittent rebellion against the government for a generation, but though at times persecution of them had been harsh, no order contemplating general massacre or mutilation had ever been issued. But as soon as Western Highlanders, the Campbells, rebel, such action is ordered. Yet simultaneously the government is summoning other clans, including 'barbarous' westerners, to help defeat the rebels. Since the 1640s the Stewarts and their supporters had turned to the anti-Campbell clans from time to time for help; but they still saw westerners in general as little better than savages. It is interesting to find Lowlanders — and Eastern Highlanders — engaged in crushing the rising referring to the western clans as 'the Mackes' or 'the Maks',[73] terms similar to the contemptuous references by the English in Ireland to the native Irish as 'the Os and the Macs'.

Though there was, in the end, no general massacre of the Argyll rebels, punishment was nonetheless harsh. Atholl was instructed to execute all heritors (men who had a hereditary interest in the land they held) who had been in arms, and one hundred of the ringleaders from among the tenants and commons. Seventeen heritors are said to have been executed as a result of this order,[74] and for several months after the collapse of the rebellion the Campbells were subject to widespread and systematic pillaging by their triumphant enemies.[75]

Suppression of Argyll's rising took only a few weeks; but these weeks undid any progress made in stamping out disorder in 1682-4. Many Highlanders had willingly turned out in arms to serve the crown against the Campbells, but once they were in arms it was impossible to stop them engaging in raiding which had nothing to do with the cause in hand; and the concentration of both clan and government forces against Argyll left many areas without protection from broken men, who seem to have exploited the situation enthusiastically. The commission for pacifying the Highlands was renewed late in 1685, but the following year it was admitted that the problem of theft and local disorder had got out of control in much of the southern and central Highlands. The commissioners reported that lack of both money and troops was preventing them from acting effectively. Lieutenant General Drummond (now Lord Strathallan) was sent into the Highlands with some troops, and soon announced that he had 'reduced the Highlands to a full quiet and peace', but as in 1683 he was wildly over-optimistic. By the summer of 1688 theft and depredation were thriving throughout the Highlands and the government seemed as far as ever from being able to cope with the problem.[76]

As throughout the Restoration period, Highland disorder presented much less of a threat to the crown than Lowland religious and political discontent, so no sustained effort to settle the Highlands was undertaken. Only once, briefly in 1685, had a Highland issue been given first priority by the government; and that was partly because Argyll's rebellion was more than just a Highland issue; the earl had hoped to act in alliance with religious dissidents in the Lowlands. It is necessary to stress this point — that there is no sign of a major and comprehensive rethinking of the regime's Highland policies under James VII in the 1680s; and that, in particular, there is no evidence whatever before James was dethroned to suggest that he planned to abolish all feudal superiorities in the Highlands. Once in exile, James apparently did woo the chiefs by promising to 'free them from all manner of vassalage and dependence on the great men their neighbours' so they might be 'freed from the tyranny and oppression of these superiours' and 'hav their sole dependence on the croun'.[77] But while successively duke of York and a reigning king, his approach to Highland problems had been much more limited than this. He had wanted to curb (but not destroy) the house of Argyll, and to encourage and support clans which had demonstrated their loyalty to the crown in the 1640s and 1650s. Accident and miscalculation had forced him, in one respect, to carry these policies much further than he intended; he had virtually to destroy the house of Argyll. The significance of this accident was great. In the 1680s, for the first time since the 1640s, the cause of the Stewarts became closely identified with hatred of the Campbells. In the 1650s Lorne's royalism had complicated the issue, and in the 1660s and 1670s favour to him as earl of Argyll had prevented the execution of his father, the marquis, having the effect on Campbell fortunes that many Highlanders had hoped for.

Argyll's feudal superiorities were forfeited to the crown in 1681 along with the rest of his property. But there was no move towards annexing these superiorities to the crown and thus making many men who had been dependent on Argyll directly dependent on the crown, as a first step towards a general abolition of superiorities. This can be clearly seen by looking at the example which is usually taken to demonstrate the opposite, that there was a general move against superiorities. As in interpreting much of Highland history since the 1650s, the test case is that of Ewen Cameron of Lochiel, as through the work of his biographer we know more about him than about any other chief.

Lochiel was in some ways the most troublesome chief in what was often the most troublesome region of the Highlands. As has been seen, in the early 1680s alone he was responsible for driving a government garrison out of Inverlochy and for preventing the commissioners for pacification from carrying out their work there. Yet he won a measure of personal favour and protection from James, presumably by emphasising his exploits against the English in the 1650s and by stressing his devotion to the crown. Moreover he evidently managed to convince James that some of the problems of Lochaber arose from the fragmented and confused pattern of landholding and feudal superiorities of the area; and James is alleged to have told him that it was a pity he should be dependent on anyone but the king.[78] But while James showed friendship to this chief, who presented himself as a loyal servant of the crown in spite of his frequent and flagrant breaches of the law, he obviously could hardly regard him as the ideal subject. He seems to have been fascinated and amused by the behaviour of this bizarre tribesman from the Gaelic north, and to have patronised him unmercifully. If in the later 1650s Lochiel had rather become the pet chief of the English, in the 1680s he was in danger of becoming James' tame savage.

Two anecdotes related by Lochiel's biographer as demonstrating his friendship with James in fact reveal also the extent to which James' favour was coloured by condescension and underlying distrust. In 1681, as part of his policy of giving at least token recognition to chiefs who had served his father and brother, James decided to knight Lochiel. He wished to carry out the ritual with Lochiel's own sword, but when he attempted to draw it the sword stuck in its scabbard, and Lochiel himself had to free it. On this James remarked that it was clearly seen that Lochiel's sword obeyed no hand but his own.[79] The comment was a humorous one, but a serious point may well underlie it, a recognition that in spite of Lochiel's expressions of passionate devotion to the king, he would give priority to the interests of himself and his clan.

Fears about Lochiel's loyalty to the crown were so strong, indeed, that when he raised men to help defeat Argyll's rebellion there were fears that he intended to join the rebels. Though Lochiel found Argyll's position as superior of some of his lands irksome, he had generally been on good terms with the earl, and when the latter landed in Scotland Lochiel was rumoured to be in correspondence with him. Suspicion of him was intensified when his men mistakenly attacked some of the marquis of Atholl's men and killed four or five of them, and Lochiel may have only escaped arrest through fear that such action would provoke the other 'loyal' western chiefs into mutiny.[80] By a hasty visit to court Lochiel won James' protection, but again the king's ambivalent attitude to him was revealed in joking remarks. James introduced his protégé at court as 'the King of the Thieves', thus indicating his attitude to the Camerons as well as to their chief, and pretended to fear that he would steal horses from the royal stables.[81] It is surprising that a supposedly proud Highland chief should swallow such insults, however light-heartedly delivered.

On the forfeiture of Argyll in 1681 Lochiel had at first seemed unlikely to benefit, for Argyll's superiorities over him were transferred to the duke of Gordon (as the marquis of Huntly had now become), who already held some superiorities in Lochaber. From the point of view of the crown the transfer thus represented a rationalisation of the confusion over superiorities in the area. But here Lochiel's friendship with James worked to his advantage, for he managed to persuade James to act on the opinion he had earlier expressed, that Lochiel should be free of such dependence on others. James forced Gordon to surrender all his rights over Lochiel, the matter being finally settled in 1688; and in addition he promised to grant Lochiel Argyll's former feudal superiority over Ardnamurchan and Sunart.[82] Thus Argyll's superiority over Lochiel was abolished as a special case, not as part of a general policy; and both James and Lochiel were ready to create a new superiority giving the latter feudal rights of men who did not belong to his clan. Feudal superiorities were to be adjusted in certain instances, but neither they nor other aspects of feudal landholding were to be swept aside in order to revive some ideal of pure and natural kin-based clan authority with which they were incompatible.

The exceptional favour shown to Lochiel over superiorities may have raised the hopes of other chiefs. In particular it is tempting to see the culmination of the feud of the MacDonalds of Keppoch with the superior of their lands, MacKintosh of Torcastle, in the battle of Mulroy in 1688 as having some connection with Lochiel's good luck. Some of the Camerons helped the MacDonalds to defeat MacKintosh and the government troops sent to help him, and the victors may well have been inspired in their defiance of the law by the belief that they too might gain royal favour if they held out long enough. Lochiel himself was held to have encouraged the MacDonalds and his arrest was ordered.[83] Thus in the short term James' favour to Lochiel may have worked against his own interests as king, by encouraging chiefs to defy the law in the hope of some eventual settlement in their favour. But in the long run his treatment of Lochiel was very much to his advantage, for it led many chiefs to have high hopes of him, and once he was dethroned (before these hopes could be disappointed) this encouraged them to uphold his cause. But what MacDonald of Keppoch, like Lochiel, objected to was not something specifically 'feudal' and objectionable in principle; it was their own dependency on other chiefs they disliked, and they had no objections to superiorities where they could benefit from them.

It is, indeed, arguable that the seventeenth century saw the triumph of 'feudalism' in the Highlands and the clan, rather than the culmination of resistance to it. Partly this 'feudalism' was forced on the chiefs as the only system of landholding the central government would recognise as legitimate; but partly also chiefs accepted it willingly because it was (and in many cases long had been) useful to them. It could reinforce their existing claims to power. It could help define — and extend — their spheres of influence. 'Feudal' primogeniture in the succession of chiefs became all but universal. The 'loyal' clans which supported the Jacobite movement after 1688 were thus much more 'feudal' than the same clans had been when, as 'disloyal' clans, they had defied James VI and his predecessors.[84] In view of the supposedly inevitable conflict between antural clan patriarchy and artificial feudalism it is ironic that when, after the 1745-6 rising, decisive government action was at last taken to destroy clanship, action was largely aimed at destroying relics of feudalism, now seen as something largely confined to the Highalnds and anachronistic in an age of progress and improvement.[85]

James VII had no plans for any great, revolutionary reforms in the Highlands. But he had destroyed the supremacy of the Campbells, and he had shown himself willing to do something to acknowledge the services of the clans which had fought for the crown in the 1640s and 1650s. Accident had thrown the dynasty and the anti-Campbell clans together in the middle of the century, but James was the only Stewart who showed them any positive favour. Their loyalty to him was very much a matter of 'Jacobitism' rather than 'Stewartism', loyalty to the man rather than the dynasty. Thus Highland Jacobitism owed much to short-term developments in the 1680s. That was the only decade in which Stewart and anti-Campbell causes were combined while the Stewarts were in power. But the longer-term tendency for anti-Campbell interests to identify themselves with the cause of the dynasty whenever the latter was deprived of power by revolutionary regimes (the covenanters; the English; the Williamites) which turned to the Campbells for support in the Highlands was also clearly important. And of course it was not purely anti-Campbell sentiments which led many clans to turn towards the Stewarts at such times. The revolutionary 'Lowland' regimes seemed to pose greater threats to the interests and the autonomy of the clans than the Stewarts they superseded; through greater zeal and efficiency in implementing the 'Stewart' policies of James VI; through religious policies offensive to many chiefs; and through the very fact that they were 'revolutionary' regimes and thus unacceptable to conservative Highlanders who took the continuance of the Stewart monarchy for granted, even though in practice they sought to ignore the demands it made on them. Thus there would have been Highland resistance to these revolutionary regimes even if they had not tended to support and use the Campbells; but the fact that they did identify with Campbell interests undoubtedly increased the scale and zeal of Highland resistance to them. The statement that 'if it had not been for the house of Argyll, there would probably not have been a Jacobite cause in the West Highlands'[86] may not be entirely true, but there is much truth in it.

In the 1640s the alliance between the Stewarts and Highland opposition to the central government of the covenanters (and to the Campbells) had been largely an alliance of expediency. Mutual suspicion and hostility were strong, and divergent ambitions obvious. But by 1688-9, when Scotland followed England in dethroning James VII in favour of William II, the alliance was much more positive; there was genuine Highland devotion to the cause of James VII which was intensified by shared misfortune (the suppression of Highland resistance and the restoration of the house of Argyll by the Williamites, and the long exile of the king).

The emergence of Highland Jacobitism posed a major Highland problem to the Williamites. But use of the general term 'Highland problem' to denote the difficulties all regimes faced in dealing with the Highlands from the sixteenth to the mid-eighteenth centuries conceals the fact that the 'problem' in fact changed dramatically between the first and the last decade of the seventeenth century. James VI had been faced with a political system in the West Highlands in which many chiefs were free to wage wars, make alliances with and against each other, and in general conduct their affairs without reference to Edinburgh. But what the chiefs concerned sought through this defiance of central authority was simply the right to ignore it. They did not deny that James was legitimate king of all Scotland. By contrast, under William II the Highlanders who resisted rule from Edinburgh were seeking not just to ignore the regime but to overthrow it by force. They were committed to replacing the Stewarts on the throne. For William, therefore, as for the covenanters in the 1640s and the English in the 1650s, the 'Highland problem' they faced was that of a direct challenge to the existence of their regimes. The common complaint in 1600 had been that many chiefs were trying to avoid taking any part in national affairs and politics. In the course of the century Lowland pressures forced such chiefs into involving themselves in national politics in order to defend their interests. Thus by the 1690s the complaint was that chiefs were seeking far too great a part in national politics; they were trying to overthrow the regime.

In the alliance of many of the clans which had formerly been the most 'disloyal' in the Highlands with the Stewarts there is paradox as well as tragedy. Both tragedy and paradox lie in the fact that the Jacobite clans, fighting to preserve their way of life and autonomy, found themselves led by circumstances into fighting for a dynasty which had shown little sympathy for them (and indeed had usually been actively hostile to them) when it was in power. With the partial exception of James VII, the Stewart kings managed to find virtue in Highlanders only when they desperately needed Highlanders to fight and die for them. James, and his son and grandson, appealed to Scottish Jacobites to fight for them though they had at heart little interest in Scotland. They sought to use Scottish Jacobites to help them gain their real objective, the English throne. Similarily they were only interested in the Highlands in so far as Highland Jacobites might help them to secure Scotland as a step towards securing England. If Scotland was important to them mainly as a back door into England, the Highlands were important as a back door into the Lowlands.

Not only was the cause Highland Jacobites fought for alien to them in this way, it was also unsuccessful. By attaching themselves to a wider cause in their attempts to protect their interests, culture and life, they brought on themselves (in the mid-eighteenth century) a much more systematic and brutal attack on clan and culture than would otherwise have taken place. The final suppression of the clans was provoked not by the centuries-old problem of Highland lawlessness, nor by the equally old hostility to Highland culture, but by the need to destroy an attempt to impose a political revolution on the rest of Britain.

Highland Jacobites backed a loser in the dynastic stakes. This was a tragic miscalculation; but it was almost inevitable. Only losers, who had already lost power in London and Edinburgh, were ready to flatter Highlanders with hopes that their interests would be given priority.

Alliance with the Stewarts brought disaster after 1745. But from the start involvement in the Stewart cause presented a more insidious threat to the interests of the Gael. Highland support for the Stewarts in their times of trouble largely arose, in the first instance, from a desire to protect Highland separateness. But the alliance involved chiefs in much closer contact than ever before with Lowland and English politicians; and the wider cause which they now fought for was based on Lowland and English traditions and values. Inevitably the chiefs were influenced by these values, and this began (or at least hastened) the alienation of chiefs from their native culture and attitudes. It is here that the paradox lies. In seeking to resist alien, external pressure on their world, they had to enter the politics of the alien world that was threatening them, and, in doing so, to begin to accept its values. The widening of the horizons of chiefs and at least some of their clansmen which this brought about is well illustrated by a development in Gaelic poetry. In the middle and later seventeenth century, poems concerned with national political issues appear and become common for the first time. In this political verse 'we see for the first time an awareness of a Scottish rather than a purely Highland identity, and of external forces pressing on the lives and sensibilities of private persons. Of course, political events are still viewed through the clan system, but their relevance to more than the immediate members of the clan is realised.'[87] The greatest of these political poets was Ian Lom; and it is symptomatic of the ambivalence of Highland attitudes to this wider world that, though he shows in his poetry his passionate involvement in national political issues, at the same time he denounces the effects that contact with this wider world has on the lives and values of chiefs. A poem which Ian Lom addressed to Lord MacDonald (in the 1660s or 1670s) complained of the frequent absences of the Glengarry chief through visits to court:

> You seem to me to be a long time in England, being ruined by gaming.
> I would prefer you in a coat and plaid than in a cloak which fastens;
> And that you should walk in a sprightly manner in trews made of tartan
> cloth.[88]

Here in the 1660s we have an early example of the type of complaint against chiefs which was to become commonplace in the eighteenth century as clanship declined: denunciation of absentee chiefs who ruined themselves by extravagant living in the south, of chiefs who alienated themselves from their clansmen by adopting alien ways, which were often most immediately evident through changes in the way they dressed. It is true that one of the earliest and greatest examples of this process is provided by the Campbells[89] whose traditional role of guardian of the interests of 'Lowland' government had exposed them to strong Lowland influence for generations; but involvement in Jacobitism hastened their enemies down the same road.

Alasdair MacColla, the great hero of the Gael, in fighting for his clan and people, had thus played a leading part in initiating political and military developments which were ultimately, in ways which could not have been predicted, to contribute to the destruction of the life and culture he had championed. The pressures of Lowland-English civilisation, political, military, social and economic, proved irresistible.

NOTES

1. W. Ferguson, *Scotland's relations with England. A survey to 1707* (Edinburgh 1977), 129.

2. Cowan, *Montrose*, 233.

3. HMC 21: *Hamilton*, i.125-6; D. Stevenson, *Revolution and counter-revolution in Scotland* (London 1977), 110-11.

4. Ibid, 216-17.

5. Ibid, 218-19; SRO, PA.11/7, ff.1v-2.

6. Stevenson, *Revolution and counter-revolution*, 145-8; SRO, PA.11/8, f.26.

7. Stevenson, *Revolution and counter-revolution*, 158,161-3.

8. [J. Drummond], *Memoirs of Sir Ewen Cameron of Locheill* (Abbotsford Club, 1842), 122.

9. Stevenson, *Revolution and counter-revolution*, 185-8.

10. *APS*, VI.ii.623.

11. J.P. MacLean, *A history of the Clan MacLean* (Cincinnati 1889), 179-83; Grant, *The Macleods*, 292-7; Drummond, *Locheill*, 94-5,96-7; Mackenzie, *Orain Iain Luim*, 265-6,289; Fraser, *Frasers*, 379-81,384; Cunningham, *Loyal clans*, 278.

12. Ibid, 278.

13. Ibid, 278; Drummond, *Locheill*, 82-4.

14. Ibid, 88,90.

15. Stevenson, *Revolution and counter-revolution*, 200-1; SRO, PA.11/11, f.25v.

16. C.H. Firth (ed), *Scotland and the Commonwealth* (SHS 1895), 185.

17. J. Gwynne, *Military memoirs of the great civil war . . . and an account of the earl of Glencairn's expedition* (Edinburgh 1822), 175-9. For other accounts of the reasons for the duel see C.H. Firth (ed), *Scotland and the Protectorate* (SHS 1899), 89 and S.R. Gardiner, *History of the Commonwealth and Protectorate* (4 vols, London 1903), iii.100.

18. Firth, *Protectorate*, 89.

19. Firth, *Commonwealth*, 220; Gwynne, *Memoirs*, 163-5.

20. McKerral, *Kintyre*, 80-102; Gardiner, *Commonwealth and Protectorate*, iii.93-4.

21. Firth, *Commonwealth*, 309,311; Firth, *Protectorate*, 111-12.

22. For the 1653-5 rising in general see Gardiner, *Commonwealth and Protectorate*, iii.85-110 the two collections of documents by Firth cited above, and F.D. Dow, *Cromwellian Scotland* (Edinburgh 1979).

23. Gardiner, *Commonwealth and Protectorate*, iii.107-8.

24. Firth, *Commonwealth*, 148-9; 'Diurnal of occurences in Scotland' (extracts from *Mercurius Politicus*) in J. Maidment (ed), *Miscellany*, ii (Spottiswoode Society, 1845), 117-18.

25. Firth, *Protectorate*, 234-7,269-82,285-8.

26. Ibid, xxxix-xliii; Drummond, *Locheill*, 110-51.

27. Ibid, 160-2; Cunningham, *Loyal clans*, 298; APS, vii.295-6.

28. Macdonald, *Clan Donald*, ii.438,439,782-3; Firth, *Protectorate*, xxxvii,288n,384.

29. Drummond, *Locheill*, 107; Macdonald, *Clan Donald*, ii.446.

30. Drummond, *Locheill*, 155.

31. Ibid, 139.

32. Ibid, 151.

33. Ibid, 162-6.

34. Cunningham, *Loyal clans*, 293-4,297,300,303.

35. Drummond, *Locheill*, 163.

36. Grant, *The Macleods*, 307.

37. G.E. Cokayne, *The complete peerage* (revised ed, 14 vols, London 1910-59), viii.342; Macdonald, *Clan Donald*, ii.441,640,757-60, iii.37-8,166-9,654-5; *Collectanea de rebus Albanicis* (Iona Club, 1847), 207-8; *RPCS, 1669-72*, 552-3; Mackenzie, *Orain Iain Luim*, 94-101,276.

38. Ibid, 78; *Letters to the Argyll family* (Maitland Club, 1839), 49-50.

39. J. Willcock, *A Scots earl in covenanting times; being the life and times of Archibald 9th earl of Argyll* (Edinburgh 1907), 115-22,131-2; HMC 5: *6th Report*, 632.

40. Drummond, *Locheill*, 168; Sir George Mackenzie, *Memoirs of the affairs of Scotland* (Edinburgh 1821), 37-8,70-2,177-80; A. Lang, *Sir George Mackenzie* (London 1909), 207-8, 211; Cunningham, *Loyal clans*, 314-15.

41. *Letters from Archibald, earl of Argyll, to John, duke of Lauderdale* (Bannatyne Club, 1829), 9,12-13,14.

42. Drummond, *Locheill*, 195.

43. MacLean, *Clan MacLean*, 184-94; J.R.N. Macphail (ed), 'Papers relating to the Macleans of Duart, 1670-1680', *Highland papers*, i (SHS, 1914), 246-9; Lang, *Mackenzie*, 208-12; Drummond, *Locheill*, 193-204; *RPCS, 1673-6*, xxv-xxvi, *1674-8*, xxii-xxiii.

44. Cunningham, *Loyal clans*, 313.

45. I. Grimble, *Chief of Mackay* (London 1965), 178, quoting A. Mackay, *The book of Mackay* (Edinburgh 1906), 439-40.

46. Grant, *Macleods*, 319.

47. B. Lenman, *An economic history of modern Scotland* (London 1977), 23,39; T.C. Smout, *Scottish trade on the eve of union* (Edinburgh 1963), 212-13.

48. *RPCS, 1669-72*, xxvi,312-13, *1673-6*, xxiii, *1678-80*, xviii,51.

49. *RPCS*, 1669-72, xxvi,222,312, *1678-80*,xviii,51;Mackenzie, *Orain Iain Luim*, 82-95,108-13,268-74,279-80.

50. *RPCS, 1661-4*, xxx-xxxi,55-6,638, *1665-9*, xiv-xv,xxv-xxviii,324-9,458,469, *1669-72*, xxv-xxvi,52-9, *1673-6*, xxii-xxiv, *1676-8*, xxii-xxiii.

51. O. Airy (ed), *The Lauderdale papers* (3 vols, Camden Society 1884-5), ii.134,137.

52. *Letters of . . . Argyll to . . . Lauderdale*, 56.

53. Ibid, 39,41; McKerral, *Kintyre*, 114-16; Airy, *Lauderdale papers*, i.261.

54. J.R. Elder, *The Highland Host of 1678* (London 1914), especially pp.16-18,34,36-9,46,62-3,80-2,84,125-6,134,136.

55. Drummond, *Locheill*, 196-8; Mackenzie, *Orain Iain Luim*, 142-3,153-8,181,292-3,295-7.

56. Drummond, *Locheill*, 198-202; HMC 5: *6th Report*, 617.

57. Sir John Lauder of Fountainhall, *Historical notices of Scottish affairs* (2 vols, Bannatyne Club, 1848), i.108.

58. Ibid, i.204-5; *RPCS, 1678-80*, xvii-xviii,1-2,34-44; *CSPD, 1678*, 468.

59. *RPCS, 1678-80*, xviii,58-9,101-4,165,169-73; Lang, *Mackenzie*, 213; HMC 5: *6th Report*, 622,628-9,632-3; MacLean, *Clan MacLean*, 194-7; Willcock, *A Scots earl*, 199,231-4; Drummond, *Locheill*, 203-4; A. Nicolson, *Gaelic proverbs* (Glasgow 1951), 136.

60. *RPCS, 1678-80*, xviii-xix,203,324.

61. Airy, *Lauderdale papers*, iii.195; Lang, *Mackenzie*, 215-16.

62. J.S. Clarke (ed), *Life of James II* (2 vols, 1816), i.703-7.

63. *RPCS, 1678-80*, xix,393-8,428-9.

64. Lang, *Mackenzie*, 213-14; HMC 5: *6th Report*, 621,633; Cunningham, *Loyal clans*, 320-1.

65. Lang, *Mackenzie*, 217.

66. Ibid, 217-21.

67. Clarke, *Life of James II*, i.709-10; Lang, *Mackenzie*, 224-5.

68. J. Dun (ed), *Letters . . . to George earl of Aberdeen* (Spalding Club, 1851), 6-7; Clarke, *Life of James II*, i.711,712-13; Lang, *Mackenzie*, 225; Cunningham, *Loyal clans*, 346-51; HMC 5; *6th Report*, 615-16.

69. *RPCS, 1681-2*, xviii-xx,65,68-9,82-4,204-5,507-15.

70. *RPCS, 1683-4*, xiv-xv,531-88, *1684*, ix-x,187-201, *1684-5*, xiv; Drummond, *Locheill*, 208-9.

71. J. Murray, 7th duke of Atholl (ed), *Chronicles of the Atholl and Tullibardine families* (5 vols, Edinburgh 1908), i.187-98.

72. Ibid, i.219*-220.

73. Ibid, i.205,208.

74. Ibid, i.246,247n. For the rising in general see ibid, i.199-264, McKerral, *Kintyre*, 120-130 and the relevant volumes of *RPCS*.

75. McKerral, *Kintyre*, 130-3; *An account of the depredations committed on the Clan Campbell, and their followers, during the years 1685 and 1686* (Edinburgh 1816); Mackenzie, *Orain Iain Luim*, 166-7,294-303.

76. *RPCS, 1685-6*, xviii, *1686*, xxvi-xxvii, *1686-9*, lxii.

77. Drummond, *Locheill*, 301; Cunningham, *Loyal clans*, 396.

78. Drummond, Locheill, 210.

79. Ibid, 205.

80. Ibid, 210-20; Murray, *Chronicles*, i.263-6.

81. Drummond, *Locheill*, 220.

82. Ibid, 207,210,216-29,231; *APS*, viii.613-15.

83. Drummond, *Locheill*, 229-31; Cunningham, *Loyal clans*, 353-4.

84. For the tendency of clans in the seventeenth century to 'feudalise' their origins by rewriting their histories and pedigrees see Skene, *Celtic Scotland*, iii.346-9,364.

85. The argument in Cunningham, *Loyal clans*, 355 that the wisdom of James' supposed plan to abolish superiorities is proved by their eventual abolition in 1747 is hardly logical; James is said to have been motivated by a wish to strengthen the clan system, while after the '45 they were attacked in order to destroy that system! Moreover it was heritable jurisdictions that were abolished in 1747, not superiorities. The Tenures Abolition Act of 1746 had destroyed the powers of feudal superiors over their vassals, though technically the superiorities continued to exist, W. Ferguson, *Scotland. 1689 to the present* (Edinburgh 1968), 154-6.

86. E.R. Cregeen, 'The changing role of the house of Argyll in the Scottish Highlands', in N.T. Phillipson and R. Mitchison (eds), *Scotland in the age of improvement* (Edinburgh 1970), 6.

87. A.A. Whyte, Scottish Gaelic folksongs, 1500-1800 (Glasgow University B. Litt. thesis, 1972), 162.

88. Mackenzie, *Orain Iain Luim*, 125,285.

89. See E.R. Cregeen, 'The tacksmen and their successors. A study in tenurial reorganisation in Mull, Morvern and Tiree in the early eighteenth century', *Scottish Studies*, xiii (1969), 93-144.

Bibliography and Abbreviations

THIS is not a complete bibliography of all works used in writing this book. It is designed, firstly, to enable readers to identify works cited frequently in the notes by short titles, and to expand abbreviations. A great many works cited only once, or cited only in the notes of a single chapter, have been omitted as it should be easy to find their full titles by looking back through the notes of the chapter concerned to the first, full reference to the work. Secondly, this bibliography contains a number of works which, though they may not be frequently cited in the notes, are useful in providing background to, or discussion of, the Highlands in the seventeenth century; or which provide information on the life of Alasdair MacColla covering more than just isolated incidents. In some cases short comments on the value of works have been made.

Sources

Aiazza, G. (ed), *The embassy in Ireland of Monsignor G.B. Rinuccini* (Dublin 1873)

APS: Acts of the parliaments of Scotland (12 vols, Edinburgh 1814-75)

Baillie, R., *Letters and journals* (3 vols, Bannatyne Club 1841-2)

Balfour, Sir James, *Historical works* (4 vols, Edinburgh 1824-5)

Black, R. (ed), 'A manuscript of Cathal MacMuireadhaigh', *Celtica*, x (1973), 193-209. A poem addressed to Coll Ciotach.

Campbell, A., 'The manuscript history of Craignish', *Miscellany* iv (SHS 1926), 177-295

Campbell, Lord Archibald, *The records of Argyll* (Edinburgh 1885)

Campbell, J.D.S., Marquis of Lorne, *Adventures in legend. Being the last historic legends of the Western Highlands* (Westminster [1898])

Campbell, J.L. (ed), 'The letter sent by Iain Muideartach, twelfth chief of Clanranald, to Pope Urban VIII in 1626', *Innes Review*, iv (1953) 110-16

Carte, T. (ed), *A collection of original letters and papers* (2 vols, London 1739)

Cobbet, W. (ed), *State trials*, v (1810)

Collectanea de rebus Albanicis: consisting of original papers and documents relating to the history of the Highlands and Islands of Scotland (Iona Club 1847)

Com Rin: O'Connell, D., and O'Ferrall, B. (eds), *Commentarius Rinuccinianus* (6 vols, IMC 1932-49)

CSPD: Calendar of state papers, domestic (London 1856-1925)

CSPI: Calendar of the state papers relating to Ireland, 1633-47 and *1647-60* (London 1901-3)

CSPV: State papers and manuscripts relating to English affairs, existing in the archives and collections of Venice, xxv-xxviii (London 1925-7)

Flower, R. (ed), 'An Irish-Gaelic poem on the Montrose wars', *Scottish Gaelic Studies*, i (1926), 113-18

Fraser, J., *Chronicles of the Frasers. The Wardlaw manuscript* (SHS 1905)

Giblin, C. (ed), *Irish Franciscan mission to Scotland, 1619-1646. Documents from Roman archives* (Dublin 1964)

Gilbert, *Contemp hist*: Gilbert, J.T. (ed), *A contemporary history of affairs in Ireland from 1641 to 1652* (3 vols in six, Dublin 1879-80)

Gilbert, *Ir Confed*: Gilbert, J.T. (ed), *History of the Irish Confederation and the war in Ireland, 1641-9* (7 vols, Dublin 1882-91)

Gordon, Patrick, of Ruthven, *A short abridgement of Britane's distemper* (Spalding Club 1844)

Guthry, Henry, *Memoirs* (2nd ed, Glasgow 1748)

Hickson, M.A. (ed), *Ireland in the seventeenth century, or the Irish massacres of 1641-2, their causes and results* (2 vols, London 1884)

HMC: Historical Manuscripts Commission. HMC publications are cited using the serial numbers recommended in Government Publications, Sectional List 17.

Hogan, E. (ed), *The history of the warr of Ireland from 1641 to 1653. By a British officer* (Dublin 1873)

Hogan, J. (ed), *Letters and papers relating to the Irish rebellion* (IMC 1936)

IMC: Irish Manuscripts Commission

Innes, C, (ed), *The book of the thanes of Cawdor* (Spalding Club 1859)

Joint print: Joint print of documents in the causa His Grace John Douglas Sutherland, Duke of Argyll . . . against Angus John Campbell of Dunstaffnage . . . Court of Session, First Division May 12, 1911 (Edinburgh 1911)

Lamont, Sir Norman (ed), *An inventory of Lamont papers* (Scottish Record Society 1914)

Leith, W.F. (ed), *Memoirs of Scottish Catholics during the XVIIth and XVIIIth centuries* (2 vols, London 1909)

Macdonald, A.J. and A.M. (eds), *The Macdonald collection of Gaelic poetry* (Inverness 1911)

Mackenzie, A.M. (ed), *Orain Iain Luim. Songs of John Macdonald, bard of Keppoch* (Scottish Gaelic Texts Society 1964). An invaluable edition of the works of the greatest Gaelic political poet of the seventeenth century, with translations.

McNeill, C. (ed), *The Tanner letters* (IMC 1943)

Macphail, J.R.N. (ed), 'Extracts from the collection of state papers in the Advocates' Library known as the Denmylne MSS', *Highland papers*, iii (SHS 1920), 90-320

Mactavish, D.C. (ed), *Minutes of the synod of Argyll, 1639-61* (2 vols, SHS 1943)

Matheson, A. (ed), 'Traditions of Alasdair MacColla', *TGSG*, v (1958), 9-93. The best, and the most extensive, collection of traditions.

Morrison, D., *The Morrison manuscript. Traditions of the Western Isles* (Stornoway 1975)

Napier, M. (ed), *Memorials of Montrose and his times* (2 vols, Maitland Club 1848-50)

NLS: National Library of Scotland

O'Mellan, T., 'Cin Lae O Mealláin', ed T. O'Donnachadha, *Analecta Hibernia*, 3 (1931), 1-61

O'Mellan, T., 'A narrative of the wars of 1641', in R.M. Young (ed), *Historical notices of Old Belfast* (Belfast 1896), 199-247

PRO: Public Record Office (London)

Rel Celt: MacBain, A. and Kennedy, J. (eds), *Reliquiae Celticae. Texts, papers and studies in Gaelic literature and philology left by the late Rev. Alexander Cameron* (2 vols, Inverness 1892-4). Vol ii contains the text and translation of Neil MacMhuirich's history.

RMS; Registrum magni sigilli regum Scotorum: The register of the great seal of Scotland (11 vols, Edinburgh 1882-1914)

RPCS; Register of the privy council of Scotland (3 series, 38 vols, Edinburgh 1877-1970)

Rushworth, W. (ed), *Historical collections* (4 vols in 8, London 1659-1701)

SHS: Scottish History Society

SRO: Scottish Record Office

Spalding, J., *Memorials of the trubles in Scotland* (2 vols, Spalding Club 1850-1)

Turner, Sir James (ed), *Memoirs of his own life and times* (Bannatyne Club 1829)

Watson, W.J. (ed), 'Unpublished Gaelic poetry, iii', *Scottish Gaelic Studies*, ii (1927), 75-91. A poem in honour of Alasdair MacColla.

Wishart, G., *The memoirs of James marquis of Montrose* (London 1903)

Secondary Works

Argyll. An inventory of the ancient monuments, i. *Kintyre*; ii. *Lorn* (Royal Commission on the Ancient and Historical Monuments of Scotland, Edinburgh 1971-5)

Bagwell, R., *Ireland under the Stuarts* (3 vols, London 1909)

Bannerman, J.W.M., 'The lordship of the Isles', in J.M. Brown (ed), *Scottish society in the fifteenth century* (London 1977), 209-40

Black R., 'Colla Ciotach', *TGSI*, xlviii (1972-4), 201-43

Brown, Archibald, *Memorials of Argyll* (Greenock 1889). Contains an appendix, pp.440-8, on Alasdair in Argyll.

Buchan, John, *Montrose* (London 1928; references are to 1931 edition)

Carte, T., *The life of James duke of Ormond* (3 vols, London 1735-6)

Clarke, A., 'The earl of Antrim and the First Bishops' War', *Irish Sword*, vi (1963-4), 108-15

Collinson, F., *The traditional and national music of Scotland* (London 1966)

Cowan, E.J., *Montrose. For covenant and king* (London 1977)

Cregeen, E.R., 'The changing role of the house of Argyll in the Scottish Highlands', in I.M. Lewis (ed), *History and social anthropology* (London 1968), 153-92

Cregeen, E.R. 'The changing role of the house of Argyll in the Scottish Highlands', in N.T. Phillipson and R. Mitchison (eds), *Scotland in the age of improvement* (Edinburgh 1970), 5-23

Cregeen, E.R., 'The tacksmen and their successors. A study in tenurial reorganisation in Mull, Morvern and Tiree in the early eighteenth century', *Scottish Studies*, xiii (1969), 93-144

Cunningham, A., *The loyal clans* (Cambridge 1932). The most ambitious study of seventeenth century Highland history available, but the interpretations presented are illogical and naive, being based on belief in the glories of divine right absolutist monarchy and on attribution of all evils to 'feudalism'.

DNB: Dictionary of national biography (63 vols, London 1885-1900)

Donaldson, G., *Scotland: James V to James VII* (Edinburgh 1965)

[Drummond, John], *Memoirs of Sir Ewen Cameron of Locheil* (Abbotsford Club 1842). A very influential work which reads back eighteenth century Jacobite attitudes into the mid-seventeenth century. The *Memoirs*, and the editorial introduction to them by James MacKnight, provided the basic arguments of Cunningham, *Loyal clans*.

Duggan, L., 'The Irish brigade with Montrose', *Irish Ecclesiastical Review*, lxxxix (1958), 171-84, 246-58. Adds very little to earlier secondary accounts.

Dunbar, J.T., *History of Highland dress* (Edinburgh 1962)

Ferguson, W., *Scotland's relations with England. A survey to 1707* (Edinburgh 1977)

Fitzpatrick, T., 'The Ulster civil war, 1641', *UJA*, new series, xiii (1907), 133-42, 155-9, xiv (1908), 168-77, xv (1909), 7-13, 61-4

Gardiner, S.R., *History of the great civil war* (4 vols, London 1893-4)

Gardiner, S.R., *History of the commonwealth and protectorate* (4 vols, London 1903)

Gordon, William, *History of the family of Gordon* (2 vols, Edinburgh 1726-7)

Grant, I.F., *The MacLeods. The history of a clan* (London 1959). A work of much greater general interest than other clan histories, as it places the clan in the wider context of Highland history.

Gregory, D., *History of the Western Highlands and Isles to 1625* (1836, 2nd ed Edinburgh 1881, reprinted 1975). A narrative survey which is still of great value.

Grieve, S., *The book of Colonsay and Oronsay* (2 vols, Edinburgh 1923)

Hill, G., *An historical account of the Macdonnells of Antrim* (Belfast 1873). A most valuable collection of information, though chaotically arranged.

Kermack, W.R., *The Scottish Highlands. A short history* (Edinburgh 1957). Very brief, but thoughtful and stimulating.

Laoide, Seosamh (Lloyd, Joseph), *Alasdair MacColla; sain-eolus ar a gaionartaib gaiage. Seosam Laoide do cuir le ceile; deantusai o Eoin MacNeill agus o Naill Mac Muireadaig sa Leabar so* (Dublin 1914). Extracts from Neil MacMhuirich's history relating to Alasdair, and from Buchan's *Montrose*, and references to some traditions, poems and music; and a brief sketch of Alasdair's life by Eoin MacNeill.

Lee, M., 'James VI's government of Scotland after 1603', *SHR*, lv (1976), 41-53

Loder, J. de V., *Colonsay and Oronsay in the Isles of Argyll* (Edinburgh 1935)

Lowe, J., 'The earl of Antrim and Irish aid to Montrose in 1644', *Irish Sword*, iv (1959-60), 191-8

McCoy, G.A. Hayes-, *Scots mercenary forces in Ireland, 1565-1603* (Dublin 1937)

McCoy, G.A. Hayes-, 'Gaelic society in Ireland in the late sixteenth century', *Historical Studies*, iv (1963), 45-61

Macdonald, A.J. and A.M., *The Clan Donald* (3 vols, Inverness 1896-1904)

McDonnell, John, *The Ulster civil war of 1641, and its consequences; with the history of the Irish brigade under Montrose in 1644-6* (Dublin 1879). Written by a descendant of Alasdair MacColla and dedicated to him and his men.

Macgill, A., 'Colkitto and the wars of Montrose', *Proceedings of the Royal Philosophical Society of Glasgow*, lxviii (1929-30), 101-27. Of little value.

McKechnie, H., *The Lamont clan* (Edinburgh 1938)

Mackenzie, W.C., *The Highlands and Isles of Scotland* (Edinburgh 1949)

McKerral, A., *Kintyre in the seventeenth century* (Edinburgh 1948). An excellent local study.

McKerral, A., 'The tacksman and his holding in the South West Highlands', *SHR*, xxvi (1947), 10-25

MacLean, J.A., The sources, particularly the Celtic sources, for the history of the Highlands in the seventeenth century (Aberdeen University Ph. D. thesis, 1939). A very useful introduction to the subject.

MacLean, J.P., *A history of the Clan MacLean* (Cincinnati 1889)

Mitchison, R., 'The government and the highlands, 1707-45' in N.T. Phillipson and R. Mitchison (eds), *Scotland in the age of improvement* (Edinburgh 1970), 24-46

Napier, M., *The memoirs of the marquis of Montrose* (Edinburgh 1856)

Nicholls, K.W., *Gaelic and Gaelicised Ireland in the Middle Ages* (Dublin 1972). A stimulating survey which provokes many comparisons with Highland conditions.

Nicholson, R.G., 'Domesticated Scots and wild Scots; the relationship between Lowlanders and Highlanders in Medieval Scotland', *Scottish Colloquium Proceedings*, i (University of Guelph 1968)

Nicholson, R.G., *Scotland: the later Middle Ages* (Edinburgh 1974)

O'Danachair, C., 'Montrose's Irish regiments', *Irish Sword*, iv (1959-60), 61-7

Reid, J.S., *The history of the presbyterian church in Ireland*, ed W.D. Killen (3 vols, Belfast 1867)

Shaw, F.J., 'Landownership in the Western Isles in the seventeenth century', *SHR*, lvi (1977), 34-48

SHR: Scottish Historical Review

Sinclair, A.M., *The Clan Gillean* (Charlottetown 1899)

[Sinclair, J.C.], *Historical and genealogical account of the Clan Maclean from its first settlement at Castle Duart . . . By a seneachie* (London 1838)

Skene, W.F., *Celtic Scotland. A history of ancient Alban* (2nd ed, 3 vols 1886-90).

Smout, T.C., *A history of the Scottish people, 1560-1830* (London 1969)

Steer, K.A., and Bannerman, J.W.M., *Late medieval monumental sculpture in the West Highlands* (Edinburgh 1977)

Stevenson, D., *Scottish covenanters and Irish confederates* (forthcoming)

Stevenson, D., *The Scottish revolution, 1637-44. The triumph of the covenanters* (London 1973)

Stevenson, D., *Revolution and counter-revolution in Scotland, 1644-51* (London 1977)

Stevenson, D., 'The desertion of the Irish by Coll Keitach's sons. 1642', *Irish Historical Studies*, xxi, no.81 (March 1978), 75-84

TGSG: Transaction of the Gaelic Society of Glasgow

TGSI: Transactions of the Gaelic Society of Inverness

Thomson, D., *An introduction to Gaelic poetry* (London 1974)

UJA: Ulster Journal of Archaeology

Whyte, A.A., Scottish Gaelic folksongs, 1500-1800 (Glasgow University B.Litt. thesis, 1972)

Genealogical Tables

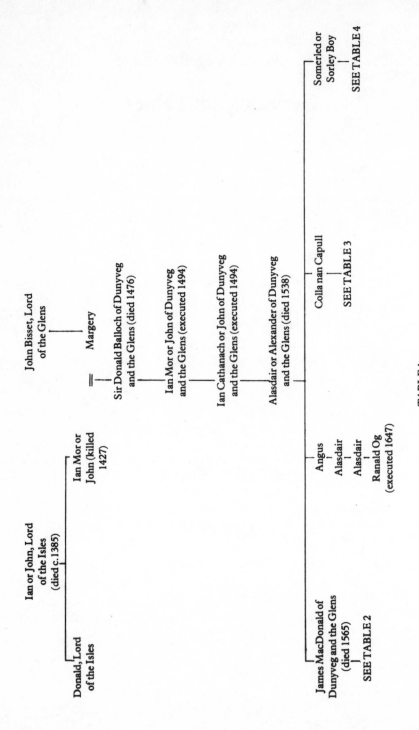

TABLE 1.

The Clan Ian Mor, or Clan Donald South

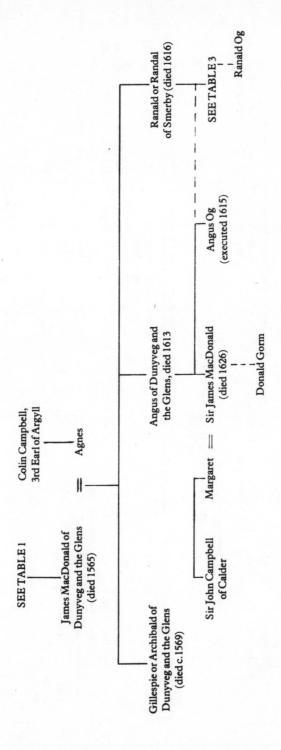

TABLE 2.
The Last MacDonalds of Islay

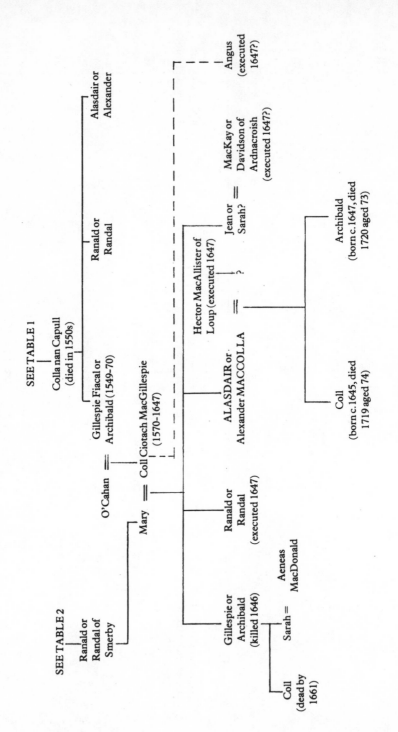

TABLE 3.
The MacDonalds of Colonsay

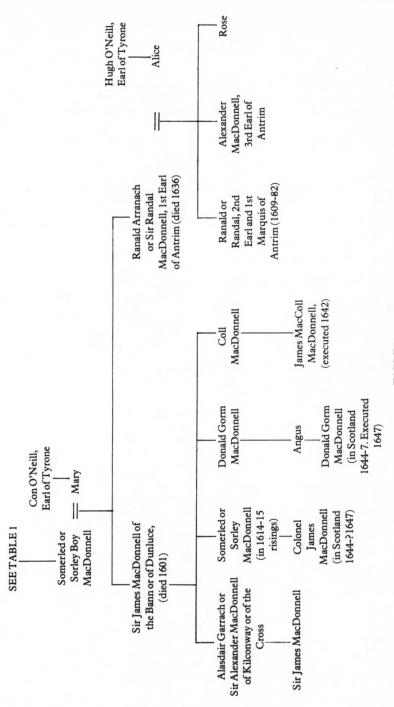

TABLE 4.
The MacDonnells of Antrim

Index

The central characters of this book, Alasdair MacColla, his three brothers, and his father, Coll Ciotach MacGillespie, are indexed under these patronymics (MacColla and MacGillespie), but all other Highlanders are indexed under the appropriate clan names, here treated as surnames.

THE SALTIRE SOCIETY

The Society seeks to preserve traditional Scottish culture and to encourage new developments in numerous fields from architecture and engineering to literature and music. Branches are active in Aberdeen, Dumfries, Edinburgh, Glasgow, Helensburgh, Highland (based in Inverness), Kirriemuir, St. Andrews and South Fife. There are Saltire representatives in Ayr and London.

Further information from The Administrator,
The Saltire Society,
9 Fountain Close,
22 High Street
EDINBURGH EH1 1TF
Tel. 031 556 1836 Fax. 031 557 1675

SOME SALTIRE PUBLICATIONS